SELECTED □ FILM CRITICISM 1931-1940 □

edited by
Anthony Slide

THE SCARECROW PRESS, INC.
METUCHEN, N.J., & LONDON
1982

In the same series

*PN
1995
.S5
1982*

ISBN 0-8108-1570-2
Library of Congress Catalog Card No. 82-10642

IN MEMORY OF
BEULAH BONDI

CONTENTS

Preface

Selected Film Criticism: 1931-1940 is the fourth volume in a series designed to provide a broad overview of contemporary American film criticism from 1896 through 1950. For this volume, reviews have been reprinted in their entirety from twelve periodicals-- Cinema Arts, Esquire, The Hollywood Reporter, Hollywood Spectator, International Photographer, Life, The Nation, The National Board of Review Magazine, The New Republic, Photoplay, Rob Wagner's Script, and Variety--to offer the reader a glimpse at popular critical reaction to 150 of the most important American productions of the decade.

As with previous volumes in this series, the editor has tried to avoid reprinting reviews that are available in other anthologies, and has made his selections from popular magazines, including Esquire and Rob Wagner's Script, as well as from trade papers, such as The Hollywood Reporter and Variety.

Background on some of the critics included here may be of interest. Meyer Levin (who died on July 9, 1981, at the age of 75) is generally considered one of the foremost Jewish-American writers of the twentieth century. His books include Yehuda, The Old Bunch, The Architect, and his best known work, Compulsion. The Meyer Levin reviews included here come from the period of 1933 through 1939, when he was associate editor and film critic for Esquire. James Shelley Hamilton (who died on June 5, 1963, at the age of 69) was the executive director of the National Board of Review of Motion Pictures from 1934 through 1945. A literate and intelligent critic, Hamilton was described by Motion Picture Herald at the time of his death as a "scholar and authority of quiet dignity." Rob Wagner (who died on July 20, 1942, at the age of

71) was editor and publisher of Rob Wagner's Script, a periodical that might well be described as Los Angeles' answer to The New Yorker. Wagner founded the publication in 1929, and it prospered thanks largely to its subscription list which included everyone of importance in Hollywood and was regularly published in the magazine to impress would-be advertisers.

Other critics in this anthology include Richard Sheridan Ames, Welford Beaton, Harry Evans, Otis Ferguson, Richard Griffith, Don Herold, and Herb Sterne. The last was a young upcoming theatre and film critic with Rob Wagner's Script, who will be featured prominently in the next volume of this series. It is interesting to compare Sterne's knowledgeable and humorous approach to that of George Blaisdell, whose career dates back to the early teens and The Moving Picture World and who is included here through his reviews in International Photographer.

Again, I would like to express special thanks to Elias Savada, for his help in checking copyright registrations at the Library of Congress in Washington, D. C. Thanks also to the staffs of the Margaret Herrick Library of the Academy of Motion Picture Arts and Sciences and of the History and Literature Divisions of the Los Angeles Central Library.

The reviews of Meyer Levin are reprinted from Esquire (August 1937, October 1937, December 1937, June 1938, and August 1938). Copyright © 1937 and 1938 by Esquire Publishing Inc.

The Otis Ferguson reviews are reprinted from The Film Criticism of Otis Ferguson, edited by Robert Wilson. Copyright © 1971 by Temple University. All rights reserved. Reprinted by permission of Temple University Press and Dorothy Chamberlain.

The reviews from The National Board of Review Magazine are published by courtesy of the National Board of Review of Motion Pictures, Inc.

Reviews from Variety are reprinted by permission of that publication and its executive editor, Syd Silverman.

Reviews from The Hollywood Reporter are reprinted by permission of that publication and its publisher, Tichi Wilkerson Miles.

Anthony Slide

x

SELECTED FILM CRITICISM:
1931-1940

☐ THE ADVENTURES OF ROBIN HOOD (Warner Bros., 1938)

Odd what makes a picture. The marquee glares with the names of Olivia de Havilland, Errol Flynn, Claude Rains, Basil Rathbone and nowhere will you find a two-inch credit for the color. This film would be dull, flat, and I'm sure unprofitable but for the work of one Carl Jules Weyle--if I've got the right man. He's listed as art director. For it is only the brilliant, amazingly versatile use of color that puts suspense and excitement into Robin Hood. One is led from scene to scene wondering what new splash of tint and texture will be revealed, instead of wondering whether Robin will be captured. Not since that first great splurge, Becky Sharp, has Technicolor been used to such effect. And this has twenty memorable color compositions, for every one in Becky Sharp.
--Meyer Levin in Esquire, Vol. 10, No. 2 (August 1938), page 82.

*   *   *

Tucked away in the old ballads that hardly anyone ever reads is the Robin Hood whose legend lives on in the Anglo-Saxon memory --lives the more glamorously the more it is merely a hazy memory. Children are given it in such books as the one that Howard Pyle wrote, and there they forget how synthetic and insipid the attempt to re-write old England in nursery terms really was, pap for heady ale, and remember a band of merry outlaws, robbing the unjust rich to help the worthy poor, roving adventurously in a Sherwood Forest colored with the unrivalled richness of imagination. Now they have a new kind of picture book on which to build their memories, this film the Warners have made in all the gorgeousness of the latest Technicolor. It is a pleasant thing to see, but the chances are very great that it will be far pleasanter to remember, when this and that detail are forgotten and imagination joins with memory to create something that the literalness of a book-page or a movie screen could never bring to life by itself.

With such a legend, which has no basis that anyone can be sure of in history, one version probably serves as well as another. This one keeps most of the best known characters--Little John, who tumbled Robin off the log-bridge with his staff, and Friar Tuck, who had to carry Robin across the brook on his back. Will Scarlet is here, a bird of paradise whose membership in the band is never

explained, and Maid Marian, a haughty Norman lady who remains
aloof from the greenwood till her hand is given to Robin in marriage for a happy ending.   There is no Alan a Dale, but there is a
fine lot of villains--a timorous High Sheriff, a poisonous, treacher-
ous Prince John, an overbearing Sir Guy, a wicked bishop, and for
low comedy a couple of Herbert Mundin-Una O'Connor mugging parts
of the kind they have been exceeding their quota on ever since they
invaded America with Cavalcade.   King Richard of the Lion Heart is
here, back from his Crusade looking very clean and well-fed, lamb-
like but pleasant, and his recognition by Robin and his men is one
of the rare moments when action and excitement gives place to real
feeling that springs out from the screen and catches the audience.

Mostly the picture is full of movement, some of it dashing
in the fine romantic costume style, some of it just sprightly.   The
excitement comes from fast action--galloping steeds, men swinging
Tarzan-like down from trees, hurling tables and chairs, rapid running sword-play, the sudden whiz of Robin's arrows coming from
no-where to startle his enemies--more than from any fear that
Robin might be worsted.   Robin is more than equal to any danger,
incredibly strong and swift and sure, politely arrogant, always flashing a smile.

Somehow the whole thing has an air of being a costume party,
a jolly and rather athletic one, with a lot of well-bred Englishmen
playing at being in the greenwood.   Their bright, fresh clothes,
their house-party kind of conversation, the clean castles and neat
forests, might all have been something an affluent host arranged for
the entertainment of summer guests.   Only Alan Hale looks and acts
as if he could be at home in the woods.

There is some charming color in the film, and quite a lot of
brilliant dazzle.   Some of the actors, like Montagu Love and Claude
Rains, might have stepped out of a history book.   The others live
up to the picture-book quality of the film, which has the supreme
virtue of a movie--except for some tedious and modernish love-
making it keeps moving.

And so another generation can get acquainted with some of the
imperishable figures of English folk-lore.   It may interest them
enough to send them to the library, to read the ballads.   Or maybe
to read a history, in which they will find that Richard did not tarry
long in England, and that the wicked John became king after all,
and such a bad king that he precipitated Magna Charta and the beginnings of democracy.   Maybe Robin Hood prepared the ground.
                                                --James Shelley Hamilton in
                                                National Board of Review Maga-
                                                zine, Vol. 13, No. 6 (June
                                                1938), pages 13-15.

☐ ALICE ADAMS (RKO, 1935)

        This department has just had another severe attack of Hep-
burn.   In Alice Adams, this girl Hepburn kept me two inches off
the downy divan of the Music Hall for something like an hour and a
half.   She makes most of the other movie queens look like spear
toters.   She bites into the human being she is portraying and makes
the juice flow.   Her Alice Adams is a foolish, lovable, lonely, little
adolescent, lying and bluffing, and holding up a chin in a world
which has her almost crushed, but with a load of sterling worth
underneath, and a quick wit and a deep vein of humor.   Can you
imagine any other of a hundred movie dolls--big ones, I mean--
giving you the real taste of a Tarkington character?   No, they just
walk through their pictures with their eyelashes and coiffeurs, and
work up into a mechanical fury when the big scene comes, with no
more real title to the name of actress than any of five thousand
girls in Woolworth's.

        Alice Adams will hurt the very hide off you.   It is painful
business, of exactly the sort you might see if you could look through
the walls of the house next door.   A sweet, honest, shiftless father,
a girl too poor and too sensitive to crash through social barriers
in her town, a mother nagging at the father because she sees how
their position is holding the girl back, a brusque brother.   If you
don't pretty nearly cry, I hate you.

        A warm paw to Fred Stone for a fine, sincere performance
as Alice's dad--his debut as a legitimate screen actor.   He has a
glorious future--and what a glorious past!
                              --Don Herold in Life, Vol. 102,
                                No. 2607 (October 1935), page
                                36.

☐ ALICE IN WONDERLAND (Paramount, 1933)

        Why mince matters?   Alice in Wonderland is, to my sober
(despite repeal) judgment, one of the worst flops of the cinema.
Paramount's first mistake was in attempting it.   The only person
in Movieland to have done it is Walt Disney.   Mary Pickford, who
once contemplated doing it, was right when she said that Alice
should be made only in cartoons.

        So--with a fine script (Joe Mankiewicz and William Cameron
Menzies), delightful music (Dimitri Tiomkin), a splendid director
(Norman McLeod), and about fifty of our best actors and actresses,
the picture, when it isn't dull, is still utterly uninspired.

        English children who still read Alice in Wonderland may get
a mild kick out of it.   I doubt if our young sophisticates will.   It's

a cinch that all the grown-ups will get is the mild fun of trying to
identify the Big Names hidden behind turtle shells and teddy-bear
skins.   Even when they do occasionally recognize a voice, they will
still wonder why all these high salaries were hidden beneath bushels
of props.   Extras, or even children, would have been adequate for
most of the parts.   No acting was required.   Indeed production costs
could have been cut tremendously by letting cheap actors play the
parts and then hiring Big Names to register five minutes of dialogue,
easily dubbed in.

The second mistake was in choosing a young lady to play the
five- or six-year-old part of Alice.   Charlotte Henry is a comely
youngster with an intelligent face, who looks as though she would be
more interested in Vance Hoyt's nature studies in Script than in
Fairyland.   She tries hard to look wonder-eyed but can't quite make
it.   And with all our wonderful kid actors!

Even so there was still a chance to make a picture of fairy-
like charm.   In all the arts there is no medium that lends itself to
fantasy like the movie camera.   By soft focus, shooting through silk,
and other technical tricks, scenes can be given an illusive, dream-
like quality that eloquently visualizes the subjective mind.   Alice goes
to sleep and dreams her trip to Wonderland, but we see both her
and her dream in hard reality, with the flat lighting and sharp focus
of the objective world.   Never for a moment are we in dreamland;
we are on Stage Four, witnessing the technical staff and prop boys
doing their stuff.   Even much of this is bad.   When Alice flies
through the air, she is obviously hanging by a wire (remember how
well that was done in Peter Pan--also by Paramount?) and when she
is falling down the well, she is still hanging by a wire.   Nor are
her skirts blown while falling.   It's hard to write a review like this,
for practically everybody who had anything to do with the picture is
a Scripter, but when a picture is a flop, it's a flop, and it's silly
to alibi.   The big mistake was in undertaking it at all.

--Rob Wagner in Rob Wagner's
Script, Vol. 10, No. 250 (December 23, 1933), pages 11-12.

☐ AMERICAN MADNESS (Columbia, 1932)

Here is the first picture that steps up and seriously considers
that little situation known as "The Depression."   The action covers
twenty-four hours.   Sounds dull?   Wait until you see it!

Why, the run on the bank is more exciting than an advancing
army!   And the scene in which the small business men rush to save
the bank by depositing their profits will bring tears.   This story
about money is more poignant than most of the sweetheart hokum of
the day!

Walter Huston, as the home-spun banker with faith in the little merchants, gives a flawless, delightful performance.

Pat O'Brien is fine as the chief teller. Kay Johnson and Constance Cummings turn in good work--but it's the picture itself that's the big thing! Don't miss it!

--Photoplay, Vol. 42, No. 4
(September 1932), page 52.

☐ AN AMERICAN TRAGEDY (Paramount, 1931)

Whether the suit of Theodore Dreiser against the Paramount-Publix Corporation was a cooperative publicity stunt; whether it was personal bell-ringing on the part of Dreiser; or whether it resulted from artistic indignation against what Dreiser calls a degradation of his art, the fact remains that the film version of An American Tragedy has become a cause célèbre in the world of cinematic art.

I have read the printed pamphlet issued by Dreiser's attorneys in which they set out, not only the details of what appears to have been an interminable quarrel between their client and the studio, but the reasons why they believe the film is a degrading travesty upon the book from which it was made.

Briefly, they claim that the book is an indictment of our whole social system, whereas the film is just an ordinary murder story. There is some truth in this contention. Nevertheless, it seems to me to be asking a good deal of a film, that must of necessity show only essential action in the space of ninety minutes running, to encompass a philosophy which Dreiser developed by the use of 800 pages.

A novel that begins with the cradle and ends with the grave, and devotes pages and pages to every little incident coloring the lives of the characters, cannot possibly be made into a film drama of equal thoroughness. Whereas the novel is usually the complete saga of a man's life, the motion picture, like the short story and the stage drama, deals only with certain definite segments. Mr. Dreiser should have known this when he sold An American Tragedy for translation into the shorter idiom of the cinema. In fact, the only way Paramount could have produced this particularly long novel to the satisfaction of its author would have been by shooting it in perhaps a hundred reels.

Mr. Bernard Shaw expresses his art in dramatic form, but recognizing its limits, he usually devotes the greater part of his books to elaborate prefaces in which he puts over his psychological and sociological notions.

Mr. Galsworthy, on the other hand, writes a play called Justice, and then takes his chances that his audience will get its

significance. Helped by the critics, a few people are led to see
that it has a deep social significance, that it is an indictment of the
cruelties of jurisprudence in his country.

This is the model followed by Josef von Sternberg, the director, and Samuel Hoffenstein, who wrote the film version of An
American Tragedy. They used the only model they could follow
within the limits of their medium. If, in telling the essential action of Dreiser's drama, they failed to put over his indictment of
our social system, it is for other reasons than those given by Mr.
Dreiser's attorneys.

Note, for instance, the fact that Clyde Griffiths' environment
and bringing-up so colored his character that he developed into a
miserable coward and weakling. Mr. Dreiser devoted many chapters
of meticulous detail to establishing this character. All Messrs.
Hoffenstein and von Sternberg could do was to show a few introduc-
tory sequences of Clyde's rotten and poisonous start in life, and
then, after his first cowardly escape from danger, to give his mother a spoken title in which she tells of the ugliness of his childhood
surroundings, and how he had been denied all the things that make
for manhood. What more could they have done in the one or two
"character-establishing" reels?

Another contention of the attorneys--that the Clyde of the
book and the Clyde of the film are in no way alike--has more merit.
I think, however, the trouble is less with the story treatment and
direction than with the selection of Phillips Holmes for the part of
the weakling. Holmes is without doubt a fine young actor, but his
whole physical, intellectual, and spiritual make-up types the high-
born aristocrat rather than the vacillating, loose-lipped Clyde of the
novel--a creature who wins sympathy because he is a product of his
environment and training, a spiritual weed.

So when a boy who looks as intelligent, handsome, and upstanding as Phillips Holmes pulls one rotten trick after another, he
does indeed become a rotter calling for little sympathy. Had the
character of Clyde Griffiths been played by a Charlie Ray doing a
bewildered weakling buffeted by chance and circumstance, we should
all have felt with Mr. Dreiser that society and not Clyde Griffiths
was to blame for the murder of Roberta Allen.

So much for the controversy in which I, reviewing studio
crimes of the past, would ordinarily have sided entirely with the
author.

But fortunately--or unfortunately--nine people out of ten who
see the picture will not have read the book. So judging An American Tragedy as "another movie," what about it? Well, undoubtedly it is one of the notable pictures of the year; a splendid
script by Samuel Hoffenstein, and corkingly photographed by Lee
Garmes.

Of the cast the big bouquet goes to Irving Pichel as the district attorney. He is smooth, suave, reserved, and speaks beautiful English in a rich, cultured voice.

Charles Middleton, the defense attorney, also contributes strongly to the effectiveness of the story. His address to the jury was highly dramatic.

Sylvia Sidney again showed that she is one of our best screen actresses capable of high moments of drama. (To think that she was programmed as a pinch-hitter for Clara Bow! Clara is a million miles outside this young lady's class.)

Frances Dee made a charming foil for the poor young factory girl and did what little she had to do with intelligence and conviction.

A large cast of lesser characters, all of whom were good.

Yes, An American Tragedy is a fine picture, and in spite of the Dreiser squawk, I think it still carries a strong sociological punch.

> --Rob Wagner in Rob Wagner's
> Script, Vol. 6, No. 145 (November 21, 1931), pages 6-7.

*   *   *

Because of the publicity that has preceded the showing of this film version of the Theodore Dreiser novel, it is impossible to review it simply on its merits as screen entertainment. Mr. Dreiser, feeling that the Paramount Company missed the purpose of his favorite brain child and distorted its characters, attempted to restrain them by law from showing the picture. You probably read something of the trial.

Director Josef von Sternberg had to take a two-volume novel and boil it down to a feature-length movie of eleven reels. The job was no cinch. Doubtless Mr. von Sternberg took a great many feet of film that have been cut out in the editing of the finished product, and we daresay that some of this deleted material might be put back in to advantage. It is impossible to believe that he overlooked some of the points of the novel that are conspicuously absent.

The one glaring fault of the film is that it does not build up a proper sympathy for Mr. Dreiser's main character, Clyde Griffiths. Through lengthy description of the boy's mental processes and a thorough review of his early environment, Mr. Dreiser presented Clyde as a victim of moral cowardice brought about, primarily, by circumstances beyond his control. These important factors are passed over hurriedly in the film, and in some instances ignored completely. For instance: Clyde's parents preached the gospel on the streets and ran a mission. The events in connection

with this phase of his life are treated casually in the picture, whereas they are vitally necessary to encourage your sympathy for this
boy whose moral upbringing had been in constant conflict with his
natural impulses.

The producers, after considerable thought, probably decided
that so many people have read the Dreiser novel that it would be
wasting film to cover these details ... which further proves the
perversity of the movie industry.   As a general rule the cinema
heads go completely moron in an effort to make the dialog and action as elemental as possible so the point at issue will not be over
the dear public's head ... then they turn right around and take it
for granted that the average movie fan has read An American Tragedy.   We do not believe the book has been read by one out of every
fifty people who will see the film--nor do we see any reason why it
should have been.

Therefore we find Phillips Holmes, the very capable young
actor who plays Clyde, working hard at a difficult task.   Without
the proper background of sympathy he appears to be a weak character who betrays a factory worker then deserts her the moment a
rich society girl notices him.   There is no evidence that he is
struggling with his better self in making his decision--in fact there
is very little evidence of mental stress and indecision when he decides to take the factory girl out and drown her and her unborn
child.

In the murder trial that follows, von Sternberg achieves dramatic moments of great power.   Many critics declare this one of
the greatest trial scenes ever filmed.   We found it very moving at
times, but far too lengthy.   Some of the film used to exploit details
could have well been devoted to more important things during the
first part of the picture.   We also found Irving Pichel's performance
as the district attorney inconsistent.   During his dramatic moments
Mr. Pichel is impressive, but his work in his more quiet moments
is filled with a smug air of importance and constant desire to mug
that are very "ham."   Emmett Corrigan and Charles B. Middleton,
as the lawyers for the defense, do excellent jobs.

The most deserving performance in the film is offered by
Sylvia Sidney as the factory girl.   Miss Sidney's role is so obvious
that her duties are much less complicated than those of Mr. Holmes,
and so, fortunately for the value of the film, she achieves much of
the poignancy that is missed in the character of Clyde.   Frances
Dee is fair as the society girl, and Lucille La Verne is reasonably
convincing in her limited opportunities as Clyde's mother.

And now that we have expressed our sympathy for Mr. Dreiser we must add that all the fuss is relatively unimportant because in
An American Tragedy the Paramount Company offers a motion picture that is far above the average.

--Harry Evans in Life, Vol. 98,
        No. 2546 (August 31, 1931),
        page 18.

☐   ANGELS WITH DIRTY FACES (Warner Bros. , 1938)

        Before Angels with Dirty Faces was previewed, those in the
know had prophesied that Rowland Brown's highly regarded story,
transferred to celluloid by Michael Curtiz, was the best thing that
had happened to James Cagney since Public Enemy. Probably our
nerves are steadier than they were then, so the new film isn't as
shocking as the predecessor it resembles, but if such a savage on-
slaught as Angels with Dirty Faces allows any time for reflection,
your thoughts may turn as mine did to Jimmy Cagney. He has
mastered the technique of motion picture acting, and whether you
can stomach such an unpleasant story or not, you're not going to
see any performances this season so perfectly timed, so dynamic,
or so breath-taking.

        To me, Angels with Dirty Faces is all Cagney, although Pat
O'Brien gives a good account of himself as the fighting priest, and
those Dead End Kids, the screen's incorrigibles, make you laugh
while seriously thinking that what they need is a juvenile annex up
at Alcatraz. Humphrey Bogart and George Bancroft are fairly convincing as Cagney's not very formidable opposition, and Ann Sheridan is merely asked to be a pretty stooge for the star, a job she's
fitted for. Otherwise the picture is a hard-hitting triumph for the
star, for Director Curtiz who makes the whole film in a tempo that
makes you hold on to your seat and wish for an emotional wind-
shield, and for Photographer Sol Polito who takes drab surroundings
like tenements and prison corridors and makes them not only interesting but almost beautiful.

        Although Angels with Dirty Faces finally points--or I think
whams out would be better--a moral, the story really appeals to
that something in all of us which makes us cheer a bold rascal.
Cagney is so honestly bad that all the piously motivated stuff about
his origin or how he reacts to the bold proposition which gives the
film a bravura ending makes any sort of morality seem tepid. To
enjoy the film, you must give in to your lowest impulses.

        The appeal is to something primitive in most of us, and
ethics be hanged, one unregenerately hopes that Cagney will shoot
or out-smart the captors who escort him to the electric chair. The
film is as hard as Hemingway, burns like a straight drink, has all
the tension of a tooth-pulling and the heartlessness of a bullfight.
                              --Richard Sheridan Ames in Rob
                              Wagner's Script, Vol. 20, No.
                              485 (November 26, 1938), page
                              12.

                    *   *   *

        It would seem that there was not much more to be said on
the screen, in the way the screen seems to have to say things,
about slum boys growing up into criminals, yet the new Cagney-

O'Brien picture, <u>Angels with Dirty Faces</u>, manages to give vigor
and a certain sort of freshness to a more than twice-told tale.
There is a difference in plot, but all the old elements are there:
the youngsters caught by the glamor of successful crime, with nothing in their impoverished lives to counteract that glamor. It is
hard to dramatize any successful rescue from such a situation, and
the device used in this film (it must have looked like such a bright
idea on paper!) seems pretty phoney, even while under the spell of
the acting of it: a gang of as skeptical young roughnecks as the
Dead End Kids can be is supposed to be diverted from their impend-
ing life of crime by reading in the papers that their hero turned
yellow before going to the chair. The big theatrical kick is that
Cagney didn't really turn yellow, he only pretended to for the sake
of its effect on the kids. Probably the kids didn't believe it any
more than the audience does.

But here are Cagney and O'Brien and the kids in their best
form, and if this could be taken as a farewell appearance for this
particular kind of thing, though it isn't exactly a climax it would
deserve a hearty round of applause. But we don't need any more
repetitions of it.

--James Shelley Hamilton in
National Board of Review Magazine, Vol. 13, No. 9 (December
1938), pages 21-22.

☐ ANNA KARENINA (M-G-M, 1935)

Old Count Tolstoy had two lives--the first as a gay, young
Russian nobleman, the second as a "dark" Russian peasant. This
is probably his best story of the first period. From it the beautiful
Clemence Dane and Salka Viertel have written an exceptionally fine
screen play. Clarence Brown's direction is superb and the cast is
tops. Yet I was not deeply moved.

The reason, I think, is that the morality of that period is
outmoded and because I can never develop great interest in the affairs of rotters. Fredric March is an officer in the Czar's guard
given to strong drink, sport and "love." In fact all the men are
roosters. (Every time I see a picture of Czaristic Russia, I can
more easily understand the Russian revolution.)

True, Greta Garbo is a high-class, high-grade woman, but
when she is cast out by high society for deserting home and son to
go loving with Fredric, the behavior of all concerned seemed very
old-fashioned. All the story lacked was a shawl and a snowstorm.
In the preview audience witnessing her calvary were many unwed
couples living happily together and in no way socially ostracized.
At least not enough to hurt.

Another handicap was the sartorial ugliness of the period.
Adrian did nobly with its demands, but the gowns were necessarily
frumpy.   And the men's military uniforms--short, unbecoming "see-
more" coats--sadly needed British tailors.

The picture, however, is a triumph for the musical director,
Herbert Stothart, and the technical staff.   The Russian Symphony
choir opens with a grand musical prologue and their singing during
a cathedral wedding is, to me, the high spot of the picture.   Cedric
Gibbons and his associates, Fredric Hope and Edwin Willis, have
given the picture magnificent production.   The snow stuff is truly
marvelous.   Douglas Shearer's "sound" is just about perfect and
William Daniel's camera work ravishingly beautiful.

> --Rob Wagner in Rob Wagner's
> Script, Vol. 14, No. 336 (Octo-
> ber 12, 1935), page 10.

*   *   *

Not that Garbo cares, but I came awfully close to coming
over to the Garbo camp, at Anna Karenina.

Either there is a new Garbo or there is a new Herold.

One of us has mellowed ... or softened.

At the start of this picture, Garbo was a quieter and sweeter
Garbo, and I sensed a lot of loveliness that I've missed--voice warm
and human and all that.   As the picture rolls on, however, they
turn on the pang, and Garbo makes the old mistake of getting out
on a limb and sawing herself off.

Fredric March (giving a very stuffed performance)--Russian
army officer--who has swiped Anna from her husband (Basil Rathbone, cold steel) and her little son (Freddie Bartholomew, a little
too adult and precise to be completely winning--he makes too many
bedtime orations to his mother)--tires of Garbo, and then the agony
arrives, as per the usual Garbo formula.

Anna Karenina has, in lesser degree, the weaknesses of most
Garbo pictures: too much circus, too much background, too much
incidental noise and hullabaloo, too many candelabra, too much show,
too much fake.   Perhaps the reason I have enjoyed so few Garbo
productions is that Garbo brings out the worst in her directors.
Sex on a high horse is what she seems to suggest to them.   If a
director has any Barnum & Bailey in him, she brings it out.   They
all want to put her in a pageant and have her stab herself in satin,
for a love she can't have, for a love which is a greater love than
the love any woman has ever had for any man; please pass the as-
pirin.

Consequently, most Garbo films have been bunk on a big
scale, and heretofore I have been inclined to classify Garbo, in that

sweeping, unfair way I have, as the bunk. Despite the fact that
Anna Karenina is still too much of a world's fair, Garbo seems
pretty honest in it, for a welcome change.

What I am wondering is, how well could Garbo act in a small,
plain room with only a table and two chairs for props, and with only
groceries and ordinary love and simple home life to talk about?
As a rule she is set in such gorgeous surroundings, and she lays
on the pomp and dignity so thick, and then wrenches the agony spig-
ot with such desperation, that it is really kind of hard to tell whether or not she is acting or bluffing.

How well could Garbo swap roles with Katharine Hepburn in
Alice Adams or with Merle Oberon in Dark Angel, where simple,
honest human emotions must be portrayed without help of elephants
and a male chorus of 200 voices?

This is from a totally convulsed Richard Watts Jr. in the
Herald Tribune: "There can no longer be sensible reason for doubt-
ing that she is the transcendant personage of the modern drama,
whether of stage or screen ... no actress has brought so much
beauty and magnificence to any form of the theater within this generation."

I wonder?

I saw Karenina and Dark Angel on the same evening, and my
choke-ometer tells me that Merle Oberon is many times a Garbo,
without half trying.
>   --Don Herold in Life, Vol. 102,
>   No. 2608 (November 1935),
>   page 24.

☐ ANTHONY ADVERSE (Warner Bros. , 1936)

First we had The Great Ziegfeld, its spectacles sustaining
our interest in the story for upward of three hours. Then we had
the two-hour Show Boat with fine music to justify its length. Next,
Warner Brothers started out to do something neither the screen nor
the stage ever previously had attempted--to entertain us with a
dramatic offering which ran without interruption for nearly two and
a half hours. A play that long would have been broken into three
acts; no one ever dared to make a dramatic picture that long.

And Warner Brothers succeeded admirably. Anthony Adverse
is one of the finest things the screen has done, an undertaking which
only superlatives can do justice to. Sheridan Gibney has done the
impossible in writing a screen play that will satisfy those who have
read the book. When he began the task, he must have felt lost in
the great distance from cover to cover, but as he roamed through it

he garnered incidents of major significance, strung them together
intelligently and with discriminating regard for their dramatic importance and interrelationship, and he gives the screen a script
which ranks among its finest literary accomplishments.

Gibney's departures from the story as the book tells it are
justified. The first duty of a photoplay is to be true to itself; it
is under no obligation to its source. Its only obligation is to the
screen audience. The picture marries Adverse and Angela to make
it cleaner by legitimatizing their son. Adverse himself is a bastard, and to make the charming boy also a bastard would have been
distasteful to any audience. Discrimination is shown in ending the
picture before the book ends, and also in disregarding the majority
of Anthony's love affairs and giving us only the more important incidents in his life. The result is an engrossing biography of dramatic power, told in the best of taste.

The picture has so many merits they cannot be set down in
a review in order of their relative importance. Each part of such
a satisfactory whole is as important as the others, story, production, music, acting being blended with rare craftsmanship, each,
when regarded separately, seemingly being the feature worthy of the
greatest commendation.

Certainly, no picture ever has been given better direction.
It is a triumph for Mervyn LeRoy. It was a monumental undertaking, even with Gibney's worthy script, to keep the story moving
forward with such precision and mounting interest, to hold the attention of the audience so long in incidents in the life of a purely
fictitious individual. The picture ran for a full two hours before
there was discernible in the crowded house the rustle of changing
positions comparable with the seventh-inning stretch at a ball game.
Mervyn's direction makes his cast just people living their lives on
the screen, not actors trying to entertain us. Dialogue is presented
as a series of intimate conversations; the drama is brought out
sharply, the romantic moments are tender and sweet, and the comedy scenes blend smoothly into the narrative without disrupting its
forward flow.

Another who plays a large part in making the picture an outstanding success is Erich Wolfgang Korngold, the master musician
who arranged the score which is almost continuous through the entire length of the film. It is an unobtrusive score, one which rarely steps to the front and demands attention on its own account, being, in fact, so completely in tune with the mood of the various
scenes I doubt if the majority of those who see the picture will be
aware of its presence except at rare intervals. But Korngold's
contribution plays a tremendous part in the production as a whole,
for to it can be attributed the sustained emotional response the audience accords the swiftly moving story.

The difficulty of pleasing a reader of a book with a picture
made from it is that of matching the reader's conception of the lead-

ing character.   That is why I never read a story I know is destined
for presentation on the screen.   When I view the picture I desire
to estimate its values as screen entertainment and not as the
screen's interpretation of something previously expressed in another
medium.   But I had read Anthony Adverse.   I had a definite Anthony
of my own, and Freddie March was a long way from my conception
of him.   I could not see March in the part, and I suppose I subconsciously expected to be disappointed with his performance.   This
morning Freddie March is my conception of Anthony.   When I fashioned the other one I must have been thinking of someone else.

The outstanding quality of March's performance is its integrity,   the force with which he makes his every word and gesture
the natural follower of what precedes it, the consistency with which
he maintains the character and makes us believe in it.   Freddie at
times has given us a lot of acting.   Here he gives us none.   He is
not pretending he is Anthony Adverse, not showing us what March
would have done if he were Adverse.   He is Anthony Adverse, and
I think he will be accepted as such by all the others who have read
the book.

Running down the list of players in the order I find them on
the credit sheet, Olivia de Havilland is next.   Olivia interests me
because she is living proof of my contention that the screen is not
an acting art, that the farther it gets away from acting the better
off it will be.   Here we have a girl of nineteen with a personality
that photographs, with an ability to absorb a part and express it
with that personality.   With only meager previous experience, she
assumes a role in an important production, pits her adaptability
against the trained skill of an outstanding cast, and makes a deep
impression on the audience.   She endows her performance with
everything it demands, responds gaily to its lighter phases, meets
with vigor its dramatic requirements; and in the poignancy of her
final parting with Adverse, the suffering we see in her eyes shows
how completely she has become the girl she plays.   That Olivia is
beautiful is incidental even though it is an important asset in building a career.

Donald Woods demonstrates again in this picture that he is
one of the young men from whom we can expect much.   He is
another whom a good appearance helps, but it is the pleasing personality back of it that counts.   As Anthony's loyal friend he is
in every way satisfactory.   Edmund Gwenn's overacting in Sylvia
Scarlett made me doubt his adaptability to screen requirements, but
certainly no one could wish for a better characterization than he
gives Bonnyfeather, Anthony's benefactor.   Claude Rains and Gale
Sondergaard are admirable as the male and female menace.   Steffi
Duna, Billy Mauch, Akim Tamiroff, Henry O'Neill, Ralph Morgan,
George E. Stone, Luis Alberni and Fritz Leiber are others deserving special mention.

The picture is mounted sumptuously by Anton Grot, all the
settings suggesting painstaking research and close attention to detail.

Tony Gaudio's camera work is superb.   There are scores of shots of arresting beauty in composition, lighting and photography.

And a word about the man through whose fingers ran all the threads which were woven together to form the pattern which will go down in history as a masterpiece of screen craftsmanship and the first picture drama to attain such footage.   Henry Blanke was the producer of Anthony Adverse.   He produced also A Midsummer Night's Dream, The Story of Louis Pasteur, Petrified Forest, and Green Pastures.   It is a record which speaks for itself.   Blanke unquestionably is a production genius, one of the few really great men connected with pictures.   He displays a sound knowledge of screen fundamentals in their relation to audience psychology.   When a man knows both the art and the box-office--well, we can expect from him the kind of pictures we get from Henry Blanke.

To Warner Brothers for the brilliant accomplishment of an enterprise so daring, salaams!

> --Welford Beaton in Hollywood
> Spectator, Vol. 11, No. 4 (May
> 23, 1936), pages 7-8.

*   *   *

I am one of several million people who tried to read Anthony Adverse and said, "I guess I'll wait for the movie."

Well, the picture is here and it is a great picture.   It has sweep and size and beauty and impressiveness and restraint.   You may take my enthusiasm with a grain of salt, however, because I expected to be disappointed.

Anthony Adverse, filmed, lasts two hours and twenty minutes. To some extent it has the book's fault of going in for length for length's sake.   It starts with Anthony as spermatozoa and traverses continents, jumps episodically through his whole life, and, wonder of wonders, does this without seeming episodic.   You are held pretty spellbound for the whole two hours and twenty minutes.

Of course, I think a picture which travels the soul of a man, within four walls, is greater than a picture which travels the earth and time, or one which leans on skulking villains and scheming villainesses or on such blatant coincidences as the accidental adoption of a boy by his own grandfather.

But life, too, is long ... life, too, has its coincidences ... so there is room for a certain number of Anthony Adverse films along with all the Mazie and Mabel films.

This picture has distinctive direction, great and intelligent direction, by Mervyn LeRoy.   There is a minimum of horses and chandeliers and roaring ham actors, and curls and cloaks and coaches.

Fredric March is quiet and winning and strong as Anthony.
Olivia de Havilland is a radiant and lovely Angela.   Other acting
honors go to Edmund Gwenn, Claude Rains and to dozens of lesser
characters.   I except that synthetic Napoleon Bonaparte.

I'd send my best friend to this film.
> --Don Herold in Life, Vol. 103,
> No. 2619 (October 1936), page
> 32.

☐ ARROWSMITH (Goldwyn/United Artists, 1932)

Producers are always changing titles foolishly.   Here was a
muffed chance to change one reasonably; the picture should have
been called "Broken-Arrow Smith."   For it is one of those darned
negative stories of futility and defeat.

Ronald Colman, purposeful young doctor, is sent to the tropics by the McGurk Institute of Medical Research to experiment with
a bubonic plague serum.   With the stupidity of a bungling amateur,
he leaves upon a table--where any servant could knock it over--a
rack of culture tubes in which, as he casually remarks, "are enough
bugs to kill the entire population."

Ronald's wife, Helen Hayes, accidentally spills some of the
dear little bacteria on a cigarette, smokes it, and dies.   Ronald
then loads up on whiskey, abandons his experiment, and beats it
back to New York, where he blatantly repudiates the McGurk Institute as though it were to blame.

I don't know yet what the big idea of the picture is, unless
it was to discredit the great privately-endowed research laboratories
that have done so much for the science of medicine.   Ronald's particular squawk against the Institute is its publicity stunts.   But why
become squeamish over that, when in this great publicity era even
the churches employ journalistic bell-ringers?   Furthermore, the
stories that are sent out from the Rockefeller Institute and the phys-
ics laboratories of Cal-Tech are stirring accounts of man's vic-
tories over the secrets of nature. Allowing for a certain journalistic
enthusiasm for exaggeration, they are nevertheless positive stories
of success that are darned welcome in a heebie-jeebied world.

Other than this story weakness, the picture has some of the
best acting and poorest tropical sets I've ever seen on the screen.
One or two actual establishing shots might have taken me to the
tropics, but so artificial were the jungle scenes and the village sets
that I was never for a moment out of Hollywood.   Our producers
should go to the Filmarte and see how Russians do these things.   If
they wish to take you to Tibet, you land in Tibet, even though the
scene is shot in the suburbs of Moscow.   Fortunately they have not

learned all of our fancy laboratory tricks for cheating reality--often
very badly.

Ronald Colman, one of our most delightfully repressed actors, is superb in a foolish and inconsistent role.   Helen Hayes,
with no such opportunity as she had in The Sin of Madelon Claudet,
proves again that she is a corking screen actress.

For three reels I was all hopped up over a big Swedish actor, evidently a recent importation, as he could barely make himself understood in English.   Then suddenly I recognized him as
Richard Bennett!   That's how good he is--a truly remarkable characterization.

Another wonderful actor is the chap who plays the role of an
old scientist.   I now learn from the credit sheet that he is A. E.
Anson.   Never heard of him?   Well, see him in this picture.

Thought for a moment that Ronald was going to run up against
something more dangerous than the bubonic plague--Myrna Loy.
Myrna is tempting enough in New York, but in the tropics...!   But
you know Ronald!   He's gone through years of cinema-sipelas, holding tight to the All Good and his British libido.

Alec Francis, Claude King, David Landau, Bert Roach, De-
Witt Jennings, and Lumsden Hare all have small parts, made big
by good acting.

Russell Hopton is exceptionally good in a minor part, and
Clarence Brooks, as a native doctor in the tropics, gives a fine
performance of an educated Negro.

John Ford's direction is better than most fellows' would have
been, with such a jumbled story.

All Sam Goldwyn productions are generously handsome.
                              --Rob Wagner in Rob Wagner's
                              Script, Vol. 7, No. 168 (April
                              30, 1932), page 10.

*   *   *

If author Sinclair Lewis finds fault with this (as Dreiser did
with An American Tragedy) he should be sent to bed without his
supper.   For everything that was in the book is here--the drama
of the doctor-scientist who risks his life and happiness so that others might live.

Ronald Colman is poised as usual, but he's more than that.
For once he has a chance to show of what actor stuff he's made.
And it's all wool and a yard wide.   He simply is Dr. Arrowsmith.

No one could have done the tender, faithful wife who makes
terrific sacrifices for the doctor's humanitarian career better than

little Helen Hayes.   These two--Colman and Hayes--are the ideal
pair for this film.   And, in case that isn't enough in the acting line,
there's the old master Richard Bennett who makes a great Sondelius.
He and A. E. Anson turn in two of the finest character performances you'll see this season.

To producer Sam Goldwyn, director John Ford, and adapter
Sidney Howard go leafy laurel wreaths for their respective brows.
Perhaps you'll say there's too much dialogue, but convincing locales
make up for it.

--Photoplay, Vol. 41, No. 2
(January 1932), page 47.

☐ THE AWFUL TRUTH (Columbia, 1937)

The Awful Truth has just won for Leo McCarey the Academy
award for the best direction of the year.   McCarey, you'll remember, was responsible for Ruggles of Red Gap, Make Way for To-
Morrow, and the early Marx Brothers pictures.

It is a light comedy, saved by a hair's breadth from the pre-
vailing crazy manner, of the six months between the interlocutory
decree and the final divorce in the lives of an otherwise ideally
mated young couple.

Questions involved are such practical issues as the custody
of the dog, the services of the common family lawyer, the choice
of a new dancing partner, the division of property.   Irene Dunne and
Cary Grant discuss these problems until divorce seems, on the
whole, more involved than marriage, and they reach an amicable
settlement just on the deadline.   Featured largely in the picture is
one Mr. Smith, alias Asta of The Thin Man, né Skippy the wire-
haired fox terrier.   Ralph Bellamy, tackling comedy for the first
time as an oil man from Oklahoma, supports Mr. Smith in the best
of the fun.

--C. A. Lejeune in World Film
News, Vol. 3, No. 1 (April
1938), page 34.

☐ BABES IN ARMS (M-G-M, 1939)

If it's true that everybody loves a baby, then Babes in Arms
is sure to become one of the best-liked films of 1939.   M-G-M
waited quite a while to convert the Rodgers-Hart success into celluloid and, before telling what Babes in Arms does for Mickey Rooney
and Judy Garland, wasn't it a pity that RKO failed to do anything
about Mitzi Green, star of the original musical, who seems to have

lost out entirely? At that, Judy Garland makes the most of her opportunity and is even better than she was in The Wizard of Oz.

In addition to acting a life-story similar to his own, Mickey
Rooney clowns, sings, dances, plays the piano and, indefatigable
youth that he is, has enough energy left to reveal an aptitude for
mimicry with impersonations of President Roosevelt, Lionel Barrymore, and Clark Gable. The film, which is the first produced by
Arthur Freed, formerly associated only with song, dispenses with
most of the original musical scores but provides agreeable substitutes. And it gives Charles Winninger and Grace Hayes (as Mickey's
parents), June Preisser (as the ex-starlet), Guy Kibbee (the friendly
judge who understands show folk), and Douglas McPhail and Betty
Jaynes, topnotch vocalists, a good chance to prove to screen audiences that they are personalities we should see more frequently.

Babes in Arms is another of the nostalgic movies which are
bound to prosper this season and, so far, the best. It mixes laughs
and tears, is concerned primarily with the plight of old-time vaude-
villians who are still good even though their offspring are better and
more resourceful in combating mechanized entertainment which
spoiled the "good old days," and it has a sort of awkward, frantic-
to-please, you-can't-beat-youth quality which makes one capitulate
easily. Its freshness and sauciness and ceaseless activity provide
a shot in the arm for the world-weary and cynical, and no picture
released in recent months, unless it was Wizard of Oz, is so likely
to make one forget the importunate war news and other distressing
manifestations of civilized existence--for which we may be thankful.

I'll be even more grateful when the miracle happens, and
Mickey at least takes an option on Man's Estate--sufficient to make
him attempt self-control and discipline a performance for the first
time. Having already proved that there is no limit to his histrionic
exuberance, the next step must be restraint, or else the youthful
mugger will finish in an unquenchable blaze of glory that will leave
him burned out before he is twenty-one. So far, directors haven't
succeeded, so it's up to Mickey himself. Or, how about some salt-
peter in his scripts?

                              --Richard Sheridan Ames in Rob
                              Wagner's Script, Vol. 22, No.
                              526 (October 21, 1939), page 16.

                    *   *   *

Superb entertainment. It has everything for everybody. It
is youth on celluloid, dauntless and joyous youth whose pluck and
enthusiasm stir your emotions even while you are laughing at their
comedy or applauding their musical numbers. In many ways it is
a remarkable picture. Its story is rather inconsequential and sheds
too many tears over the departed vaudeville days in which the present generation is in no way interested, and therefore cannot join in
the tear shedding, but I can not recall any other picture which was
so continuously entertaining as this one.

That Judy Garland and Mickey Rooney are a pair of extraordinarily gifted youngsters was an opinion expressed by the Spectator
long before either gained much prominence, but even so, there was
some element of surprise in what a great combination they make
when teamed in a vehicle expressly for them.   In fashioning their
screen play Jack McGowan and Kay Van Riper cleverly worked in
the complete bag of tricks of each of the co-stars, thus, by bunch-
ing their hits in one production, enabling the two to bring the full
force of their talent to bear on their public.   And victory will be
theirs wherever Babes In Arms is shown.   It should be one of the
box-office smashes of screen history.

The spirit of youth dominates the production, thus making it
choice entertainment for adults.   It is wholesome--just good, clean
fun, with a note of serious optimism running through its entire
length.   Whoever dug up all the talent deserves a distinguished service medal.   Betty Jaynes scores a triumph.   She has a glorious
singing voice combined with knowledge of how to use it, and in addition has a personality which alone could make her a favorite.   Exactly the same thing can be said of Douglas McPhail.   In the two of
them Metro has a prospective co-starring team.   June Preisser is
another promising young miss with an ability to look dumb and prove
otherwise.

In this picture the adults were up against exceedingly stiff
competition, but Charlie Winninger, Guy Kibbee, Henry Hull and
Margaret Hamilton managed to attract attention.

Cedric Gibbons again gives us some of the artistically imposing settings he has taught us to expect from him, the closing sequence having a background of arresting dignity and beauty.   Dolly
Tree enhanced the visual attractiveness of the production by designing gowns which appeal with force even to the male eye.   Ray June's
photography brings out all the pictorial values of each scene, and
Frank Sullivan's film editing is another contribution meriting commendation.

Busby Berkeley gives the whole production admirable direction
except in one scene in which Rooney addresses his troupe of youngsters.   He has his back to them while he talks, to bring his face
and all the others into the camera.   More effective direction would
have been to have had Mickey entirely surrounded by his hearers
until we lose sight of him but hear his voice coming from the middle of the huddle.   But that is only one scene, and there are scores
which Berkeley directed most ably.   Producer Arthur Freed certainly
can take a bow for having been the guiding influence in one of the
best pieces of entertainment Hollywood ever has offered the world.
                          --Welford Beaton in Hollywood
                              Spectator, Vol. 14, No. 14
                              (October 28, 1939), pages 7-8.

☐ BABES IN TOYLAND (Hal Roach, 1934)

Chalk up another victory for the Decency Leaguers for stirring the studios to such charming wholesomeness.   This is a grand
holiday picture and the kids will love it.

Artistically, however, it has definite faults--the biggest being
indecision as to whether it is intended for a musical or an old-fashioned gag comedy.   It starts off musically, and to me the high
points were the songs and choruses, especially the duet between
Little Bo Peep (Charlotte Henry) and Tom Tom the Piper's Son
(Felix Knight).   Charlotte is lots prettier than she was in Alice in
Wonderland, and Felix sings gloriously and fills the eye handsomely.

Laurel and Hardy are at their best as Dum and Dee, assist-
ants to the Toymaker (William Burress).   Their gags are swell and
their timing perfect.   Henry Kleinbach gives a remarkable characterization of the symbolic Fairyland dirty heavy, and Florence Roberts
is perfect as the Widow Peep who lives in a shoe.

Bogeyland is ugly, lacks comedy and runs much too long.
The final battle between the toy soldiers and the bogey men starts
off bang! with a trick shot of the soldiers, but in the actual fighting
the human toys are not stiff and mechanical enough.

Gus Meins and Charles Rogers direct with speed, whimsy and
excellent taste--not a rough nor vulgar note throughout.   Camera
work of Francis Corby and Art Lloyd, excellent.   But this is one
picture that cries out for color.

Frank Butler and Nick Grinde wrote the screen play, and as
is always the case, the screen play is the picture.

Curiously enough, one of the best deserved credits was
omitted from the cast sheet--the fellows who fabricated the three
little pigs, the cat-and-the-fiddle and other props.
                              --Rob Wagner in Rob Wagner's
                                Script, Vol. 12, No. 298 (De-
                                cember 22, 1934), pages 8-9.

                     *   *   *

Most of the pictures I have said were good, I was just kid-
ding.   The three really important pictures of all time are: The
Birth of a Nation, Three Little Pigs, and Babes in Toyland.   The
last of the three was loosed on the world about Christmas time by
Laurel and Hardy, and if you have missed it, I urge that you have
Junior and Sissy drag you to it.
                              --Don Herold in Life, Vol. 102,
                                No. 2599 (February 1935), page
                                35.

☐ BACK STREET (Universal, 1932)

Honesty, like most of the virtues, has its dull side. Back
Street, Universal's new picture, which has reopened the Carthay Circle Theatre under Fred Miller's direction, tries to keep to the out-
lines of Fannie Hurst's book, and just escapes the dullness that dogs
so many fidelities. Picture makers still, apparently, haven't made
up their minds whether their job is making novels, plays or movies.
John Stahl, who directed Back Street, and Junior Laemmle, who
sponsored it, seem to have chosen fidelity to their book--at least to
the latter part--instead of fidelity to their medium; the result is
more a testimony to their sincerity than it is to their esthetic perception.

Back Street proceeds on the screen like the successive chapters of a novel, gently unfolding its narrative with the placidity of
a meadow stream. All the potential dramatic elements of this story
of a left-handed wife have been curbed and harnessed by discreet
hands, until there is very little left of the underlying drama but good
taste and a kind of reminiscent romantic pathos--what James Huneker
used to call the "pathos of distance."

Back Street essays to tell with historical perspective in settings and backgrounds the story of a sweet girl, betrayed by Life
and Circumstance--in the person of a Stuffed Shirt--over a period
of thirty-two years, ranging from 1900 to today. This mistress--in
a day when mistresses were not so favorably under the public eye
as today--found that her swain valued his position more than divorce
and remarriage. She accepted his mandate; acceptance by no means
singular in the days before the Great Female Emancipation.

But no jewels and fine gold were her portion for these years
of devotion. All she got for hiding out in the back streets of what
passed for civilization--the social, mental and moral back streets
of her day--on call at every moment to give spiritual and emotional
sustenance to her Galahad when he needed it, all she got out of it
was her keep--two hundred dollars a month, which is, of course,
the ironic point of Fannie Hurst's tale.

This is undeniably a story worth telling. The usual trajectory
on the Present or Victorian Past is one to penetrate and expose the
hypocrisies of that sappy and foolish time. Mr. Laemmle and Mr.
Stahl saw fit to forego such sardonic pleasures. They tried instead
to paint the plaintive panorama of an enduring love. But the net result of their steady effort to keep the erring husband from being
disclosed as a hypocritical villain allows him to slide depressingly
into a characterization of a moping cluck. A fortunate paralytic
stroke takes him off in the end--doubless some intimation of the
wages of sin.

In this day of pratfalls, kicks in the antipays and socks to
the jaw, you might believe that such gentle telling of a harsh drama

would be a relief; on the contrary, I found myself wishing for the fresh air of today's candor and social truth telling. After all, why portray the past unless it is to show that we understand now why the poor wretches labored on so blindly and so trustingly in their futilities; as a future daylight may indeed show why we are limping and halting in ours!

As a production, Back Street has its pleasant side, an amusing and not too elaborately punctilious evocation of beer gardens and horse cars in Cincinnati, and the bourgeois habits of the decade. Miss Irene Dunne does very well with Ray Schmidt, Fannie Hurst's beleaguered heroine; John Boles tries nobly to bring the Other Woman's Husband to life, but finds it hard going. ZaSu Pitts flashes for a brief moment; George Meeker does a potential Henry Ford with conviction and authority.

William Bakewell is within an inch of a great role, but the blue print of the action makes no provision for that extra inch. As the son who intervenes between his father and his father's mistress --for all the reasons of outraged pride, family loyalty, etc., of the day, Mr. Bakewell promises savory dramatic excitements, but the gentle principle which seems to guide the production is in the way and the promise petered out.

I must concede, however, that the final scene achieved some dramatic novelty. The dying lover asks his critical son to call his mistress on the telephone; through numb and nerveless lips he tries to mumble her name, and expires. This is treated in effective cinematic fashion. Closeups of the dumb telephone instrument are more effective here than the actors' faces.

--Rob Wagner in Rob Wagner's
Script, Vol. 8, No. 183 (August
13, 1932), page 8.

*   *   *

The story and spirit of Fannie Hurst's book are here exquisitely translated to the screen--and we can hear state censor boards groaning with rage as they do not dare to ruin, with their clumsy shears, this lovely story of unconventional love. This is the tale of a seemingly ordinary girl forced by fate to tread the lonely back streets of life, sacrificing everything for her man and becoming a character of rare beauty. In this role Irene Dunne rises to new heights. She can make the hardest-boiled shed a tear. John Boles does his best work as the young banker for whom the girl stays in the background, content to see him rise to fame.

The motion picture in one of its finest forms--a story that will follow you from the theater, tugging at your heartstrings. Do not cheat yourself by missing Back Street.

--Photoplay, Vol. 42, No. 4
(September 1932), page 52.

☐ THE BARRETTS OF WIMPOLE STREET (M-G-M, 1934)

       The Barretts of Wimpole Street is of course one of the major
pictures of the year, and I am going to pick on it more mercilessly
than I would if it were a less pretentious attempt.   It presents itself
as a tremendously important production, and isn't.   Perhaps its
chief fault is that it tries too hard; it advertised itself widely as
having three of the world's greatest stars.   But if it did not happen
to contain two exceptionally human performances by Maureen O'Sullivan (as one of the lesser Barrett sisters) and a water spaniel, it
would be almost too stiff to take.

       Norma Shearer (not, in my opinion, one of our great screen
actresses) is, in this, pleasantly restrained and dignified, but still
fails to intimate much of the intellectuality that Elizabeth Barrett
must have had.   Miss Shearer seems, rather, just a good looking
girl and Hollywood wife and mother, getting her picture taken from
attractive angles.

       Fredric March bounds into the story with the backslapping
vim and cheerio vigor of a successfully syndicated daily newspaper
poet, instead of approaching the role with the warm, gentle charm
and quiet humor which I prefer to think that Robert Browning must
have had.   I shouldn't have been at all surprised to have seen Mr.
March's Mr. Browning take out a pad and ask for Miss Barrett's
order for a set of books on the installment plan.

       Charles Laughton (in my opinion one of our really great
screen actors) here is so melodramatically villainous that he completely lacks authority.   Such a father as he depicts would have
scattered his family years ago; he gives no hint of any virtues between which and his tyranny his children might have felt themselves
torn.

       The "comedy relief" in this supposedly great film is awful.
There is one man who stutters, a girl who lisps, and a servant
who gets laughs (usually at the wrong time) by walking as if she had
wheels under her hoop skirt.
                              --Don Herold in Life, Vol. 101,
                                No. 2597 (December 1934),
                                pages 34 and 53.

☐ BECKY SHARP (Pioneer, 1935)

       Color is the important thing to sell in this picture and there
is no doubt of the fact that the color item will sell.   The main
credit for its success belongs to Robert Edmond Jones in this production, and it will make audiences sit up and wonder why color
isn't in general use.   To the very big credit of the actors, the di-

rector and the writer be it said that the novelty of color never for
a moment overshadows their contributions.   Their work is the important thing to the picture, but color is the thing to sell.

The tale of late Napoleonic era strumpet, Becky Sharp, is a
familiar one to many who have seen the story done in pictures before and known to millions who have read the classic Vanity Fair.
It is a joy to meet the familiar characters again, done in the
sprightliest manner that has yet been attempted.   Faragoh has done
an excellent job of making the dialogue practically up-to-the-minute
in its humor and implications.   Also, he has made no compromise
with the story and that is perhaps its weak point, because it is a
kind of realism that not many can appreciate and leaves the picture
definitely for the class trade, except for the fact that the color is
something everyone must and will want to see.

It is by far the best thing in direction that Mamoulian has
done.   It has charm and flavor and an appreciation of the medium
that is rare.   His groupings are things of joy and they all have the
feeling of spontaneity.   He has done very well by color and has
smartly saluted the artistic talents of Robert Edmond Jones.   Mr.
Jones is solely responsible for the settings (and they are magnificent), for the costumes and for the art work, and they are all something to be seen, admired and deeply appreciated.

For acting, there couldn't have been a better choice than
Miriam Hopkins for the role of Becky.   The vitality of the girl, the
sly humor, the complete understanding of the witch that was Becky
Sharp are breathtaking as a series of vivid portraits.   Nigel Bruce
is delightfully the idiotic and amusing Joseph Sedley, Alan Mowbray
a dashing and grand Rawdon Crawley, and Cedric Hardwicke a superb masculine counterpart of the feminine Becky as the Marquis of
Steyne.   Alison Skipworth briefly booms her way through a few
scenes and is heartily entertaining.   Frances Dee is quite lovely as
the gentle sap, Amelia.   And excellent individual characterizations
by Billie Burke, William Stack, Ottola Nesmith, Doris Lloyd, Colin
Tapley, Elspeth Dudgeon and all the lesser players in the cast.

Still further credit must be given to photographer Ray Renna-
han, whose camera work in several sequences draws forth spontaneous applause, and the musical scoring by Roy Webb cannot be overlooked.   It, too, is important to this new novelty, color that is
destined to become the natural way to make pictures.

> --The Hollywood Reporter, Vol.
> 27, No. 37 (June 14, 1935),
> page 3.

*   *   *

Color is here!

So what?

The greatly hullabalooed Whitney million dollar Becky Sharp, with the new Technicolor three component color process, is here, and I am not the least bit excited. I don't believe it will revolutionize motion pictures one iota of a revolution.

At least, not until they learn how to keep all the actors from looking like roast turkeys.

There is no sex appeal in a gal who looks as if she were in the last stages of scarlatina.

In the first place, we don't see color in real life to any such extent as they give it to us in this picture. Things are colored in the world in which we live, but rather dully and grayly colored-- whereas in Becky Sharp they are shriekingly brilliant. The colors are the colors of souvenir post cards (which are certainly zero as an art form)--vivid, livid, disturbing and distracting. You see colors when you should be having emotions. If Technicolor can give us color without giving us color, then they'll have something.

Color is just one more thing to get the producers' minds off of their real job. This is proved definitely in Becky Sharp, which is, despite the valiant efforts of attractive Miriam Hopkins, a dull, boresome picture, which dullness and boresomeness are only intensified by the gaudy splendor of the color film. Some shots in which the color is subdued or simplified are magnificent, but it remains a question as to whether or not color can be kept in its place in the creation of a full-length film.

Experimentally, Becky Sharp may have great significance, but, per se, it is just a chromo.

> --Don Herold in Life, Vol. 102,
> No. 2605 (August 1935), pages
> 43 and 45.

☐ A BILL OF DIVORCEMENT (RKO-Pathe, 1932)

This picture makes history. Not since Greta Garbo first flashed before screen audiences in The Torrent has anything happened like this Katharine Hepburn. This girl from the New York stage is not only a fine actress--she is a great personality. Not beautiful, measured by Hollywood standards, she has something more than beauty--that thing, whatever it is, that makes the great, great.

In giving her first mention, we do not mean to take the glory from John Barrymore who gives the greatest performance of his life. Billie Burke, who plays his wife, reaches dramatic heights of which you would not think her capable. David Manners and Paul Cavanagh are excellent.

The story is unrelieved by humor, insanity is its theme, but it is terrific in its power.

--Photoplay, Vol. 42, No. 6
(November 1932), page 56.

*   *   *

A fine play about a man, his wife and daughter, made into a fine picture, dramatic, moving, extremely well done.   John Barrymore will surprise even his admirers, and the rest of the cast acts superbly.   An altogether unusual film, both artistically and as entertainment.

--National Board of Review Magazine, Vol. 7, No. 7 (September-October 1932), page 21.

☐   BIRD OF PARADISE (RKO, 1932)

Lavish settings, gorgeous photography and the spirited musical score, plus good acting by Dolores Del Rio and Joel McCrea, give this a good rating.   Young moderns will thrill to the love scenes, as romantic and daring as any recent film has offered, but the story about a native princess and a white boy will seem out of date.   The film actually cost its producers a million dollars.

--Photoplay, Vol. 42, No. 5
(October 1932), page 54.

*   *   *

There are many factors in RKO's Bird of Paradise that will assist in bringing this spectacular and melodramatic production to the attention of that larger public always attracted by a really unusual picture.   In the course of its running there are several major jolts--surely four or five--meaning sudden, hazardous happenings that fall without warning.

One of these and a sample one is during the boisterous behavior of a volcano in an adjoining island, the detonations sounding like the ripping explosions coming from massed artillery.   Joel McCrea as Johnny walking along the beach sees the ground under his feet part a foot or more.   Everybody out front sees it, too, with a resulting genuine scare.

The screen play by Wells Root, Wanda Tuchock and Leonard Praskins is described as having been suggested by Richard Walton Tully's play.   The theme is the sacredness of the person of the chief's daughter--Luana, played by Dolores Del Rio.   She is tabu, or taboo, to all outside the princes.   In that category, of course, Johnny is out.   Therefore when he flirts with Luana he is courting death.   And flirt he does, and flirt Luana does, much.

Pictorially the picture stands out. RKO chiefs, realizing the possibilities of a subject the exteriors of which were to be photographed in Hawaii, assigned an unusually strong crew. Four photographers were given screen credit--and that you will note if you follow the screen happens very seldom. These are Clyde De Vinna, who has had wide experience in tropical lands; Edward Cronjager and Lucien Andriot. Lloyd Knechtel supervises the photographic effects--and these are employed to a large and successful degree.

One of the initial shots is of a large white yacht topped by a mass of white sails smashing through tumbling waters at a lively speed. It is an impressive shot, none of its effectiveness being lost by reason of the recording camera being close to the level of the sea.

It is unlikely Del Rio in the course of her life will be assigned to a part that will match in difficulty that of Luana. She is seen as a native girl, one who dances as a native surrounded by natives. With memory of the remarkable Reri in Murnau's Tabu still keen it is out of reason to expect any other than a full-fledged South Sea islander to make good in a parallel part. The player is slight where her agile predecessor possesses great physical power with paralleling skill as a dancer. Del Rio is entitled to praise for her really fine work.

For the lovers of the romantic as well as of the beautiful and picturesque in backgrounds there are many warm if attractive moments. The scenes of the American boy and native girl honeymooning on an island otherwise uninhabited contain remarkable examples of waterfalls and rocks and tropical verdure.

Some of the followers of these fervid situations may get a smile and a lessening of the illusion when they note a wrinkle in the not quite invisible gauze brassiere imposed on the feminine lead--a gesture on the part of some one to offset a possible censorial squawk in spite of the obvious absurdity and incongruity of such action considering the surrounding circumstances.

Other players include John Halliday and Skeets Gallagher. King Vidor directs.

--George Blaisdell in The International Photographer, Vol. 4, No. 7 (August 1932), page 31.

☐ BLONDE VENUS (Paramount, 1932)

Calm realism rubs elbows with hasty improbability in The Blonde Venus, the much-talked-of new picture directed by Josef von Sternberg and starring Marlene Dietrich, the post-Garbo darling.

The impassive, slightly cadaverous Marlene, in The Blonde Venus, is a woman who takes life with both hands and rough-hews it to her ends. She passes from utter devotion to hopeless renunciation. She toys with defeat and despair with the maddening assurance of womankind, which realizes always that there are two weapons in life which are veritable Excaliburs--physical beauty and a sound heart.

From wife, to harlot, to popular woman of the theatre and back to wife is the gamut Miss Dietrich must pass. Her parade is a goose-step of confidence. Indeed, this is the true character of the part she plays, that of Helen Faraday, a woman who values as nothing the conventional requirements of propriety when she is faced with the grinding problems of true morality.

The theme is old as life, and almost as interesting. Helen Faraday has a sick husband but no money. She gets the money by the oldest, quickest and best method available to beautiful women. And she gets it from Nick Townsend, an attractive and gallant fellow played by Cary Grant. When Edward Faraday discovers the source of his wife's money, he repudiates her, snatches from her the five-year-old Johnny Faraday, and carries on in the fury of outraged righteousness. Helen thereupon adopts despair, becomes the sexual chattel of whoever appears, but finally recovers herself. Finally, she meets Nick again, visits Faraday in an effort to see her child, and becomes reconciled to him at the kiddie's bedside. Nick chivalrously disappears.

Acting honors, Miss Dietrich must share with Dickie Moore, playing the youngster, Johnny Faraday. Johnny's success, on the other hand, is entirely based on the lines written for him by Jules Furthman and S. K. Lauren. The child's lines, simple, strong and completely true, are psychologically the soundest this reporter has heard on the screen. Each bit of dialogue in which Johnny takes part is a delight to the mind.

Herbert Marshall does well in the part of Edward Faraday, the injured husband. Here again, the writers saw life as it is. For Edward, after straining at one gnat of infidelity--swallows the camel of prostitution. Nothing is truer than this wage of obstinacy.

Mr. von Sternberg--or shall we say, in the face of the formidable "von," Freiherr von Sternberg?--is a director of force and instinctive cunning. His manner of handling continuity of scenes is impatient but sound, something like the prose of the De Goncourts. He wastes no time on matters which would bore the injudicious. Here is where improbability rears its horrid head.

The story, to our mind, came to one logical end when Helen staggers out of a flophouse, degraded beyond recall, with the waters of death beckoning to her. We admit that the story should not be allowed to end there. A come-back is too sweet to reject. But the interval between Helen's crushing defeat and her immense success

as a cabaret singer a few months later, is covered only by a trifling
dialogue en passant.   We also admit that harlots do come back and
sometimes gloriously.   But we submit that here is where the drama-
tist and the director must exercise their utmost skill and penetra-
tion.   We would have cheerfully foregone many shots of trains and
steamers for the sake of one sharp episode showing Helen's struggle
to regain her integrity.

The cast of The Blonde Venus is large.   Everybody did the
job well.   Special mention is deserved by Gene Morgan and Robert
Emmett O'Connor, who played the two vaudeville managers.

The Blonde Venus should be a howling box-office success.   It
has all the ingredients.   It fills the eye, it prods at the tear-ducts,
it does not tax the intelligence.   To be just, it ladles out generous
portions of emotional truth.

> --José Rodriguez in Rob Wagner's
> Script, Vol. 8, No. 189 (Septem-
> ber 24, 1932), page 8.

*   *   *

This picture attempts to de-glamorize Marlene Dietrich.   She
is a down-to-earth person and is exotic only in a few sequences.
But her exotic scenes remain the best and you are not quite convinced by her other type of work.   It is a mother love story, and
besides smooth direction, there is the unforgettable Herbert Marshall
as the soul-torn husband, and charming little Dickie Moore.

> --Photoplay, Vol. 42, No. 6
> (November 1932), page 58.

☐   THE BRIDE OF FRANKENSTEIN (Universal, 1935)

Out of the several pictures with great possibilities that have
come along in a month, it is oddly enough The Bride of Frankenstein
that puts up the best show.   Advertised as a chiller, this film turns
out to be something else, having a lot of jollification, nice fancy,
elegant mounting--there is, in short, beauty as well as the beast.

James Whale's whole method of production has been one of
going as easily as possible on the supernatural.   The everyday note
is stressed continually--as in the petty bombast of the chief burgher
after the monster's capture, as in the pathetic business of having
the Thing burn his hand and, with every man's horror turned against
him, find a friend in the blind hermit.   And for macabre good humor, there is the role of the scientist who uses his power over the
monster to get Frankenstein's collaboration on a mate for the poor
brute.   With the good assistance of Boris Karloff, the producers
have made their wild story rather human, and the audience gets it.

In background, atmosphere, dramatic invention, The Bride of Frankenstein will stand up as one of the best of the year. The episode of the electric storm is an astonishing bit of well-sustained imaginative play. There are traces of Caligari, particularly in the stylized woods and crag of the first chase sequence (a quite breathless and eerie sort of affair), but the point is that in such matters Caligari is gone one better, cardboard backdrops not being here quite so much an end in themselves. In short, a great deal of art has gone into the planning and making of whole portions of this film, but it is the kind of art that gives the healthy feeling of men with their sleeves rolled up and working, worrying only about how to put the thing over in the best manner of the medium--no time for nonsense and attitudes and long hair.

> --Otis Ferguson in The New Republic, Vol. 83 (May 29, 1935), page 75.

☐ BRINGING UP BABY (RKO, 1938)

In view of the heavy thought that has recently gone into the question Is Humor Best for Us?, I am happy to report that Bringing Up Baby is funny from the word "go," that it has no other meaning to recommend it, nor therapeutic qualities, and that I wouldn't swap it for practically any three things of the current season. For comedy to be really good, of course, there is required something more in the way of total design than any random collection of hilarities. There must be point--not a point to be made, which is the easy goal of any literary tortoise, but a point from which to start, as implicit throughout as the center of a circle. Bringing Up Baby has something of the sort. The actual story goes into the troubles of a paleontologist who first offends a prospective angel for his museum, then his fiancée, and then gets into the wild-goose affairs of a girl and her leopard and terrier and other family members, ending up in jail and of course in love. That could be done in two reels. What puts the dramatic spirit into it is the character of the harebrained young thing who gets him mixed up in all this.

Katharine Hepburn builds the part from the ground, breathless, sensitive, headstrong, triumphant in illogic, and serene in that bounding brassy nerve possible only to the very very well bred. Without the intelligence and mercury of such a study, the callous scheming of this bit of fluff would have left all in confusion and the audience howling for her blood. As it is, we merely accept and humor her, as one would a wife. Cary Grant does a nice job of underlining the situation; there is good support from Barry Fitzgerald, Walter Catlett, May Robson (the leopard was better than any of them, but is it art?). The film holds together by virtue of constant invention and surprise in the situations; and Howard Hawks' direction, though it could have been less heavy and more supple, is essentially that of film comedy. All of which could be elaborated,

techniques analyzed, points cited, etc. But why? Bringing Up Baby
is hardly a departure; it settles nothing; it is full of an easy inviting
humor. So do you want to go or don't you?

> --Otis Ferguson in The New Re-
> public, Vol. 94 (March 16, 1938),
> page 165.

☐ BROADWAY MELODY OF 1936 (M-G-M, 1935)

Looks as if Leo intends to chase the Warner boys up a
tree. In any event he's gone after their "Big Musical" crown and
is wearing it--temporarily?--with jaunty triumph. He has substi-
tuted sheer beauty for size in dance ensembles (Albertina Rasch and
Dave Gould), scores it with the best music yet (Nacio Herb Brown,
Arthur Freed, Edward Powell and Alfred Newman) and introduces a
whole bunch of new and sensational talent.

The biggest stand-out is Eleanor Powell, who can act, sing
and dance amazingly well. Besides which the girl has a whole load
of that elusive quality called personality. Cast in a role of the
country gal dreaming of Broadway triumphs, like that of Katharine
Hepburn in Morning Glory, she impersonates Katharine in her dream
lines, and not only does she do it to the finest gradation of posture
and accent, she looks so much like Kate as to be almost uncanny.
As for her dancing--you ain't seen nothin'.

In my opinion Jack Benny is the brightest and most original
smart-cracking comedian on screen or radio. In this picture he has
as a side-kick (he's more than a "feeder") Sid Silvers, who clicks
with a swell brand of his own comedy. A grand team.

(As master of ceremonies at the preview, Jack Benny said,
"Most of you will no doubt expect me to plug for Jello, my radio
sponsor, but naturally that would be entirely out of place on an
M. G. M. program. However I feel that it is my duty to tell you
that Jello comes in six flavors...!")

Una Merkel, of course, is her usual bright and beautiful
self. Robert Taylor will be new to many--he's a real find. A
new dance team, Vilma and Buddy Ebsen, click notably.

For an individual hit, Robert Wildhack, in his famous snoring
stunt, literally panicked the preview audience.

Even the old backstage story has many new twists and exceptionally bright dialogue. Credit Jack McGowan, Sid Silvers and
Harry Conn.

Roy del Ruth again proves that he's tops in big musicals.

A rare orchid to John Considine, Jr. , producer.
                              --Rob Wagner in Rob Wagner's
                                Script, Vol. 14, No. 333 (Sep-
                                tember 21, 1935), page 10.

☐ CAMILLE (M-G-M, 1937)

        Greta Garbo may have been built up by glamour and mystery,
but she will stay on the heights by great artistry.   I haven't seen
all the famous Camilles, but I never expect to see one as satisfactory as this little Swedish ex-milliner.   As a prostitute she is gay,
indifferent and disillusioned.   When love comes she is utterly convincing, and in approaching death she is sublime.

        Some of the critics have kidded Robert Taylor, saying he is
nothing but a beautiful boy.   In this picture he acts, perhaps not
triumphantly, but darned well.   For much of which we must no
doubt credit George Cukor, the director.   But Robert will grow;
that's obvious.

        Lionel Barrymore has only one big scene, but he plays it
with his usual sincerity.   He convinced not only Greta but the audience that Robert's marriage to her would be fatal to both.

        Henry Daniell, as the rich baron, gives a fine performance
of restraint and aristocratic manners.   Laura Hope Crews is gorgeously rowdy and Lenore Ulric injects a rich, rare and particularly
racy comedy into her part.

        Elizabeth Allan handles her bit with her usual charm, and
Jessie Ralph fits her part perfectly.   Rex O'Malley is fine--as are
all the lesser characters.

        Zoë Akins, Frances Marion and James Hilton have prepared
a perfect script from the old Alexandre Dumas fils novel and play,
and David Lewis has given the story rich and handsome production,
with Adrian coming across with the most beautiful gowns seen on
the screen in a long time.

        But one thing I can't understand: Why is it that after all the
care Douglas Shearer must have gone to, to get perfect sound recording, that at a press preview they turn over the sound projection
to a deaf person who "steps up" the dialogue until the characters
fairly shout?   At times Laura Hope Crews rattled the rivets in the
roof-beams.   At other times the characters would be speaking what
is considered "normal" (but too loudly for a normal listener) when
suddenly some one would bust out like a machine gun.

        With fine recorded music, a beautiful production is no longer
at the mercy of a bum organist, but apparently it is still at the

mercy of noise-loving sound projectionists.
                                        --Rob Wagner in Rob Wagner's
                                        Script, Vol. 16, No. 400 (Janu-
                                        ary 30, 1937), page 10.

☐ CAPTAIN BLOOD (Warner Bros. , 1935)

Abaft, scums, or I'll bash yer bloody brains out on yon binnacle! Yes, mates, that's the talk in this new spoke of the torture
cycle.   And Captain Blood lives up to his name even if, after wad-
ing knee-deep in blood, he doesn't get one drop on his pretty shirt
or even prettier pan. Also this is swash-drammer on the raging
main, even if the sails and halyards hang limp throughout the main's
ragings.   Unlike its "Bounteous" rival, this saga of the sea also
packs a pretty gal, even though she has to slosh hither and yon in
a pretty white-satin ball gown.

But after all, it's only make-believe (though no one can make
me believe that Englishmen were ever so bloody crool, human
skunks so odorless and seamanship so punk), and kids who still like
"piruts," matrons whose domestic mates are wash-outs, and college
lads who go nuts over pretty girls in satin flounces, will no doubt
simply eat this pitcher up. In fact though the whole nautical ome-
lette left my timbers without a shiver, I'll bet you 100,000 pieces
of 8 against just one piece of 8 that the bloody carnival will be a
box-office wow.

Errol Flynn, a newcomer, is a handsome, personable rascal,
but a bit theatrical and posey.   And where did he, a ragged slave,
get such pretty, well-tailored uniforms after he captured that ship?
(Why from "Gowns by Milo Anderson," you poor cluck!)

Olivia de Havilland is a pretty wench (good olde English
worde) and after Errol had been looking into the piratical pans of
Guy Kibbee, David Torrence, Frank McGlynn, Sr. , Ross Alexander,
Robert Barrat and--heavens, what an interminable crew!--it was
easy to understand why she looked good to him.

But if you should ask me--which you probably won't--Lionel
Atwill is the most believable character in the whole dreadful debacle.

Hal Mohr's photography is grand, but I can't rave over the
miniature stuff.   It looked very little-boyish.   In the battle stuff,
three huge ships under full canvas within a hundred yards of the
shore switched around like bobbing corks.   After a battle that shot
down everything including the flagpole at the Warner studio, the
victors line up on the deck of a vessel that could put right to sea.

As I said before, it's all make-believe, so what the heck?

Nobody but a silly artist--or a still sillier sailor--will notice such things.

--Rob Wagner in Rob Wagner's
Script, Vol. 14, No. 348 (January 11, 1936), page 13.

☐ CAVALCADE (Fox, 1932)

The internationality of art is a commonplace truism.   Whistler learned from Hokusai; Foujioka, now exhibiting at the Exposi-
tion gallery, sat at the feet of Matisse; every country making motion pictures is contributing to the culture of the cinema.

Cavalcade is shot distinctly in the Russian manner.   A background of tremendous historical events tells the story, which we see
reflected in the lives of the principal characters.   Four years of
war are shown to us subjectively in a rapid kaleidoscope of lap-
dissolved shots of death and destruction, accompanied by terrific
noise.   Perhaps the most effective shot of the picture is the awful
drama of the sinking of the Titanic shown merely by a simple and
direct suggestion to the intellect.

At the time of Queen Victoria's Diamond Jubilee in 1894,
England was at the height of her greatness and Alfred Austen, the
poet laureate, celebrated the event in a grandiose poem called
"Processional. " In the midst of the cheering another poet by the
name of Rudyard Kipling shocked the nation by coming forth with a
poem called "Recessional, " in which he sounded a prophetic warning
of the future--"Lord God of Hosts, be with us yet, lest we forget,
lest we forget. " Cavalcade is an epic of that extraordinary proph-
ecy.

That's why Cavalcade is a difficult picture to review.   It is
easy to describe the obvious; not so easy to make plain the mark-
ings on the soul of a nation brought about by stupendous historic
events and shown on the screen by the montage method.   All I can
say is that Frank Lloyd (and it's a director's picture) approached
his huge canvas with the assurance of a master, and delivered all
and perhaps more than Noel Coward wrote into the original stage
play.

I was in London during the Boer War, at the time of Queen
Victoria's death and funeral, and the fidelity with which the scenes
of this period were made shows that anything can be reproduced in
Hollywood.   William Darling has performed a miracle of art directing.   All that was missing at the Queen's funeral was the drizzle.

Another artistic triumph is the all-British cast.   No American howsoever good--or howsoever important his studio contract!--
could have been equal to the complete British flavor the story demanded.   Nor did Frank Lloyd yield to the temptation to introduce,

for box-office reasons, a single American. Once I heard, just for
an instant, "Yankee Doodle," and I feared the worst. But, no--.

You all know Clive Brook, Beryl Mercer, Herbert Mundin,
and Billy Bevan--well, they all came through gloriously. Of the
newcomers, Diana Wynyard has the biggest role, and she gives a
remarkable performance of a thoroughbred Englishwoman glorified
rather than embittered by her sufferings.

Of the others Una O'Connor as the homely maid of the household gives a performance as clean-cut as a cameo. Merle Tottenham, as a typical moronic skivvy, dominates every scene she is in.
Others of the cast do equally well. Indeed there is not one weak
color on Frank Lloyd's palette.

It's a grand show, mates.

Gosh, I nearly forgot to mention Ernest Palmer, the cinematographer. His work is entirely worthy of his magnificent subject.
The same goes for the musical direction of Louis de Francesco.

Reginald Berkeley did the screen play and Sonia Levien the
continuity from Noel Coward's play. Noel should thank them handsomely.
                              --Rob Wagner in Rob Wagner's
                                Script, Vol. 8, No. 206 (Janu-
                                ary 21, 1933), page 8.

                        *   *   *

Very rarely a film succeeds in presenting not only a poignantly human story, but also in conveying the sweep and power of
world events against which the humans work out their lives. It is
this rare achievement which makes Fox's version of Noel Coward's
stage success, Cavalcade, so outstanding. Starting with a heart-
broken upper middle-class mother (Diana Wynyard) sending her officer husband (Clive Brook) to the Boer War, it portrays his safe return and happy years rearing their two boys, until maritime disaster
takes one (John Warburton), and the World War snatches the other
(Frank Lawton) on Armistice Day. Yet at the end the aged and
broken parents still carry on with indomitable British spirit. Woven
through this, their butler (Herbert Mundin) and maid (Una O'Connor)
live out the rise, decline and death under drink of a Cockney parent,
while their daughter (Ursula Jeans) rises to fame via the music hall
stage.

A cavalcade, yes--a kaleidoscope, too--yet through it all
sounds the mighty tread of history's march, portrayed in epic scenes
that still blend beautifully with the detailed human sorrows and joys.
Magnificently staged and every role, major and minor, is outstandingly done, especially the comedy bits by Beryl Mercer, Tempe
Pigott and Merle Tottenham. You must see this!
                              --Photoplay, Vol. 43, No. 4
                                (March 1933), page 59.

☐ THE CHAMP (M-G-M, 1931)

There isn't a machine-gunning in it.   There's no more sexiness in it than there is in an annual crop report.   No colossal sets;
no song-and-dance routines....

But boy-oh-boy, is The Champ one grand picture!   It is--it's
one of the best talkies of the year, and if you don't get many times
your money's worth out of it, you'd better see a psychiatrist.

Wallace Beery is an ex-heavyweight champ, who's slid down
the toboggan via booze and gambling, until he's just a Tia Juana
bum.   Jackie Cooper is his son--and the love between them, Jackie's
supreme faith in his dad, is a thing beautifully played by these two
artists.

As the story unfolds, you'll howl with laughter, you'll thrill
at exciting scenes--and, suddenly, you'll come up against a bit that'll
tear your heart out.   Whether you're old or young, woman or man,
you'll cry at least once, and you won't be ashamed.   There's never
been an actor who can yank tears from audiences as Jackie Cooper
can.   And there's never been an actor who can play a no-good bum
and still make you love him as Wally Beery can.

Direction (by King Vidor), story, dialogue, photography--all
grand.   Don't miss The Champ.

--Photoplay, Vol. 41, No. 1 (December 1931), page 47.

*   *   *

One night, years ago, I sat with D. W. Griffith at a first
night showing of his newest picture.   "Hear that, Rob?   When they
start blowing their noses I know I've got 'em!"   For nose-blowing
is the embarrassed "out" of the proud Nordic when tears begin to
flow.   During two or three scenes of The Champ, the nasal trumpet-
ing and sniffles sounded as though the whole audience had been suddenly stricken with the epizoodic.

Of course there is nothing more heart-wringing than the fa-
ther-and-son equation, and given a father and son like Wally Beery
and Jackie Cooper, leave it to Frances Marion to emerge the champ
wringer of them all.

It was like this: Wally Beery is a great big, good-natured,
tender-hearted, moronic slob who became the world's champion prize
fighter.   Irene Rich married him in his glory, but with his cheap
vanity and weakness for booze, his glory was short-lived, and after
he had degenerated into a bum, Irene divorced him.   By some
queer judicial quirk--or more likely, for story purposes--their child,
Jackie Cooper, was awarded to the husband.

The story opens with Jackie and Wally living in comparative squalor, Jackie trying to keep Wally sober enough to stage a fighting comeback.   During a temporary flushness Wally buys Jackie a horse and enters him in the Tia Juana races.   Comes Irene and her new husband, Hale Hamilton.   Irene recognizes her child and wants to take him away from his bad environment.   After much to-do, Wally decides to give Jackie up "so the kid will have a chance."   Fine, except that Jackie runs away from his rich mother and returns to Wally.

Then for the big punch.   Wally is in training for the championship fight.   Drink, late hours, bad heart; he hasn't a chance. He has lost Jackie's horse at gambling and things look dark.   In the fight Wally is cut to ribbons, but a lucky poke when he's all but out gives him the championship.

But the wages of victory is death, and in that scene--well, at Noah's Ark the deluge was on the screen; in The Champ it is the audience that is deluged.   I floated out into the court of the Chinese Theatre in such a flood of tears I never "touched bottom" until I got on to the high ground of the parking station.

Yes, Frances Marion has written a box-office knockout (the Chinese Theatre was jammed at the Sunday matinee).   Wally Beery gives the best performance of his moronic screen life.   And as for Jackie Cooper, he hereby wins my vote for next year's Academy award.

(It is absurd, of course, to say that a mere child like Jackie Cooper is as great an artist as Lionel Barrymore, who would glorify any character he undertook, while Jackie has very definite limits. But the Academy awards are based upon individual performances and Jackie's individual performance in The Champ will stand up with that of the finest actors of any age.)

Irene Rich has grown even richer in the talking pictures and her mother stuff was put over with fine restraint and a pleasant lack of sentimentality.

Hale Hamilton gives his usual finished performance in the role of the rich husband and Roscoe Ates makes a very good fight trainer.   In each picture Ates is using less and less of his stammering.   A great mistake, as it was one of the funniest of human idiosyncrasies.   Apparently, however, Ates seems to reason that audiences will really think him a stammerer if he does it all the time.   He should care what they think if he can get those rare and precious laughs.   Which being the case, Edward Brophy steals the acting honors from him in the same sort of role.

The dialogue of Leonard Praskins is crisp, human, and to the point.   No long editorial or narrative speeches.

Cedric Gibbons does a swell job with the sets, and Gordon Avil's camera work, except in the paddocks at Tia Juana, is excellent.

Again, to get even with King Vidor because of his well-known disrespect for writers, I mention him last. But again I have to admit that he's one grand director.

--Rob Wagner in Rob Wagner's
Script, Vol. 6, No. 145 (November 21, 1931), page 6.

☐ THE CHARGE OF THE LIGHT BRIGADE (Warner Bros. , 1937)

This long awaited picture has arrived with a bang, figuratively and literally. A gorgeous and beautifully produced saga of India and the Crimea, simply bursting with excitement and battle stuff. Perhaps too much of the latter as, especially toward the end, it completely smothers the fragile story of the old, old theme of the two brothers in love with the same girl, the loser making the supreme sacrifice.

I am a poor judge of mystery dramas and battle stories, as I can't solve mysteries even when explained in the inevitable courtroom scene, and I can stand only about so much battle-noise and confusion.

But up to the shambles I was intensely interested. The direction (Michael Curtiz) is superb; the sets, especially the palace interiors (Jack Hughes), are rich and convincing; the photography (Sol Polito and Fred Jackman) stunningly beautiful; the sound (uncredited) exceptionally fine, especially in its perspectives. I should like to credit some one for the gorgeous military costumes, but surely they don't come under the head "Gowns by Milo Anderson"!

If Errol Flynn's first acting was in Captain Blood, he is a wonder and traveling fast. A handsome, personable chap, he enacts the leading role with fine spirit.

As the lone romantic note in the midst of chaos, Olivia de Havilland is both beautiful and charming. A grand cast of troupers in which C. Henry Gordon reaches high in the part of an Indian prince. Donald Crisp puts over a wonderful character in the person of Olivia's father. His lines are spoken with decision and his usual Crispness. A good lesson to the mumblers and mouthers.

Henry Stephenson, of course. And Spring Byington--delicious. And lots prettier than most of the kid stars. Patric Knowles is a romantic chap, always the gentleman. I wish David Niven had had a bigger part, and G. P. Huntley, Jr. I like those fellows a lot.

Can't name them all, but not one miscast.

I have only one serious criticism of the picture--the (apparent?) cruelty to the horses in the battle scenes. They must have

been tripped, injured and possibly killed.   In one shot a horse in
the middle distance remained on his back, his legs stiff!

There were also too many stunt men doing high dives off
walls into nets.   Surely every man shot in battle does not pitch forward.   But it was the horse stuff that got me.   Wait till the "Animal Defense League of England" gets a wallop at those battle scenes!

--Rob Wagner in <u>Rob Wagner's</u>
<u>Script</u>, Vol. 16, No. 399 (Janu-
ary 23, 1937), page 12.

☐ CHRISTOPHER STRONG (RKO, 1933)

The society folk were tired of playing treasure hunt, so somebody offered a prize for the perfect husband and another prize for
the girl over twenty-one who'd never had a love affair.   Helen
Chandler rushes off to get her father, Colin Clive, who wins the
perfect husband prize.   Katharine Hepburn, a famous aviatrix, turns
up and wins the other prize by confessing her lovelessness.

But when perfections meet, look out!   Colin falls for Kate
and Kate for Colin.   You can almost understand Clive's defection,
knowing his sidekick, Billie Burke, who is one of those awful mar-
tyred wives who chokes on her vowels and soul-stuffs all over the
works.   On the other hand, Kate is purposeful, efficient, almost
masculine, and breaks aviation records.   That's unromantic enough,
but in addition, she wears jodhpurs, and when jodhpurs walk across
the field, sex goes into a tailspin!

Then, looking at it from Kate's point of view, Colin is rich,
aristocratic and "perfect," but the most lugubrious lover who ever
necked with a stricken conscience.

No, it was just one of those love things that simply wouldn't
jell, so Gilbert Frankau, the author, sends Miss Hepburn up for an
altitude record, drops her thirty thousand feet to mortuary fame and
a bronze tablet, and sends Mr. Clive sobbingly back to join his
doloroso spouse.

The only real understandable love breaks loose between Helen
Chandler and Ralph Forbes, and the fact that he is married doesn't
bother her.   While waiting for him to come across, she meets Jack
La Rue, who wrongs her in jaunty Continental fashion.   Ralph over-
looks her impatience and--clinch!

Colin Clive is a fine actor, and does a swell job, in spite of
Dorothy Arzner's insistence upon his gloom.   (I have a feeling that
Dot has it in for us men.)   Ralph Forbes and Helen Chandler both
do well, but Billie Burke is too throaty and theatrical.

However, it is Katharine Hepburn's show, and if you can restrain your laughter at her jodhpurs, she'll give you an eyeful of
one of the most fascinating personalities of the screen.   I again insist that she play Jeanne d'Arc!

--Rob Wagner in Rob Wagner's
Script, Vol. 9, No. 222 (May
13, 1933), pages 9 and 19.

*   *   *

This is Katharine Hepburn's second feature and her first
starring venture.   Point of high interest to the trade was whether
she would repeat her initial smash impression in Bill of Divorcement.   New release justifies the hopes of the girl's well-wishers,
and does so under rather trying circumstances in that the story is
a weak vehicle for a new star.   Weak, that is, in the profound appeal that was inherent in A Bill of Divorcement, however flamboyant
it may be in theatrical situation.

The people in this picture are merely glamorous stage puppets; they never once touch human reality.   Picture is a peculiar
compromise between an effort to produce a class subject and a desire to reach for the cinema generality.   It falls down on both ob-
jectives and is saved only partially by a fine performance of this
newcomer and capital team work by an expert supporting cast.
Story is handled in the manner noted recently in Radio's class output in the respect that it drawls when it aims most for brisk effect
and drags lamentably at many points.

Star role, that of an English aviatrix, is a sort of step-sis-
ter to the ingenue part of Divorcement so far as it makes of her a
svelte and elegant sort of tomboy; but there the family resemblance
ceases.   Relationship between Sydney of Divorcement and Lady Cynthia of Christopher Strong is less than superficial and only the in-
sinuating quality of Miss Hepburn gives them anything in common.

The new picture is overloaded with playwright device that is
just that and nothing more.   Lady Cynthia, the aviatrix, picks her
dramatic moment of sorrowful renunciation to break the world's altitude record so she can commit suicide in a tailspin from 35,000
feet.   That couldn't happen anywhere but in a scenario.   So that the
scene becomes just a screen stunt, arresting enough as a stunt, but
leaving it pretty hard for a sincere actress to make her sentimental
moment register for anything but a side-show gasp.

Footage is abundantly supplied with similar moments, action
studied mainly for footlight effect.   Sometimes Miss Hepburn coaxes
to an illusion, but the others seldom get a chance to break through
the story's artificiality.   So they make themselves as graceful and
agreeable as the circumstances permit.

Billie Burke has grown camera wise since her first picture
and manages the not especially engaging role of an old-fashioned

matron with much skill. Colin Clive is saddled with a part that
probably nobody could make register as anything more than a background, a middle-aged man who falls earnestly but distractedly in
love with the heroine to her destruction. Clive must have been a
little uncomfortable and he looks it. The rest of the people do not
especially matter, being merely a fringe of gay young things, though
Helen Chandler and Ralph Forbes acquit themselves satisfactorily as
a pair of amusing young lovers.

Physical production is exceedingly well managed, and the
camera work is notable in a day when fine photography is taken for
granted.

                              --Rush in Variety, Vol. 110, No.
                              1 (March 14, 1933), page 14.

☐ CIMARRON (RKO, 1931)

Why is it that in all these pioneer pictures the hero always
talks about Destiny and Empire-building? We've known a lot of
pioneers, each and every one of whom went out after land, gold,
oil, or just adventure and damfoolishness, leaving historians of patriotism like George M. Cohan and Jim Cruze to paint 'em as Sons
of Destiny. Besides, Will and I thought we'd ended all that hokum
in Two Wagons--Both Covered. * We proved that to attempt to found
an empire in this here Republic was pretty near to treason. Another
"besides": Our pioneers--Will's and mine--went west to found an
empire with a crate of roosters and one bull. These "Big Trail,"
"Great Meadow," and "Cimarron" pioneers went forth with less than
a bull.

I don't know whom to blame for Yancey Cravat--mebbe Edna
Ferber or mebbe Howard Estabrook. But no matter who invented
his character, it's pretty ham. Looking for all the world like William Jennings Bryan in his younger days, I'll bet sixteen to one that
Richard Dix would have recited the "cross of gold" speech if they'd
given him a chance. And Dix is a good actor at that.

Some grand opening shots of the Oklahoma land rush--tem-
pestuous and exciting. But as many of the rushers were headed for
choice acres miles and miles from the starting line, it is hard to
believe that they would exhaust their horses in the first few furlongs
by racing like runaway fire wagons. However, that's motion pictures. Horsemen always ride at full tilt whether the goal be the
water trough at the east end of the studio lot or the Grand Canyon of
the Colorado two hundred miles away.

---

*A 1924 parody short of The Covered Wagon, starring Will Rogers
and directed by Rob Wagner.

Irene Dunne is the second in importance in the cast and her
reserve is in delightful contrast to Richard's lion-heartiness.   So
reserved is she in fact that when Richard comes in, shot right
through the arm, she doesn't so much as rise from her chair to
remove his shirt or bathe him.   However, perhaps she noted that
his prop wound didn't in the least interfere with the use of that
member.   The only other arm we ever saw shot that way hung limp
and inert.

Miss Dunne's work improved with the years and in the last
sequence, as a Congresswoman, she was truly magnificent, and I
can easily subscribe to Will Rogers' enthusiasm for her banquet
speech, always remembering, however, that Will's interest was
largely edited by her defense of the Oklahoma Indians.

All in all, however, this picture largely belongs to the character people, the best of whom, in my opinion, are Roscoe Ates,
the stammering printer, whose age creeps on with amazing verisim-
ilitude, and Edna May Oliver, who puts over a pursy old New Eng-
lander with most repressed and delicious comedy.   William Collier,
Jr. , makes a better kid outlaw than many of the standard western
heavies and George E. Stone does a Jew peddler without clowning
the part.

As an "epic" the picture is much better than most of those
claiming that grandiose title and Wesley Ruggles has directed the
various sequences and bridged the time lapses with fine artistry.

Also, the camerawork of Eddie Cronjager is superb.

The tag to me is an artistic blunder.   No doubt it was "necessary" to bring Richard Dix back, but I never wanted to see Yancey Cravat again after his last domestic desertion.   Personally, I
should like to round up all the "empire builders" on the one hundred
and tenth floor of the Empire Building and push them off.

However, after all my crabbing about the old pioneer hokum,
Cimarron is darn good entertainment.
                              --Rob Wagner in Rob Wagner's
                                Script, Vol. 5, No. 114 (April
                                18, 1931), page 8.

                    *   *   *

The talkie version of Edna Ferber's thrilling novel of pioneer
days in Oklahoma is by far the finest thing Radio Pictures and
Richard Dix have ever done.   The picture carries all the sweep and
power of Ferber's best seller.   Not only is the land rush sequence
one of the most exciting ever shot, but Dix's portrayal of Yancey
Cravat gives him new screen rating as one of our finest actors.
One of the year's best pictures.
                              --Photoplay, Vol. 39, No. 3
                                (February 1931), page 54.

☐ THE CITADEL (M-G-M, 1938)

A fine, exciting and dramatic picture of the struggle of a
young doctor in England to justify himself, his ideals and his profession.   The background is new and interesting and the incident is
noteworthy for its effectiveness.   There are splendid performances
by Robert Donat and Rosalind Russell and a wealth of exploitation
material.   It's a triumph for American production in England and a
treat for American audiences.   Give it the gun, it's a grand production.

Taken from the best seller of the same name, the picture
has managed quite remarkably to take only the very best parts of
the book and has made excellent changes in the story that the book
could have stood.   The screenplay has improved the drama and
logic one hundred percent.   It is, in reality, an expose of the panel
system and private nursing homes of England.   It traces the career
of a brilliant, young doctor who almost starves by fighting authority
out loud and by the wrong method.   He is then caught in a web of
his own weaving: catering to neurotics at fancy fees and trading
patients with doctors who are not representative of the medical profession.   He manages to redeem himself after his best friend dies
because of inadequate surgery on the part of one of his "friendly"
doctor associates.

King Vidor has brought forth a really beautiful picture that
has any number of moments that are touching and moving due to excellent directorial management.

Robert Donat, as the young doctor, is a very, very good
actor and gives a most legitimate reading of his part that makes it
a standout of its kind without unnecessary heroics.   Rosalind Russell gives one of her very best performances as Donat's wife and
best friend and severest critic.   Ralph Richardson is a knockout as
the cynical, besotted surgeon who redeems himself through his faith
in Donat and then is killed by his disappointment in him.   He's been
seen here before and he should be seen much more often.   Dilys
Davis is excellent as a money-grubbing shrew and there are fine
performances on the part of everyone in the cast with a too small
part for Emlyn Williams, whose acting rates far more.

The musical scoring of the picture is more than impressive
. . . it's arresting in spots and plays a great part in the dramatics
of the picture.   The photography is tops, particularly the scenes in
the mines.   Altogether Ben Goetz has one of the finest productions
of the year and a picture that will cause plenty of talk here and
abroad.

--The Hollywood Reporter, Vol.
48, No. 16 (October 22, 1938),
page 3.

*   *   *

Better than <u>Arrowsmith</u>, as good (though not so important)
as <u>Louis Pasteur</u>, the greatest thing King Vidor has done since <u>The</u>
<u>Crowd</u>, and a personal triumph for Robert Donat, entitling him <u>as</u>
<u>well</u> as his director to serious consideration for Academy awards.
Such, before enthusiasm had been qualified by reflection, were my
thoughts after seeing M-G-M's picturization of A. J. Cronin's <u>The</u>
<u>Citadel</u>, produced by Victor Saville in England, and the best <u>news</u>
to cross the Atlantic since the peace of Munich.

To silence readers of the novel, Dr. Cronin himself approved
certain important story changes, and as a result the screen play is
a model of economy, balance, and dramatic unity; flawlessly blending action and the year's finest screen dialogue to reproduce various
aspects of British life and character, from the Welsh mining dis-
tricts to Mayfair and Harley Street.   The acting is so good that
run-of-the-mill Hollywood Thespians will probably stage a wholesale
exodus, fleeing with their costly chattels and vanity.   I think I'll
retract that statement though--because Hollywood really respects
accomplishment, and the preview of <u>The Citadel</u>, which had even the
aisles choked with enthralled spectators, was received with enthusiasm appropriate to Hedy Lamarr's knock on a gentleman's door.

In a short review it is impossible even to begin to enumerate
the excellences of what I may happily describe as a real motion picture.   I need not tell a million book readers that <u>The Citadel</u> is the
quite conventional but engrossing story of a doctor's discovery that
his own profession can stink to high heaven.   Although the picture
is entertaining always, immensely moving, and rich with pungent
characterizations, it indirectly wallops the tar out of medical hypocrisy,
tips its hat to socialized medicine, gives decent and high-minded
medicos a fair deal by showing what they are indeed up against--
mainly ourselves, from the stupid miners who run Dr. Donat out of
town because he wants to help them and they want pink pills instead,
to the dowagers chastely in love with the bedside-manner and too
rich to be jilted.

In general, <u>The Citadel</u> is a remarkable picture because it
sticks to its job, doing what the stage or novel can't; but in addition, this production bears the imprint of intelligence and good taste
--rare in even the best of films.   Mr. Vidor never descends to the
obvious or the cinematically trite.   His treatment of the industrial
towns suggests Arnold Bennett at his early best.   I think the miners,
their families, and that amputation performed in the crumbling tun-
nel would have pleased D. H. Lawrence.   And if this begins to
sound a bit literary for a movie notice, then I may be excused when
I say that <u>The Citadel</u> has the bite of reality.   It has inevitability.
It hurts.   It makes one pity.   Makes one feel shame and indignation, and, since <u>Zola</u>, when has a movie done just that?

In lighter moods, when Donat joins the fashionable practition-
ers in golf, there is some choice satire.   On the romantic side--
although Rosalind Russell is a sort of Leora, to men more of an
ideal wife than a nocturnal pastime--the film concentrates on that

novelty, fidelity, instead of frolic.   To mention only one instance of
cinematic genius: Vidor's subtle handling of the Italian delicatessen
owner (Mary Clare).   When the Italian's child undergoes an operation, the camera compresses the whole thing into two facial close-
ups, cuts to the daughter's feet once more dancing ecstatically,
averts tragedy, affirms happiness in a lightning stroke!   Even
Frank Capra could learn something from King Vidor, and if that
doesn't express approval, I'll give up!

But not before saluting Robert Donat as a better actor than
any we have over here, with the exception of Paul Muni who occu-
pies a different niche, and setting up a little typographic Hall of
Fame for a cast which includes Ralph Richardson, Rex Harrison,
Emlyn Williams, Dilys Davis, and Penelope Dudley Ward.

--Richard Sheridan Ames in Rob
Wagner's Script, Vol. 20, No.
484 (November 19, 1938), page
12.

☐   CITY LIGHTS (Chaplin/United Artists, 1931)

It has taken three years for Charlie Chaplin to film his challenge to the talkies.   The answer is not altogether successful.   The
weakness of his reply lies, I think, in having compromised with the
new idiom by using sound effects and mechanical music and revert-
ing in an astonishing degree to the use of the printed titles which in
his silent days he always considered an inherent weakness to pantomimic story telling.

I agree with Charlie that his screen character should never
speak.   The illusive, gnome-like Charlie (Charlot--Carlos) has become a symbol somewhat akin to Pierrot and Puck and symbols
must not come to corporeal life.   This does not mean, however,
that he cannot function in a real world.   In the days of silent pictures all of our screen characters were more or less unreal, but
the moment they found voice they became completely human.   Our
minds are now so completely adjusted to that fact that the pantomimic yammering of lips that are silent seems a bit absurd.   Not
even the genius of a Chaplin can read just the world's mental processes to an outworn idiom.

No doubt a degree of this partially unsuccessful experiment
is due to the inadequacy of the sound treatment.   In the silent pictures a master organist could "play the picture" with music appropriate to every mood and introduce sound effects that were hilariously amusing.   This was possible, of course, only in first-class
theatres; in small towns where Mamie might play "Hearts and
Flowers" during a storm, the results were terrible.   It was natural, therefore, that Charlie should have welcomed the mechanical
synchronized score, for in this way he could completely control the
character of the musical accompaniment.

But in this, his first experiment, the scoring is not satisfactory. The high notes screech, the low notes are faint or entirely missing, and none has the richness or gentleness of the organ. It is too bad Charlie didn't have Walt Disney score the picture. This boy has become the great master of perfect synchronization, amusing sound effects, and rich orchestral accompaniment.

I hope that in his next picture Charlie will accept the tremendous advantages of the audible screen even to the point of dialogue--not for his own character--but for all the others. Let Charlie (as he always has) come from Nowhere, live his short, silent, illusive moment in a world of reality, and then again disappear (as he does once more) into Nowhere. In fact, I think a little deaf and dumb figure, listening with his eyes and pantomiming his answers, playing his Jack-the-giant-killer role in a world of real giants, would be a more wistful, pathetic, and amusing character than if his world were also illusive.

Also I think that Charlie's three years of puzzlement and preparation for City Lights has taken some of the edge off his spontaneity. His opening gag on the statue is classically amusing; he has some wonderful new twists to a prize-fight sequence, but several of his gags, though well done, are very old--especially the one of Albert Austin eating the soap and blowing bubbles and the one where the blind girl winds the wrong piece of yarn and unravels his undershirt. A pansy gag in the locker room I felt was unworthy of his good taste.

In my opinion, next to The Kid, this is the best story Charlie has ever told, and in the last sequence where he meets the girl whose eyesight has been restored by his bounty, the drama rises to a pitch he has never before achieved.

Harry Myers came into his own in A Yankee in King Arthur's Court. Then for years he just stalled along in inconsequential parts. In City Lights he returns magnificently. He has a bigger part than / even Miss Virginia Cherrill, who was beautiful and charming, and he played his role with consummate comedy and fine finish.
--Rob Wagner in Rob Wagner's Script, Vol. 4, No. 104 (February 7, 1931), page 6.

*   *   *

After three years of careful preparation, Charles Spencer Chaplin's film, City Lights has reached the screen, and in our opinion it is well worth the wait. The point which seems to be the primary point for discussion is the fact that there is no conversation in City Lights. The success of this silent film does not mean Mr. Chaplin has proven that the talkies are inadequate or unnecessary ... it merely proves again what we have known only too well ... that Mr. Chaplin's knowledge of pantomime is so profound that the medium through which he expresses his art is secondary. While

the arguments are raging to and fro as to the relative merits of
this film and the better talkies, it may be well to remember that
the stage has a parallel in the person of Ruth Draper. Miss Draper can take a bare stage and a chair, and without the use of a
single line of conversation amuse an audience for an entire evening.

City Lights presents some of the most amusing comedy and
moving pathos ever filmed.

With the passing of years Mr. Chaplin's sense of comedy
takes on added depth and color. His art is a difficult thing to analyze, but as a feeble effort we should say this:

Mr. Chaplin's comedy is born of human understanding ... a
comedy that makes you laugh from the heart more than from the
abdomen, and leaves such a thin partition between the two organs
that you are ever receptive to his sudden transitions from smiles
to tears.

Perhaps the most appealing characteristic of this little tramp
figure is his spirit of good sportsmanship. He is the living embodiment of the old wheeze about "the man worth while is the man who
can smile".... Fate has kicked him in the pants until the ragged
little trousers seem to be holding their own by nothing more material than the indomitable spirit of their owner--a spirit that can
make you forget the safety pins and patches and cause the tattered
garments to take on an air of superlative gentility.

The story is not unlike a picture that Harry Langdon did
some time ago ... the love of a ragged tramp for a blind girl.
The big difference comes at the end of the film ... and wait until
you see the Chaplin finish. Sitting directly in front of this reviewer
was one of the hardest-boiled dramatic critics in New York, and
there were unmistakable tears in the gentleman's eyes, of which he
seemed singularly unashamed. The picture closes with surprising
abruptness, so we warn you to keep a handkerchief ready.

It might spoil some of your fun to discuss the gags in detail,
so we will just make appreciative mention of a few. The outstanding situation is the millionaire who, when he is drunk, takes Charley
to his home and treats him like a brother--but when he sobers up,
fails to recognize the tramp and has him kicked out of the house.
The gag runs through the film, and never fails to get a big laugh.
It is grand comedy and (if you care to look for it) presents a fine
touch of satire on fair-weather friendships.

Other situations deserving mention are the prize fight scene,
during which Charley manages to keep the referee between him and
his opponent; the cigar-lighting episode; the business of trying to
concentrate on the statue of a horse in a store window while he
steals guarded glances at a statue of a nude; stepping from a Rolls
Royce to pick up a cigar butt; the first scene--the public unveiling
of a statue--the sound of the voices of grandiloquent speakers repre-

sented by musical instruments--then the unveiling which finds Charley asleep in the arms of the statue.

One thing we did not like, and can see no excuse for its being left in the film, is the scene in which Charley acts effeminate while a pugilist is undressing.   Bad taste and entirely out of step with the picture.   There are one or two other touches that are suggestive of smut, but are excusable.

A great amount of credit is due Harry Myers for the support he offers the star in the role of the drunken millionaire.   Superb performance.   Virginia Cherrill as the blind girl, Florence Lee as her mother, and Hank Mann as the prize fighter are also excellent.

An indication of the success of City Lights in New York can be estimated from the boxoffice.   The daily receipts have averaged nearly ten thousand dollars--with hundreds of people being turned away.   Mr. Chaplin will undoubtedly make another two or three millions from this film--and deserves to.   He is a very great artist.

> --Harry Evans in Life, Vol. 97,
> No. 2521 (February 27, 1931),
> page 20.

☐ CLEOPATRA (Paramount, 1934)

When C. B. DeMille is at his best, he's the grandest pageanteer of them all.   And this picture tops anything he has done. A huge canvas of magnificent splendor (including every archaeological prop and gadget known to Rome), the cavalcade moves on through the familiar story, yet the drama is in no way overwhelmed.   Indeed (thanks to Waldemar Young and Vincent Lawrence--screen play --and Bartlett Cormack--adaptation) every character comes to life, despite his sartorial strangeness and the remoteness of the action in time and place.

Rome was materialistic and sensual, and Cleopatra (who was not so darned spiritual herself) played up to those weaknesses to the (literal) queen's taste.   After reducing Imperial Caesar to wax, she went after Marc Antony, and the world knows what she did to him.

The big punch, of course, occurs aboard her royal barge as it moves idly along the Nile.   In these scenes, C. B. cuts loose and puts on dances that will make you blink--if a censor, gasp!-- and then when Tony takes the chloroform, the dancing gals pull silken curtains across the royal couch so that we can't see what's going on.   But imagine goings-on taking place with only a curtain separating the goings-oners from the gallery!   However, as peeping toms were no doubt thrown to the crocodiles, the arrangement was oke in those far-off days.   Nor can I see how "the church" can ob-

ject, for you can't expect people to behave like Christians some
eighty-odd years before there was any Christianity.

Then, what better motivation for throwing away an empire
than Claudette Colbert? Gosh, I hope she doesn't appear at my
court with the pinnies she wears in this picture! And when you behold Henry Wilcoxon, you'll understand why Cleo fell for him--truly
the noblest Roman of them all.

A big cast, perfectly chosen--amazing how much Warren
William looks like the bust of Caesar in the Louvre--gorgeous sets,
wonderful sound effects, authentic props and beautiful cinematography.

Yes, this is a notable comeback for our greatest showman.

While passing credits, permit me to congratulate the bull for
his modest demeanor while sirens of the Nile slithered about him
in the most sensually provocative manner. I trust the cameramen
kept their minds on their marriage vows.

> --Rob Wagner in Rob Wagner's
> Script, Vol. 12, No. 289 (Oc-
> tober 20, 1934), page 10.

                    *   *   *

It would be a shame to have the Cecil B. DeMille type of
movie die off like the dinosaur. I am quite a noisy and obnoxious
rooter for subdued, conversational movies which get nowhere in particular (like One More River), but, just the same, I do get an ata-
vistic kick out of watching 5,000 extras running up 400 Cecil B.
DeMille steps and down again, whether it means anything or not.
And I like to see 50 horse-drawn chariots coming at me head-on
with a great clatter of cocoanut shells. And I gasp at Mr. De-
Mille's conception of high life in any era, though I realize he may
be a caterer at heart, rather than a great artist. The point is,
he's no piker. Whatever else he may be, he's grandiose. What a
boon he would be to the Roosevelt administration and the New Deal
if they would only make him Secretary of Extravagance!

Mr. DeMille's Cleopatra is a circus. And I mean just that.
It has the gaudy splendor and the magnitudinous phoniness of something done by Mr. Ringling, but it satisfies. It tells, with probably
no authenticity whatsoever, the story of the love affairs of Cleopatra
with (1) Julius Caesar and (2) Marc Antony, with 8,000 extras just
outside the door ready to go to war or to go into a dance at Mr.
DeMille's beck, and does he beck! Claudette Colbert is easy-going
and human as Cleopatra, and her naturalness and restraint make an
effective contrast with Mr. DeMille's pompous and artificial background, and he no doubt deserves credit for thinking of that. Warren William is a good and hungry-looking Caesar, and Henry Wilcoxon is a manly Marc Antony with romantic disdain of haircut.
The principals are all actors to the n-th degree, the extras are

beautifully regimented, the horses are magnificent, and all that it
lacks are elephants and peanuts.

--Don Herold in Life, Vol. 101,
No. 2595 (October 1934), page
30.

☐ THE CRIMINAL CODE (Columbia, 1931)

"A few more such pictures and the public will demand a reform of our penal institutions." That's what people have said at
the production of each and every one of the prison stories that have
been released in the past two years. We only wish it were true.

"It's pictures like All Quiet that will end war." So said nine
reviewers out of ten. But habits of thinking and ancient institutions
are not so easily killed. The news weeklies from Europe show
scarcely anything but marching soldiers yipping for war. As for
All Quiet, it has precipitated more violence in Europe than the story
records.

But if there is one picture that should make us thoughtful regarding modern penology, it is The Criminal Code, which shows that
our "eye for an eye" criminal code on the outside breeds a "tooth
for a tooth" code within prison walls. Furthermore, it is as inex-
orable, cold, and relentless as our criminal code. In other words,
our criminals, instead of regarding our penal institutions as places
of friendly rehabilitation, consider them enemy camps of punishment
and degradation.

This theme was slammed over to us in the stage play by
Martin Flavin, and it is slammed over again in the film version very
well done by Fred Niblo, Jr. The chances are, however, that the
basic lesson is lost to most fans in their immediate interest in the
principals. Here indeed was a place in which the Russian treatment
of bringing the background forward and playing down the importance
of individuals would have been wonderfully applicable to the purpose
of the author.

An ugly story softened a bit by the beauty of the boy victim,
Phillips Holmes, the charm of the girl, the character of the warden,
Walter Huston, and the splendid direction of Howard Hawks. Even
the cameraman, James Howe, facing the ugliest possible backgrounds,
got a certain pictorial beauty into the scenes.

Here is one time that an unhappy ending was changed to a
happy one without injuring the story. Walter Huston is simply magnificent in his role, and although it seemed cruel to cast so beautiful a boy as Phillips Holmes in such a grim part, perhaps that's
what gave his character poignancy.

DeWitt Jennings in the part of the cruel prison guard gave a performance second only to Huston. Jennings is usually cast in the most unpleasant roles, but his artistry invariably gives tremendous strength to the story. He is without doubt one of the screen's finest artists.

Miss Constance Cummings is new to me, but she acted her part with a fine repression and great subtlety.

The part of the warden's old maid sister, which was played for comedy on the stage, was cut to practically nothing in the film. Ethel Wales made the best of a slim role.

Boris Karloff, the prison butler, working domestically for the warden, gave an extraordinarily fine performance as a sinister monster who suffered death in order to kill Jennings according to the inside code.

A fine picture that seems to me to raise Howard Hawks right up with the best of our directors.
                                        --Rob Wagner in Rob Wagner's
                                        Script, Vol. 5, No. 106 (February 21, 1931), page 8.

                         *   *   *

Put The Criminal Code down on your list of preferred attractions for 1931. Here is one of the rare sights of screen and stage (we used to say "stage and screen")--a powerful, melodramatic story in which the writing, directing and acting is characterized by intelligence. Last year the piece was a stage success, but when Columbia Pictures bought the movie rights it was a foregone conclusion that certain events in the plot would have to be changed for general motion picture consumption ... which caused a lot of people to sigh regretfully in anticipation of another literary murder in Hollywood. Fortunately the piece fell into the hands of Fred Niblo, Jr., who amputated small bits of discolored conversation, grafted a shiny, new tail onto the opus, and completed the operation leaving only a small scar that is hardly noticeable unless you happen to be a scargazer.

The second good break for the vehicle came along in the person of Howard Hawks, a director who evidently has sense enough to respect the good works of others. Then Walter Huston was hired to play the lead. Mr. Huston is, of course, a very fine actor, but his long, successful career has never seen him more effective than in this motion picture. Running Mr. Huston a surprising close race for honors is Phillips Holmes, a young actor whose recent efforts proclaim unusual possibilities. He has the perfect combination of looks, voice and real ability ... and, as a personal note, we might add that his attractive unassuming off-screen personality should be a big help in keeping his head the proper size.

From a standpoint of news value, the most interesting character in the cast is Constance Cummings, who disposes of an exacting role with such neatness that one can hardly believe this is her first screen assignment. Miss Cummings went to the coast to play the female lead in The Devil to Pay, Ronald Colman's latest picture. According to a report passed on to us by a responsible person who was on the scene, Miss Cummings was the victim of bad makeup, which may have been partly her own fault, and unsympathetic treatment, which was not. As a consequence she was let out after the film was about a third completed, and the entire thing re-made with Loretta Young taking her place. From here Constance walked right onto the Columbia lot where a bit of patience on the part of the producers was rewarded by a performance that is most deserving.

While we're raving, which opportunity is not afforded often, we want to nominate Boris Karloff as the most quietly terrifying criminal we have ever seen in a prison film--which is quite a statement considering the number of "Boo!" faces that have been assembled for jail scenes during the past year. Mr. Karloff's menacing figure and deep, hollow voice will cause delightful shivers to romp up and down your spinal cord.

Commendation is also due the work of DeWitt Jennings, Mary Doran and Clark Marshall.

Swell show.

--Harry Evans in Life, Vol. 97,
No. 2517 (January 30, 1931),
page 20.

☐ DARK VICTORY (Warner Bros. , 1939)

For an evening replete with anguish and excellent acting, you can't do better than to seek out Dark Victory, one of the most lachrymose, heart-breaking, withal absorbing, dramatic studies the American screen has given us. Bette Davis is the star and her rather nervous impersonation of the hapless heroine who finds both love and supreme courage during the course of her tragic last ten months on this troubled (yet very desirable, when you come to think of it) earth, provides at least several scenes which are probably without parallel in screen history; scenes which this individual and gifted actress won't be able to surpass, I'm afraid, if she acts until she's a hundred. (Miss Davis, and I don't suppose you need to be told, will, unless she retires to devote herself to wagging tails, be on the screen much longer than any of her glamorous contemporaries less concerned than she with vigorous characterization, self-exploration, and technical improvement.)

With the exception of a final sequence which was so wrong that sensitive previewers winced (it has probably been cut!) Edmund

Goulding has directed Dark Victory with imagination, crafty theatri-
calism, and emotional sincerity, so that the heroine's protracted
suffering never becomes maudlin.   The supporting players respond
nobly to the exacting demands of a wordy script.   George Brent has
never been better than he is as the brain surgeon who marries his
doomed patient.   Geraldine Fitzgerald, trained in Dublin's Gate theater, plays with rare competence and sensitivity hard to describe,
Miss Davis's secretary-companion whose devotion to her friend is
infinitely touching.   Cast in a sympathetic role, Humphrey Bogart
is the horse-trainer who grimly believes in the sportsman's code and
is responsible, in a scene of taut passion, for bringing the heroine
to her senses before she squanders what is left of life on round after round of hysterical sensuality.   Max Steiner's musical score
contributes much to the film's effectiveness.

--Richard Sheridan Ames in Rob
Wagner's Script, Vol. 21, No.
510 (May 27, 1939), pages 21-22.

*   *   *

Dark Victory is the kind of movie that will tear you to pieces
if you give in to that sort of thing, and leave you wondering, after
your emotions have calmed down, why you ever let yourself be
moved by something so obviously aimed straight at your tear ducts.
It does not take any long wondering to arrive at Bette Davis as the
answer.   It's her show, her special kind of show, all the way
through.

It has a plot that sounds pretty grim, about a girl with a
brain growth that can be removed once but is sure to come back
again, fatally.   No happy ending possible.   But it is not so grim to
watch as it is fascinating, being managed with a good deal of theatrical effectiveness and blessed with a performance of its chief role
that is genuinely human and moving.   At first you are inclined to
think this is just another of those mean parts with which Miss Davis
has made such a reputation, a spoiled rich girl who drinks and
smokes too much and delights in being disagreeable.   But almost at
once you begin to suspect that it is not a nasty disposition but some
physical ailment that is wrong with her, and--though rather tenta-
tively--you hold yourself ready to extend a bit of sympathy.   For a
little while there is the rather morbid interest of finding out what is
the matter with her, then the more ordinary movie satisfaction of
seeing her apparently cured, a new creature all gaiety and generosity
and in love with her doctor.   But!   Soon you and he know that she
is doomed: the end will come, suddenly but surely and in no very
long time, and she must be kept ignorant of it, and happy.   The
doctor, of course, falls in love too.   Then she accidently finds out
the true state of things, and there is bitterness and readjustment to
go through, a thorough ennobling of character and a slow, sacrificial
ending in which she sends him away and dies alone.

The Camilleish, East Lynnish qualities are fairly well disguised by a brisk, up-to-date script and a set of characters that

might have walked in from the generally accepted Long Island of
smart fiction.   Edmund Goulding knows how to direct such a script
with slick, quick persuasiveness, though he could not restrain himself from wringing the last drop of agony from the ending, and
crowning it with what must have been meant for a choir of angel
voices.

He had a good cast to help him.   Such dependables as Henry
Travers and Cora Witherspoon in their respective specialties, Ronald Reagan developing abilities in the line of sympathetic comedy,
George Brent solemnly kindly but with more substance to him than
usual, and Geraldine Fitzgerald proving that her brilliant acting in
Wuthering Heights was no flash in the pan.   But chief of all Bette
Davis, whose gamut corresponds with the most minute precision to
the requirements of this part.   She has never before seemed to be
so entirely inside a part, with every mannerism and physical aspect
of her suited to its expression.   If she has deserved medals before,
in parts of more dramatic validity, she deserves the prayerful
gratitude of Dark Victory's authors for putting life into something
that must have looked pretty improbable on paper.

--James Shelley Hamilton in National Board of Review Magazine,
Vol. 14, No. 5 (May 1939),
pages 16-18.

☐ DAVID COPPERFIELD (M-G-M, 1935)

This is Big Production Stuff, with the Greatest Galaxy of
Stars Ever Shot on One Lot.   And all that sort of thing.   But to
this reporter, who is not impressed by names nor excessive ballyhoo, it is just another picture, too long and, except for a few
flashes, rather dull and tiresome.

Dickens' stories all seem to start in the rain and hold to
that low meteorological level throughout.   There are too many characters, for the most part mean and miserable and wearing the ugliest clothes in the history of human society.

The high spots of the picture are the acting of little Freddie
Bartholomew, Jessie Ralph, Elizabeth Allan, Una O'Connor, Lennox
Pawle and Basil Rathbone.   Lew Stone plays a sick part sickly;
Madge Evans has a colorless blonde role; Edna May Oliver gags
her part too unctuously; Maureen O'Sullivan is sweet; Roland Young
is miscast as Uriah Heep--not oily enough; Lionel Barrymore is
wasted in a part any character man could have done; Herbert Mundin is in for only a couple of flashes; and W. C. Fields as Micaw-
ber looks like the Cruikshank character, which to a modern audience
seems like a deliberate comedy role.   Frank Lawton simply could
not follow little Freddie Bartholomew as David grown up.

Of the whole I should say that Basil Rathbone puts over the most convincing performance, as he made you hate his guts.

This negative critique is no reflection upon the artistry of these exceptional actors, nor the direction of George Cukor, but results from the story material. However, the picture is "pure" and at the preview one could hear Joe Breen's purring way over at the Hotel Roosevelt.

The only really bad stuff should be laid at the door of the technical department. Picture storms are ridiculously terrifying. Wind is wind, but why these wind-machine monsoons? And the storm at sea made in bath tubs! No ship nor sailor could last five minutes in the storm that raged within the Chinese theater when I saw this picture.

I'm sorry to write thus about a sincere effort to put over the "classics" (Universal did better with Great Expectations), but perhaps the piece was over-ballyhooed. In any event, I was not stirred (except by Basil Rathbone--the "dirty dog") and I have my doubts--.

However, I've been wrong before, and I hope for Dave Selznick's sake I'm wrong again.

--Rob Wagner in Rob Wagner's
Script, Vol. 12, No. 302 (January 19, 1935), page 8.

*   *   *

Bon bons and boom booms to David Copperfield, just about the finest thing that ever came out of the studios, even if it is as long as the Dickens and perhaps, naturally, more like a string of pearls than a modern photodrama. This is that rare thing and miracle, a picture that seems inspired rather than assembled on a production line. It has captured the manner and essence of a masterpiece.

Mr. Hugh Walpole turned in a script which honors its source, George Cukor's direction is likewise reverential, and a magnificent cast seems fired by its contact with an immortal work. This sounds, I know, like the rave of a county seat weekly over the annual high school play at the town hall, but I'm willing to bust a gallus and risk an outburst of superlatives over David Copperfield.

I believe, however, it is too painful in spots for children.

--Don Herold in Life, Vol. 102,
No. 2600 (March 1935), pages 35-36.

⬜ DEAD END (Goldwyn, 1937)

Being an artist, my first interest is pictorial. Here is one
of the seldom masterpieces. Hogarth at his best. And bettered.
Hats off to Norman Bel Geddes, Richard Day, and Gregg Toland.
The slums and "Fifth Avenue" juxtaposed--the slum casting its
shadows on a chromium goldfish bowl, the bowl mocking the slum.
No, Hogarth never painted so terrible a picture.

And the drama: equally sinister. A bow to William Wyler.
Goldfish swimming in among water rats; many characters in the
bowl--rich wasters, beautiful blonde kept girl, uniformed door-man.
In the streets, gangsters, tarts, and water rats. A mosaic in
which the dramatis personae make up a huge Tapestry of Sin--for
excessive poverty and excessive wealth are both sinful.

This, written a week after I saw the picture, is just an impression. Yet of the characters, the boys on their way to Hell
were the most impressive. Next, Humphrey Bogart, gangster, and
Allen Jenkins, his man Friday, persist strongly in my memory.
And Marjorie Main. Too bad Will Hays made Claire Trevor tuber-
cular rather than syphilitic. Such terror shouldn't be softened.

It is essentially a director's picture. Wyler must have had
sympathetic support from Merritt Hulburd, associate producer.

Fifteen years ago, there was in Hollywood an amusing part-
nership--Rob Wagner and Norman Bel Geddes. It was my job to
"sell" Norman to moom-pitchers. I landed him at Universal, and
how long did Norman last? Oh, perhaps thirty minutes. They
thought him completely nuts. After a few years in New York, Norman was saying nuts to them all. But who was I to bet on Norman
Bel Geddes? Just another nutty artist.

The opening title shouts "SAMUEL GOLDWYN" in the biggest
type ever screened. Next we get the main title, "Dead End produced
by SAMUEL GOLDWYN." Then, after the cast is named, we are
informed that this is a SAMUEL GOLDWYN Production.

Thus, I ask forgiveness for kidding Charles Rogers' large
type, and add another orchid to the memory of Irving Thalberg who
never so much as permitted his name on the screen.
                                    --Rob Wagner in Rob Wagner's
                                    Script, Vol. 18, No. 428
                                    (September 11, 1937), page 10.

*   *   *

This is Goldwyn's reverential translation of the Broadway
stage success, dealing with the lives of a bunch of frustrated people
down by New York's East River. The story concerns an architect
(Joel McCrea) who dreams of better things but never achieves them,

a shopgirl (Sylvia Sidney) whose shoes are worn out with picketing, Baby-Face Martin (Humphrey Bogart), a local killer, who comes back after ten years to find his girl walking the streets, and his mother hating and disowning him, a bunch of toffs from the adjoining hotel, forced into this unsavoury area by building operations, and a crew of ragged boys of the streets, Baby-Face Martins in embryo, who live like wharf-rats, stealing and hiding, bullying and swimming.

The boys are the picture. They have been lugged across a continent to recreate in Hollywood the peculiar filth and frankness of the Manhattan tenements. Their language has been toned down for the microphones, but their faces tell unprintable things to the camera. They are the real stuff, and not even Mr. Goldwyn can glamourise them, past-master though he is in this peculiar art.

The film itself, except for two first-rate camera sequences, is more theatre than cinema. It is played in one vast tenement set, and suffers, at moments, from claustrophobia. There is no brilliant coup de cinéma, like the barrel-organ climax of Winterset, to resolve and excite the final moments. But within these limits it is a remarkable film, hard-hitting and honest. The sound-track, separately recorded in Manhattan, carries all the bedlam of the East Side river-front. Bogart is Baby-Face Martin, Dillinger, Legs Diamond and all the rest--the composite Public Enemy. The small parts are alive. The scene frequently crawls with horror. Dead End is a précis of an urgent document, if not quite a first-rank film.

--C. A. Lejeune in World Film
News, Vol. 3, No. 1 (April
1938), page 34.

*   *   *

Sidney Kingsley's great play reaches the screen with all of the power of its thought-provoking drama intact. There are no compromises with the basic theme of the original. It remains a grim slice of life, ending, as it begins, in futility. A highly effective theatrical reenactment, Dead End is magnificently played by each and every member of its tremendous cast and flawlessly directed by William Wyler.

That the production bears the name of Samuel Goldwyn is an asset not to be disregarded in computing the boxoffice future of this attraction. Goldwyn has set a standard that ticket buyers have learned to respect. Dead End is a work worthy of the Goldwyn trademark, and should take its place well toward the top of the year's finest pictures. With Merritt Hulburd as associate producer, production investitures are beyond criticism.

Lillian Hellman's sensitive regard of dramatic values is always apparent in her screenplay craftsmanship. It is less of a narrative and more of a closely knit series of incidents that depict in swift, vivid strokes its story of New York tenement life.

Dead End takes its name from those short streets of the
East Side that terminate on the river front.   Here fashionable apartment houses meet the slums.   Here restless hoodlums run riot,
their idols the gangsters, their ambitions to live as their heroes do.
They respect no law nor order.   Reform schools mark their end.

William Wyler scores a veritable triumph in his lucid direction of the complex drama.   No contributing factor to the power of
the scene escapes his attention.   His guidance of the six young actors from the original Norman Bel Geddes production is nothing short
of masterful.   This only serves to cement the deserved acclaim
Wyler won with These Three.   In Dead End, he again looks clearly
and intelligently into the adolescent mind.

Of the six boys, reams could be written of their amazing
performances.   Billy Halop's Tommy is a memorable characterization of which even veterans of the theatre would have right to be
proud.   No less potent are the portrayals of Bernard Punsly as the
dumbly worshiping Milty, Gabriel Dell as T. B. , Huntz Hall as
Dippy, Leo B. Gorcey as the cowardly Spit, and Bobby Jordan as
Angel.   The role of the "rich kid" is well played by Charles Peck.

With such strength in the juvenile assignments, it is doubly
notable the adult stars so brilliantly distinguish themselves.   Yet
Sylvia Sidney is splendid as the girl who aspires to better environs,
and Joel McCrea takes added acting stature in his effortless playing.
Humphrey Bogart does with rare intelligence his flashy public enemy,
a job that will be rated among his finest on the screen.   Wendy
Barrie is excellent as a wealthy dilettante, and Allen Jenkins outstanding as the gangster's pal.

Playing in only a single sequence, Claire Trevor makes a
lasting impression in her role of the street girl.   Marjorie Main
is superb as the tragic mother, a beautiful bit of character work.
Adding fine support in brief, impressive moments are James Burke,
Minor Watson, Ward Bond, Elizabeth Risdon, Esther Dale and
George Hubbert.

Richard Day's set of the Dead End street must share liberally
in credit for the picture's rare mood.   Gregg Toland's photography
is exquisite in light and shadow.   The roundalay of deserved praise
must include mention of Alfred Newman's musical direction, Omar
Kiam's costuming and Daniel Mandell's editing.

> --The Hollywood Reporter, Vol.
> 40, No. 38 (July 30, 1937),
> page 3.

☐ DINNER AT EIGHT (M-G-M, 1933)

Here is a society drama done in the Grand Hotel manner--
and with no more plot.   Billie Burke, a snooty socialite, having

captured Lord and Lady Whoosis, is to give a dinner, and the show is merely a series of episodes characterizing the various people invited, with a mere thread of a story woven into the pattern.

Lionel Barrymore, the husband of Billie Burke, is a shipping magnate in the clutches of Wally Beery, a cheap, vulgar financial racketeer.   Wally is invited for business reasons.   Jean Harlow is Wally's glamorous but vulgar wife gone simply ga-ga with the thought of meeting a lord.

Marie Dressler is an old trouper, and a sweetie of Lionel's youth.   She is invited for sentimental reasons.   Eddie Lowe is a doctor married to Karen Morley, but naughty with Jean Harlow. As the family physician, he and Karen are invited.

Jack Barrymore is a vain, hard-drinking movie actor headed for oblivion because of the talkies.   He's invited as a "celebrity." (This is the part that Conway Tearle had panicked New York with.) Others in the cast: Lee Tracy, Madge Evans, Jean Hersholt, Louise Closser Hale, May Robson.

With such paints you can expect a brilliant canvas and George Cukor has painted it.

I did not see the play, but Frances Marion and Herman Mankiewicz have written a sparkling script, many of the sparkles no doubt having originated in the brilliant wits of Donald Ogden Stewart (additional dialogue by).

Individual credits are impossible, but Jean Harlow is entitled to a bow for shining brightly amid this "georgeous galaxy of stars."

It isn't fair to spill the best gags, but I can't resist repeating the tag.   The gang are at last going out to dinner.   Jean Harlow, wishing to impress Marie Dressler, says: "You know, I've been reading a book.   It's all about civilization or something.   A nutty kind of a book.   Do you know that the guy says that machinery is going to take the place of every profession?"

Marie looks Jean up and down and noting her slithery sexiness replies: "That's something you never need to worry about, dearie."

--Rob Wagner in Rob Wagner's
Script, Vol. 10, No. 234
(September 2, 1933), page 8.

*   *   *

Again a strong studio puts in most of the stars on its lot, adds some freelancers, plus a plot that was a smash hit on Broadway--and emerges with a grand evening's entertainment, if you don't mind a mixed-up affair.

Lionel Barrymore's wife (Billie Burke) decides to give a dinner, and invites the stage and screen has-beens, Marie Dressler and John Barrymore, Wally Beery, an uncouth financier and an uncouth wife to match in Jean Harlow; philanderer Eddie Lowe and wife Karen Morley, and Phillips Holmes, engaged to Madge Evans.

And then what a mix-up! The guests of honor depart for Florida, Lionel has a heart-attack, John ends all when his agent, Lee Tracy, tells him he's through--and so it goes. But if you like all-star entertainment--here it is!

--Photoplay, Vol. 44, No. 3
(August 1933), page 55.

☐ DR. JEKYLL AND MR. HYDE (Paramount, 1932)

Our dual personalities, our good self and our bad self, have always fascinated artists who have forever been trying to picture them as separate entities. In The Picture of Dorian Gray, Oscar Wilde attempted it by perpetuating the beauty in Dorian's face throughout years of sin while, with every debauch, his portrait grew steadily more bestial. Max Beerbohm used a similar device in The Happy Hypocrite. A man whose face was monstrous with sin fell in love with a pure girl, and in order to win her wore a beautiful wax mask. When finally a woman out of his past scratched it from his face, lo and behold, the monster had disappeared! Because of his newly-pure life, his face had grown to look like the beautiful mask of virtue.

Robert Louis Stevenson, more daring in putting over his character's preachment of separating dual personalities, went the whole way by actually creating two complete physical egoes of the same man--Dr. Jekyll, the virtuous, and Mr. Hyde, the monster.

All of which is easy to write about but darned hard to show realistically and convincingly.

For instance, one might easily suppose that Dorian's degenerating picture was merely a reflection of the young man's mental guilt, and Beerbohm's wax face presupposes that his sweetheart would never suspect the fantastically absurd cheat. But Stevenson's device is the most childish of all, for it harks back to the fairy tales wherein the witch, by merely waving a wand, changes a prince into a donkey, or vice versa.

One might get by with such a sensational phenomenon were it treated symbolically, but in this Paramount production Samuel Hoffenstein and Percy Heath stuck to the realism of the book. We see Dr. Jekyll in his chemical laboratory, a trick-set filled with retorts, alembics, tubes, vials, and furnaces--every gadget known to science and a few extra ones invited by the property department--the

purpose of which is to impress us with the wonders of chemical
science.   Like the alchemist of old we see him mixing his mysterious brew, drinking it, and then presto! changing from a gentleman
to an ape-man before our very eyes! Wonderful--but much too
Grimm for our credulity.

(Even as realism these laboratory scenes are absurd for the
reason that Dr. Jekyll leaves the place for days at a time with
everything burning and boiling full tilt.)

That's why the picturization of the Stevenson tale is not convincing.   One can easily understand a virtuous man taking a drink
of such potency that it will make a beast of him.   We have seen that
every day since booze became so rotten.   But to have the drink
change his high brow to that of an anthropoid ape and grow Ingagi
fangs where but a moment before the dental equipment was perfect
is too grotesque to be taken seriously.

If, however, you can hurdle this attempted rationalization of
the fantastic technique of the fairies, you will be gripped by a wonderful picture, well directed by Rouben Mamoulian, and superbly
acted by Fredric March and a bang-up cast.   Besides which the
sets are simply gorgeous and the camerawork of Karl Struss nothing
short of marvelous.

Rose Hobart, a beautiful, aristocratic type of girl, plays the
sweetheart of Dr. Jekyll with dignity, poise and charm, while Miriam Hopkins as the victim of Mr. Hyde's lust repeats her triumph
in The Smiling Lieutenant.   Holmes Herbert, Halliwell Hobbes, and
Edgar Norton, the butler, complete a perfect cast.

When the pictures first began to show double-exposures,
much dramatic interest was lost because the audience was too busy
figuring out how the actor could be shaking hands with himself.
Much of the intended horror of Dr. Jekyll and Mr. Hyde is lost in
marvelling at the trick camera work.

A masterly attempt to picture the impossible, but never once
did I feel a sense of horror.
                                        --Rob Wagner in Rob Wagner's
                                           Script, Vol. 6, No. 151 (Janu-
                                           ary 2, 1932), pages 9-10.

                              *   *   *

Type.   The old Dual Personality thriller.

Credits.   Fred gives one of the greatest screen characterizations ever presented.   Miriam continues to climb the ladder to
stardom.   And loud cheers for the makeup man and technicians who
were responsible for the amazing transitions Fred makes from the
gentlemanly Jekyll to the monster Hyde.   More and louder cheers
for Director Rouben Mamoulian.

Comment. Too starkly hair-raising for nervous people and children. The one weak spot is the love interest between Fred and Rose. And Rouben, whatever gave you the idea of letting Rose collapse on the keyboard of the Steinway? "They laughed when she fell on the piano. "

Decision. Yes (if you can "take" it).
--Harry Evans in Life, Vol. 99,
No. 2564 (March 1932), page 38.

☐ DODSWORTH (Goldwyn/United Artists, 1936)

It's the old gag of a woman in her "dangerous forties" playing with the fires of repressed desires. Paralleled by the old gag of a man whose life is full and exciting with industrial achievement while his wife has nothing to do but play bridge with her small town sidekicks and dread growing old.

Thus the play starts. Walter Huston has sold his auto factory to the trust and at last he and Ruth Chatterton were to catch up with Life by a trip to Europe. Walter's excitement is in navigation and visiting historic spots. Ruth's is for social glamour. She is rich and personable and naturally--well, you know those handsome foreigners. Their manners are most alluring; their customs not so good. Ruth goes completely haywire, first with David Niven (who, after she refuses to finish what she's started, warns her that the European waters are too deep for her), next Paul Lukas who ravishes his women by simply "giving them looks, " and finally Gregory Gaye, a much younger German nobleman.

In the meantime Ruth and Walter quarrel; he finally finds comfort with Mary (Dear Diary) Astor.

Sinclair Lewis, who wrote the book, did not have them realize that they'd both been wrong and then "wash 'em up" by having husband and wife rush into a happy-ending clinch. And what do you think? Neither did Sam Goldwyn, producer, and Sidney Howard (screen play by)! Which is a glorious triumph of art over cinehoke.

That, however, is not the only triumph. Will Wyler's direction is nothing less than superb. Not one "movie" cliché or "surefire" gag. Such naturalness has rarely been seen on the screen. Of course he had magnificent pigments with which to paint. Walter Huston reaches his dramatic zenith not only in Zenith, but in Paris, Rome and Naples. And Ruth Chatterton, playing in a picture not of her own choosing, is again a great actress. Mary Astor (cheers from the previewers) accounts for much that was recently revealed about her private life. She certainly has a way with her. David Niven gives a perfect picture of the patent-leather foreigner who would ga-ga any American small-town gal. A grand job. Gregory

Gaye is boyishly charming as the German nobleman, and his mother,
Mme. Marie Ouspenskaya, etches a remarkable portrait of a poor
but aristocratic German baroness.

Even the bits are beautifully played. John Payne, confront-
ing his first-born, expresses the usual masculine bewilderment with
exquisite comedy. Odette Myrtil, Spring Byington and Harlan
Briggs make much of their still smaller parts.

Richard Day's sets are, as usual, rich and beautiful; Rudolph
Mate's camera work superb; Omar Kiam's costumes in excellent
taste; and Alfred Newman's musical direction gently in the background where it, in this picture, belongs. And let me offer a
happy hand to Oscar Lagerstrom for truthful and pleasing sound.
Sam Goldwyn still holds his place far out in front.

> --Rob Wagner in Rob Wagner's
> Script, Vol. 16, No. 383 (Octo-
> ber 3, 1936), page 10.

*   *   *

When we estimate the values of the various contributions to
Dodsworth, we find it is the director's picture. We have had complete and elaborate productions before, well written screen plays
and thoroughly competent performances, but extremely rarely have
we had them blended with the skill displayed by William Wyler in
his direction of the Sinclair Lewis story. It is a beautiful job, one
that finally establishes young Wyler's right to recognition as one of
Hollywood's really great directors.

Although I have not seen Willie Wyler for three or four
years, my ego is inflated a little more by each step he takes in
his forward progress. As I stated in my review of his These
Three, something he directed when he was a mere boy gave me
the impression that some day he would be a director of distinction,
an opinion I recorded in the Spectator at the time, thus constituting
myself his original discoverer. The feeling of proprietorship is so
strong within me, I am inclined to bow when I hear him praised.

What Wyler learned when the screen was silent is evidenced
in his technique to-day. He attaches importance to the camera and
displays intelligence in its use. In every Dodsworth scene there is
story value in the composition. When the story is being advanced
by dialogue, when what the characters are saying is more important
than what they are doing, all of them are included in the shot, thus
holding the scene as a sustained pictorial unit without any of that
hopping about from one unnecessary close-up to another. This
treatment adds value to such close-ups as are necessary in other
sequences. In his grouping of characters in their relation to the
settings, Wyler obtains striking compositions which Rudolph Mate's
camera brings to the screen as beautiful examples of the art of
photography. As something to look at, Dodsworth is a joy.

In its human aspects it is an offering of dignity and compelling power to provide you with a treat you rarely can experience in a motion picture house. Wyler does not entertain us with actors playing parts. He shows us a group of quite ordinary human beings, doing things natural for them to do and unaware that we are watching them. The excellence of the performances is the greatest tribute to the excellence of the direction. Never have Walter Huston, Ruth Chatterton and Mary Astor appeared to better advantages --in fact, never have Ruth and Mary given us anything approaching their understanding characterizations in this picture.

Paul Lukas comes back to us in Dodsworth after too long an absence from the screen. He is a player we can not see too often. David Niven and Gregory Gaye are two others who strike a satisfactory masculine note. A brief bit is made into a big scene by the outstanding artistry of Maria Ouspenskaya. As a married couple with staunch convictions, Spring Byington and Harlan Briggs do splendidly.

There is one brief scene in Dodsworth that is a cinematic gem. John Payne, a youth I never saw before, married Kathryn Marlowe, Huston's daughter. The scene I refer to shows Payne coming into the hospital room and seeing his son for the first time --about a minute of it altogether, but an example of inspired direction and acting. Payne does not know what to do with his hands; he wants to touch the baby, and is afraid to. The scene strikes a human note, powerful in its simplicity.

Some music by Alfred Newman is scattered through the production. It is rather strange that a production reflecting so much screen intelligence in all other respects, should reflect a total lack of it in its musical treatment. It is ludicrous to have spots of music in a motion picture, but before producers learn why, they will have to take a course in motion picture elementals.

To Samuel Goldwyn and Merritt Hulburd, though, must go credit for one of the season's greatest pictures. Sam paid $160,000 for the rights to the story. To justify the investment a great picture had to be made from it, and Sam saw that such a picture was made.

> --Welford Beaton in Hollywood
> Spectator, Vol. 11, No. 13
> (September 26, 1936), pages 8-9.

☐ DRACULA (Universal, 1931)

Recommended for the mystery-minded. It's creepy and thrilly but it could have been better, and before it's over you're pretty confused about this vampire (a bat-like demon, not a lady in black negligee) business. Bela Lugosi fixes his victims with hyp-

notic eyes and everybody in the audience says, "OOH." Helen
Chandler does grand work as the terrified heroine and you'll get
your spinal chill.

                              --Photoplay, Vol. 39, No. 4
                              (March 1931), page 57.

☐ DRUMS ALONG THE MOHAWK (20th Century-Fox, 1939)

Drums Along the Mohawk is a triumph of color and beauty.
Rarely, since color came into pictures, has its use had such opportunities as in this production, and 20th-Fox has gone the limit on it.
But aside from the color and its great scenic investiture, the picture has little to offer aside from sterling performances by Claudette Colbert and Henry Fonda, in parts that required every ounce
of their abilities and the fine hand of John Ford to make them interesting.

Unquestionably the story has been wrung from the pages of
early American history, detailing the efforts of those small groups
of people who lived in the Mohawk Valley and had to fight for their
existence against the intrusion of the Tories and Indians.   However,
the theme has been used so many times (but certainly not with the
beauty of this production) that, in the opinion of this reviewer, audiences will weary of its re-telling, even with the background in which
20th-Fox has placed it.

The story pace has a tendency to become slow too often.
Whether it was the fault of the direction or the writing, it was hard
for us to tell, but the slowness dimmed all efforts to build suspense
and certainly took most of the intentional thrills out of the production.   In addition, it seemed to us that much of the story's effectiveness was sacrificed in the strife for production beauty, which it
always attained.   Accordingly, the picture should be recorded as a
great scenic, lavishly done and cast.

Certainly no feminine player lends herself better to color
than Claudette Colbert.   She has never been more beautiful, and
her work, particularly all her scenes with Henry Fonda, was top
notch.   Fonda was perfectly cast in the role of Gilbert Martin, a
young farmer of the American party who took his new bride to the
Mohawk Valley to settle.   Another fine contribution to the cast was
Edna May Oliver in one of those parts that only she could do with
such fine effect.

Among others who stood out in the exceptionally large cast
were Eddie Collins, Jesse Ralph, Francis Ford, Arthur Shields and
Robert Lowery.

John Ford has always been a master for characterizations,
and his direction here with his individual characters and their group-

ings highlighted this mastery.   However, the general movement was, for the most part, slow and tedious.

That color is improving is evidenced by the extreme beauty of this subject.   The effects that the Technicolor photography accomplished were at times breath-taking, if you are only the least bit color-conscious.

The picture should be sold on its magnificent scenic investiture, for nothing that could be said could measure up to what has actually been accomplished in that direction.

--The Hollywood Reporter, Vol. 54, No. 33 (November 3, 1939), page 3.

*   *   *

At two-for-five, the Technicolor postcards which constitute most of Drums Along the Mohawk should fetch five dollars.   The backgrounds have the contrived look of funeral sprays, the tints are unreal, and the locale a bit puzzling since the studio sent the unit to Utah to film the Mohawk valley and then had eucalyptus trees in the foreground.   (Now you don't have to tell me that eucalypts have been grown in various parts of the country since their introduction in California.   But not in New York, prior to the Revolutionary War--or will annoyed research experts tell me that there are native trees which are dead-ringers for eucalypts?)   Even if the Mohawk valley had looked more like itself, the characters of the Edmonds novel do not come to life on the screen.   The atmosphere is not convincing.   One never believes for a moment that one is experiencing, vicariously, terrors and tribulations endured by hardy backwoods folk during the Revolutionary War.

Indeed, although conscious comedy was probably not the aim of the producer, large chunks of the pseudohistorical Drums are probably the funniest bits of early Americana we shall see until Hedy Lamarr, as announced in the not too dependable press, appears as Pocahontas.   Miss Claudette Colbert who fell from grace in Maid of Salem (wherever did producers get the idea that she is a Puritan maid?) is hopelessly inadequate and cruelly miscast as a frontier wife who walks through her role as if on French heels. Even when menaced by Red Men--and the Indians in Drums would make you laugh more only if they appeared in a Disney frolic--la Colbert has chic.   But only an ungrammatical phrase could describe the way in which she has been photographed: "Claudette never looked worser."   Poor Henry Fonda, one of the "realest" people on the screen, and a gifted interpreter of homespun heroes, has seldom appeared to such disadvantage.   The only participants who may look back upon Drums Along the Mohawk with any relish are probably Edna May Oliver, scrumptious as a Colonial dame, domineering, quick-tempered, and loyal to her four-poster; and John Carradine, appearing briefly as a Tory mischief-maker, who gives you an entire character with a few deft strokes.   I can't remember when a well-

governed performance has been more effective, and repression has
never been Carradine's forte.

No one is sorrier than I that John Ford got mixed up with
Drums, and if his name weren't flashed on the screen you'd never
suspect for a moment that he had anything to do with the film. I
don't wish to bore you with an examination of facts which might
support the theory that the screen has never coped successfully with
the Colonial or Revolutionary periods as dramatic material, but
I'm ready to forgive Ford, as I forgave Frank Lloyd Maid of Salem
(influenza's aftermath made me indulgent then) because I think the
subject is formidable. It can be tackled successfully, yet; but
Drums Along the Mohawk represents another fumble.

If the film scores commercially, I have no other alibi to offer than the fact that Darryl Zanuck's eager public has become so
inured to trash after Suez and Jesse James that it can now swallow
his cinematic castor oil, sufficiently disguised, and will gag at
nothing. Respecting the public's taste, I am dumfounded by such an
admission, but while I should wish to hide from such a film as
Drums Along the Mohawk, I'm bound to admit that there are people
who buy French postcards, believe English propaganda, and some
who paid their good money to witness Abie's Irish Rose. Who said
ours was not an age of minor miracles?
                                        --Richard Sheridan Ames in Rob
                                        Wagner's Script, Vol. 22, No.
                                        529 (November 11, 1939), pages
                                        18-20.

☐ DUCK SOUP (Paramount, 1933)

Remember the song, "Oh, Gee, It's Great to Be Crazy"?
That's the theme of all Four Marx Brothers' pictures. Loading up
on foolish powders, they get together in a padded cell and go completely booglie. When they emerge, they have the skeleton of
another classically mad movie. In the case of Duck Soup they had
the collaboration of four other nuts--Bert Kalmar and Harry Ruby
(story, music and lyrics) and Arthur Sheekman and Nat Perrin (additional dialogue). The result is a celluloid cataclysm of such
idiotic fun that one is absolutely converted to the theme song. It
certainly is great to be crazy.

My only complaint is that the darn thing moves so fast that
the moment I tried to memorize one joke, another and better one
was on the way. Coming home Ye Real Ed said, "If you don't stop
laughing, I'll take you over to Doc Reynolds (Cecil) and have you
tapped for the simples."

The basis of homeopathy is that "like cures like," and in a
world that has gone completely haywire I can suggest no better medicine than Duck Soup.

This particular madness is staged in a mythical kingdom--
without a king! But it has a prime minister, Groucho, who keeps
slapping the face of Louis Calhern, ambassador from a rival kingdom, until he brings on war. A war to end war, if the writers of
war stories have any sense of humor. "Remember, men," shouts
Groucho, "we are fighting for the honor of Mrs. Teasdale, which
is a darned sight more than she ever did for herself!"

Harpo does a Paul Revere. While dashing through a village
he looks up and through a window he sees a peach of a girl going
to bed. He dismounts, puts the feed-bag on the horse and enters.
(Fade.) Cutting back a little later the camera panorams beneath
the bed. We see the gal's shoes, Harpo's shoes and the horse's
shoes. The full shot shows all three in bed--the horse in the middle!

In another scene one of the madmen--I've forgotten which--
while burgling, turns on what he thinks is the combination to the
safe. It's a radio and never have I heard "The Stars and Stripes"
played so loud. Nor can the fellow stop it because he has broken
the lever. He chops the machine to kindling and throws the wreckage out the window but Sousa marches on.

There are gorgeous sets and rich costuming. As the royal
horse guards march by in the palace, the madmen play upon their
steel helmets like Swiss bell-ringers!

When war is declared, the huge mob of courtiers sing a gorgeous patriotic hymn weaving hither and yon in great mass movements like the recent colossal Jewish pageant in New York. This
is the high spot of excitement--and delicious satire.

A swell cast, but of course the big end of the fun is furnished by the Marxes. However, Margaret Dumont--Mrs. Teasdale
--makes a grand foil for Groucho. And sings well. Then there is
Ed Kennedy (strangely enough his name is omitted from the credit
sheet). Ed plays a long routine between Chico and Harpo and holds
up his end nobly. The look on his face when he discovers he is
sitting on the submerged Chico in the bath tub is one of the funniest
things in the picture.

Finally a magnificent bow to Leo McCarey for his direction.
There's the lad who knows timing! When I was directing Will
Rogers at Roach's, Leo was an assistant director. In his first
directorial effort he took two almost unknown "red-nosed comics"
and by playing the old gags to slow tempo, he made them famous. ·
No doubt you've seen 'em--Laurel and Hardy. Not that they didn't
have it in them. But they had never before been given a chance to
shine.

--Rob Wagner in Rob Wagner's
Script, Vol. 10, No. 245
(November 18, 1933), page 8.

☐ A FAREWELL TO ARMS (Paramount, 1932)

The spiritual collapse of the boys and girls at the front and
how they sought escape in alcohol and sex is beautifully told in Hemingway's novel, and Frank Borzage has translated it to the screen
with fine artistry.

Against a background of war marvelously photographed in the
Russian montage manner by Charles Lang, we follow Gary Cooper
and Helen Hayes through an intense and hopeless love to its inevitably tragic end.   Miss Hayes, of course, is fine, but Gary Cooper
is the surprise.   His stilted aloofness is gone and we see a new
Gary--sensitive and warm.

The final sequence bothered me, however.   The obstetrics of
human motherhood are shocking enough, but the physical background
of a Caesarean operation with its mechanical paraphernalia robs the
miracle of childbirth of much of its sentiment.

The death scene also loses much of its tragic tenderness because of cinematic necessities.   Though life is slowly ebbing, Miss
Hayes, propped up in bed, is far too strong physically and emotionally to make the scene convincing.

Jack La Rue enacts the role of an army priest with feeling
and intelligence; Miss Mary Philips, as another nurse, does a fine
piece of work.   And Adolphe Menjou creates one of his most colorful and delightful characters.   Altogether, Paramount has produced
a beautiful picture.

                    --Rob Wagner in Rob Wagner's
                      Script, Vol. 8, No. 203 (Decem-
                      ber 31, 1932), page 8.

                    *   *   *

The memory of this poignantly tragic love story of Ernest
Hemingway's, laid amidst the brutal futility of the World War, is
one that will linger for many days.

Scenarists Benjamin Glazer and Oliver H. P. Garrett kept
their eyes on both Hemingway's novel and the censors without apparent compromise.   And Frank Borzage merits another bright feather
in his directorial cap.

Helen Hayes, a nurse, falls in love with Gary Cooper, an
American who has enlisted in the Italian army.   Torn between love
and duty, Gary returns to the front, and Helen to the tiny Swiss
village to await the coming of their child.   Sensing her peril, Gary
deserts, fighting and dragging his way back to her.   He arrives a
few minutes before she dies while armistice bells ring about them.

The performances of Helen Hayes and Adolphe Menjou are
among the outstanding of the year, while Gary Cooper probably does

the best work of his career. Jack La Rue and Mary Philips contribute splendid performances. And Cinematographer Lang must not be forgotten.

The scenes showing the retreat of the Italian army after the great defeat at Caporetto are especially magnificent. A picture you should see.

--Photoplay, Vol. 43, No. 3
(February 1933), page 57.

☐ FLIRTATION WALK (Warner Bros. , 1934)

If there are three kinds of music I like they are Hawaiian music, marchin' music, and Dick Powell's singing, and Flirtation Walk is jammed with all three. This musical is fortunate in its choice of locales: Hawaii and West Point. The U. S. Army (which I suppose we have to have) helped the producers in both places. In Hawaii, Dick Powell, a buck private, is (he thinks) high-hatted by a General's daughter and a lieutenant, and he makes up his mind to chin himself up to their level by going to West Point. Which he does. Not, however, until we have been given a lot of dances by a beachful of Honolulululus. Then follow fine shots of indoor and outdoor life at West Point. Ruby comes there as the Supt. 's daughter, and Dick writes the academy show, and that makes a musical of it.

Ruby Keeler may not be the best actress in the world, but I wouldn't care; there is nobody who is fresher or more appealing, acting or no acting, than she. Dick Powell has something of this same non-factory flavor, and Pat O'Brien helps any picture.

--Don Herold in Life, Vol. 102,
No. 2598 (January 1935), page
34.

☐ FLYING DOWN TO RIO (RKO, 1933)

The trouble with "big smash numbers" is that they are likely to smash not only the story--if any--but everybody that gets in their way. This picture is a good example of an over-effort for sensation and originality. The story is weak enough, but what there is of it is smothered by "production stuff. " The two principal characters, blond Gene Raymond and dark Dolores Del Rio, became mere marionettes trying to compete with Niagara Falls, Paine's Fireworks, and a National Air Circus.

Which would no doubt be O.K. if the production stuff were overwhelmingly beautiful. But it's not. Some fine music and several swell songs, but the big dance numbers are pictorially confusing. Over-elaboration of sets and decorations, together with flat lighting cause the dancers to become all mixed up with the background like the jumble of a busted kaleidoscope.

The big novelty number shows the gals doing their stuff while strapped to the tops of airplanes flying over Rio de Janiero. The remarkable "cheating" by process shots was achieved by Vern Walker and his staff.

But what these shots do to the story. A bunch of Americans have flown down to Rio to put on a show such as we see in our own Cocoanut Grove. Meanies forestall a license. So the boys pull the airplane stunt. O. K. as far as the movie audience is concerned, but how the hotel guests a mile below can see the show is a bit puzzling.

Out of all this confusion, however, emerges one figure who manages to attract attention--Fred Astaire. This chap has charm, a fine flair for comedy, and how he can dance! To my mind, he is pretty nearly the show.

> --Rob Wagner in Rob Wagner's
> Script, Vol. 10, No. 251 (De-
> cember 30, 1933), page 10.

*   *   *

Flying Down to Rio is a badly written musical film which has two outstanding features. The first is a dance sequence featuring a new Argentine hoofing routine called "Carioca." Colorful, well executed, and much better than the usual mob scenes of team dancing. But, as is usually the case when the movies get hold of something good, they didn't know when to quit.

The second item, and one of real importance to movie fans, is the performance of Fred Astaire, who bears out the prediction of this department that he would click in the talkies the first time he was given a suitable opportunity. In his first film, Dancing Lady, he appeared with Joan Crawford, and for some reason the cameraman never seemed to quite know where he was. I mean to say that you would get a very clear view of Miss Crawford's dancing, but Mr. Astaire seemed to elude the lens. Because of his inability to stay in front of the camera for any length of time at a stretch, Mr. Astaire did not appear to be doing very much. In Flying Down to Rio Fred made friends with the cameraman before the picture started, so he does all right.

Which reminds me of a conversation that took place between Mr. Astaire and some of his friends after he had made Dancing Lady. They were discussing the dismal subject of the hereafter, and what they wanted done with their mortal remains.

"When I die," said one of them, "I want to be cremated. How about you Fred?"

"Oh, no," replied Mr. Astaire. "When I die I want to be
buried in a Crawford-Gable movie."

> --Harry Evans in Life, Vol. 101,
> No. 2587 (February 1934), page
> 38.

☐ FOREIGN CORRESPONDENT (Walter Wanger/United Artists,
1940)

Alfred Hitchcock has delivered to Walter Wanger, for his distribution through United Artists, the best picture that has ever carried the Wanger name and a great piece of screen entertainment for
the whole picture business. It's a stand-out hit and an individual
triumph for Mr. Hitchcock.

Foreign Correspondent has but one burden--its title. We believe that too many people are going to be kept away from the picture because of it; that is, kept away until one of their neighbors
rushes to them with the information that it is the best picture of its
type this great business has ever turned out. It's a thriller from
beginning to end and will keep any audience on the edge of its seats
every minute of its running. It would take Mr. Hoover and all his
G-Men even to attempt the deciphering of its plot, and they would
miss, as will any audience, and it's that missing that makes it such
a great show, plus the manner in which Mr. Hitchcock leads up to
all his major (and minor) events.

It's a simple plot in the writing, but the manner in which it
has been directed and its magnificent cast of players make of the
yarn something entirely unique in this business--a picture that's always far ahead of the audience. It's a story of a young reporter,
delegated by his New York paper to cover Europe before the declaration of war to keep his sheet informed on what is actually happen-
ing in the paper's effort to have something to print on the European
situation other than the publicity handouts of the various govern-
ments. The reporter, played by Joel McCrea, gets hold of a yarn
that's almost too hot to handle and, in addition to the yarn, becomes romantically involved with a young lady, played by Laraine
Day, whose father turns out to be the arch-conspirator of the whole
European setting. But this foreign correspondent finally comes
through with the story and the girl.

No description of the plot, however great its detail, would do
justice to the masterpiece that Alfred Hitchcock has put on the
screen. His manner of staging the intrigues shifts the blame on
first one and then another, and when you finally believe you have
the character pegged, you get another switch. At last, when Hitchcock eventually tells you who he is, you say to yourself: "Well,
how's he going to end the thing? How's he going to piece the thing
out?" But he does, and how convincingly.

This Britisher, too, sees things through different glasses than the ordinary director. He goes in for realism to the nth degree. Take the instance of photographing one of his best scenes in the rain and in heavily clouded weather, and pitch against the background the tops of hundreds of umbrellas, moving up the steps of a building that is housing a peace conference. Then a murder is committed. The most important member of the peace conference is shot and then the race under the umbrellas in an attempt to find the murderer. That's a thrill for you. But soon you find out it's not the fellow that you thought was murdered. It's his double, with the whole thing plotted for the kidnapping of the real character so that the Germans can question him.

And imagine the bombing of a big trans-Atlantic Clipper ship, with all the action taking place INSIDE the ship instead of the way most yarns would have it done--the action outside the ship with the actual scenes of the bombing. And the little touches that Hitchcock puts into scenes that, under another hand would be of no consequence! Everything's important to that fellow in the making of a picture, and that's why Foreign Correspondent is so good.

Joel McCrea has never been better in his acting career. He is most convincing in his every movement, with every word of his dialogue. The same can be said of Laraine Day. She has not had much of a career, but from this picture on she will become important. And imagine Herbert Marshall playing a heavy! True, a refined heavy, but nevertheless unusual and fine piece of casting, and Mr. Marshall does it as few others could. And Albert Basserman! Well, everything that Herr Basserman does is good, but this is better. One of his scenes was rewarded with applause. Not that his others didn't merit it, nor those of the other players. The story was so tense, the audience did not want the running of the picture disturbed by applause, but they couldn't deny Basserman. Bob Benchley did a great bit with his Stebbins: "I've been over here for twenty-five years reporting for my paper." Edmund Gwenn was swell in a small bit, as were Harry Davenport and Eduardo Ciannelli.

To give credit to the rest of the cast, probably the largest speaking cast ever assembled for a picture, would take up a couple of pages. Suffice that they were all good.

The writers of the picture, Charles Bennett and Joan Harrison on the screenplay and James Hilton and Robert Benchley on the dialogue must thank Alfred Hitchcock for his magnificent handling of the yarn. There was nothing brilliant about the dialogue nor the originality of the screenplay.

The photographing of this subject was a tough assignment for any cameraman, because of the demands in realistic lighting and settings, and that it came through in the manner it did is a great tribute to Rudy Maté.

Foreign Correspondent is big enough to surmount its title, but the wise exhibitor should sell and sell and sell, for he has a picture to back up any guarantee of good entertainment.

--The Hollywood Reporter, Vol. 59, No. 25 (August 28, 1940), page 3.

*   *   *

Alfred Hitchcock is a cinematic stylist who has shown himself at his best when handling I-spy thrillers. He has, from time to time, turned his attention to other subject matter, but the man's more rabid enthusiasts, among whom this scrivener must be listed, insist that he is never in better form than with a perambulating saga of international intrigue--preferably one that limits its melodramatic happenings to a few crowded hours. From such threads has he many times woven a tapestry of tension, excitement, and entertainment. After such typical examples of Hitchcockiana, and not so long ago, one exited from the picture palace a little breathless and quite exhilarated.

However, since the map of Europe has changed and because of some of the instruments of that change, one views Foreign Correspondent with a difference. The fifth column has proved its efficaciousness; spies have ceased to be figments of pulp-paper and celluloid. What once supplied us with pleasant titillation of the nerves has become a dread reality. The hooded figure is no longer a thing of printed matter or screen shadows, but something dire that moves among us. We have discovered that when it strikes it is not with a prop dagger.

Because of the fast-moving panorama of actual events abroad, the Hitchcock formula now bludgeons where it once patted, horrifies where it once supplied adventure-delight. Today, Foreign Correspondent strikes too close to home to be mere amusement. It is, without doubt, a picture to be seen, being admirably directed by Mr. H., with no small share of the merit of the film due to the designing skill of William Cameron Menzies. Joel McCrea is very good indeed as the never-say-die journalist and Laraine Day gives the heroine assignment considerable charm. The real acting honors, we believe, go to Herbert Marshall, Albert Basserman and that able funnyman, Robert Benchley.

There is one matter with which we take exception. Recognizing the fact that people are neither black-black or white-white, it still should be apparent that now is no time to glorify traitors, as is done here. The arch-spy does his damnedest to betray his adopted country; he is responsible for murder, torture and similar pleasantries, only to have a "This was a man!" oration read to his memory after what is meant to be an heroic, and redeeming, death scene. The dispassionate view may very well be a laudable British virtue, but here it seems to have been stretched just a bit too far.

--Herb Sterne in Rob Wagner's Script, Vol. 24, No. 568 (September 28, 1940), page 16.

☐ 42nd STREET (Warner Bros. , 1933)

    If you want to know what I think of this show--as though it
makes a difference!--I'm giving it a lotta stars in Liberty!

    It's a musical. But it's more than that. It's a darned good
story of the making of a musical (Bradford Ropes, author; Rian
James and James Seymour, scenarists), full of fine heart interest,
splendid acting, swell music and gorgeous production numbers.

    Warner Baxter, as the tempestuous director of the show,
does the best job of his career. Bebe Daniels glamours all over
the works and sings and acts with spirit. Una Merkel and Ginger
Rogers as a couple of hard-boiled showgirls are terribly amusing,
and Dick Powell, the lad who made audiences like even a radio
crooner, sings delightfully. Best of all is Ruby Keeler, who plays
the newcomer in the show business and then riots them with her
good looks and dancing.

    That everybody in the picture acts as though he liked his
part is darned creditable to Lloyd Bacon, who has given us the
best musical since Broadway Melody.
                                      --Rob Wagner in Rob Wagner's
                                      Script, Vol. 9, No. 209 (Feb-
                                      ruary 11, 1933), page 9.

                         *   *   *

    Highly entertaining story of backstage musical comedy life.
Ruby Keeler, who is Al Jolson's wife, offers a wide-eyed, naive
performance which assures further roles which demand the appearance of innocence.   There are so few gals for these exacting character parts. Cameraman Sol Polito offers ingenious shots of Busby
Berkeley's excellent dance routines, and several tunes are catchy.
There's one risqué laugh. A man emerges from a door saying to
a girl, "... so the other fellow says, 'Well, what do you think I've
got down here--a duck?'" (Tch-Tch!)
                                      --Harry Evans in Life, Vol. 100,
                                      No. 2578 (May 1933), page 39.

☐ FRANKENSTEIN (Universal, 1932)

    Motion pictures are still in their infancy. For a while it be-
gan to look as though they had grown up, when bang! they instantly
became infantile again.   Little children have two passionate urges--
one, to make mud pies and snowmen, and the other to go "boo!" and
frighten their playmates. Grown-up infants like to do the same
things--they wish to create "monsters" to frighten people.

Before Universal shows us the film version of the old, old fairy tale of Frankenstein a fellow comes out and warns the audience that it is about to be horrified and anybody who can't stand for "monsters" had better leave.   In other words, he says "boo!" Those with childish minds enjoy a delicious thrill of fear.

But to grown-up people the story of Frankenstein is pretty childish.   It hasn't the romantic beauty of Pygmalion falling in love with his beautiful Galatea, or yet the horror of The Golem which, by the way, was filmed in Italy some twenty years ago and was infinitely better than Frankenstein.   For the Golem was a magnificent monster of stone, so huge and heavy that when it started on its depredations it walked through villages with the destructive power of a tank.   The human monster of Frankenstein is not very much more powerful than its victims.

Nor as a work of art can much be said for this Universal Production.   Arthur Edeson gives us a few examples of his magnificent photography in the opening sequences of the grave robbing, but after that the camera work is pretty poor, edited no doubt by James Whale's direction, or the demands of the sound engineers.

After seeing London Bridge I expected great things of James Whale, but his direction of Frankenstein is ridiculously old-fashioned.   His crowd scenes look as artificial as grand opera, especially when the villagers set out with torches and clubs to hunt the monster amid the papier-mâché mountains.

All the old Mack Sennett scare-sequence gags are used to give us the creeps--a goofy windmill atop a mountain of rocks (windmills are always in the valleys!); a lot of pseudo-scientific gadgets intended to impress the unscientific; bringing the thing up-to-date with talk of ultra-violet rays; and pulling the big punch in a thunder storm.   The only thing omitted is the comedy relief of a frightened coon.   Yes, there was the grandest of the old comedy-studio props, a skeleton!

No, I'm afraid Universal has tried too hard to frighten me. Evidently the word-of-mouthers feel the same way, for Andy Anderson, Bev's most beautiful cop, had no trouble handling the crowd trying to hurry by Warner's Theatre.   Or perhaps the crowd was trying to avoid Graham McNamee and a bunch of Godawful shorts.

The only ones who seem to have had any fun with Frankenstein were Garrett Fort and Francis Faragoh who wrote the screen play.

Colin Clive is a personable chap but he sings his lines in the old-fashioned stage English.   Perhaps he cawn't speak in any other way, but it's too broad and mushy for my western ears.

Mae Clarke is a perfectly beautiful girl made almost ugly by axle-greased lips.   Boris Karloff's make-up is truly remarkable

and what acting he does is very fine. But why didn't the technical
fellows invoke the old comedy-studio piano wires so that he could
lift his victims above his head and toss them about like toys?

                              --Rob Wagner in Rob Wagner's
                                Script, Vol. 7, No. 158 (Febru-
                                ary 20, 1932), page 10.

                          *   *   *

If you like mystery and spooky pictures, here's your meat.
It's strong stuff, and not for faint-hearted folks. It introduces a
successor to the late Lon Chaney, who out-horrors anything Chaney
ever gave us.

The opening scene is a funeral. A mad surgical genius creates a monster and, no matter how well you know the story, to
watch that mechanical man come alive is a breath-taking, sensational experience you won't forget.

Boris Karloff plays the monster. During the making of the
picture he lost twenty-one pounds. You won't wonder when you see
him. He's great, as is Colin Clive as Frankenstein. The direction
and photography are magnificent. And, whether you like it or not,
you'll be held spell-bound.

                              --Photoplay, Vol. 41, No. 2
                                (January 1932), page 47.

☐ THE GARDEN OF ALLAH (Selznick/United Artists, 1937)

It is thirty years since Robert Hichens penned the desert romance that entitles him to consideration as a bulwark of middle-
class literature. In its long and successful career the book has
convinced myriad frustrated spinsters that the Sahara is a hot-spot
inhabited solely by hootchie-cootchie exponents and avid, if soul-
scarred, lovers. Statistics also prove that the patronage of sand
diviners has increased by leaps and bounds since that long-ago publication date, with thousands of gullible foreign metaphysicians an-
nually overrunning Biskra to salaam before the native brand of ho-
cus-pocus.

Filmed twice in the "silents," the current adaptation emerges
as one of the most beautiful, heady and synthetic strips of celluloid
ever to run through a projector. Its visual enchantment probably
won't overwhelm as box office bait, but the four-sided tug of war
between God, the World, the Flesh and the Devil is going to be
mighty popular with the ladies; and that despite a theme which is
not so much intrinsically old-fashioned as not of-the-moment.

Traveling through the lands which lie between Casablanca and
Saigon, one's fingers itch for a color camera; without "hues" the

images of the East lose greatly. Hichens' major merit is in his
jeweled prose which evokes the North African locale; the Selig and
Rex Ingram versions were shot in black and white which castrated
the novel's primary allure. Fortunately David Selznick realized
this, used Technicolor to create a cyclorama sufficiently authentic
to transubstantiate a chromo plot into a chromatic feast. Avoiding
the overbrilliance of past tinted epics, the picture has been held
down to half tones ... groups of compelling beauty, sweeping vistas
of desert lighted by fragile dawns and tiger sunsets. The Kalmuses
should be eternally grateful to Lansing Holden, W. Howard Greene
and Hal Rosson for exhibiting their process to such advantage.

The screen play and direction have devised a series of Ben
Ali Haggin tableaux that replace dramatic action. The tale of the
renegade monk who marries a devout Catholic girl is always secondary to the composition and acting. The original is followed with
precision for the most part, but it's regrettable that Count Anteoni
was so ruthlessly sheared, for Basil Rathbone gives a glyptic show.
The Mohammedan angle, so persuasive in the written work, has
been lifted so that there's not a single shot of muezzin or mosque.
Eyebrows will be raised at the "Arab" types used for atmosphere;
they look as though they've just been plucked off Olvera Street and
for some reason (fear of halation?) the European men are dressed
in dark worsted suits rather than in the white linens usual to hot
countries.

Julia Marlowe contended that only a skillful technician could
play a "good" woman interestingly; Marlene Dietrich does just that.
My idea of the screen's most entrancing gal escapes at last from
the black-crêpe-and-diamonds enchantresses that have so long entrapped her talents, to create a character that is sharply defined,
subjective and, believe it or not, spirituelle. Color gives Marlene
a new reality ... but I prefer her as the shadowy heroine of black
and white close-ups.

Casting Charles Boyer as the brooding monk who breaks his
vows was a perspicacious stroke. Probably no other actor could
have given so completely moving a performance. Great! Tilly
Losch (début) is a ravishing Ouled Nail undulator, dances a solo
that will get raves from everyone but the censors. C. Aubrey
Smith once again is excellent. Direction by Richard Boleslawski is
restrained, creates a mood that is continuous and haunting.
                              --Herb Sterne in Rob Wagner's
                                Script, Vol. 16, No. 398 (Janu-
                                ary 16, 1937), page 10.

                    *   *   *

Since life and art are progressive, some day, soon, a story
sturdy enough to hold up in black and white will, when coupled with
the Technicolor, combine into socko b. o. It resolves itself down
all over again, in color cinematurgy or in the normal screen hues,
that it's the story first. The rest are merely production niceties

to enhance and embellish but never sufficient to sustain on their own.
Accordingly Garden of Allah, so sumptuously and impressively
mounted by David O. Selznick, impresses as the last word in color
production, but a pretty dull affair.   It'll come out all right chiefly
on the ballyhoo and the marquee values of the stellar pair, Dietrich
and Boyer.   Especially so for the matinee trade.

        The b. o. answer finds itself in perhaps the No. 1 feature
money-maker in color, Trail of the Lonesome Pine, to date, where
the prismatic camera enhancement had the advantage of a romance
which, despite its backwoods familiarity, could almost stand up in
ordinary black and white camera treatment.

        Selznick's Garden of Allah is the last word in coloring.   It
is optically arresting and betimes emotionally gripping but, after a
spell, the ecclesiastic significance of the Trappist monk whose
earthly love cannot usurp his prior secular vows peters out completely.

        After their romantic safari into the Sahara--when the French
captain and the count learn of Boyer's desertion from the monastery
--the renunciation of earthly emotions, as Miss Dietrich escorts the
monk back to sanctuary, somehow misses fire.   It doesn't click
emotionally; it's vapid in its romanticism, once the premise is established; and irises-out on an impression of the sands of the desert
which have grown cold 20 minutes before the final camera portrait
shot.

        The cinematic portraiture combines with the expert trouping
of the stellar twain in bolstering the proceedings, but not quite
enough.

        As a motion picture, the screen is asked too much of.   The
demands to reflect emotions into satisfying film drama are almost
beyond the medium.   In literature, Hichens' novel could word-paint
something which neither the lens--on the face of it a more advan-
tageous medium--nor the screen artificers could achieve.

        Miss Dietrich and Charles Boyer are more than adequately
competent in the leads although sometimes slurring their lines.   But
in the main they impress in the difficult emotional roles.   The support is likewise ultra.   Basil Rathbone, C. Aubrey Smith, Tilly
Losch (making her screen debut in a Bagdad cafe dancing sequence,
and okay in what she does), Joseph Schildkraut (who almost steals
the picture with his exaggerated oriental ingratiations) and John
Carradine as the sandseer leave nothing wanting.   The color is particularly flattering to Miss Dietrich who has also taken off a little
weight.   In the flowing capes to which she is so partial, the color
camera has caught her at her photographic best.

        Running time of 80 minutes, while not abnormally long, ap-
pears longer, which is invariably a tip-off on calibre of script and
direction.   Yet Boleslawski has done an expert technical job in moti-

vating the action and the Lipscomb-Riggs continuity has been wisely
sparing of dialog. Which leaves the impression that the "action,"
such as it is, isn't sufficiently actionful. Shots and more shots of
the desert, silhouettes against sunsets, caravansaries into the Garden of Allah (as the Arabs call the Sahara), bivouacked Bedouins,
et al. do not make for cinematurgy. It's good incidental by-play,
but that's all.

Nor is Boyer's struggle between worldly pursuits and his return to Trappist celibacy any great stirring premise, save for the
femmes. Garden of Allah as matinee fodder thus impresses favorably, which in one aspect augurs well for its box-office.

Max Steiner's score is second only to the gorgeous color
cameraing, among the major contributory aspects. His music has
really been called upon to collaborate with the histrionism in pitch-
ing the emotions, and he achieves it in no small measure. Lansing
C. Holden's color direction and the W. Howard Greene-Hal Rossen
cinematographic collaboration more than fulfill requirements from
the lens adjunct which, in a production of this nature, is no small
component.

> --Abel (Abel Green) in Variety,
> Vol. 124, No. 11 (November 25,
> 1936), page 14.

☐ THE GAY DIVORCEE (RKO, 1934)

Fred Astaire! There is a name you're going to see in lick-
erish lights as big as the building ordinances will permit 'em. For
Fred has raised tap and ballroom dancing to a Great Art. Also he
can act--deliciously. Also he has more personal charm than Maurice Chevalier. Ye Real Ed says he has more sex appeal standing
a foot away from a gal than most of the sex-apple-knockers have in
a clinch. Further and more, Pan Berman has put him in a production in which all his talents and charms shine gorgeously.

As you see, this review is becoming a rave. And while
I'm at it, let me celebrate Ginger Rogers. She had one whale of
a job in playing and dancing up to the star, yet she did so in a
manner that makes a monkey of me for all my past reviews of her
work.

Alice Brady does another of her inimitable morons. (I'll
bet anything she would be grand in drama, but when one is stuck
with a character on the screen, well--you know.) Eddie Horton--
never funnier. He even does a little dance, and the fans howl.

But where has Eric Blore been all my celluloid life? He
has only two or three short scenes, but those scenes would save
any doubtful picture. The preview audiences cheered!

Then there is Erik Rhodes (this must be a Swede year) who plays the part of a professional corespondent with a most refreshing exuberance.

This newest musical comedy has brilliant lines, gorgeous music and exceptionally beautiful production numbers, but its greatest excellence is dancing, not only by the stars, but by the ensemble. One thing you can chalk up to this Decency thing--it has put long flowing skirts on the women and thereby restored the rhythm essential to fine dancing. In fact, the added jazz numbers with the usual bare-legged syncopaters come as a decided anticlimax.

The credit sheet lists a forbidding number of artistic heroes, but I can't overlook the musical direction of Max Steiner, nor the one very original song, Cole Porter's "Night and Day."

But to return to Fred Astaire--he is as graceful as a dik-dik, and not much bigger, cleaner cut than Valentino and with a gentility that raises a musical comedy into something as exquisite as a Barrie play. Who says good taste and virtue don't pay?

--Rob Wagner in Rob Wagner's Script, Vol. 12, No. 289 (October 20, 1934), page 10.

*   *   *

The Gay Divorcee is a propaganda film for more Fred Astaire dancing.

If I had the choice of choosing between death for what some pudgy U.S. senator might consider our proper national righteousness and of dying for what Fred Astaire might consider an important new dance step, I'd take a million deaths in the latter cause.

The Gay Divorcee is, as a whole, pure delight, and when the lithe, jaunty Mr. Astaire has the floor, it becomes thrillingly pleasant. His inventive footwork, his nimbleness of ankle and cerebellum, and his sense of humor expressed in dance, song and acting, are something for mankind to be proud of in one of its representatives. I imagine he is a type on which the gods dote.

The movie is an elaborate derivation from the musical comedy of the same name in which Mr. Astaire starred. Several new songs are introduced, including "The Continental" which involves a dance with kisses in the clinches--oh, coryza, here you come!

Ginger Rogers, no great shakes as an actress, puts a song over surprisingly well, wears a dress captivatingly, and serves adequately as an Astaire dancing partner, though I'll confess I didn't watch her carefully when Mr. Astaire was around. The plot is of love at first sight and the goings on when the young lady discovers (or so she thinks) that her lover is a professional corespondent in divorce cases and has apparently been assigned to her apartment in a seaside hotel.

--Don Herold in Life, Vol. 102,
No. 2598 (January 1935), pages
30-31.

☐ GOLD DIGGERS OF 1933 (Warner Bros. , 1933)

The success of 42nd Street naturally prompted Warners to a repeat--always a dangerous game, for while one might enjoy a single banquet, two banquets in a row make a pretty big dish, and even though the second banquet may be better cooked, it won't be relished like the first.

Despite the yips in the trade press, I don't think this picture tops its immediate predecessor, though it has most of the original cast and the dancing numbers are exceptionally beautiful.

42nd Street had distinct unity. It was a simple story of the making of a great musical show; this one is largely concerned with the adventures of three gold diggers, most of their digging taking place away from the theater. Of course, there's a show, but it could have been left out without injuring the story.

Another structural weakness, in my opinion, is the attempt to build a big production number out of the depression. Done splendidly in the manner of a great Max Reinhardt pageant, it nevertheless is a dour, gray let-down from the effervescent glories of carnival. There certainly is nothing glamorous in long parades of mud-and-blood-soaked soldiers and equally long lines of broken-spirited breadliners.

Mervyn LeRoy has done well with the material, but I think the material is a bit confused.

Dick Powell gets a swell break, and while Ruby Keeler is charming as usual, the camera was not kind to her and she didn't dance enough.

Ned Sparks acts well in a part similar to Warner Baxter's in 42nd Street, but his diction, always pitched in the same high, tempestuous key, is monotonous. He should occasionally lower his voice, have a few gentle moments.

Joan Blondell has the hardest role, appearing mostly in the off-stage sequences, and shows a fine artistry. But even she, usually so careful of her make-up, wears heavily varnished lips.

Guy Kibbee and Warren William, as the gold-dug suckers, deliver with their usual finish, but Aline MacMahon clowns her part to absurdity.

Nor do I think Ginger Rogers was a happy choice with which
to open a great musical spectacle; she sang her number with spirit,
but she is not pretty enough to key the picture to beauty.

This all sounds a big negative, but there is enough splendor
and lively business to make a fine show.   Had I not over-banqueted
on 42nd Street I might even have considered it a great show.
                              --Rob Wagner in Rob Wagner's
                                Script, Vol. 9, No. 225 (June
                                3, 1933), page 8.

                    *   *   *

If you thought 42nd Street was good, you have a date with
any theater showing this one.   It's another Ruby Keeler show that
has everything 42nd Street did!

To start things off, chorine Ruby is in love with Dick Powell, a penniless song writer.   But when things look hopeless, Dick
digs up money, the show goes big, and zowie!   In pops Warren
William, brother of the show's "angel," from staid old Boston.   No
chorus girls in his family.   No sir!

What to do?   Ruby's roommates, Joan Blondell and Aline
MacMahon, decide to work on Warren and his co-killjoy, Guy Kibbee, and we'll let the film tell what happens to them.   But it's
rich, we promise you, and at that it's only the foundation upon
which Director Mervyn LeRoy and dance impresario Busby Berkeley
have built music, ensemble numbers, and acting that are splendid.

Coming to performances, Ruby still wins you at sight--al-
though she has too little to do.   Dick Powell, especially in his song
numbers, is a treat; while Warren William, Aline MacMahon and
Guy Kibbee turn in the excellent work you might expect from such
artists.   But the surprise of the show is the new Joan Blondell.
Cast as a traditional gold digger, she achieves absolutely compelling
emotional power.   Wait till you hear her lead that "Forgotten Man"
finale!   Ginger Rogers and Ned Sparks, too, are delightful.
                              --Photoplay, Vol. 44, No. 3
                                (August 1933), page 54.

☐ GONE WITH THE WIND (Selznick, with M-G-M, 1939)

Like a skyscraper, Gone with the Wind is impressive, first
and foremost, because it is big, bold, and overwhelming.   It flab-
bergasted the critics, including this one, chiefly because after having been publicized so long and so arrogantly, and having been so
long in patient preparation, it surpassed expectations.   In this respect it is unlike most modern creative works of epic proportions--
the dramatic trilogies, hour-long symphonies and novels which ap-

pear in sections--which seem portentous before they are finished
and offered to the public but later, although their creators' ambition
and industry are praised, prove disappointing.

Gone with the Wind is undoubtedly a screen milestone, if not
a masterpiece. Frankly, I wouldn't know a masterpiece if I saw
one, unless it had been sanctioned by Time, possessed the proper
academic credentials, and required considerable study before one
could understand why it came to be so highly regarded. And even
then I might have my own notions. If you wish to believe that
Gone with the Wind is the greatest motion picture ever made, dwarf-
ing everything that came before and practically annulling any that may
come after, go to it! The daily and trade press are behind you,
and I'm only a few steps behind them.

Since the film is the triumphant result of almost perfect collaboration, it invites no comparison with past films bearing the hall-
mark of virtuoso directors. This is no reflection on Victor Fleming who did a difficult job well, but he would probably be the first
to admit that G. W. T. W. derives its excellence from many sources,
with special credit going to the art department. Since the film is
almost twice as long as the best of yesterday's films, it had opportunities (and faced dangers, too!) that some earlier epics didn't
have. Technicolor, its artistic possibilities at length realized, was
also a tremendous factor in making this picture different from others. Besides, we mustn't be forgetting Margaret Mitchell, without
whom there wouldn't have been any picture or an expectant audience
of millions.

My personal tribute to Gone with the Wind requires few
words and no expression of critical opinion. The film's power is
indicated by the fact that your reviewer, a fidgeter by nature, never
once shifted in his seat after it had begun; furthermore, he scorned
the intermission, still under the picture's spell, impatient for it to
resume. Such an admission, I think, would argue that whereas the
novel was hailed for its "sheer readability," the motion picture
holds one's attention to an equal or even greater degree.

The picture as a whole is so well integrated that one does
not concentrate on individual performances except in retrospect.
Vivien Leigh, with her lynx eyes and determined chin, is as vital
and varied, as magnetic as the Scarlett of the book. When you look
your last at her, you know that she must go on; she is so much a
living character that you swear she won't fade out before "The End"
flashes on. Rhett or wrong, Clark Gable makes a handsome, virile
figure of the Charleston buccaneer and lady-killer. Olivia de Havilland, the serene and gracious Melanie, gave what was, to my mind,
the finest performance of all, a lustrous creation. And even an incomplete report must laud Hattie McDaniel for the haunting pathos
of her stairway scene, Butterfly McQueen for her hysteria during
the siege of Atlanta, Ona Munson for the brief perfection of her
Belle Watling. Bestow the other laurels yourself, but you will be
kept busy. And if I've neglected Leslie Howard, perhaps it's be-

cause he began to fade after a few scenes and I was hardly aware
of him finally--except for the sound of a distinctly British accent.

Cinematically, the picture has more surge and sweep during
the first half, but since Sidney Howard's adroit adaptation mirrors
the novel faithfully, one regrets only passively that the dramatic
exploration of human relationships, in the second half, proceeds
from the general to the specific until the tragedy of a whole people
is nearly forgotten and we leave the theater carrying the image of
an audacious yet essentially worthless woman in our minds.

It is probably futile to protest that Gone with the Wind is a
stirring narrative which lacks significance. The same thing might
be said of Mourning Becomes Electra which is sufficiently great
when viewed only as superb melodrama. Scarlett O'Hara is a fascinating creature of blood and fire but, to one spectator, Melanie
quietly dominates the story, and it is she who is the real victim of
the Civil War. The Scarletts survive and flourish through hell and
high water, but the Scarlett we see, tear-stained and whimpering,
as the film ends, postponing reality until the next day, is the same
girl-woman we met in the first scene, and remains an enigma. Is
that why she has fascinated millions?

> --Richard Sheridan Ames in Rob
> Wagner's Script, Vol. 22, No.
> 535 (December 23, 1939), page
> 16.

*   *   *

The word about Gone with the Wind--if you haven't heard it
already--is that it is about on the same level as the novel from
which it was derived. It is exceptionally long, as the book was,
and it isn't likely to disappoint those who liked the book, who number so many that no one else counts very much. If as a book it
was a great novel, as a movie it is a great picture. Need greatness be defined? Obviously all the time, effort, talent and money
that have gone into the making of the picture were employed to
satisfy a certain public, the phenomenal multitude of readers who
made the book one of the astonishing successes of the century. The
movie had to tell the same story to the eye and ear that the book
told in printed pages, and its success as a pictorial narrative is
the only fair thing to judge it by.

There is an intermission in the middle of the picture (merci-
fully, because sitting still so long is physically onerous no matter
how interested one may be), and there are those who think the film
would have been better if it had ended just there. That would have
been a logical enough ending in a way, if the story had been only
about what the war did to Scarlett O'Hara, the determination that it
led her to. But there is another interest than that--how did she
carry out her determination? And what, on the one hand, became
of her infatuation for Ashley, and on the other hand what came of
that strange combination of antagonism and attraction between her

and Rhett Butler?   Of course, after another ten or twelve reels, the end is still uncertain, but there is nevertheless the satisfaction of watching that fascinating cat-and-dog conflict between Scarlett and Rhett for a while.   It was probably never-ending.

The adaptation of so much material to the screen was a tremendous job.   Sidney Howard did it remarkably well, keeping the multitude of characters in good perspective, all in their relation to Scarlett, yet each one clear and individual.   The story itself, though Scarlett is always the center of it, has a broad beginning, with the bitter plight of Georgia and the Yankee army steadily advancing. Gradually it converges, its emotion and landscape narrowing, till it becomes all Scarlett and Rhett, and the other people closely involved with them.   And it always keeps moving.

Victor Fleming, in his direction, has been content to tell his story as clearly as possible, with no fancy work or lingering on "touches. "   When the story calls for something impressive he does it, as in the scene in the railroad yard when Scarlett picking her way among scores of wounded soldiers lying on the ground, who look like thousands, suggests as much of the devastation of war as a terrific battle scene would have done.   Or when Scarlett shoots the marauding Yankee, or when Mammy (so magnificently played by Hattie McDaniel) leads Melanie up the stairs to the room where Rhett is brooding over his dead child, and in a single scene sums up all the woe and despair that has filled the house for days.   It is an achievement to have kept so long a narrative from never flagging, or getting wearisome.

The casting is another stroke of excellence.   It was an inspiration to give the part of Scarlett to an unknown actress, unassociated with other parts, and Vivien Leigh is completely Scarlett O'Hara, with no aura of other characters about her.   Everything about her is triumphantly right, just as with Clark Gable, for whom the part of Rhett Butler might have been especially written.   Olivia de Havilland embodies the gentleness and nobility of Melanie without becoming over-sweet, just as Barbara O'Neill, in her brief appearance as Scarlett's mother, embodies the dignity and aristocratic refinement of a lady who is the mistress of a great southern plantation.   Hattie McDaniel and Butterfly McQueen have vividness and depth as two of the slaves.   The whole enormous cast is full of people who do excellently what they have to do in filling out the picture.

Faults could be found if one were looking at this film merely as a motion picture of Georgia in the war and reconstruction days; that it leaves too many important things untouched, that it has no historical perspective, that it provides no ethical or social comment on its characters or events, finally that it is still a novel more than it is a motion picture.   But none of those things were intended, or really to be expected.   It is enough that Margaret Mitchell's novel should have been put on the screen so satisfyingly for its millions of readers.

--James Shelley Hamilton in National Board of Review Magazine,
Vol. 15, No. 1 (January 1940),
pages 19-20.

□ THE GOOD EARTH (M-G-M, 1937)

M-G-M's devoted, daring and costly filming of the widely-
read Pearl Buck novel of Chinese peasant life will arouse sharp
contrasts of opinion. It is a biographical narrative that comes close
to revealing the soul of a great and ancient people, and in so doing
it probes deeply the common heart of mankind, arousing a sympathy
that all will feel. It is, too, a pictorial masterwork.

On the other hand its episodic form, embracing a whole generation of loosely-connected events, its insistent note of harrowing
hardship and tragedy, its present length of more than two hours,
and its foreign locale with American players in the principal roles
will tend to make it caviar to the mass American audience. Despite
the fame of the book and the presence of Paul Muni and Luise Rainer in strong portrayals, it will have to be sold with vigor to return
any large profit. Fortunately, it is meat for effective exploitation.

The golden thread of motive throughout is love of the soil--
of that Good Earth without whose bounty man must starve. For the
little plot of ground one endures everything. Plagues come to the
little family in the north of China--a great storm at harvest-time,
drought and dreadful famine and, later, the locusts--but it fights its
way out of them all, unconscious of its own dauntless heroism.
Americans will be vividly reminded of what has happened recently in
part of our own middle west.

The story focuses on a young Chinese farmer of the poorest
class. He is Wang, the role portrayed with consummate artistry
by Paul Muni. It is his wedding day and he goes with boyish excitement to bring home the bride he has never seen, a woefully
homely but industrious slave girl who is the best that he can afford.
This is Luise Rainer's role and it is the most bizarre given a
woman star in a long time. Miss Rainer, fresh from laurels won
as the sparkling Anna Held in The Great Ziegfeld, here divests herself of every shred of good looks and animation to bring to life with
compelling persuasiveness the downcast and doggedly devoted farm
wife whose whole life is one of unremitting toil, briefly punctuated
by child-bearing. She seldom speaks and seldom ever smiles but
she is a powerfully dominant influence throughout the story. Highest credit must go to the courageous Miss Rainer.

Following the childish merriment of the wedding events, comes
the first climax--a vividly pictured electric storm that threatens the

ripe grain. There is wild haste to garner the crop, and the wife, though expecting her first baby within the hour, joins in until she drops. Wang's ingenuous pride in this first son is one of the bright spots of the picture.

The faithful wife's industry brings a measure of prosperity and little by little more land is added to the farm. Then comes the drought. The fields dry up and the farm animals die of thirst or are eaten for food. Hunger reaches a desperate pitch. The pot on the stove contains nothing but earth and water. Wang is persuaded to sell the land for a pittance but the wife intervenes, as always. Stumbling with weakness they join the tragic trek of the starving, southward to the city. There they are kept alive by begging and a little inhuman labor.

Revolution comes to the city. The wife is swept along in the mob that loots the palace, and is left unconscious. Reviving she finds a bag of jewels. With these as capital they escape to the north. But the wealth goes to Wang's head. He covets a pretty dancing girl in the exquisite person of Tilly Losch, taking her into his home as a second wife, only to find that she is amusing herself with his youngest son.

He has alienated family and friends. Then the locust invasion comes and all forget their differences in a climactic battle to save part of the crop. This unique sequence is vividly and dramatically presented. A trick of the winds among their hills aids the fighters. The crop is saved and the family reunited. But now the ever-patient wife patiently dies, leaving Wang humbled among his ripe fields.

The screenplay delivered by three top-rank writers, except for its inevitable fault of construction, is an able and continuously engaging presentation of characters and situations. It is sparsely but pungently dialogued without any attempt to use a Chinese idiom and is recited in plain though somewhat varied American accents, except by Miss Rainer, whose slight French accent is not disturbing, but rather helpful.

Sidney Franklin's direction has much to commend it, especially in his handling of mass movement outdoors. Many of these scenes are marvellously impressive. His unfolding of the personal drama has emotional power but may be too deliberate and emphatic to sustain the illusion of an oriental atmosphere. It was a difficult and perhaps an impossible undertaking. Considerable credit reflects on Albert Lewin, who supervised the picture under Irving Thalberg.

The highest praise must go to Karl Freund for photography of thrilling artistry; to the technical staff for an infinitude of properties and sets of authentic flavor and interest, and for several marvels of make-up; and to Herbert Stothart for a score built from authentic Chinese themes that adds immeasurably to the atmospheric charm of the narrative.

Honors to the supporting cast are plentiful.   Charles Grapewin presents a tragic and moving personification of oriental fatalism
as Wang's father, and Walter Connolly aptly captures the vein of
serio-comedy as his self-important and wily uncle.   Tilly Losch's
dance is a thing of rare beauty and Jessie Ralph as Tilly's avari-
cious promoter is not beautiful but realistic.   Keye Luke as Wang's
college-trained older son adds an unexpected touch of modernity.
Roland Got, Soo Yong, and Suzanne Kim give first aid in sustaining
the Chinese color.

--The Hollywood Reporter, Vol.
36, No. 42 (December 7, 1936),
page 3.

* * *

My illiteracy ("ignorance of letters or books"--Webster) has
one advantage.   Like five or ten million others who will go to see
this picture, I haven't read the book.   Consequently, I attended in
the critical raw.   Discounting the usual "terrific" and "colossal"
ballyhoo, what of the picture itself?

My final reaction was tremendous admiration for Irving Thalberg for having the courage and high artistry to order its production.   For this is no light fare, not even roast beef and Yorkshire
pudding.   It is black bread and cabbage soup.   Rougher even than
that; it is the fight of the people of the soil to survive in spite of
the wrath of God.   The story conflict is not between virtue and vice;
but between a single family and the greater heavies of nature--flood,
famine and insect plague.

Strangely enough, prompted by our recent floods, I had just
written how the Chinese had helplessly faced these terrors for centuries, whereas the white race had gone out to conquer them.   And
that is the "top" of this grim story--a younger son returning from
college led his folks in a successful battle against a plague of locusts.

With the slow unfolding of the grim lives of these Chinese
peasants, it was only natural that the story-tellers should play up
the violence of battle.   But I felt that the storm was too tempestuous, the drought sequences too long, the revolution too crowded and
repetitious, and that there were too many grasshoppers.   My critical side-kick didn't agree with me.

The greatest single triumph of the picture--other than the
superb direction of Sidney Franklin--was, to me, the extraordinary
characterization of O-Lan given by Luise Rainer.   Crushed, brow-
beaten, and humiliated as a slave girl, she became, as a slave
wife, one of the most wistfully loving and pathetic figures imagin-
able.   Yet beneath her obedient humility lurked such a passion for
a few miserable acres of the soil that she became a magnificent
symbol.

To the beautiful Miss Rainer's everlasting credit, not once did she try to put over Miss Rainer. She was the crushed, bovine peasant up to her pathetic death. Not so Paul Muni. As fine as was his acting, he did not look the "brother to the ox" that he was supposed to be. Toward the end, after he had cut his queue and was wearing his hair very U. C. L. A. , he looked more like Paul Muni than the character Wang.

Walter Connolly also had some difficulty in sublimating his personal ego. Charley Grapewin was right up with Miss Rainer-- amazing make-up and understanding of his role.

Tilly Losch was also a triumph of Jack Dawn's gelatinous surgery. And her pantomime was superb.

The real Chinese actors all delivered finely, but I was so impressed with the make-up of the white actors--you couldn't tell which was which--that next week I shall write at length about this extraordinary development in what has become a new art.

Haven't room to give detailed credit to the individual authors, superb camera work, sets, costumes, music, and sound. But I must express delight in reading that Script contributor Harry Oliver was Cedric Gibbons' assistant on the sets.

Albert Lewin did a grand job in carrying on Irving Thalberg's last, and probably greatest, production.

Have just learned that the big credit for The Good Earth sets goes to Harry Oliver who began them under Irving Thalberg and continued under seven directors, while Cedric Gibbons was in Europe. He built the farm with its many terraces up at Chatsworth. Smart of Frank Whitbeck finally to enlist Harry's artistry in building the huge spectacular street effects leading from Wilshire Boulevard up to the entrance of the Carthay Circle Theater. Fairs and pageants are the huge canvases Harry needs to paint upon. He won all prizes at the Dallas fair, and you all remember his Gold Gulch down at San Diego.

--Rob Wagner in Rob Wagner's
Script, Vol. 16, No. 401 (February 6, 1937), page 8.

☐ GOODBYE MR. CHIPS (M-G-M, 1939)

Not again this year, and perhaps not for many another, does your reviewer expect to endorse so wholeheartedly a film which will appeal to patrons of all ages and every taste and be treasured until their dying day by many of them. That film, introduced so uncritically, is James Hilton's Goodbye Mr. Chips, now presented as it should be, prefaced only by a newsreel and Donald Duck's touching encounter with a penguin, at the Four Star, a house whose name by now is synonymous with the word "quality."

Indeed, about the happiest man in town ought to be Bruce Fowler, the theater's urbane manager, whose recent good fortune included The Citadel and Pygmalion. Not only must he inform the waiting line, at seven o'clock, that there's nothing behind the fourth row, but he must feel a bit like a benevolent deity as he observes the faces and hears the remarks of the customers reluctantly homeward bound. I couldn't help telling him, while struggling with the urge to remain for another show: "I like your picture, but I like the audience even more." Just when the future of motion pictures appears so gloomy, it is heartening to hear those audience "raves," and no postscript for Mr. Chips could have been more perfect than that provided by a dapper member of a contingent of Military School boys who addressed his awed and moist-cheeked gang with: "It sure was--well, a super picture!" Blessings on thee little man--you said it!

Apart from its cinematic cunning, notable production, direction, and the overwhelmingly beautiful performance given by Robert Donat in the titular role, Goodbye Mr. Chips has had an interesting history. The novelette from which the film has been so sympathetically adapted, first appeared, in this country, in the Atlantic Monthly, a publication seldom combed by studio readers for potential screen material. Nevertheless, as I fear I once before stated, via radio, the Atlantic's editors were directly responsible, in one way or another, for such screen classics as Mutiny on the Bounty and the still-to-be-appreciated Slim, and they welcomed Ernest Hemingway when, but for Scribner's, the others, and most notoriously Cosmopolitan, were turning him down. Mr. Chips pleased Atlantic readers (incidentally, the film is less cloyingly sentimental and much stronger than the original tale) and simply went to the head of one A. Woollcott, a heady creature whose state of encomiastic intoxication he generally makes alarmingly public. As a result, a slim, sentimental volume became a best seller, just about Christmastime when books priced at $1.25 are invariably popular, and the movies eventually caught on.

Years have passed, and everyone thought Goodbye Mr. Chips had turned to sugar in M-G-M's story commissary, but fortunately we were wrong, and while the film credits the late Irving Thalberg with its being, no one can lament procrastination after viewing Sam Wood's result, produced in England where the climate seems to favor the cinema, by Victor Saville; cast to perfection, with the womanly Greer Garson, young Terry Kilburn capably handling four generations of himself, John Mills in one marvelous scene and Paul Von Henreid in a great many; and elevated to Academy award stature by Donat (who really earned his Oscar last year) in one of the most winning, self-obliterating acting performances it has ever been my pleasure to see. To put it bluntly, you can believe every foot of Goodbye Mr. Chips without believing that you've seen Robert Donat, and that ought to reveal what kind of acting appeals to me.

Mr. Chips is an elegiac, atmospheric vignette, in film form, devoted to the life of a square-peg schoolmaster who eventually found the right groove with the aid of an understanding and admiring woman he met on an Alpine pinnacle. Chips was humble, shy, and probably the victim of numerous neuroses which the photoplay does not bother to explore, but he had a great capacity for love, and when the woman who had made a man of him died, in childbirth, that capacity for love was transferred to a whole school, and what happened after that should be seen to be admired in an ever discreet and heart-warming filmplay, rather than described. One reviewer liked Goodbye Mr. Chips for its reticence, for its taste, for its calm in an era of cinematic confusion. He hopes you will like it as he did, although aware that there are bright and brittle people who will regard the film as they would a marshmallow sundae and pour over it an acid sauce of intellectual disdain. These people read very well, but I'd prefer not to know them. In fact, I think Goodbye Mr. Chips will wear better, and I am very happy to welcome it in to an addled world.

--Richard Sheridan Ames in Rob Wagner's Script, Vol. 21, No. 510 (May 27, 1939), pages 20-21.

*   *   *

Very much worthwhile. The story of an unimportant man made into a picture which becomes important by virtue of the excellence of the performances and the skill of the script writers and the director. Of course, James Hilton must not be overlooked. He it was who made Mr. Chips a person and put him between the covers of a book, thus entitling Mr. Hilton to take a bow every time we pay a compliment to Mr. Chips as a person or as a picture.

In its bid for box-office favor, the picture has two things to overcome--its length and Alexander Woollcott. A screen offering must have more physical body to it, must be built on a more exciting scale, to entertain the average audience for two hours, and it has to be somewhat better than one can be to live up to Woollcott's estimate of its virtues. As an intimate study of one man's life it will satisfy intelligent audiences, but the over-exploitation to which it is being subjected will prepare the general public for more than it will get.

Accepting the picture for what it is, it certainly is a production of which Metro has reason to be proud. Beautifully directed by Sam Wood, it comes to the screen as an emotional symphony which will cause your heartstrings to vibrate in response to its bid for your interest in a cavalcade of happenings to a lovable man across a span of sixty-nine years. Robert Donat makes us love the man, sympathize with him, share his joys and sorrows, the performance being in every way a remarkable demonstration of powerful and understanding characterization.

But Donat by no means is all the picture. Greer Garson is
in it--very much in it, even though her appearances are brief in
comparison with those of Donat.   The wooing and winning of the
gracious young woman and the few short years they are together as
man and wife, are presented in scenes which run the emotional
scale from gaiety to the tragedy of death, scenes played quietly,
tenderly, graciously--screen acting rarely equaled.

To American eyes the picture's physical background will come
as something refreshingly new, and its presentation of life in an
English school with centuries of traditions handed down from fathers
to sons who have been students there, also strikes a note of newness which will entertain our audiences.   Another asset is the simplicity of the story, its down-to-earthness, its being about someone
who might be a member of your family or mine.   And Sam Wood
tells it simply, without extravagant gestures or striving to stress
points.   But he makes it greatly human and ably sustains its mood
as such.

There is something about an English cast that always appeals
to me, smoothness, clearness of diction--a suggestion of good breeding extending back a long way.   There are many excellent performances, but those of Donat and Miss Garson stand out as cinematic
treats long to be remembered.   Donat, of course, we have seen
before, but Greer Garson comes to us as something new, a lovely
something with that strange something which stirs us emotionally
when we look into her eyes and share with her the feelings they
reveal to us.

--Welford Beaton in Hollywood
Spectator, Vol. 14, No. 4 (May
27, 1939), page 8.

☐ GRAND HOTEL (M-G-M, 1932)

Here it is, the picture in which you may see Garbo, Crawford, both the Barrymores and Wally Beery in a magnificent two
hours you'll never forget.   With that cast why wouldn't it be good?
Wait a minute, Vicki Baum's successful play was not fool-proof,
and Eddie Goulding deserves a cheer for making a smooth running
story.

Adjectives fail us when we describe the work of Lionel Barrymore, the man who really wanted brother John to have the best
part, and yet was compelled to give a vital performance that will
go down in the saga of the cinema.   Hold on, Garbo fans, that
doesn't mean Garbo is any less glamorous.   She's great, but the
story is not all Garbo.

Joan Crawford gives excellent competition and moves up along
her ladder of successes.   John Barrymore is fascinating every min-

ute. Wallace Beery has a scene, after he kills the baron, that
stacks up along with the greatest. Lewis Stone and Jean Hersholt
--excellent.

You may argue about who deserves the most praise and not
get anywhere, for the picture, as a whole, steals the show. It is
produced on a scale of grandeur that the stage couldn't touch. If
you don't already know the story, telling it would take the edge off.
You can't miss this.

--Photoplay, Vol. 41, No. 6 (May
1932), page 49.

*   *   *

Great indeed is M-G-M's Grand Hotel--in many respects. It
is an absorbing subject, as it is bound to be because of the interpretation given the various characters by the highly skilled players
assigned to them. Even second rate drama as it rides in the lines
takes on a larger significance when read by either of the Barrymores, by Garbo or Crawford or Wallace Beery or Stone, not to
mention Hersholt or Robert McWade, Purnell Pratt, Ferdinand
Gottschalk, Rafaela Ottiano or Tully Marshall. Grand Hotel is not
a single track story. If you say that it is and that Kringelein is
its head and front then you must concede that through the whole
course of the tale Garbo does not touch the main theme of the drama. Of it she is a thing apart. And when love comes to Grusin-
skaya following her determination to call life quits, comes to her
in the guise of a thief hiding in her room, what a glorious creature
she is and what an appealing and altogether charming picture she
paints of the woman fired and raised by a delayed love from the
depths of melancholy!

As seen at the Chinese in Hollywood early in May the subject
was handicapped by an incoherence in enunciation, by an indistinct
dialogue, through the first half of its projection. The writer was
ideally seated, practically in the centre of the house. Nevertheless
others in the neighborhood were overheard complaining. The latter
half of the picture was seemingly entirely normal and understandable.

No one who has followed the screen for any length of time
is likely to look on a dialogue between Lionel and John Barrymore
or the latter and Greta Garbo or any one of many combinations
which so casually are formed in this production without being deeply
impressed with the rarity in screen drama on which he is looking.
There never has been anything like it before in the case of acknowl-
edgedly successful screen players.

Some years ago when it was suggested to Ad Kessel that he
make a picture with Bill Farnum, Bill Hart and Doug Fairbanks, a
trio at the time very chummy as well as popular, Kessel threw up
both hands. "It's a great idea," he declared, "but we'd never get
the money out."

That was well over fifteen years ago, and the policy of the industry never has changed materially. That all these years the industry may have been overlooking a bet very likely will be demonstrated by M-G-M when the returns come in from Grand Hotel. That it will be a success is out of the question, meaning a financial success.

It should be a financial success as a reward for the daring and the farsightedness of those who disregarded hidebound tradition and blazed a production trail.

It should be a financial success even as it is an artistic success in spite of the fact the auditor looks upon it from the viewpoint of one more or less detached, one to whom the varied issues are of more or less unconcern personally, in spite of being thrilled by the individual who may hold the floor for the particular moment.

The production is one to be seen more than once, and with every reason to believe that a second viewing will be enjoyed more than was the first.

Edmund Goulding directed the script and adaptation from the novel by Vicki Baum.

> --George Blaisdell in The International Photographer, Vol. 4, No. 5 (June 1932), page 32.

☐ THE GRAPES OF WRATH (20th Century-Fox, 1940)

Perhaps, like the Joads, your reviewer just ain't "kissin' people." Thus, while he admired The Grapes of Wrath and considered it a finely intentioned and notable contribution to the screen, he wasn't swept off his feet as were some others. Unlike them, he didn't capitulate completely to the John Ford picture, and his remarks, therefore, are likely to be reserved rather than an outpouring of demonstrative critical affection.

First, let's consider what's obvious. Grapes is a forceful, honest, artistically disciplined, and deeply sympathetic picturization of the Steinbeck novel. The startling realism of its photography sets the mood for the story to follow: you need expect no sweetness and light, no artificiality. In this picture the American cinema intends to come to grips with life, and it does. The honesty and directness of Grapes of Wrath, the courage of its producer in throwing controversial material smack in the face of the large public which has been coaxed into thinking that it couldn't think--these accomplishments are indeed heartening and deserving of praise, and maybe that's why some critics fell overboard in evaluating the film. They wanted to show their appreciation because the screen had come of age.

It is never wholly pleasant to see a long novel you've liked condensed into film form, because cuts are obligatory. I might have enjoyed Grapes of Wrath more if I had never read the book, but Nunnally Johnson's adaptation is reasonably deft, and except for my hunch that Grapes would have been magnificent as a four-hour picture, with the crossing of the Colorado coming just before intermission, and the flood (now omitted) as a climax, about all one could expect from anyone under the circumstances. The dialogue retains its flavor, although it has been washed off, and the new ending is satisfactory--although it comes with disquieting suddenness just after Tom has departed.

Mr. Ford has assembled a cast which couldn't have been bettered. His opening sequences are spellbinding in their stark and simple beauty, but the film loses something the novel had when the Joads start their long journey along Highway 66. It is understandable why Ford concentrated on the ever-steaming Joad truck and practically ignored the Great Migration. Time had to be observed, and if the trek of the "Okies" could be indicated by a few signposts, well and good. Yet the strength and the poignancy of many Steinbeck chapters depended on the friendships of the road, the mutual aid, the common hopes and fears of thousands traveling toward the Promised Land. The epic quality is absent from the picture. The deaths of Grandpa and Grandma are not as dramatic as they might have been (there's no attempt at suspense in the case of the latter); Rosasharn's "condition," boldly referred to, for the screen, never produces anything, dramatic or otherwise; although three references are made to natural functions, the Joads' hunger is barely suggested, and, except for the scene of the starving children in the camp, these people to whom food is the prime necessity are never shown eating their sidemeat or fried dough. At times one might think that Mr. Ford deliberately slights the senses and emotions and addresses his film to the spectator's intellect.

Nevertheless, The Grapes of Wrath has many fine and beautiful moments. It is a courageous, compassionate film, almost austere in its simplicity. And while this remark doesn't come within the province of film reviewing, I wish all our legislators would be compelled to see it at least a dozen times!

--Richard Sheridan Ames in Rob
Wagner's Script, Vol. 23, No.
545 (March 9, 1940), page 16.

*   *   *

This isn't one of the films that need a lot of explaining to tell why they deserve to be called great. Unlike so many movies that are now counted among the masterpieces it doesn't have to have footnotes to call attention to its importance or its excellencies. The book from which it was taken has prepared a lot of ground for what to look for, and a lot of speculation about whether Hollywood would dare to put it on the screen honestly and sincerely has created a good deal of curiosity about how it would turn out. To those who

know something about John Steinbeck's novel it is enough to say that
the picture is way ahead of anything even the most hopeful had much
reason to expect.   To everyone, readers of the novel or not, one
simple statement tells the truth: here is a film that belongs up
beside--at least--the best the screen has ever done.   And you have
only to see the film to see why.   What it is is as apparent as the
sun in the sky on a clear day.   Whether you like it or not is a
question of your personal reaction.

   It is all beautifully direct and literal, like clear-cut themes
in a symphony.   You can go back and discover new effects in the
orchestration, which is unobtrusively elaborate, but the main motifs
are announced from the first and maintained till the end.   There is
Tom Joad, on parole from prison, going back to his family on their
farm.   The shell of a farmhouse, deserted, the family blown out
by dust-storms and tractor-farming.   The family, found again, setting out westward in their junky old truck, for work and a place to
settle on the soil once more.   The long trek west, over the endless
inter-state highways, joining the miserable stream of other families
driven away from their own birthright and seeking a promised land
of home and work again.   Managing somehow to make the truck keep
holding together, and managing somehow to eat, the Joad family
jolts through New Mexico, Arizona, at last to California, dwindling
as it goes: Grampa dies, Grandma dies, Noah just disappears,
Connie gets too discouraged and runs away.   And in California there
are thousands just like them, people looking for work in a place
where the workers are too many, the jobs too few.

   Nunnally Johnson had to do something more with Steinbeck's
book than cut pages out of it and paste them together.   He had to
dramatize it, which meant concentrating its essence while he built
it to mounting action and emotion.   A lot that Steinbeck might have
done to his novel in the way of economy and good taste (good taste
not in the parlor, prissy sense but in the sense of clean cutting instead of haphazard, emotion-driven chopping) has been accomplished
in this dramatization, but no one can say that Steinbeck's spirit or
intention has been anywhere betrayed.   What shifts in incident and
emphasis have been made are all to the good.   Some may say, as
some have said, that the picture only scratches the surface of the
truth, or that it would have been more generally representative if
Tom Joad had been an ordinary decent citizen instead of a jail-bird.
Well, Tom is a decent citizen--that he was in jail and came out
not hardened into a criminal, not "mean-mad" as his mother put it,
gives him just that special strength of character above the dead-
level ordinary, that rock-bottom touch of the heroic, which puts
lift and thrill into the semi-mystical words he speaks to his
mother in their last farewell; his renunciation of an individual
life to become a part of the fight for the hungry, the beaten.
the knocked-about miserable--everywhere.   And as for just
scratching the surface, by making the story a family story,
perhaps to some a mere "mother-love" story, with the final
implication that families--those primal units of mankind--cannot
be crushed and destroyed but go on generation after generation

preserving the seed and spirit of human life--what audience, or what individual, could endure a picture that told them these families are not enduring and persisting but actually dying off, that there is no hope at all? Steinbeck told his tale of hopelessness, eloquent in arousing pity and indignation but pointing no way of remedy. The picture, in Tom Joad and Ma Joad, lets a bit of light in by a hint that the spirit of man is not to be conquered and snuffed out. And, less mystically, there is the government camp, switched toward the latter part of the picture where its contrast with the previous wretchedness is more effective, unobtrusively, and without specific pointing, suggesting that there is a way, slow perhaps and with a long difficult road ahead of it, to remedy the conditions that blight so many lives. If that be New Deal propaganda, make the most of it--and note, as compensation, that the manager of the camp in the person of Grant Mitchell is not a stalwart enough crusader to throw a scare into the rugged individualists.

If Nunnally Johnson's script narrows the gist of the story to only what happens to the Joad family, John Ford in his direction has spread it wide again, in the way that only a movie can do. With the magnificent help of Gregg Toland's camera he has created a whole vast section of country and a multitude of people to embank his main stream. Countless subtleties of movie photography have gone into the universalizing of the Joad family's modernized ironic version of a covered-wagon journey to a new land. One supreme example is that entrance to a camp, shot from the jostling truck, where the shacks as well as the people seem to be tumbling and fleeing. Over and over again the camera has supplied details, of meanness, brutality, misery, pity, human fellowship, that no narrative or dialogue could possibly reveal. And the use of sound is as eloquent as the use of picture--silence filled with meaning by the far-off sound of a train whistle, or a rooster crowing in the dawn, or the eternal theme of the truck coughing and sputtering and rattling along its endless road. There is, too, Ford's fondness for mist and shadows and music--but all in their place here, integral and rarely mannered.

The chief thing about the acting is that it almost never seems to be acting at all. Perhaps John Carradine and Grant Mitchell give an occasional impression of doing their stuff, but the rest, from the most casual extra to the stars, might have been caught, without costume or make-up, in some episode of actual life. Henry Fonda and Jane Darwell are the most important because they embody the main spirit of the drama: they both fill their parts with such life, the life that lies back of mere looking and speaking, that they are more than mere actors in a movie. Other people are less important only because they are less in the foreground, but just as much an element in the livingness of the picture--people like John Qualen and Russell Simpson and Charles Grapewin and Doris Bowdon, if it isn't invidious to name a few out of so many.

One wants to believe that The Grapes of Wrath is a milestone in movies, that the daring which went into its production will

prove something about the theory of what the public wants that has
so restricted the subject matter of motion pictures. If it is a milestone, by turning out to be a box-office hit and leading producers to
tackle other important problems of life with equal honesty and effectiveness, it will go down in the history books. It proves that
Hollywood can lead the world in serious as well as merely entertaining pictures; it has done its kind of thing so supremely well that
it is a fair test. If it is a box-office failure--which so far it
doesn't appear to be--it is a proof, not that Hollywood is unrespon-
sive to the times and the needs of the times, but that movie audiences are indifferent and hostile to real life on the screen. In that
case The Grapes of Wrath will not be a milestone but a magnificent
monument over a lost cause.

> --James Shelley Hamilton in Na-
> tional Board of Review Magazine,
> Vol. 15, No. 2 (February 1940),
> pages 16-18.

☐ THE GREAT DICTATOR (Chaplin/United Artists, 1940)

        A lot happens in five years these days, and in that time you
can learn a lot and forget a lot. That is why so many people who
have been waiting for another Chaplin picture, made more and more
impatient for it by delays and rumors, don't know quite what to
think now that The Great Dictator is here. If it were just a new
picture, and not a New Chaplin, they would enjoy it and acclaim it,
as thousands upon thousands will anyway. But if they are among
those who are always solemn about Chaplin, expecting him to be
not only a great comic but a great tragedian and social commentator
as well, they won't be satisfied with just taking what they get and
enjoying it: they will have to ponder and analyze about Art and
Meanings and Social Satire, with all their preconceptions about such
things, and the result of all this searching thought will perhaps puz-
zle them by not adding up to what they thought they were going to
get in the Masterpiece they were all set for. This will be because
of what they have learned, and even more what they have forgotten,
in the years of waiting.

        Movies have developed a good deal since Modern Times, and
the world has changed even more, and unless you keep that pretty
carefully in mind you don't realize the extent to which expectation
of what a new Chaplin picture would be has subconsciously keyed itself up to a point that forgets what Chaplin has always been. Except for some of the two-reelers we don't get much chance to see
Chaplin films after their season of newness is over, and so we have
no chance to check our memory of them with all that was actually
there. Chaplin--it's a temptation to say more than any other man
in the world--is a figure that lives mostly in our memories, and
what each remembers is shaped and colored by a personal reaction
to him, all the more vivid for the personal feeling that infuses the

memory. We remember him, and forget a great deal about his different pictures except as the frame in which he himself was so unforgettable.

The Great Dictator is its own kind of film, a completely Chaplin kind, and no other kind in the world. It is not only the climax of Chaplin, so far, but a résumé of Chaplin's whole growth, in his picture-making and in the evolution of his social conscience--a statement that is practically a quotation from Terry Ramsaye, who so far as I know is the only commentator who has noted this fact, as well as the fact that you must go back to Griffith's Intolerance for another motion picture that is so completely one man's personal expression of his attitude on something about which he feels deeply and passionately.

There is practically no plot: a Jewish barber looks so much like Hynkel (Hitler) that eventually he is mistaken for the dictator and finds himself in the dictator's shoes about to broadcast to the nation. The rest of the picture is the rambling, episodic sort of thing that a Chaplin picture has always been. There's the old Charley, hat, shoes, walk, with the old-time ragged gentility and gallantry, up against a world of mishap. (Ah, but here is a world of more than mishap, a world of colossal evil, and he can't just walk away from it, over the horizon, swinging his cane, to some new adventure.) There are the same tumbledown settings, obviously just painted scenery. The same story-book girl, the object of his shy adoration. There are old gags, bobbing up like old friends, with some new twist to them perhaps but bringing the same old laugh. All of the barber episodes are much as Charley has always been, slithering along on the fine edge between the funny and the sad, but always safely funny. From the prologue in the Old War (it might have been something out of Shoulder Arms), through the barbershop days when Hynkel forgot the Jews for a bit, till his escape from the prison camp in the uniform that made him mistaken for the Phooey, the picture might have been made before talk came to the films--it is, in truth, a lot like an early talkie.

But without talk Chaplin couldn't have been Hynkel. The gods in their wisdom made Chaplin hit upon a make-up from his earliest days that destined him to be the inevitable parody of Hitler in appearance, but something even higher in the right ordering of things bestowed on him the gift to conceive and utter the astonishing, devastating speech that spurts from his lips when he is Hitler vocal. Every move of his as the dictator is absurd enough to be funny, and sharp enough to be a cutting exposure of some trait in the Fuehrer's mania, but the bitterest venom of his characterization comes out in the indescribable jargon, utterly untranslatable yet completely understandable, which is the utterance of Hynkel in his greatest furies, and which is certainly one of the most remarkable things that the talkies--or anything else--has ever presented in the form of speech.

The world-shadowing figure of Hitler--did you think it couldn't be brought down to the dimensions of a movie screen, pinned there

to be laughed at, without lessening its horror? It can't be laughed
away? A madman is no subject for farce? Take a look at Chaplin's Hynkel--and after you've adjusted it to what you expected, or
hoped for, take another look. You're likely to find that Chaplin's
genius, working subtly and artfully, has burned up to its greatest
creation in this--not caricature--portrait. That it can be laughed
at is perhaps useful: it puts this titanic demon into some proportion with other men, a creature that somehow, some time, can be
swept aside.

     The bit of plot in the picture landed Chaplin, the author, in
a situation that just couldn't be resolved. When the little persecuted
barber had to appear in the dictator's place before the world, what
was there for him to do? Anything but a bombshell would fall flat.
The only bombshell was for the picture to gather itself together--
all its meaning and purpose--and speak straight out in the voice of
Chaplin as the man who made it all. It may not seem in the character of the barber--it is emphatically in the character of the whole
picture. What seems to so many an artistic aberration, and perhaps not the most eloquent oration ever uttered, is maybe the most
useful thing about the film: and certainly Chaplin made this film
not merely to amuse, but to stir. In that speech Charlot--Charley
the little man--really found his voice, and millions of people will
know the meaning of it.

     It is easy to find technical shortcomings in The Great Dic-
tator, ways in which it doesn't line up with the stream-lined slick-
ness of continuity, photography, sets, lesser characters, that have
become a commonplace in our studios. As a job of picture-making
Chaplin has been content to do things just about as he has always
done them. He has been himself, but with a further reach. And
his grasp has equalled his reach. What other man in motion pictures has put so much time, so much money, so many gifts, into
the sincerest expression he could achieve of what he feels about the
most important thing in the world today? That will be remembered
long after all the other pictures of this year have been forgotten.
                              --James Shelley Hamilton in Na-
                                tional Board of Review Magazine,
                                Vol. 15, No. 8 (November 1940),
                                pages 10-12.

□ THE GREAT ZIEGFELD (M-G-M, 1936)

     A great picture from any angle--production, acting or story.
Three hours is long, even for a stage play; it's a still bigger load
on the screen. Yet I was interested with nearly every foot of it,
and at times enthralled.

     Yes, it's the story of the greatest pictorial artist of the
stage, glorified by screen technicians who have achieved spectacles

that Ziegfeld dreamed, but couldn't have encompassed on the biggest
stage in the world.

The story begins at the Chicago World's Fair with Ziegfeld
exhibiting Sandow, the Strong Man, in poor competition with Frank
Morgan's Little Egypt.   Then, Ziggy's signing Anna Held, his glorious years of the Follies, his marriage to Billie Burke (Myrna Loy),
and his death after the financial debacle of the depression.

Luise Rainer plays Anna Held and while she deliberately shied
away from Anna's glorious pompadour (which, by the way, swept
America as the fashionable headdress...), she reproduced the famous French girl's charm, intelligence and noble heart.   It is not
generally known that after Anna left Ziegfeld she became victim
to a strange ailment--a softening of the bones--and died in a New
York hospital.   Ziggy was loyal to the end and often visited her.
Indeed, it was his loyalty to the poor girl that helped endear him
to Billie Burke.

Structurally, however, the story misses in one respect.   It
gives the impression that Anna Held dominated the fuller years of
Ziegfeld's life and that Billie Burke was merely a short final flash.
Just the opposite is true.

Will Powell looks very much like Ziegfeld as I remember
him, as a young man, and he must have felt the part deeply, for
he gives a magnificent performance.   The same for Frank Morgan
who goes through the story as Ziggy's friendly enemy.   Myrna Loy
is, of course, ravishingly beautiful and it is no wonder that her
charm and performance has met with the generous approval of the
real Billie Burke.

Strange experience for Patricia Ziegfeld, society and sports
reporter on young Bill Rogers' paper across the way, to see herself
as a child with Will Powell and Myrna Loy as her parents!

I quote from her own column:

> It is a strange sensation to see one's own family por-
> trayed on the screen and it is more amazing and quite a
> thrill to suddenly see someone representing one's self age
> seven, and I hate to admit it, much better behaved than I
> ever thought of being....

A long cast in which Fannie Brice plays Fannie Brice grand-
ly.   Reginald Owen is Ziggy's distressed bookkeeper and clicks
handsomely as usual.   The same for Ernest Cossart, as valet for
both Frank Morgan and Ziggy.   Nat Pendleton is not as handsome
as Sandow, but his physique is nearly so.

Naturally Adrian and Cedric Gibbons and the camera boys
have a glorious field day and many of the ballets and big production
numbers justify the overworked word, colossal.

I quote again Patricia Ziegfeld:

> I have never seen such beautiful musican numbers on
> any screen, especially the Melody Number, conceived by
> John Harkrider, who should certainly get the praise and
> credit due him. He designed costumes for Daddy for eight
> years and when he came out here he took up set designing
> as well.

The credit sheet is too long to include all the deserved bouquets. But we must add cheers for William Anthony McGuire for
story, Robert Z. Leonard for direction, and Hunt Stromberg for
production.

--Rob Wagner in Rob Wagner's
Script, Vol. 15, No. 363 (April
25, 1936), page 12.

*   *   *

The Great Ziegfeld is about how Flo the Showman started as
the son of a respectable musician, barking for a muscle-man act on
the World's Fair midway, how he went from a shoestring to dazzlements in the Broadway theater, and back to the shoestring, and back
again to greater dazzlements, making stars and marrying women;
how he got old and broke and died that way, leaving over the street
a legend that is brighter than the lights. We have had romanticized
biographies of show people before, but this is apart from them in
scale if nothing else: three solid hours of tunes, girls, specialty
numbers, and all the bustle of people and events in the lean and fat
years of a national figure. The movie is fantastic, yet curiously
appropriate, its atmosphere matching the topsy-turvy reality of all
this blare and tinsel. Too glib for real life, it is persuasive for
all that--possibly just because of that.

To take Ziegfeld as legend, as he was felt across the footlights and known to stars in ascendancy, the picture would properly
be something like this, full of glamorous types, color, brash spec-
tacularism. The only other way to do such a figure--why and how
he did it, what it took from the country and what it left--would be
to do a book, to be more sober and thorough and first-causey--and
inevitably to lose the principal radiance identified with the name.
Of one whose energies dazzled the eyes and ears of an immediate
(also fleeting) moment, it would be rather barren to write a book:
the truth would be truer and more precisely gauged, but to those
who had known the blandishments it would be partly false, the statistics of moonshine without its magic, and who cares anyhow.

The Great Ziegfeld is full of many matters, too many for re-
counting and certainly too many for its own good. Even if it didn't
run on forever, there is no excuse for the lag in the first part, the
long-drawn-out death, the stage-spectacle material in the last half,
etc. And since it does run on, everything should have been tightened
--not in the tremendous job of cutting those miles of negative, but

in boiling down the script, saving a line here, combining two scenes
into one there.

The best acting part is that of Luise Rainer, whose Anna
Held is gay, touching, and just about right, though probably not
Anna Held.   William Powell is a plausible Ziegfeld, dressy, flashy,
mostly surface; and for solid support there are Fannie Brice, Frank
Morgan, Reginald Owen, Ernest Cossart, etc.   The story has nice
fun and sentiment, but its setting and numbers are even more important to its effect, one bit of gorgeous flummery standing out
above all: the "Pretty Girl" number, serving as a first-act curtain
and also as an example of the best to be done anywhere--a revolving
stage, surmounted by a great spiral staircase that sweeps up, covered with girls, as the circular curtain rises and the spiral turns,
the spectacle spreading to a climax.   In the end it is this general
atmosphere of hysterical lavishness and aimless splendor that stands
out from The Great Ziegfeld--the unreal made actual by our knowledge that such things did happen here, and that there is a like fever
of aimless glitter and lavishness still in the world--people building
the pyramids for a night, the Hanging Gardens for a finale, Ziegfeld's ghost having apparently gone west.
--Otis Ferguson in The New Re-
public, Vol. 87 (May 13, 1936),
page 18.

☐ HIS GIRL FRIDAY (Columbia, 1940)

With the original Hildy Johnson of the Hecht-MacArthur newspaper yarn, Front Page, metamorphized into Hildegarde Johnson and
played by Rosalind Russell, Columbia has made a fast-moving, always interesting picture out of the story.   There may, and probably
will be those who will say it is not up to the former version, but it
nevertheless furnishes good entertainment.

In the present version, Hildegarde is the former wife of the
editor, played by Cary Grant, and, instead of wishing to retire, as
did Hildy, she wants to marry an insurance salesman (Ralph Bellamy).   It is to prevent this marriage that the complications, instigated by Grant, ensue.   Also, the twist of making the star reporter
a woman gives opportunity for some new situations, of all of which
good advantage is taken.

Miss Russell plays Hildegarde for all there is in the role and
scores a fine personal triumph.   And right here credit should go to
the dialog writers who gave her and the other characters lines that
really sounded as if newspapermen were talking.   Grant is both
suave and forceful as the editor, giving delightful emphasis to some
of the sly humor in his role, especially when he and Hildegarde are
re-united at the finish.

Ralph Bellamy is good, as always, as the insurance salesman, and John Qualen does a capital job as the psychopathic criminal. Molly Malloy, as his one friend, is excellently played by
Helen Mack, especially in her emotional scenes. The scene in the
press room in the courts building is as striking as ever, and the
reporters, played by Ernest Truex, Porter Hall, Cliff Edwards and
others are very good, as are all the others in the cast.

Gene Lockhart, in a role smaller than his usual ones, was
excellent.

Howard Hawks maintained a fast pace in his direction, overlooking no chance to inject punches into the picture, and as producer
he did an equally good job. Joseph Walker's photography is well up
to standard.

The writers have, wisely perhaps, toned down the language of
the original version, although it is still lusty entertainment.

                              --The Hollywood Reporter, Vol.
                              55, No. 5 (November 30, 1939),
                              page 3.

☐ HOLIDAY (Columbia, 1938)

Bright and up-to-date is this seasons-old Phillip Barry opus,
for Donald Ogden Stewart has brushed eight years off the hide by
putting in a line about John L. Lewis. And it seems that even today young men with the possibilities of stuffed riches before them
have longings to chuck it all and descend among the people, to find
out, as films poetically put it, what strange new spirit is astir in
the wurruld. Cary Grant is the self-made youth who handsprings
his way out of the millionaire's home mausoleum, with the millionaire's second daughter on his back. The democratic daughter is
played by none other than Katharine (poison-at-the-box-office) Hepburn, who, at least in this opus, is poison mighty tasty to swallow.

                              --Meyer Levin in Esquire, Vol.
                              10, No. 2 (August 1938), page
                              82.

                          *   *   *

Holiday ... is an old friend it is pleasant to see again. It
is a strictly in-doors thing, devoted to that infinitesimal section of
people in the highest money-brackets, and concerned with acquiring
and keeping great wealth, or escaping it; but it has been freshened
up in its talk and people, and is bright entertainment.

                              --James Shelley Hamilton in Na-
                              tional Board of Review Magazine,
                              Vol. 13, No. 7 (October 1938),
                              pages 19-20.

☐ THE HUNCHBACK OF NOTRE DAME (RKO, 1939)

One with nothing in it to justify its making--the most horrible thing the screen has given us--a ghastly story made more ghastly by the treatment given it.   There was a streak of human feeling running through the Hunchback in which Lon Chaney starred, and we could look upon Lon's Quasimodo and feel sorry for his deformities.   There is no feeling, only boredom, in RKO's version, and we cannot look upon Laughton without getting the willies.   His is a revolting make-up, and his performance is a travesty on acting, meaningless strutting and mumbling about as pleasant to watch as the progress of a slug across a patch of mud.

The original Hunchback made money, made Lon Chaney an outstanding star.   The story was told on a silent screen which glamorized it.   We saw mobs howling and individuals screaming, and were no less impressed by virtue of our hearing nothing.   Music was played softly as the shadows moved across the screen, and our imaginations functioned to make everything real to us.   It was the medium which entertained us--the manner in which the story was told.

Producer Pandro Berman evidently thought the success of the first picture was due to the horror content of the story.   He proceeded to tell it in a realistic medium, to make horror more horrible, to rasp our nerves with the din of discordant sounds, with the crash of music, by leaving nothing to our imaginations to interpret to suit our individual tastes.   The result is the most completely unpleasant picture I ever saw, the most unnecessary nervous shock the screen has given us.   And that is not only my opinion; the restlessness of the large audience registered the same feeling, and it was expressed generally in the after-preview comment.

There are many excellent individual contributions to the picture, an imposing production, impressive performances and brilliantly enacted scenes, but as assets they are nullified by the lack of appeal of the offering as a whole.   No degree of merit can make entertaining a sustained attack on our nervous systems.   Maureen O'Hara gives a superb performance, as do Thomas Mitchell, Sir Cedric Hardwicke, Edmond O'Brien, Alan Marshal, Walter Hampden, Harry Davenport and many others.   Photography and all other technical features were in competent bands.   William Dieterle's direction is particularly impressive in intimate scenes in which lines are read in tones soothing to ears which have been assailed with too many discordant sounds.

A feast for those who love to have a thoroughly unpleasant time in a film theatre, but I can see nothing in it for others.   Any values it might have for study groups are offset by the strain students would be under while viewing it.   Producers should not assume it will repeat the success of the silent version, as the two have little fundamental similarity.   Owing to its great cost, the price

to exhibitors probably will be too great to assure profitable showing.
                              --Welford Beaton in Hollywood
                                Spectator, Vol. 14, No. 18
                                (December 23, 1939), page 15.

                              *   *   *

       Only the movies can produce a spectacle like The Hunchback
of Notre Dame--but in the present instance I'm afraid the vast ex-
penditure wasn't justified.   Possibly audiences are anxious to feast
their eyes on a full-size reproduction of the cathedral again.   William Dieterle has filled the cathedral square with thousands of dis-
orderly and clamorous Parisians.   His street scenes, the crowning
of the King of Fools, the realistic presentation of filth and poverty,
superstition and terror, tortures and persecution appropriate to the
Dark Ages, offer evidence of careful preparation and precise craftsmanship.   But they also retard a film which needs more spontaneity,
which lacks sharpness of outline and derives most of its vitality
from the performance of Charles in the title role.   A good bit from
Walter Hampden and Sir Cedric Hardwicke, too!

       Overlong and cluttered, The Hunchback doesn't actually de-
mand the spectator's undivided attention until Quasimodo rescues
the lovely Esmeralda (Maureen O'Hara) from the scaffold and instals
her, with himself as devoted protector, in a tower of Notre Dame.
Here she sits placidly while the monster with the tender heart re-
pulses the mob attacking the cathedral--chortling to himself as he
hurls slabs of stone and finally decants a cauldron of scalding lead
upon the rabble far below.   The hunchback's counter-offensive becomes exciting, even if you know what to expect after seeing the
Lon Chaney version of the Hugo classic.
                              --Richard Sheridan Ames in Rob
                                Wagner's Script, Vol. 22, No.
                                535 (December 23, 1939), page
                                17.

☐ HURRICANE (Goldwyn, 1937)

       This is a great picture.   On more than one count it goes far
beyond anything ever filmed.   The hurricane that fills its last 1500
feet with awe and terror is supreme spectacle.   The film is also
the most masterly and moving marriage of music and picture ever
achieved, and is truly great as a pictorial work of art.   Lastly, it
is a compelling drama of powerful emotional appeal.

       With The Hurricane, Samuel Goldwyn insures his fame as
one of the supreme makers of motion pictures of our time, and this
high rating will be confirmed at the boxoffices of the world.   There
is no type of theatre-goer that will be immune to the spell of enchantment that the picture weaves and it should break attendance
records far and wide and for months to come.

The widely read novel of Charles Nordhoff and James Norman Hall, authors of Mutiny on the Bounty, has been faithfully followed and magnificently brought to life. The adaptation by Oliver
H. P. Garrett and the screenplay by Dudley Nichols admirably capture both the spirit and the drama of the story. It is the tale of
a great love, and of great heroism and suffering for that love.
That the lovers are simple natives of a South Sea island makes no
difference in its romantic appeal, and the elements of hair-raising
adventure but strengthen the heart-tug of the pair's devotion.

John Ford's direction of the work will be acclaimed as his
most distinguished achievement. For breadth of canvas, for emotional and dramatic power, and for capture of beauty in mood and
movement, it stands high in film annals. He must share honors
with many important contributors, including his associate, Stuart
Heisler, but his own contribution is unmistakable and memorable.

Ranking high among those who have brought creative genius
to the making of the picture is Alfred Newman, who wrote the music score and directed it. There is a 12-minute overture before
the picture opens. It is meant to set the mood and does with beauty
and power.

The score itself carries through almost the whole of the 105
minutes of running time, and is comparable in its form and its musical quality and invention with the orchestral part of the great music dramas. From the lyric loveliness of the gay marriage festival
early in the picture, through the growing menace of events up to and
including the howling turmoil of the hurricane, it builds movingly and
magnificently, its pulse-beat carrying the spell to almost unbearable
heights.

Another notable contribution is the staging of the hurricane
scenes, the work of James Basevi and his assistant, R. T. Layton.
It is almost unbelievable that such stunning effects can be achieved
deliberately, and their realism markedly advances the industry's already marvellous technical capacity.

For the photography nothing but raves are possible. Bert
Glennon on the sets and Archie Stout and Paul Eagler in their capture of tropic beauties on a long expedition to the South Seas in
preparation for the picture, have made an unforgettably glamorous
contribution, aided notably by the photographic effects devised by
R. O. Binger. To this credit for visual distinction must be added
the art work of Richard Day and Alex Golitzen.

The work of the cast is on a par with the picture's other excellences. Terangi, the heroic lover, is handsomely and powerfully
realized by stalwart Jon Hall, splendid in action and showing just the
right degree of native impassiveness to make the character true.
Marama, his wife, is exquisitely realized in the exotic beauty and
melting tenderness of Dorothy Lamour. A notably veracious and
sympathetic portrait of the hard-drinking but deeply understanding
Dr. Kersaint, is delivered by Thomas Mitchell.

Mary Astor, as wife of the French governor of the island, fills her role with distinction. The governor, a stiff-necked martinet whose unyielding rulings precipitate the conflict, stands out strongly in the able hands of Raymond Massey. C. Aubrey Smith as the island's devoted and heroic priest draws an unforgettable portrait. John Carradine is excellent as the cruel prison warden at Tahiti, and Jerome Cowan makes his rather negative role of the ship's captain stand out.

The native chief is played with impressive dignity by Al Kikume. Layne Tom Jr., and Kuulei DeClerq make touching contributions as native children, and there is an eye-filling bevy of Polynesian beauties that includes Mamo, Movita, Reri, Francis Kaai and Pauline Steele. Minor but efficient contributors are Flora Steele, Mary Shaw, Spencer Charters and Inez Courtney.

Merritt Hulburd, in charge of production under Mr. Goldwyn, wins a distinguished service mark for a big and difficult job exceedingly well done.

--The Hollywood Reporter, Vol. 42, No. 21 (November 5, 1937), page 3.

☐ I AM A FUGITIVE FROM A CHAIN GANG (Warner Bros., 1932)

Talk about "roast beef cut thick"; this picture is sorghum and sowbelly, and your enjoyment(!) of it will depend upon your film dietary strength. Paul Muni, medaled hero, returns from the shambles of war full of pep and high purpose. Vainly tramping the country in search of work, he meets up with an evil companion who makes him an innocent partner to a hold-up. Ten years in the chain gang!

The apparent purpose of the author and director is to show that "Man's inhumanity to Man" reaches its most terrible depths in our Southern prison camps--five or six reels of horror that would turn the tummy of a Torquemada. Degraded in stripes, hobbled in heavy chains, worked like beasts, fed upon filth, beaten by brutal guards, the pitiable victims are pictured as nothing less than loathsome monsters.

Muni escapes from the dreadful hellhole twice, but the final fade-out shows him still a hunted fugitive, utterly hopeless of the future.

If the story is true, one wonders whether, after twenty centuries of Christianity, our civilization is worth saving. And if the story is only half true, we should think very carefully before growing horrified over the "atrocities" in Russia or Manchuria. As my German primer said, "People who glass legs have should not on the ice go."

What with the recent "sweat-box trial" in Florida, Jim Tully's book, Laughter in Hell, and this godawful film, Dixieland is certainly on the spot. (Not that we Northerners are entirely spotless!)

But as has often been pointed out in these columns art has nothing to do with subject matter, and this picture is so well-done that it will no doubt disarm every censor.

There are several screen actors whom I can "see" in the part of James Allen, but only a fellow with the social consciousness of Paul Muni could have put so much feeling into the part. Many other characters appear as the long tapestry of horror unfolds, but they are merely passing figures of Muni's calvary.

However, with all due respect to Paul Muni's artistry and the splendid acting of the cast, it is essentially a director's picture, and Mervyn LeRoy, young and gentle as he is in real life, has wielded his megaphone like a six-pound sledge and has driven home his story with such blows that even the horror-hounds who have been eating up the Draculas, Golems, Freaks, and other "monster" entertainment are likely to be shocked.

It will be interesting to learn how the picture will go south of the Mason and Dixon Line, for not only does it portray the lowest point of man's cruelty to his brother, but it shows the state authorities as ignorant apologists for the medieval tortures of punishment.

It's a grand picture if you can stand strong meat. But don't take little Edgar or Vivian.

> --Rob Wagner in Rob Wagner's
> Script, Vol. 8, No. 196 (November 12, 1932), page 8.

*   *   *

Powerful and timely story, packed with suspense and stark cruelty, that points an accusing finger at the prison chain gang system. Paul Muni gives a strong performance as the returned soldier, anxious to get away from routine, who becomes an accomplice in a crime and is sentenced to ten years on a chain gang. With Director Mervyn LeRoy, he has given us a fine, vivid, but depressing picture.

> --Photoplay, Vol. 43, No. 1
> (December 1932), page 58.

☐ IF I HAD A MILLION (Paramount, 1932)

Eight stories by eighteen authors. I expected it to be one of those darn things with no unity or continuity. But while the eight stories are eight distinct pearls, they are hung on a good stout cord, and at the end is an epilogue that ties them all together.

It wouldn't be fair to tell any of the plots as the biggest kicks and laughs come from the surprises. As you might guess, the shortest and funniest one was made by Lubitsch.

However, I can't resist telling of the gratification of just one repressed desire. When Wynne Gibson, a tart in a speakeasy, found herself with a million dollars, she took the swellest suite in the swellest hotel in town, and then indulged in the greatest luxury she could think of--she went to bed alone!

All the headliners on the Paramount lot are in the picture, but it is three grand old-timers who grab the gravy--Richard Bennett, as the millionaire, W. C. Fields as the old vaudeville cutie of Alison Skipworth, and May Robson as the inmate of an old ladies' home. These are hard days for the young folk; with little children challenging interest from below and old troupers from the top, they have to step pretty lively to hold their places.

Yes, it is a great show, and it packs more surprises, laughs, and good acting into it than half a dozen ordinary pictures. Judging by the crowds and laughter at the Paramount Theatre, it should be one of the biggest box-office successes of the year.
                                    --Rob Wagner in Rob Wagner's
                                    Script, Vol. 8, No. 200 (December 10, 1932), page 8.

                                    *   *   *

Paramount tossed in their best writers, directors and stars-- and out of this Jack Horner pie they have pulled a perfectly grand picture.

A fabulously wealthy eccentric, played superbly by Richard Bennett, selects eight names at random from the city directory and presents each with a million dollars. The picture in a series of episodes reveals the lives of these people before and after they received the million.

Played gorgeously by Gary Cooper, George Raft, Wynne Gibson, Jack Oakie, Charles Laughton, May Robson, Charlie Ruggles, Gene Raymond, Frances Dee, Mary Boland, and a splendid supporting cast, with seven major directors contributing episodes, the result is a smooth and expert picture. Don't miss it.
                                    --Photoplay, Vol. 43, No. 2
                                    (January 1933), page 57.

☐ I'M NO ANGEL (Paramount, 1933)

One little bright-minded, healthy woman has done more to
clarify the murky waters of sex than Freud, Jung and Havelock El-
lis combined. For generations we have been inclined to look upon
sex relations as something morbid and shameful. Then along comes
Mae West in She Done Him Wrong and with joyous abandon she drags
sex out into the open and laughs at it. When Paramount had that
classic film in production, many of the executives wondered just how
far the public would go for the glorification of a prostitute. But the
public responded healthily and hilariously, and almost overnight Lady
Lou became an international character.

Mae West has repeated her formula in I'm No Angel. Again
we see her shamelessly and joyously selling her charms to anybody
who can provide her with pretties. The reason her film character
is lovable rather than offensive is that we see only her jungle tactics
of tracking down the male and none of the results.

Frankly she announces, "When I'm good, I'm very, very good,
but when I'm bad, I'm--better," and the smile and the little m-m-m
at the end sound so cozy that even a puritan would be utterly dis-
armed.

In this picture Mae is a cootch dancer in a side-show. Edward Arnold, the manager, induces her to put her head in the lion's
mouth, a stunt that lands her in the Big Time stuff in New York.
Here at last she can give up her smalltime cuties and go after
"silk hats." Her first victim is Kent Taylor, who shoots the works,
and when Mae goes Saks, Tiffany and penthouse, she's just about
the most glamorous creature you ever saw. Off to save Kent from
the clutches of the siren goes Cary Grant, a big Wall Street friend.
Mae likes Cary's proportions, and when she learns that he is even
richer than Kent, she gives him the works. When Mae gives a man
the works, he becomes simply wax in her pretty hands.

Out of her past arrive Edward Arnold and Ralf Harolde and
we get the dramatic menace. Cary, disillusioned, tries to scram
out. A breach-of-promise suit in which Mae makes monkeys of the
defense witnesses, gets herself over to the judge, and has the jury
ga-ga. Cary calls off the suit and returns to the charming gold-
digger. The tag line is too good to tell.

Perhaps the picture is not as sensational as She Done Him
Wrong; nevertheless Tira the lion tamer is a more interesting character than Lady Lou. Contrary to those who think Miss West merely a single-shotter, I feel sure she can repeat and repeat on her
extraordinary characterization, for despite its fundamental "sinful-
ness," it has exceptional charm and is one upon which to hang the
amusing weaknesses of my supposedly strong and vigorous sex.

As usual, Miss West, besides playing the leading role, wrote the original story, the screen play and the dialogue, which makes her the only other artist of the screen in Charlie Chaplin's class.

The cast is long and important, each one doing his part as though he enjoyed it. Wesley Ruggles' direction is fine throughout.

> --Rob Wagner in Rob Wagner's Script, Vol. 10, No. 239 (October 7, 1933), page 10.

*   *   *

Only the blue noses will be able to resist the humor of Miss West's close-lipped, loose-hipped utterances. Critics may be inclined to think she is putting it on pretty thick--unless they take time out to watch the audience. Then you see why she is considered the most important name in Hollywood at the present time.

> --Harry Evans in Life, Vol. 100, No. 3585 (December 1933), page 44.

☐ IMITATION OF LIFE (Universal, 1934)

Yes, there are other problems in life besides sex. For instance, the problems that arise from miscegenation. Children born of black and white parents may be black, mulatto or white. If black or mulatto, they can easily take their places with their own people. If white, they face a tragic future, for while the physical ego may be pleased, the spirit meets a racial impasse. In their own hearts, they feel cursed.

That is the story William Hurlbut built from Fannie Hurst's original into one of the best screen plays yet. The central characters are Louise Beavers and her daughter, Sebi Hendricks as a child, and Fredi Washington grown up. This is a big starring role for Miss Beavers and she carries it amazingly well on her handsome black shoulders.

For box office purposes it was no doubt necessary to play up the names of Claudette Colbert and Warren William, and William Hurlbut wove in a parallel story with great adroitness, but the fact remains that the really gripping drama centers about the black Mammy ("For God's sake don't say 'Mammy'; call yourself 'Mother'!") and her embittered white daughter.

With complete resignation regarding her color, Miss Beavers demanded little of life, but in death she exhibited the usual naive Negro compensatory wish--a swell funeral. This was a difficult scene to shoot because the morons in the audience were bound to regard the funeral as comedy. That John Stahl keeps the dramatic note is a tribute to his intelligence, artistry, and above all, his feeling.

Baby Jane Quigley, Claudette's daughter, is one of the most beautiful and charming children of the screen. Grown up, the role is taken by Rochelle Hudson, who enacts the part of a romantic schoolgirl in love with her mother's fiancé with extraordinary conviction. The tragic role of Miss Beavers' grown up daughter is handled by Fredi Washington superbly. The fans howl at the dead pan of Ned Sparks, but there is not the least shading in his lines and to me the monotony of his delivery is terribly grating.

Claudette Colbert again proves that she is lots more than just one of the most beautiful girls on the screen; her generosity in throwing every possible scene to Miss Beavers, reveals a fine artistic spirit. Warren William as usual gives a splendid interpretation of his part.

After all is said and done, John Stahl deserves the praise; he succeeded with a subtle and difficult theme.

Sets, sound and cinematography all excellent.
--Rob Wagner in Rob Wagner's Script, Vol. 12, No. 296 (December 8, 1934), page 8.

*   *   *

This adamantine critic had a tear on his alabaster cheek at Imitation of Life, and he pronounces it one of the truest and most poignant pictures of recent weeks. It merely tells the life stories of two admirable women, one white and one colored, and of their joys and troubles with their respective daughters. One mother is a hard-working young widow, making her living by peddling molasses. A colored mamma comes along and offers to work for almost nothing if she can get a home for herself and little girl.

This team of mothers goes far. Delilah makes luscious pancakes. Her mistress gets the idea of opening a pancake shop, and then of marketing a pancake flour, and that brings wealth to both women. The daughters grow up. There are no sour notes in this fine movie. Claudette Colbert and Louise Beavers are both perfect as the mothers. The nearest I came to disappointment was in Warren William; he's a little too nicey and too voicey and dappery to fit well into a story otherwise so untheatric.
--Don Herold in Life, Vol. 102, No. 2599 (February 1935), page 35.

☐ IN OLD CHICAGO (20th Century-Fox, 1937)

Here is veritably colossal spectacle, welded to great drama
in a splendid unity that makes it one of the greatest works of screen
art ever presented.   Many indeed, will consider it unequalled in the
annals of the industry.   Whether or no, it is an unquestioned triumph for Producer Darryl F. Zanuck, a magnificent entertainment
of universal appeal, and a "must" for every theatre patron in the
world.

Chicago's great fire of 1871, which destroyed 1, 800 buildings,
climaxes the drama.   It is a marvelous technical and directorial
achievement and is almost overwhelming in its emotional impact.
The fire scenes last about 20 minutes and build steadily in terror
and awe.   No music is used in the background of sound, but instead
a crescendo of interwoven noise that is shatteringly expressive.

The story starts 17 years earlier, with the O'Learys and
their three small sons trekking across the prairies by wagon toward
fast-growing Chicago.   As they near the goal, Pa O'Leary is killed
in a runaway and the indomitable Mollie, who later owned the famous
red cow that started the fire, goes on to give her boys the chance
in the city of which their father had dreamed.

There is a lapse of years and the drama then centers on the
rise of the two older boys to positions of power in the wide-open
town.

The first, played by Don Ameche, becomes an upstanding
lawyer and is drafted by the reformers to run for mayor and clean
up the city, especially that part of it known as The Patch, an area
of wooden rookeries, gaudy saloons and unbridled license.

It is in The Patch that the O'Learys live and it is there that
the second son, played by Tyrone Power, is growing rich with a
big dance hall and saloon, in partnership with Alice Faye, cafe
singer.   This second son plays the game of politics according to
the loose rules of The Patch, and thus the two brothers come into
a conflict that mounts steadily until the elder, now Mayor, is killed
in the fire.

Credits for the monumental production are inevitably many
and must without exception be unstinted.   At the top stands Darryl
Zanuck, whose greatest achievement it is, and Kenneth Macgowan,
his associate, responsible for a thousand perfected details.   With
them is to be included Henry King, the director, whose vision has
united personal drama with big spectacle in a compelling singleness
of aim and a sure grasp that makes each enhance the other.

The story by Niven Busch gives solid body and climbing intensity to the drama, and the screenplay of Lamar Trotti and Sonya
Levien sustains the vigor of conflict, captures the colorful atmosphere of the period and strongly individualizes some 35 characters.

For the special effects in the fire scenes honors go to the technicians, Fred Sersen, Ralph Hammeras and Louis J. Witte, to H. Bruce Humberstone, director in charge of this material, and to Daniel B. Clark, whose photography makes it so notable. Photography of the rest was in the hands of Peverell Marley, who earns encomiums.

Four new songs of popular excellence are introduced by Alice Faye. They are "In Old Chicago," by Mack Gordon and Harry Revel, and "I'll Never Let You Cry," "I've Taken a Fancy to You," and "Take a Dip in the Sea," by Lew Pollack and Sidney Mitchell. Music direction by Louis Silvers is notably good.

An eye-filling feature are the period sets by William Darling and Rudolph Sternad, with decorations by Thomas Little, to which must be added Royer's costuming, especially in the period gowns for Miss Faye.

The cast is a strong one, both histrionically and for marquee appeal. Power is exceptionally forceful both as lover and man of affairs, rising to heights beyond anything he has done. Alice Faye, lovely and appealing, also qualifies in emotional scenes. Ameche, as lawyer and leader, is magnetic and virile. Alice Brady, as the warm-hearted and courageous Molly O'Leary, scores notably, and so does her Irish brogue. Tom Brown, as the third son, is less in evidence, but delivers delightfully, especially in his love scenes with the attractive June Storey. Andy Devine as Power's comedy henchman gives needed lightness to many grim scenes, and Brian Donlevy, as a crooked politician and rival candidate for mayor, gives his opposition sinister smoothness.

Phyllis Brooks, daughter of Senator Berton Churchill, adds pretty rivalry for Power's favor, and J. Anthony Hughes as the prophetic Pa O'Leary of the prolog scores. Sidney Blackmer is in briefly as an imposing General Phil Sheridan, and among the many lesser roles some who stood out were Paul Hurst, Tyler Brooke (as a specialty singer), Harry Stubbs, Spencer Charters, Thelma Manning and Ruth Gillette.

--The Hollywood Reporter, Vol. 43, No. 17 (December 31, 1937), page 3.

*   *   *

Over-exploitation is a handicap it will have to overcome. I had read and heard so much about it that I expected it to give me one of the cinematic thrills of a lifetime. Instead I saw only a rather good screen offering, worth seeing for its historic interest and in spite of bad casting for the part of leading man; with a physical spectacle at the end which is absurd to compare with the earthquake in San Francisco or the hurricane in Hurricane. In Old Chicago has a fire--one burning building multiplied by hundreds, and depends for its thrill on multiplication of something we all are used

to seeing--wood burning.   In the other pictures we are presented
with two of nature's most furious and terrifying rampages--physical
manifestations beyond man's power to stop, lessen or divert.   A
fire can be put out.   In Chicago there merely happened to be at
hand nothing to put the fire out.   The advance hullabaloo about the
fire sequence had prepared me for something extraordinary; I found
just a fire accompanied by a terrific noise and which delayed the
story while it was burning.   As I suffered through the sequence, I
thought how easily it could have been made effective enough to have
given In Old Chicago a place among the greatest achievements of the
talkie era to date.   If Darryl Zanuck understood what gives a picture its soul as well as he understands how to make it physically
impressive, he would have expressed the drama of the fire sequence
with music.   When talking pictures emerge from this adolescence
there will be no more such awful uproars as that in Chicago.   But
before that time is reached I am afraid we will have to grow a new
crop of producers.

     While I am crabbing about this Century picture I might as
well trot out the rest of my objections before mentioning its strong
points.   I cannot see Tyrone Power in the part he plays, that of a
dominating, saloon-owning, unscrupulous political boss.   Not only
is he too young now to be convincing in such a part, but he never
will be old enough to play it acceptably.   He is not the type.   In
addition to that, he is given a wholly unsympathetic characterization, his treatment of the woman who loves him and whom he is
supposed to love, being too callously selfish to make him an acceptable romantic leading man.   He does the best he can with the
part, but someone else should have played it.   Not so, however,
with Alice Faye, whose acting and singing are strong features of
the production.   Don Ameche, too, gives a fine performance.   But
it is Alice Brady's picture.   She responds to Henry King's sympathetic direction with a thoughtful, human and appealing performance which reveals again what a superb actress she is.   I hope her
appearance in this picture definitely puts an end to her casting in
jittery parts.   Brian Donlevy, Andy Devine and Tom Brown also
distinguish themselves.   In all its technical departments In Old
Chicago is a notable production.   The recreation of the Old Chicago
is a triumph for the Century art department.   The opening sequence
is both acted and photographed beautifully.   The home life of the
O'Learys gives the picture all its emotional appeal, thanks to the
masterly and understanding direction which always is characteristic
of Henry King's work.   Produced with appreciation of its possibilities, the picture could have been one of the most notable of the
year.

                              --Welford Beaton in Hollywood
                                Spectator, Vol. 12, No. 31
                                (January 22, 1938), page 7.

☐ THE INFORMER (RKO, 1935)

At last this season is privileged to view a Hollywood production which for sustained brilliance of technical accomplishment can
bear comparison with the best recent importations from other lands.
The picture is the work of John Ford, a director who has done
distinguished work before, its story is based on one of the better
novels of that sometimes powerful, sometimes incorrigibly mere-
tricious Irish realist Liam O'Flaherty. The Informer in Dudley
Nichols' excellent version, gives a more dramatic, a more richly
documented, and an even more terrifying impression of the Black
and Tan troubles in Ireland in 1922 than one received from Mr.
O'Flaherty's novel. This is the result partly of the greater objec-
tivity imposed by the screen medium, partly of Mr. Ford's superior
detachment toward his materials. Gypo Nolan, the underworld drifter who sells his comrade for twenty British pounds, gains in reality through being presented in terms of direct action rather than in
the often diffuse interior monologues of Mr. O'Flaherty's more Dos-
toevskian manner. Victor McLaglen, under the superb direction,
contributes to this impression of a greater solidity and roundness
by giving one of the most memorable screen portrayals of the year.
It matters little that the megalomania with which he endows the
twisted little introvert of Mr. O'Flaherty's conception gives to the
character a somewhat more heroic quality than is appropriate. The
modifications of the original are all in the direction of a better
realization of the character and theme in strictly cinematic terms.
At the same time Mr. Ford has not ignored the drama played out
in Gypo's consciousness before, during, and after the betrayal. In
fact, the greatest importance of the film consists in its experimenta-
tion with the means of rendering subjective moods and states of
mind on the screen. What may be called the total mood, the emotional ambience surrounding the theme and the subject, is created
and sustained by the lighting--a uniform semidarkness splotched
here and there with the sinister glow of street lamps. Not only
does the dimness through which people and objects are glimpsed in-
tensify the atmosphere of hushed terror of Dublin under the Black
and Tans, but it also serves to reflect the miasmic confusion of
Gypo's guilt-laden consciousness. By this means outer and inner
world are interfused; rarely has an American picture achieved such
a consistent unity of emotional tone. It is reinforced rather than
broken when doors thrust open in the fog reveal by contrast the
lighted interiors of police stations, restaurants, and bawdy houses.
(The scene in the middle-class lupanar is one of the most unforgettable, as it is certainly the most astonishing, in the recent American cinema.) But it is not by lighting alone that Mr. Ford has
built up the unity of effect which makes this film so remarkable.
Using musical accompaniment in the way that it was most effectively
used in the silent film, recording Gypo's "second voice" or voice of
conscience, and trailing both music and voices on the soundtrack as
a dissolve device, Mr. Ford has striven to integrate all the newer
resources of the medium and restore to it that identity which it has
tended to lose since the introduction of sound. What is most signifi-

cant of all perhaps is Mr. Ford's rediscovery of the uses of silence. Not only is the dialogue reduced to a minimum, but it is sometimes blocked out entirely for the sake of pantomime and other effects reminiscent of the silent film.   At times this leads to results which may be considered artificial and unnatural, which can be defended only as a type of stylization.   When Gypo comes to the revolutionary headquarters to be examined, he and the others are forced to stand silently for several moments while a picture of his betrayed comrade burns in the fireplace.   But the intention behind the effort is one of the things which make this film the best that has come out of Hollywood in a very long time.

> --William Troy in The Nation,
> Vol. 140 (May 22, 1935), page
> 610.

*   *   *

The movies have rarely tried to look at modern Ireland with modern eyes, in spite of the riches of dramatic material to be found there.   The reverberations sent through the world by Synge and Joyce and O'Casey have awakened no echoes in California, though in recompense we have been spared the Mother Machree, Macushla Mavourneen kind of thing that might have resulted if Hollywood had ventured timidly into Irish romance.   There were some Kelleys paired off with Cohens, a pleasant little vehicle manufactured for bringing John McCormack to the screen but remembered, if at all, for bringing Maureen O'Sullivan to America, a husband-wife-lover affair set in a Dublin uprising--these are all the evidence movie makers have given of any interest in the Emerald Isle.

Which is one reason The Informer comes with such novelty and vitality.   Another is that Liam O'Flaherty's novels have little in them of the stuff from which ordinary movies are made.   Mr. O'Flaherty fights fiercely against having any sentimental and romantic illusions about his country and countrymen: he goes in for a bitter realism that seems inspired by something pretty close to hatred, and the Irish traits he delights to picture range all the way from braggart blackguardism to blarneying hypocrisy, with little pity for any but the stupid and bewildered.   His books would be a stiff dose for the ordinary audience if they were put on the screen in the key he wrote them in.

Dudley Nichols and John Ford have struck a somewhat gentler strain from the harp of old Erin.   One with his scenario, the other with his directing, they have made of The Informer something that popular sympathy can more conventionally respond to.   They have romanticized the motive for Gypo Nolan's turning informer, making him do it for a girl--as if hunger were not an effective enough reason.   All the women in the story have been stereotyped into lay figures used to suggest the usual heart interests of commonplace fiction, and do not count very much.   But these little compromises have left intact what is essential to the tragedy of a man who was the victim of his own character.

There is probably no blacker form of sin against one's fellow man, to the Irish, than turning informer, as Gypo Nolan did in the Dublin days of revolt when the Black and Tans tyrannized over the city.   An outcast even among the rebels, to gain the twenty pounds reward offered by the British he betrayed his pal Frankie McPhillip, who had been hiding in the wet hills and sneaked into the city on a dark foggy night to steal a quick visit to his mother and sister.   By morning the informer was caught, tried and shot.

In the hours from early evening to dawn, in the murk of the Dublin slums, Gypo's inevitable punishment stalks him.   Brutal and stupid, a brawny man who always needed his pal Frankie's brains to guide all his actions, he is lost and desperate with Frankie gone. With his pocket full of money he can buy companionship from a crowd of riff-raff who follow him from bar to bar, and he can buy momentary forgetfulness and elation from liquor, even a feeling of goodness by an impulsive gesture of sentimental generosity.   But the money, drunkenly scattered here and there, piles up into evidence against him, and at last he has to confront the rebels' tribunal, where his wild and futile lies are worse than a confession.

There is a grim splendor to it, both as a tragedy and as a motion picture.   Fundamentally it is honest in intention and sincere in execution.   The man's character is truly understood and truly portrayed, with the inevitability coming from its own nature that great tragedy always has to have.   The film illustrates powerfully the old dictum that character is destiny.   Gypo might have lived a sneaking, sordid life to a dreary old age, drifting to its end with no drama at all, but once his slow wits got the idea of going after that twenty pounds he had to step out of the gutter of aimless futility and fight the consequences of his act, with all that was in him dragged up into the glaring illumination of a final crisis.

The writer of the scenario dealt honestly and ably with the O'Flaherty character, and encompassed it in a framework that follows the best motion picture technique.   John Ford has directed it with a fine eye for picture effect, both atmospherically and dramatically. Occasionally he slips into old movie ruts that seem outworn--fade-ins to supply deficiencies in the audience's imagination, for instance, that must seem quaint and unnecessary at best to any alert audience of today.   But subtle and powerfully suggestive is the way he has paralleled the blind twistings of Gypo's inner nature with an exterior presentment of dark foggy streets peopled with dim figures and dimmer shadows, with the action erupting into some place of light and noise whenever Gypo emerges into positive activity.   The players, given what the script called on them to do, he has managed well, with much more conspicuous success with the men than with the women.   The acutely Mater Dolorosa aspect of Frankie's mother must be held against him--any director who wanted to could surely have subdued her.   But Margot Grahame, as Katie, in her earlier scenes, is a real person, not to be blamed for the unfortunate piece of writing that sent her like a blurred carbon-copy of innumerable movie heroines to plead for Gypo's life at the end.

The dominating actor is Victor McLaglen, who shines all the brighter for all the worthless parts he has had to play in the past. He is completely sunk in the sodden body and mind and soul of Gypo Nolan, a creature of the slums pushed on his fumbling way by only the most primitive instincts. Yet, without ever noticeably playing for sympathy, he manages to present a figure that is somehow pitiable. Most of the other men are good, too, with J. M. Kerrigan topping all of them, not merely because he has the only richly authentic brogue in the whole picture, but for his portrait of a grasping Irish toady that for sheer brilliance surpasses even McLaglen's performance.

Pictures like this come rarely, and it will make an interesting test of how justified people are who insist that audiences are eager for better films than producers provide.

--James Shelley Hamilton in National Board of Review Magazine, Vol. 10, No. 6 (June 1935), pages 8-9.

☐ INTERMEZZO (Selznick International, 1939)

Most beautiful presentation of the triangle theme that memory can recall as it travels backward across all the cinematic years. On the scroll of film fame it enscribes the names of a new director and a new star. I am aware Gregory Ratoff directed other pictures, but there was nothing in his previous ventures to even hint at the power he reveals in Intermezzo, power generated by gentleness, by feeling, by deep human understanding. The new star is Ingrid Bergman, whose power is as great as Ratoff's, as gentle, as understanding. What nature denied her in the way of the Hollywood standard of beauty is compensated for by a great soul which makes her beautiful.

I am writing too soon after seeing the picture to be altogether rational in recording my estimate of the ability of the Swedish star. The spell she cast over me last night lost none of its vigor during my night's sleep. She makes me forget other performances I have seen and rate her now as the screen's greatest feminine star--not actress, perhaps, because Ingrid Bergman does not act. She feels, and makes her audience share her feeling. She is a more tender Garbo, a more gentle Bette Davis--a great person.

Even though George O'Neil wrote a great screen play, he gave director and players little in the way of story. What story there is has been told on the screen a thousand times: Husband falls in love with his daughter's music teacher; she returns his love; he is a world famous violinist; she becomes his accompanist on a concert tour; she sees the hopelessness of their love; she leaves him; he returns to his family. There you have this picture's ver-

sion of the old, old story.   But as you sit in front of the screen
you will think you never saw it before; it will come to you as a
new love story, a stirring, beautiful one of tremendous emotional
appeal.   It is screen story-telling at the peak of perfection.

Leslie Howard, the nominal star of the picture, never gave
a finer performance on the screen, but in all his scenes with Ingrid
Bergman your eyes see only her.   The center of the stage moves
when she moves.   Edna Best, for more than a decade one of my
favorite English players, is perfect casting in the role of Howard's
wife.   John Halliday, too, has a part cut to the measure of his
ability and personality.   All the others in the cast fit perfectly into
the pattern.

An outstanding feature of the production is the photography of
Gregg Toland.   His lighting is extraordinarily effective.   Scorning
screen traditions, he shows us the faces of players moving in shadows even when speaking lines, and his shadow effects always are
beautiful and play a big part in creating and sustaining the mood of
the scenes.   Merely as something to look at, Intermezzo is a treat.
The art direction of Lyle Wheeler is responsible for some strikingly
artistic settings.   Music plays a big part in the picture, but that is
something which belongs in Dr. Ussher's department.

It took some courage on the part of David Selznick to endeavor to make such an old story look new.   The results are vastly
to his credit.   He is destined to become one of the leaders in the
screen world, and is in a position to take advantage of the changes
in production and distribution which will follow the revolution in the
industry now underway in federal circles and aggravated by the war
in Europe.   By and large, Dave Selznick is proving himself to be
a really great motion picture producer.

> --Welford Beaton in Hollywood
> Spectator, Vol. 14, No. 13 (Oc-
> tober 14, 1939), pages 5-6.

☐   THE INVISIBLE MAN (Universal, 1933)

There are two very good reasons why the version of H. G.
Wells's The Invisible Man is so much better than this sort of thing
usually turns out to be on the screen.   The first is that James
Whale, who is responsible for the direction, has taken a great deal
of pains with something that is usually either reduced to a minimum
or altogether ignored in these attempts to dramatize the more far-
fetched hypotheses of science--namely, setting.   Ordinarily we are
precipitated abruptly and without warning into the strange and violent
world of the scientific romancer's imagination.   We are given no
time to make our adjustment to the magic of this new world which
is so different from the world to which we are accustomed.   The
result is, of course, that we never truly believe in this new world;

it is too abstract, too intellectually conceived, to take us in very
successfully through our feelings. For this reason one is always
tempted to lay down as a first principle for writers and directors
dealing with the extraordinary, the principle that to respond to the
unusual we must first be reminded of the commonplace. And James
Whale's success in observing the principle makes one more convinced than ever that it should be regarded as a general one. He
begins with a carefully documented picture of a small country inn
in England: the people, the furnishings, the whole atmosphere are
not only instantly recognizable but also so particularized as to have
an interest in and for themselves. The background is solidly
blocked in so that we have no uncertainty as to the reality of the
people and the places with whom we have to deal. Everything is
made ready for the invisible man to step in and perform his marvels.

Now the only problem for the director was to make the best
possible use of his idea--an idea which happens to be ideally suited
to the talking screen insofar as it is impossible to imagine it being
equally well treated in any other medium. For the wretched scientist who had made himself invisible still has a voice. A body
without a voice we have had on the silent screen, but not until this
picture have we had a voice without a body. And in Wells's novel
the sight of the printed words on the page cannot be so disturbingly
eerie as the actual sound of Claude Rains's voice issuing from empty chairs and unoccupied rooms. The problem for Mr. Whale, then,
was to miss none of the opportunities for humor, pathos, and metaphysical horror which this rare notion opened up to the sound camera. How admirably he has succeeded it is impossible to indicate
without reference to the numerous instances in which his ingenuity
surprises our habitual sense patterns. It will be enough to mention
the books hurled through space by an invisible hand, the cigarette
smoked by invisible lips, the indentation in the snow of the shattered
but still invisible body. Also one must point to the effectiveness of
not showing the visible features of the scientist until, in the last
few feet of the film, death restores them to him. Of Claude Rains's
richly suggestive voice it is not too much to say that it is hardly
less responsible than the direction for the peculiar quality of the
picture as a whole. The preternatural compound of Olympian merriment and human desolation which are its overtones lends a seriousness that would otherwise be lacking. But taken either as a
technical exercise or as a sometimes profoundly moving retelling
of the Frankenstein fable, The Invisible Man is one of the most re-
warding of the recent films.

--William Troy in The Nation,
Vol. 137 (December 13, 1933),
page 688.

☐ IT HAPPENED ONE NIGHT (Columbia, 1934)

Once, while trying to explain to a Frenchman in Paris how
American boys and girls were brought up together without the ever-

lasting consciousness of sex, I told him how we used to go canoe-
ing on Belle Ile.   "Ah, you Americans have ice in your blood!" he
exclaimed.

That's the way I felt about Clark Gable during the nights he
spent in auto camps with Claudette Colbert, with only a blanket hung
on a clothes line separating their cots.   Especially when Claudette,
fleeing from her father to an unhappy marriage, almost pleaded with
Clark to "understand" her.   I'll bet there were times when Clark
said to Mons. Capra, the director who usually soft-pedals even
kissing in his picture, "Aw, Frank, have a heart!"

But perhaps that's why the picture is so charming.   Fast
moving, spirited, and full of hilariously amusing incidental business,
it builds to a finish that simply panics the fans.

En route in the night bus from Miami to New York the gang
bursts into song about the gal on the flying trapeze, the contagion
of which all but had me joining in the chorus.   There is another
equally amusing episode in which Clark explains to Claudette the
etiquette of hitch-hike signalling.

Clark used to say that he couldn't understand his popularity,
for as an actor he was "ham."   Maybe he was at first, but the
son-of-a-gun has certainly learned how to act.   He plays the part
of a news-hawk with warmth, spirit and an exquisite sense of humor.   As for Claudette, well they'd have to build a "Wall of Jeri-
cho" a lot stouter than a Navajo blanket to keep me off-side.

Walter Connolly plays the rich, indulgent dad with his usual
élan and fine art.   And Roscoe Karns strikes ten as a yap on the
make.

Samuel Hopkins Adams wrote a peach of a story, and Robert
Riskin kicked through with the liveliest script of the year.

But after all, it's Frank Capra's picture.
                            --Rob Wagner in Rob Wagner's
                              Script, Vol. 11, No. 263 (March
                              24, 1934), page 8.

                    *   *   *

One of those stories that without a particularly strong plot
manages to come through in a big way, due to the acting, dialog,
situations and direction.   In other words, the story has that intangi-
ble quality of charm which arises from a smooth blending of the
various ingredients.   Difficult to analyze, impossible to designedly
reproduce.   Just a happy accident.

It starts off to be another long distance bus story, but they
get out of the bus before it palls and it is not handicapped by the
restraint that locale always seems to impose.

Plot is a simple one. The headstrong, but very charming
daughter of a millionaire marries a suitor of whom her father does
not approve. She quarrels with her father on the yacht off Miami,
and the girl goes over the rail. She seeks to make her way to
New York, with the old man raising the hue and cry. Peter Warne,
who has just been fired from his Florida correspondent's job, is on
the same bus. The story is thin and frequently illogical, but the
action carries it along so fluently and amusingly that there is small
chance to take time out to argue the plausibility.

But the author would have been nowhere without the deft direction of Frank Capra and the spirited and good-humored acting of
the stars and practically most of their support. Walter Connolly
is the only other player to get much of a show, but there are a
dozen with bit parts well played.

Miss Colbert makes hers a very delightful assignment and
Gable swings along at sustained speed. Both play as though they
really liked their characters and therein lies much of the charm.

One Night proves two things. A clean story can be funnier
than a dirty one and the best way to do a bus story is to make
them get out and walk.

--Chic in Variety, Vol. 113, No.
11 (February 27, 1934), page
17.

☐ JEZEBEL (Warner Bros. , 1938)

In Jezebel Warners has its greatest film achievement and the
industry an exceptional attraction of smash proportions. It is a
compelling emotional drama that draws with relentless clarity the
portrait of a self-willed girl. This portrait, as projected by Bette
Davis, is one of deep beauty, power and understanding. Though
not a wholly sympathetic role, it is a marked departure from anything she has had recently and again shows to brilliant advantage
her emotional command.

The story is laid in New Orleans, beginning in 1850, and
climaxes three years later in the great yellow fever epidemic. It
concerns a group of the socially elite of the period; pictures with
sumptuous detail the life of the times among aristocrats of the deep
south; and builds slowly, but with steadily rising emotional power,
to the disaster of the epidemic, the tragedy of which is emphasized
by ignorance of control or curative measures.

In this environment the tale is told of a headstrong girl,
reckless and self-willed, who is too sure of the man she loves and
who, when she loses him, sets out to get him back at all costs.
Her ways and means wreak havoc with all the lives she touches,

but in the end, by a supreme self-immolation, she starts on the way to redemption. As the picture closes she is seen on the way with the fever-stricken man of her desire to the leper island where she will nurse him to the end.

Henry Fonda carries the other half of this dramatic conflict and an exceedingly vigorous and keenly detailed portrayal he gives it. When Fonda breaks with the girl and disappears in the North he marries Margaret Lindsay and later brings her home. Then the conflict becomes a triangle, with woman pitted against woman, and this situation not only greatly intensifies the drama, but gives Miss Lindsay a chance for emotional playing that scores for her notably.

Present also in this social circle is George Brent, Bette's ex-fiancé, and the antagonism between him and Fonda gives a valuable secondary element of conflict, which comes to a head in one of the two duels and gives Brent a spirited acting part that he delivers with appealing dash.

Excellent in support is Fay Bainter as Bette's aunt, drawing a cameo of a southern gentlewoman that stands out for sensitive restraint and graciousness. Excellent also is Donald Crisp as a doctor of the period, trying to rouse his community against the fever threat. Richard Cromwell is upstanding as Fonda's younger brother. Henry O'Neill draws a fine type as Bette's guardian. Spring Byington as another of the group, and Margaret Early as her pretty young daughter, join with Gordon Oliver and Janet Shaw in filling out a charming picture of the period, and Theresa Harris, Eddie Anderson, Stymie Beard and Lou Payton head the colored contingent.

The screenplay from Owen Davis's stage play, for which hearty credit is due Clements Ripley, Abem Finkel and John Huston, is an able and penetrating piece of dramatic writing, capturing emotional and character values with fine perception.

William Wyler's direction is the major factor in giving this fine and dignified work its dramatic verity and depth. It is in all respects a notable job. The production given the play by Henry Blanke captures on a large scale the romance of the old South and the terror of the city under the scourge. Ernest Haller's camera gives excellent value to the contrasted moods, and Max Steiner's admirable score, under the direction of Leo F. Forbstein, adds rich atmosphere.

--The Hollywood Reporter, Vol. 44, No. 23 (March 8, 1938), page 3.

* * *

They talked so long about making Gone with the Wind, that Warner's made Jezebel, to put an end to the suspense. Bette

Davis, more restrained than usual, sometimes subtle, and nonetheless powerful, does the wilful Southern belle to a crisp. The usual duelling scene, also plantation singing, and an inexplicable bit where the negro servant, asked to have a mint julep by a massa who has been to the north, says it wouldn't be proper, and compromises by taking his to the kitchen to drink. Seems almost like someone was trying to say something there, but succeeded in holding it in.

--Meyer Levin in Esquire, Vol. 9, No. 6 (June 1938), page 89.

☐ JUDGE PRIEST (Fox, 1934)

Dudley Nichols and Lamar Trotti certainly did well by Our Irv, for they have taken the famous Cobb character and woven about it one of the most delightful stories ever told on the screen. Though Will Rogers is physically unlike the dear old Judge of Irv's stories, he fulfills his spirit gloriously. I once said that Will was a personality, not an actor. I was wrong; Will can act. In this story, he is a Southerner, accent and all, and the way he impersonates Stepin Fetchit is a riot.

John Ford begins the picture with a "slow Southern drawl" which gives one a chance to become acquainted with the characters, fill the eye with beauty, and laze along with just a suggestion of coming drama, the calm preceding the storm, emphasizing its arrival.

The drama is built around the silently mysterious figure of David Landau, a village blacksmith. The major conflict is between Judge Priest and the bombastic senator, Berton Churchill, who wants his job. The love interest--secondary in this story--is carried by young Tom Brown and the very beautiful Anita Louise. The fun, and there is lots of it, besides Will's philosophical blurbs and his tenor singing with the cullud gals, is put over by Stepin Fetchit and those three grand musketeers of comedy--Charlie Grapewin, Roger Imhof and Francis Ford. Ford has a running gag that simply panicked the preview audience.

As Juror No. 12, he is in a quandary to find a place to spit. He contemplates everything from hats to overshoes. Finally he shoots at the court spittoon, and every time the bailiff moves it farther away, his marksmanship is tested. Finally the bailiff has him stymied, but darned if Francis doesn't shoot a "dog's leg" and ring the bell! Cheers, and the proud juror exhibits his sharpshooter medals.

One of the high points of the picture is the performance of Henry Walthall. Twenty-five years ago he rose to fame as the Little Colonel in The Clansman. Now we see him as a Confederate little minister who betrays the confessional to save a man from an

undeserved sentence. He tells his story from the stand in one of
the longest and most quietly dramatic scenes ever filmed. He is
beautiful to look at, his voice is rich and resonant and his pantomime wonderfully restrained. It is a part that should again lift
him to stardom.

Space doesn't permit elaboration on the fine work of all the
principals, Ford's excellent direction, the authentic settings of William Darling, the wonderful "sound" of Albert Protzman and the
musical direction of Samuel Kaylin. Incidentally, the two "screen
play authors" also wrote the lyrics!

It's a grand picture--the best Will Rogers ever made, and
Sol Wurtzel should be purring happily for having produced it. And
Irv Cobb for the fidelity of his story spirit.

> --Rob Wagner in Rob Wagner's
> Script, Vol. 12, No. 286
> (September 29, 1934), page 8.

*   *   *

I regard Will Rogers and Kin Hubbard as the two best all-
American humorists of my time. Kin was perhaps better than Will
because he had sense enough not to overproduce. He realized that
no humorist should write more than two paragraphs a day, and that
even then he would produce some chaff. (The fact is, no real
humorist should write any paragraphs a day.) And Kin was under
no obligations to any string of polo ponies; when I knew him his
stable consisted of a ten-year-old Franklin.

Will Rogers has enough ripe, round, sound wisdom to make
the human race ashamed of itself (which is perhaps a humorist's
prime function), and I reverence him. I say this, thoroughly conscious of his large output of drivel, and deeply sickened by his
back-slapping, his mighty-fine following, his terrible Sunday newspaper articles, his exaggerated hemming and hawing and ain'ting,
his systematic boosting of aviation ... and most of his movies.

This is all in place here, because it leads up to Will in his
latest picture, Judge Priest. Most of Will's pictures have been in
the department of his overproduction, but I believe Judge Priest is
worthy of him at his best. Judge Priest drags groaningly at times
and takes a good half hour to get wound up, but it has tastes and
flavors that make it well worth while.

> --Don Herold in Life, Vol. 101,
> No. 2597 (December 1934),
> pages 53-54.

☐ KING KONG

It is too bad that "colossal" and "super-colossal" have been
bandied about so freely--for here is a real hair-raiser to which
those terms are appropriate.

The story, conceived by the late Edgar Wallace and Merian
C. Cooper, deals with the adventures of Fay Wray, Bruce Cabot
and Robert Armstrong, entangled with Kong, a monster ape fifty
feet high.   Caught by savages, Fay is offered as a sacrifice to the
ape.   But Kong fancies her, as a man might cherish a dainty flower,
and fights dinosaurs on her behalf, until Fay's companions, using
gas bombs, catch him for exhibition in New York.

While in Gotham he breaks loose, seizes Fay, and--but from
there on we'll let the film speak for itself.   Suffice it to say, you'll
get thrills such as the screen rarely affords.
                                    --Photoplay, Vol. 43, No. 6
                                      (May 1933), page 46.

                    *   *   *

Here is the horror picture to end all horror pictures.   The
only way to top this one would be to make a newsreel of the Ar-
menian atrocities.   Yet King Kong holds enough of the sensational,
the novel and the macabre to claim attention from any film fan.
Its woman appeal may be questionable, but there is no record that
the femmes have stayed away from other productions of this ilk.
Radio has been grooming this one as a special.   It will make more
money if it is shoved right out to the first runs for a quick cleanup.

Nothing quite like Kong has been engraved on raw stock before.   The closest parallel is Lost World, but that silent never had
so intimate an association between the human beings and the prehistoric monsters as Kong, and therefore never became as chilling.
Both as producer and co-author, Merian C. Cooper is entitled to
take the first bow on Kong.

Yet there are as many little flaws to this production as would
be expected in so wildly improbable a yarn.   Despite the year of
technical work on the animals, their movements are still mechanical
and unreal and the 50-foot gorilla that carries the film's title is at
first sight disappointingly machine-like.   It is only in the sum total
that the picture packs the wallop that will bring in gate receipts.

There is just enough story on which to hang a love interest,
and an excuse to exhibit the monsters, but that story is the best
part of the production.   Carl Denham is an explorer-producer, not
unlike Cooper, who made the picture.   He sails with a tough crew
for an uncharted South Pacific island after picking up a destitute
girl in New York to provide the sex appeal.   The island has never
been visited by whites before, and when they arrive the natives are

about to sacrifice one of their girls to Kong, the multi-sized ape
on the other side of the island, imprisoned behind a 100-foot wall.

Natives kidnap the white girl and offer her instead to the
monster, who is so struck by her beauty that he spares her, carrying her away to his lair.   This is tipped off in a foreword that
says "the Beast was rendered weak by Beauty," which is strictly
a tipoff and essential.

Crew, including the hardboiled mate who has fallen in love
with the girl, goes to her rescue.   Most are killed but the rest
save the girl.   Kong follows them, is knocked out by gas bombs
and brought to New York as a freak.   He escapes and turns the
town into a shambles before he is killed by police airplanes as he
roosts on the mooring mast of the Empire State Bldg.

In addition to Kong, there are numerous other over-sized
mammals, reptiles and birds of the prehistoric ages which he fights
and kills.   He also accounts for plenty of humans.

Horror scenes are often too long and as such border on the
ridiculous.   Film needs trimming in these spots.

Four actors comprise the cast, Robert Armstrong, as the
film explorer, Fay Wray, the girl, who had little to do but scream;
Bruce Cabot, her sweetheart; and Frank Reicher, the ship's captain.   All turned in above-par performances.

Unusually good photography and beautiful jungle settings deserve mention.   Same goes for Murray Spivak's sound effects, with
plenty of them scattered through the film, and a musical score by
Max Steiner that heightened each dramatic scene.   Technical staff,
headed by Willis O'Brien, who did similar work on Lost World,
made this picture possible.

--Daily Variety* (February 17,
1933), pages 3 and 6.

☐ KITTY FOYLE (RKO, 1940)

Put down a mark of distinction for RKO.

Kitty Foyle is a big hit; probably as big a hit as this organization has ever had, and it will get more circulation than the book
Christopher Morley wrote that made of this picture such sensational
entertainment.

---

*This review was written almost a month prior to the official open-
ing of King Kong, following a February 13, 1933, preview of the
film at the State Theatre, Long Beach, California.

Credit Sam Wood's great direction and Ginger Rogers' exceptional acting for most of the success of the picture. Both contributions were as bright as could possibly illuminate any hit. Of course Mr. Morley's book is the basic reason, but without good old Sam Wood, and Mr. Wood without Ginger Rogers, it would be pretty hard to conceive of such a hit. And, too, you must credit David Hempstead and Wood for having the courage to settle the big question that's bothering every studio--leading men--through casting not only one, but two unknowns for such important assignments. Unknowns, for the reason that no other producer or director has had the courage to give Dennis Morgan and James Craig chances at really good parts. But both the boys rewarded Wood and Hempstead for their gamble and their actions should give encouragement to a lot of other producers who have felt that, without one of the big names for a leading man, there's no use starting a picture.

Kitty Foyle will probably go down in the picture history book as one of the finest love stories ever told. It will be recorded in the minds of the ticket buyers, particularly the women, for years and years as a great picture. It might, with proper handling, be ranked as one of the year's outstanding moneymakers. For it's all that and still some. And coming from RKO, which has been sort of down in the mouth for quite a while, it becomes more important, even a greater contribution to the big forward step the whole picture business is taking.

Morley's story was fine picture material and the script must have been something approaching perfection to photograph. For months and months your Hollywood Reporter has informed you that Kitty Foyle was the best of all best sellers, so there's as big an audience waiting for the release of the picture as has anticipated screen entertainment for a long time. And that audience will love the story of little Kitty Foyle, from the backwash of Philadelphia, meeting and falling in love with Wyn Strafford, of the main line Straffords, of Darby Mills, Pennsylvania. Every ticket buyer will be rooting for that little girl to win her happiness with the man she loves, and none of them will deny her right to that happiness. They will admire her courage in facing the world on her platform and, although many of them will be disappointed, their reason will prompt them to agree with Kitty that her everlasting happiness was with Mark Eisen, the young doctor, who was more down to Kitty's level, but they will all know that Kitty will go to her deathbed loving Wyn.

It was great story material, but even greater direction, for you must take into consideration that Sam Wood had two boys to whom Ginger Rogers had to make love and accept their love making, and these boys were not up in that bracket before. And, too, Miss Rogers, though probably furnishing no great problem for her director, nevertheless had a part that exacted every ounce of her ability and then some, and Wood brought them all through more brightly than Kitty's crystal of the girl on a sleigh-ride. It was easy to recognize where writing stopped and direction started in this picture, and that's why Sam Wood's credits must go up in bigger lights, if there are lights that big.

Dennis Morgan, who was formerly known around town as Stanley Morner, and a singer, certainly divested himself of both name and avocation, for through his performance as Wyn Straf- ford, he becomes the actor--par excellence.   And Jimmy Craig has been beating at studio doors for a couple of years, pleading for a chance, and once he got it, jumps himself up into the front line. Theirs are two sterling achievements and are certain to give them sufficient recognition to stay up in the chips.

The rest of the cast was more than capable, although all playing no more than bits, for the whole picture was on the shoul- ders of the three top players.   Eduardo Ciannelli as Giono, the speakeasy proprietor, stood out, along with Ernest Cossart as Pop Foyle.   Odette Myrtil caused this reviewer to wonder why she is not being used in more pictures.   Katharine Stevens, who happens to be Sam Wood's daughter, stuck out like a sore thumb in a couple of short scenes, as did Mary Treen.

Nothing short of a blitzkrieg could stop the success of Kitty Foyle.   It belongs in the top allocation and merits the longest runs. It's exceptional entertainment.

--The Hollywood Reporter, Vol.
61, No. 2 (December 17, 1940),
page 4.

☐ LADY FOR A DAY (Columbia, 1933)

A story about an old apple seller's love for the daughter who believes her a society dowager.

May Robson as Apple Annie gives an unforgettable perform- ance.   Her drunk scene with the social chatter is an all-time clas- sic; Warren William, Guy Kibbee, Ned Sparks and Glenda Farrell as the smart cracking lowlives who play fairy godmother are grand. Jean Parker is the romantic interest.

Highbrows may call this hokey but it's the kind of hoke that makes the movies and the world go round.   You'll scream with de- light when all the riffraff prepare to impersonate quality folks at the reception, you'll thrill with suspense when the real guests arrive, and you'll breathe the breath of living drama with Annie in her final triumph.

--Photoplay, Vol. 44, No. 4
(September 1933), page 56.

*   *   *

But if you were as disappointed as I was with Tugboat Annie, and want to recompense yourself by witnessing a character performance worthy of Miss Dressler's more inspired moments, see Lady for a Day. May Robson is simply superb.

Which reminds me of the fortunes of a movie actress. Take Dinner at Eight and Lady for a Day. In the first May Robson is a cook for two scenes. In the second she is the lady for a day.

In addition to Miss Robson's work, the film's assets include Damon Runyon's swell dialog, and fine performances by Guy Kibbee, Warren William and Ned Sparks. From these names you would think it was a Warner Brothers picture. It isn't. The film was made by Columbia Pictures, and this is how President Harry Cohn gets away with it. First he selects a story that suits him. Then he goes around to the studios who have players on contract and picks suitable stars who are not working at the moment. In this way Harry gets the best players without having to keep a mess of them on contract, and the other studios get an income from their unemployed help.

Lady for a Day is an example of how well this method can work. It is one of the best pictures in months.

--Harry Evans in Life, Vol. 100, No. 2583 (October 1933), page 43.

☐ THE LIFE OF EMILE ZOLA (Warner Bros. , 1937)

The Warner boys are the cinema's greatest enigmas. Building their reputation on musicals and girl shows, they suddenly tackle intense, timely dramas--I Am a Fugitive from a Chain Gang, The Black Legion, etc.--do them amazingly well, then--bingo!--in the face of critical doubts, they produce Pasteur, a biographical masterpiece, and top even that with a (yes, "terrific," "colossal," "stupendous") supermasterpiece, Zola.

Biographies like those of Barnum and Diamond Jim Brady may possess elements of entertainment, but, after all, Barnum was but a showman and Brady a gourmet. Pasteur and Zola on the other hand were world figures, the latter the center of one of the greatest dramas of the age. So, besides being characters of heroic proportions, their life stories are of tremendous interest, and, as produced by Warner's, of historical information. And they are more stirring--if we can judge audience reaction as observed preview night--than the most hair-raising melodrama ever produced!

Paul Muni is magnificent in the title role. He changes from a warring young radical to a fat, soft, flattered bourgeois; then, stirred by the injustice done the Jew, Dreyfus, again into a terrific crusader. That, dear fans, is superb acting.

The other characters--and what a tapestry!--are equally convincing, all appreciating their opportunities and rising to them,
particularly Joseph Schildkraut as Dreyfus and Vladimir Sokoloff as
Paul Cézanne.

Bet you never heard of the authors and scripters--Heinz
Herald and Geza Herczeg--but they have written a story that not
only shows every facet of Zola's personality but portrays perfectly
the many historic characters of the Dreyfus scandal and then builds
and builds to its inevitable climaxes.   I well remember the thrill I
had in reading Maitre Labori's defense of Zola.   I was even more
thrilled in hearing Donald Crisp thunder those historic philippics.

Strangely enough, the anti-Semitic angle of the story which
was of such tremendous importance at the time is scarcely touched
upon in the picture.   The fact is, Dreyfus was chosen to be the
goat of the scandal simply because he was a Jew.

Space limits my enthusiasms for other individual performances, but I must commend William Dieterle's superb direction
which is masterly, not only in sweep but in the smallest detail.

Then there are the superb photography of Tony Gaudio; the
rich sets by Anton Grot, especially the Pantheon; the authentic costumes by Milo Anderson and Ali Hubert; the unobtrusive musical
direction of Leo Forbstein.   I can even understand giving screen
credit to Perc Westmore for his make-up (the aging Zola and Dreyfus)!

Creditable not only to Hal Wallis, Henry Blanke, and the
Warner Brothers, Zola even raises America's cinematic preëmi-
nence.   "Horrible Hollywood" indeed!
> --Rob Wagner in Rob Wagner's
> Script, Vol. 18, No. 428
> (September 11, 1937), page 10.

*   *   *

Another great characterization by Paul Muni.   The photoplay
is weighty but solid.   At times, the story of Dreyfus dominates the
story of Zola, especially since Joseph Schildkraut plays Dreyfus
beautifully.   The Christlike closeup of Schildkraut in the release-
from-prison scene really becomes the climax of the picture.   Muni
just manages to top it with the dogged intensity of his trial-scene
expression.   Gale Sondergaard is splendid as Mme. Dreyfus; most
of the other players are so ordinary that it is difficult at times to
keep the characters in mind.   Erin O'Brien Moore's Nana and Mor-
ris Carnovsky's Anatole France are exceptions.   Direction is pon-
derous.   But nevertheless the great theme of the story is delivered
with relentless effort.
> --Meyer Levin in Esquire, Vol.
> 8, No. 4 (October 1937), page
> 121.

☐ LITTLE CAESAR (Warner Bros. , 1931)

Ah, yes, we know--you're all fed up on underworld stories.
Well, all right--but before you take a solemn vow never to see one
again, do catch this one. Little Caesar is the latest and not far
from the best of them, thanks to the grand dirty work of Edward
Robinson, as lethal a gangster as ever wore grease-paint. Doug,
Jr. takes second honors.

> --Photoplay, Vol. 39, No. 1
> (December 1930), page 112.

* * *

If you like movies about racketeers, you'll get a big kick out
of Little Caesar. The objection that this department has always expressed regarding films glorifying the American gangster is overcome to a great degree in this production because of Edward G.
Robinson's masterful portrayal of the leading character. From
start to finish he is nothing more than a tough, conceited Wop gun-
man, whose likable qualities are never stressed to make you think
he is anything else. If you read the book, which is also very interesting, you will be pleased to know that Little Caesar's farewell
speech is preserved on the screen.

The absence of women in the life of the leading character
does away with the refining influence of love interest, which is a
relief. The cooing, such as it is, is done by Douglas Fairbanks,
Jr. , and Glenda Farrell. Mr. Fairbanks does as well as anybody
could with a part that is nowhere near worthy of him. Lord knows
why they wasted him on it. Miss Farrell makes a small part seem
even less significant than it is.

Recommended for Mr. Robinson's exceptionally fine performance.

> --Harry Evans in Life, Vol. 97,
> No. 2517 (January 30, 1931),
> page 20.

☐ LITTLE WOMEN (RKO, 1933)

Being the only allegedly educated person in these United States
who had never read Little Women, nor even knew what it was all
about, I approached the film version in a perfectly objective state
of mind. What I saw was a picture of American family life before
the age of gasoline and bungalow courts. The charming loveliness
of well-bred New England life during the Civil War period.

With Father off at the front, Mother was bringing up her four
daughters according to the best Emily Posting of the time. At first

I was a bit disturbed by the sizes and ages of the girls who were
supposed to be mere adolescents. All but Joan Bennett, who played
Amy, a twelve-year-old kid--and looked it. The fine artistry of the
other three, however, soon squared off the anachronism, even the
long-legged Katharine Hepburn managing somehow to register extreme youthfulness.

Indeed, one of the best scenes in the picture shows Jo running through the woods and vaulting fences like a young deer, a fine
lesson to every eighth-grade girl in Los Angeles. Strangely enough,
the only other person I ever saw on the screen who could run with
speed and youthful abandon was Nazimova (aged 40!) in Barbary
Sheep.

Joan Bennett gives just about her best performance. Jean
Parker in an exceptionally sweet and sentimental role makes it ring
true by her own intrinsic sweetness. Frances Dee, whom I have
considered one of the best of our younger actresses, takes another
firm step toward stardom. But it is Katharine Hepburn who raises
what might have been an over-sentimental cry-fest into art.

Add to these the excellent work of Spring Byington as the
mother, Henry Stephenson as the rich and grouchy but kindly neighbor, Edna May Oliver, so like my own imperious grandmother,
Paul Lukas as a gentle professor, and Douglass Montgomery, who
gives one of the best performances of a juvenile I've ever seen, and
we have as fine a cast as was ever assembled in a single picture,
and that's not excepting any of these popular all-star casts that are
supposed to slay one.

Still add the sympathetic understanding of Kenneth Macgowan,
the supervisor, and the nice subtlety of George Cukor's direction
and we have a picture that, though dipped in syrup, ranks right up
top.

While I am raving, let me hand a large bouquet to Sarah Y.
Mason and Victor Heerman for turning in a script that is a triumph
of light and shade. Henry Gerrard's camera work stands right up
with the general excellence of the production.

Katharine Hepburn again proves that she is not a freak nor
a single-shotter, but a consummate artist. Don't think for a minute, however, the picture is all Hepburn. Far from it. In the
whole pattern there is not a weak thread nor a dull color.

--Rob Wagner in Rob Wagner's
Script, Vol. 10, No. 250 (December 23, 1933), page 10.

*   *   *

Mr. Cukor's personality is so predominant at all times he
must be included in the cast. One of the finest pictures ever made.

Hock your watch and take the whole family.
                    --Harry Evans in Life, Vol. 101,
                      No. 2586 (January 1934), page
                      44.

☐ LOST HORIZON (Columbia, 1937)

        But a good film is not to be made by spectacular touches
alone, as can be seen from The Lost Horizon, which appears to be
Mr. Hilton's rewrite of She with a little reverse English and something of a special screwball in the way of cosmic thought.   Frank
Capra made it with evident care and faith, and Frank Capra has
made living screen fiction out of nothing at all and a few bent hair-
pins with such steady ease that we have come to expect seeing him
walk on the waters any minute now.   But something has happened.
The picture has its spots of charm, some really big adventure moments in Tibet, and the good work of Ronald Colman and Edward
Everett Horton.   It is a big, expensive job and perhaps the capital
letters and blast of horns with which it is being opened on the two-
a-day time can be interpreted as happy days for it and lots of
money.   Nonetheless it strikes me as little more than moxie and
noodles, being in total mawkish, muffed, and as mixed up as the
only figures by which you could describe the general effect--e. g.,
by saying in one breath that the Master's hand was not steady on
the throttle because in diving off the deep end he had landed on the
horns of a dilemma and laid a pretty terrific egg.
                    --Otis Ferguson in The New Re-
                      public, Vol. 90 (March 17, 1937),
                      page 168.

                    *   *   *

        To those honestly concerned with the development of the mo-
tion picture as an art, Frank Capra has endeared himself above
most producers of films.   One after another, his pictures have ap-
pealed both to the exacting few who have demanded that the screen
be bright with truth as well as vivid motion, and to the many whose
demands at the box office have made the whole art of the screen
possible.   But in Hollywood's mushroom growth there has always
been the unfortunate obstacle of a tendency to run (as in the copying
of ideas, forms, effects) before one could walk, and many of the
most arty attempts have tripped over this obstacle.   Frank Capra
never tripped because he never came anywhere near such an obstacle.

        But after getting himself a name for being a sort of magician
in the movies, he apparently began to take seriously a lot of things
the movies (as he knew them) had never heard of.   In Lost Horizon
he seemed to see both a smashing adventure story and an excursion
into philosophy that would stun everybody.   So he and his right-hand

script writer (Robert Riskin) went to work on what is all too obviously an "epic."

Lost Horizon in the Capra production for Columbia is mani-
festly high adventure with no expense spared.   The plane Ronald
Colman boards rises stirringly above the rebellion of the Chinese
masses and rides stirringly through the night as Colman and his
younger brother discover that they are being kidnapped along with a
hodge-podge of passengers (an erratic E. E. Horton paleontologist,
an Isabel Jewel embittered sickly woman, a Thomas Mitchell ruined
banker risen from plumber, etc.).   The plane takes them into Tibet,
higher and higher into the mountains, and their chance crack-up
leads into the highest adventure of all--their discovery of a sheltered
lamasery where the cross purposes of winds and mountains, private
careers and universal revolutions, fade away in an atmosphere of
June and good-will.

Up to this point it is still tense adventure stuff.   But at this
point Capra leaves an action-spectacle for a romantic-Utopia in
which he is no longer at ease.   It turns out that Ronald Colman (an
Anthony Edenish diplomat) has written some of the clearest philosophy of his day, and that for this reason a Grand Lama (instigated
by The Girl) has shanghaied him hither to be Grand Lama Presump-
tive.   Life in the lamasery, which is already getting too prolonged
by reason of its miraculous climate, diet and general unworldliness,
is thus extended to include romance, many pastoral shots, a natural
conflict between the brothers and their love affairs, and some state-
ments about the world that come even sillier from a Hollywood
Grand Lama than they would from Arthur Brisbane.   Ronald Colman is tricked, after having been made Grand Lama, into thinking
he has been tricked; he goes out into the terrible winds again and
after desperate adventures forsakes the world once more to return
to his waiting sweetheart for the fade-out.   Meanwhile there have
been perhaps seven minutes in which the hand of Frank Capra might
be considered visible, if palsied.

For the rest of it, no one could say who made the picture.
It is mounted with elaborate heaviness, but on tissue paper.   It
abandons action for thought, and then spreads the thought so cosmic
and wide that it cannot be any deeper than half-way tide over mud
flats.   The sets constructed (to life size) for the strange region of
Shangri-La are alone worthy of Ahs and Ohs: the evident care in
casting and acting stands out above the average run of most productions; but then there comes all this serious statement of the improbable that could be set forth effectively only in burlesque, and
these random light-comedy effects that become burlesque against
such a background--and in the end a person doesn't know where he
is, except that he is nowhere as far as pictures are concerned.
This film was made with obvious care and expense; but it will be
notable in the future only as the first wrong step in a career that
till now has been a denial of the very tendencies in pictures which

this film represents.

                              --Otis Ferguson in National Board
                                of Review Magazine, Vol. 12,
                                No. 3 (March 1937), pages 11
                                and 14.

☐ LOVE AFFAIR (RKO, 1939)

Love Affair is by all odds an impressive picture. It strives hard to be great. It succeeds in being distinguished in certain moments. But for the most part it must rely upon the pull of its lead names for boxoffice effect. For as entertainment it can hope only for mixed reactions and split opinion squarely for, or against.

The play is halved in two distinct moods and therein lies its conspicuous difficulty. The transference from the flighty first chapter to the drab second presents an awkward problem, complicated by the separation in the latter of the two principals who have together occupied the former exclusively.

The story itself is thin, relying on the abilities of producer-director Leo McCarey and of Irene Dunne and Charles Boyer to charm the audience into an affinity for two story-book characters. Boyer is a foreign playboy, Miss Dunne an American entertainer. Both are engaged to marry in America when they are picked up by the cameras aboard an ocean liner.

They play at love-making, provocatively and charmingly. McCarey has presented them against entrancing backgrounds and given each every opportunity to be as fascinating as possible. But their lines are neither as charming nor as amusing as their effete presentation might imply.

They part at the gangplank, uncertain of their futures and pledged to meet at an appointed place on an appointed date, if they find it impossible to continue apart. The date finds both prepared for reunion, but Miss Dunne is struck by an auto while on her way to the meeting.

The ensuing chapter lacks the inspiration of the preceding. The wanted sympathy for Miss Dunne proves elusive, but is gratifyingly recaptured finally when the two lovers are reunited.

McCarey has invested his picture with rare moments of charm, and many of its passages will undoubtedly have a cloying effect on feminine audiences. The approach is so deliberately diffuse, however, that the picture at times borders on monotony, and puts the talents of the players severely to test.

Performances of both Miss Dunne and Boyer are beautifully matched, and individually their portrayals are distinctly praise-

worthy. Both roles are peculiarly demanding, requiring unusual assurance with fine appreciation for the delicate nuances.

Among the supporting characters, Maria Ouspenskaya is superb as Boyer's elderly grandmother. Also briefly registered is
Lee Bowman as Miss Dunne's loyal fiancé, Astrid Allwyn as Boyer's
intended bride, and Maurice Moscovich.

Technically the picture is outstanding in photography, musical scoring and artistic backgrounding. Two musical numbers,
"Wishing" and "Sing My Heart," sung effectively by Miss Dunne,
will add copiously to the picture's exploitation values.

--The Hollywood Reporter, Vol.
50, No. 28 (March 10, 1939),
page 3.

*   *   *

The new films following Stagecoach, which added much needed
zest to our winter screen rations, are refreshingly different and
reveal the studios in a frolicsome mood. Three of them can be
recommended, with or without reservation, and all three contain
elements of surprise, a quality recently conspicuous for its absence
in most of Hollywood's product.

The first half of Love Affair, Leo McCarey's film with Irene
Dunne and Charles Boyer, adapted from a story by Mildred Cram
and the director, fully realized its cinematic possibilities and impressed me as a superior romantic comedy; leisurely to be sure,
but then one wished time to savor many excellencies, to indulge in
a few private dreams, and to shed furtive tears during the scenes
which Maria Ouspenskaya played so superbly, together with the principals, in the sunny quietness of an enchanting old house in Madeira.
The exuberant characters and their relationships were entirely plausible. The film moved spontaneously and gracefully, was photographed to perfection by Rudolph Maté, and its decorum made one
nudge one's neighbor proudly and whisper, "There's nothing so wrong
with Hollywood. "

But alas, there is something wrong, and since the trouble
has reached epidemic proportions, Love Affair must bear the brunt
of one reviewer's rising indignation. After reaching an important
and stirring climax, when destiny prevents Miss Dunne from keeping
a poignant rendezvous with her lover, the film did a Humpty Dump-
ty, and as it dragged on, maimed and spineless, it became evident
that no one had had the necessary surgical skill to put it together
again. The picture had simply lost its direction, unity, and mood,
and although future audiences may not notice such imperfections,
many previewers were heard to grumble because the story didn't end
sooner, before the orphanage sequences introduced so many unnecessary new characters when what we wanted was more of Dunne and
Boyer and the much more dramatic clash of their emotions.

Although each film had a different theme, such recent well-made and potentially healthy cinematic exhibits as Made for Each Other, Stagecoach, and Dark Victory all blundered after splendid beginnings.   Made for Each Other erred in its uncontrollable melodrama and lavish use of clichés.   Stagecoach started out with too much plot and didn't know how to release ballast after soaring to exciting heights.   Dark Victory, in which case a mere snip of the shears can remove an unsightly blemish, added an anticlimactic sequence after achieving a stunning climax.

Sagging middles and sloppy endings wouldn't matter so much if the films mentioned were not meritorious, sufficiently so to make Hollywood's severest critics optimistic about the future.   But inasmuch as movies can be timed to the split second, thoroughly previewed, cut, re-edited, and even reshot when portions are found wanting, I am at loss to account for the sort of helpless floundering afflicting the better films.   Are the studios subtly trying to beat double features by so tiring audiences with the second half of otherwise excellent films that they will wearily believe they have seen both an A and a B and be drowsily content with quantity instead of quality?

All the actors in Love Affair, whether essential to the story or not, contribute animated performances, but the unexpected sensation of the evening was a glowing "bit" performance by an unknown actress who earned an ovation as a blustering landlady.   I say "unknown actress" because, after the preview, pandemonium prevailed in the foyer as reviewers demanded the actress's name, while R. K. O.'s publicity staff looked shamefaced, and even Mr. McCarey, so I was told, couldn't recall the name of the player who had worked only one day in order to become celebrated overnight.

She is Ferike Boros, and my face is scarlet because I've admired her work before, yet failed to recognize her when she dominated the screen.

--Richard Sheridan Ames in Rob
Wagner's Script, Vol. 21, No.
500 (March 18, 1939), page 16.

☐ LOVE ME TONIGHT (Paramount, 1932)

What a picture! First, you have Chevalier (and last, you have Chevalier, and all through this riot of entertainment you have Chevalier)--zat Maurice who captures you with his risqué songs, his magnetic smile and his rakish straw hat. And, adding her beauty and lovely voice, you have that delightful Jeanette MacDonald. And those two ridiculous Charlies--Ruggles and Butterworth. And C. Aubrey Smith, who plays a doughty old duke and puts over a solo as inimitably as Maurice. Then there is Myrna Loy. And others equally good. The story? About a lowly tailor who woos

a princess.   The music?   Woven through the whole picture like a
brilliant symphony, accented with some of the catchiest tunes of the
season.   You'll surely be humming, "Isn't It Romantic?" or we
miss our guess.

                              --Photoplay, Vol. 42, No. 5
                              (October 1932), page 52.

☐ MAKE WAY FOR TOMORROW (Paramount, 1937)

      Make Way for Tomorrow is the picture that Leo McCarey,
the Paramount director, had to fight for.   He had read Josephine
Lawrence's novel, The Years Are So Long, and was convinced it
would make a good picture.   Paramount was so dubious that Mc-
Carey (he made Ruggles of Red Gap) offered to waive his salary
and accept a percentage of the profits instead.

      So Mr. McCarey deserves chief credit for one of the finest
things Hollywood has done this year.   It is a human, absorbing,
comic and pathetic tragi-comedy of an old couple, married fifty
years, who are unable longer to support themselves and are compelled to call upon their children.   Pa Cooper (Victor Moore) is
"adopted" by one daughter; old Lucy (Beulah Bondi) by a married
son; and then their troubles begin.   Not that the children are merciless brutes, or that the parents themselves are without blame.   But
misery is theirs and, after a touching reunion and second honeymoon, the two old people part; forever, we are made to suspect.
                              --Frank S. Nugent in Cinema Arts,
                              Vol. 1, No. 2 (July 1937), page
                              32.

                      *   *   *

      By now, everybody knows this is the "surprise picture of the
year."   By its very unpretentiousness as a production it touches the
heart of everyday American life, exposing the tragedy of circumstance which makes it impossible for people who really love each
other to take care of each other.   The children of the old couple
are shown as decent souls, at bottom, who despise themselves because of the hurt they have to bring to their aged parents.   The
acting at times possesses an almost careless realism: as though
the players for once had abandoned technique, and given themselves
to the screen as people.   The scenes are caught off-guard.   At
moments, as when the young doctor is examining the cantankerous
old man, there is a sense of intrusion into an actual home.   The
doctor even seems to be a poor actor, because he so completely
lacks the polish usually given to such parts.   Credit for all this
must go to Director McCarey, but certain members of the cast go
beyond anything a director could have given them.   Beulah Bondi's
performance as the old lady couldn't be surpassed.   Victor Moore
as the father, and Thomas Mitchell as the worried, helpless son

are way ahead of the usual standard of film acting, but a degree below Beulah Bondi in this.

                                    --Meyer Levin in Esquire, Vol. 8,
                                      No. 2 (August 1937), page 101.

☐ MAN'S CASTLE (Columbia, 1933)

    I've often repeated that high art was not concerned with sub-
ject matter. Here is a simple little genre story of vagabonds living
in a city dump, but acted and directed with such superb artistry
that it becomes a thing of exquisite beauty.

    Spencer Tracy, a bindle stiff, makes a precarious living
parading the streets as a sandwich-man. He picks up Loretta
Young, a drifter, and takes her to his shack down on the Pali-
sades. Here in the shanty city of the down-and-outs they find happiness that Riverside Drivers dream about but seldom achieve.

    Only five characters--Spencer, rough in manners, but gold
inside; Loretta, who reads her man like an open book and loves the
heart of him; Walter Connolly, a night watchman and a Bible nut
who grows flowers in the dump; Arthur Hohl, a sensual-minded bum
"desiring" Loretta; and Marjorie Rambeau, a burnt-out, hard-drinking old prostitute who tries to show Loretta the way of happiness.

    With a charming little story told in simple narrative, Frank
Borzage, one of our best directors, has taken these five characters
and painted a never-to-be-forgotten picture.

    "What a performance!" said Frank Capra, sitting beside me
in the crowded Warner Theatre (the preview section had been pre-
empted by Outlanders!). He was referring at that moment to Spencer Tracy. Loretta Young is altogether convincing, and as for Arthur Hohl, Walter Connolly and Marjorie Rambeau, they give superb
performances. Helen Jerome Eddy makes her bit stand out like a
cameo, and Glenda Farrell vamps as only she can do it.

    No wonder the preview audience gave the picture a long and
enthusiastic hand.

                                    --Rob Wagner in Rob Wagner's
                                      Script, Vol. 10, No. 247 (De-
                                      cember 2, 1933), page 9.

                            *   *   *

    This is the saga of a roughneck you wouldn't put up in your
stable. The horses might complain. That's an idea of how it might
strike the genus homo chancing to hear it. A picture that goes contrary to normal entertainment appetites and tastes, its possibilities
of going places look slender at best.

Spencer Tracy, playing the title role opposite Loretta Young, is cast in his most distasteful role.

The New York censors toyed around with it rather menacingly before it was in shape for approval in the Empire state. Then, even after meeting certain requirements of the scissor brigade, the picture has nothing left that's eligible for recommendation by the local sewing circle or the Y. W. C. A.

In short, it's a story of a worthless mugg who rudely picks up a homeless girl and transports her to a shanty town, where he and other no-goods reside in one fashion or another. The story attempts to justify it all by reformation of the calloused, smart-cracking hero via marriage to the girl when she is about to become a mother. Just to further bring out the character Tracy plays, he attempts a holdup two hours after the hymeneal ceremony has taken place so that he can toss the money in his wife's lap and run away. It's that kind of a character, the kind that develops not the least vestige of sympathy.

Some of the wisecracks Tracy is called upon to read are of the roughest, most inconsiderate kind, in view of the sympathetic understanding and actions of the girl to whom they are delivered. Such things as "shut up or I'll pour that stew down your back" could hardly be accepted as ever leading to true affection, no matter how softened by the tempering of circumstances.

It's that way for Tracy throughout. He leaves on that long-awaited-for freight in the end, with his wife, for some kind of honeymoon. The story forgot that he might have gotten a job after all that had happened or made some honest effort to do anything except fall victim to the haunting whistles of freight train engines. Loretta Young does a noble job as the little girl who stands nearly everything.

Locale is almost entirely in a shanty village, where little more than sheets of tin and some garbage was necessary. The few miniatures employed look phoney.

Marjorie Rambeau, Glenda Farrell, Walter Connolly and Arthur Hohl are in supporting assignment, none of them of more than passing importance, but all well done. Miss Rambeau again plays a drunk.

--Char in Variety, Vol. 113, No.
3 (January 2, 1934), page 13.

☐ THE MARK OF ZORRO (20th Century-Fox, 1940)

This department has small faith in shades, specters and poltergeists. But it will admit to something in the nature of a

"turn" on glimpsing the late Doug Fairbanks in the lobby of Grauman's Chinese, following the preview of the dialogued Mark of Zorro. Busy ruminating how integrally the original had been inter-
twined with Doug's career, then suddenly seeing him through the
theater throng, was a shock. A double-take brought the realization:
The "apparition" was a wax figure of the star that has stood in the
same foyer-spot since the days of The Gaucho.

Well, if Doug had been present at the preview, he would undoubtedly have been enthusiastic about the new version of one of his
pet stories. The new Mark of Zorro has the same reckless, in-
fectious spirit of adventure, the same carefree mood of gallantry
and idealized romance. The 1940 film is quite as successful as was
the Fairbanks vehicle in its day. And no higher praise can be paid.

A great measure of the film's quality must be attributed to
the remarkably fluent direction of Rouben Mamoulian. His touch
lends much of that impudent charm with which he imbued The Gay
Desperado a few seasons back. His collaboration with the cameraman (Arthur Miller) results in an amazingly fresh pictorial treatment of the old days of young Los Angeles, through the medium of
low-key lighting and a literate application of the quick-shot. Mamoulian never bends the knee to formula; each sequence is worked
out in individualistic manner. Individuality is something which Mr.
Zanuck's sponsored handiwork usually lacks. Excluding the John
Ford films, The Mark of Zorro displays more cinematic skill and
art than any motion picture that has been manufactured at the Fox
factory since "Twentieth Century" was added as a prefix and Zanuck
insisted that the same old stories be treated in the same old box-
office manner.

Not that this tale of a New World Robin Hood is not boxoffice. Unless my divining mirror is hopelessly out of kilter, it will
net a fortune, despite an obviously high production budget. A popular film needn't lack freshness, novelty, and imagination. However, when a producer's mind is exclusively on the till, those three
virtues all too frequently fall into desuetude.

John Foote's script has pace and tension, and there is a
persuasive musical score by Alfred Newman. The early transposition of "The Curse of Capistrano" was a bit more bloody and ruthless. While the Zorro of old scarred Z into the foreheads of all
his opponents with his sword's point, today he practically limits his
initial to walls, furniture, and similar inanimate objects. There's
one exception: he rips the letter into the chest of a particularly
heinous scoundrel. The story has been tightened, the sociology
broadened and stressed. All of which doesn't in the least lessen
the impact of the delightful chasings, leapings, and adolescent heroics.

The cast, without exception, lives up to the high production
level. There have been times when Ty Power has lacked definition
and perspective on the screen. As the devil-may-care swordsman

who returns to California from Madrid and sets about righting the
peons' wrongs, Power is emphatic and authoritative.   By day a fop,
by night the free-lance zamindar Zorro; it's really a dual role assignment, and Ty neatly differentiates the antithetical parts.   Linda
Darnell is accurately lovely as the damsel in distress and there is
an excellent performance by J. Edward Bromberg.   Eugene Pallette
as a rotund, peppery padre scores in an assignment that resembles
Friar Tuck.   Basil Rathbone, as the arch-villain, has the chance
to strut, frown, and glare to his heart's content.   It's a major exercise in deep-dyed acting which happens, this time, to fit the period and texture of the story.

　　　　The Mark of Zorro is a movie, in the finest sense of the
word.   See it and have yourself a time.

> --Herb Sterne in Rob Wagner's
> Script, Vol. 24, No. 574 (No-
> vember 9, 1940), page 16.

☐ MAYTIME (M-G-M, 1937)

　　　　With the most glorious musical score yet to be heard on the
screen, Maytime is literally a triumph for all concerned.   Hunt
Stromberg gives it an exquisite production that must have taxed even
the great resources of MGM.   The direction of Robert Z. Leonard
is to be ranked with the best of this fine craftsman's work, and the
technical contributions bespeak a smooth functioning organization.
Both in performances and in voice, Jeanette MacDonald and Nelson
Eddy rise to new heights, with magnificent support headed by the
flawless playing of John Barrymore.   The screenplay by Noel Langley is a beautiful job, making unforgettable this deathless love story.

　　　　And if all of this and more is not tremendous boxoffice, Hollywood might as well stop making motion pictures.   Maytime has
everything to make it a smash attraction of the highest caliber--
powerful name draws, great and beloved music, a haunting story of
a great love, and the finest of productions on all counts.   It is
ticketed for certain record-breaking business.

　　　　The plot is told in flashback, opening in 1905.   It is May
day, and an elderly recluse is moved to tell her story to a young
girl who has quarreled with her beau over pursuing an operatic
career.   The old lady has had a career.   She was Mornay, the
great prima donna, and in 1865 she sang at the court of Louis
Napoleon.

　　　　The scene moves back to this success and the others that
followed.   The star's career has reached its peak and her maestro
proposes marriage as his price of her fame.   In gratitude, she
consents.   Then she meets a young singing student and with him
enjoys a single Maytime afternoon of romance, a romance that must

last her a lifetime, for she feels bound by her bargain.   Their second meeting years later ends in tragedy.

Langley's screenplay is based upon the original play by Rida Johnson Young.   The writing and dialog by Langley are exceptional, not only in projecting a mood but in maintaining it.   Leonard's direction is likewise notable for the mood of the piece.   His sure and steady hand is always apparent.   There is fine sincerity in his work.

It is a temptation to hail a new Jeanette MacDonald, for this is unquestionably her greatest performance.   She portrays an old lady and a breath-takingly beautiful young girl with unprecedented skill.   And her singing surpasses everything she has done before.

Concerning the music, there are many credits and all deserve unstinted praise.   Herbert Stothart served as musical director and adapter, and his original compositions include "Virginia Ham and Eggs," "Vive l'Opera" and a student drinking song, all sung by Nelson Eddy.   Even more noteworthy is the act of an imaginative opera called "Czaritza," based upon Tschaikowsky's Fifth Symphony. It has an amazingly understandable book, and is effectively staged by William von Wymetal, responsible for operatic sequences.   The excellent special lyrics are credited to Bob Wright and Chet Forrest.

Sigmund Romberg, composer of the original Maytime, is represented by the always lovely "Sweetheart" song, "Will You Remember?"   Its melody motivates the entire story.   Among the other music is the Page aria from "Les Huguenots," "Carry Me Back to Ole Virginny," "Episode Patriotique," "Les Filles de Cadiz," and "Santa Lucia."   Snatches of other operas are devised into a montage of success with arrangements by Stothart and photographic effects by Slavko Vorkapich.   Recording throughout betters even the expected high standard of Douglas Shearer.

The acting of Nelson Eddy is distinctly improved and he is in his usual fine voice.   No one but a John Barrymore could have been so impressive as the maestro.   Comedy honors are a walkaway for Herman Bing as a music teacher.   Lynne Carver scores splendidly as the girl of 1905 and Tom Brown is excellent as her suitor.

All the other parts are bits, but standing out are Rafaela Ottiano, Paul Porcasi, Charles Judels, Guy Bates Post and Anna Demetrio.

Photography by Oliver T. Marsh is superior.   To heighten the effect of the romantic sequences a colored filter is used.   Other bows are due the art direction of Cedric Gibbons, and his associates, Fredric Hope and Edwin B. Willis; the gowns by Adrian; the dances staged by Val Raset; and the film editing by Conrad A. Nervig.

--The Hollywood Reporter, Vol.
38, No. 13 (March 4, 1937),
page 3.

☐ THE MERRY WIDOW (M-G-M, 1934)

A Lubitsch production always marks the high point in Hollywood's yearly schedule. And once again he has held that position. The Merry Widow is dated in costume and humor--and somewhat in music--but our greatest director of sophisticated comedy has brought it to life with a gorgeous bang.

Handicapped as she was by the flounces and bustles of the '80's, Jeanette MacDonald nevertheless looked more beautiful than ever, and sang with greater spirit (except in the train sequence in Monte Carlo, which still stands as an all-time high).

Maurice Chevalier, again the Smiling Lieutenant, seems destined always to enact the Parisian playboy, yet he is the only one who can do so without the slightest offense. And even though he can't sing for sour apples, his personal charm compensates, and he once more teams up with Miss MacDonald in delicious love-making.

Next to Lubitsch, the greatest credit must go to Ernest Vajda and Samson Raphaelson for the scintillating new humor of the grand old opera, handed fortunately to a superb bunch of comedians--Edward Everett Horton, Una Merkel and George Barbier. Even the lesser roles of Minna Gombell, Sterling Holloway, Herman Bing, Donald Meek and Ruth Channing were handled in the exquisitely restrained but hilariously amusing Lubitsch manner.

While the music is glorious, I felt the need of a singing partner for Miss MacDonald. But for the dancing (Albertina Rasch) I have nothing but cheers. The Merry Widow waltz which swept the immense floor of the palace was a triumph of beauty and good taste. It was also a delightful relief from the geometrical "big production" numbers of our usual musicals in which shapely gals attitudinize but do darned little dancing.

Cedric Gibbons has designed many notable sets, but this was the first time I heard a preview audience applaud one.

Needless to say, Oliver Marsh's camera work is perfect, as is the sound recording of Douglas Shearer.

> --Rob Wagner in Rob Wagner's
> Script, Vol. 12, No. 295 (December 1, 1934), page 10.

*   *   *

I'll bet Mr. Ernst Lubitsch could bake an angel food cake in the middle of a U.S. Steel plant. I mean, I can't imagine how any man can produce such finespun humor and such exquisite beauty among the gargantuan confusion and under the cruel pressure of one of the monster picture mills. The man must have the soul of a Fritz Kreisler and the hide of a U.S. marine sergeant.

Maybe you ought to pass me my bib, but I think The Merry
Widow is the best picture I've ever seen.   It could easily have been
(aside from the music) the most boresome thing in the world.   Any
revival of an oldtime costume operetta could be.   And I confess I
went a little braced, having forgotten Mr. Lubitsch's knack of making the dead not only walk but trip a delightfully light fantastic.   He
has wisely canned the story of the old stage Widow completely and
had the boys cook up a new one more to his own notion.   And with
the burden on his shoulders of spending $1,500,000 he is as irre-
sponsible as a bird in a tree and as effervescent as a glass of
champagne.   Everybody within megaphone distance seems to catch
his spirit; he makes consummate artists out of even the most numy
of his supernumeraries; why, he is the first man in Hollywood to
make Sterling Holloway get a haircut.   He touches each incident
with the fluffiest playfulness and daubs the whole with a gorgeous
beauty.   He can tell his leading woman how to hold her little finger
or direct the sway of a ballroom full of extras ... just right.   He
is eloquent with doorknobs, and makes even a hardwood floor voice
his art.

As for Chevalier, no other living man could carry with such
grace and conviction the absurd role of egotist and large-scale
boudoirist he is asked to play as Danilo in The Merry Widow, and
Jeanette MacDonald is beyond compare among the singing stars.
                                        --Don Herold in Life, Vol. 101,
                                            No. 2597 (December 1934), page
                                            34.

☐ A MIDSUMMER NIGHT'S DREAM (Warner Bros. , 1935)

For some time the shy clarions of Warner's publicity department have intimated that the costly teaming of the Bard of Avon and
the Wizard of Salzburg has produced the screen's Divine Comedy.
Whether true or not, and despite such lush honkings, the studio
which gave the screen its voice has now endowed it handsomely with
its first poetic spectacle.

For those who had expected the worst, let it be said at once
that Shakespeare has not suffered in the slightest.   As a matter of
fact, Max Reinhardt's A Midsummer Night's Dream would have been
an infinitely better motion picture if Shakespeare had contributed
less to it.

Considered cinematically, his diffuse fantasy provided too
much scenario.   In this respect the Dream is an unfortunate choice
for the first major film Shakespeare.   Unfortunately, too, the creative camera is much more persuasive and varied in its effects than
audible poetry.   Since the Dream contains little cerebral action, no
subtle emotion that can be projected in pantomime, we have actors
stopping in their tracks, brought to the audience in close-ups, and

then struggling desperately to utter poetry in a manner faintly commensurate with their four-figure salaries.

I feel certain that valiant efforts must have been made by William Dieterle to put life into these static spoken interludes. I feel equally certain that even trained Shakespearean actors could not have accomplished the superhuman task of battling the genius of the camera. When speech is absent and the beautiful, soundly contrived Mendelssohn-Korngold score paraphrases the Reinhardt spectacle, we get rapid movement, thrusts of imagination and sometimes sheer loveliness. But the constant contrast of this with the spasmodic progress of the plot and the grappling with the spoken word serves largely as an irritant.

At least it did with me. Put it down as a prejudice, if you like. It may seem ironic, but to me Shakespeare's lines meet with too much competition on the screen and often come off badly. The stage found that out, too (I think some will agree) when Robert Edmond Jones, Norman Bel Geddes and others, overwhelmed the plays with their very intelligent and possibly misguided productions.

There remains mention of the sociological factor, before tossing out the bouquets. A Midsummer Night's Dream should reach millions of folk who know Shakespeare only through textbooks or hearsay. With this production Hollywood may show them the poet's humanity and emphasize the entertainment he provides. In this sense the Dream is probably front-page news, like Social Security, and the Warners, who have emptied their jeans magnificently, may go down in history as the New Dealers of the motion picture. Time and the box office will tell. What I most fear is that critics and public alike may be stampeded into the belief that a spectacular and well-intentioned picture is the apotheosis of all film achievement. Quite contrariwise, this observer feels that the screen will find its greatest inspiration from within itself and not from classical sources.

The most impressive performance in the Dream was delivered by James Cagney, who made Bottom poignant in his transformation and soundly farcical at other times. The comedy antics of Joe E. Brown, Frank McHugh, Hugh Herbert and Otis Harlan are bound to be popular. Ian Hunter's brief role was artistically right and Victor Jory's Oberon a creature of splendid poise and power, marred visually by too much lipstick. Grant Mitchell was effective as Egeus but Mickey Rooney's Puck was florid and overloud, obviously a fault of direction. Pictorially Nina Theilade's evanescent dance was the high point of the film--a camera gem. And closely seconding it, Oberon's majestic departure, the extravagant billowing of his black mantle, a fantasy in itself.

Hal Mohr must be saluted for his photography, Max Ree for his costumes, Anton Grot for art direction. Leo Forbstein executed the intricate musical score perfectly, though someone forgot to do something about Anita Louise's voice.

Opinion must be divided about the relative responsibility shouldered by Reinhardt and Dieterle in filming their collaborative show.   But I think it would be nice, for once, to laud the producer who brought all these people together, who gave them carte blanche and the cash to create a Warner triumph.

--Richard Sheridan Ames in Rob Wagner's Script, Vol. 14, No. 337 (October 19, 1935), page 10.

                              *   *   *

Shakespeare is, of course, essentially a bore.   Now, wait a minute.   Give me a vol. of Shakespeare and a hammock, and I get something.   I like it (though I'll confess you don't catch me that way oftener than about twice in a lifetime--when I can't find my current Photoplay).   Give me Shakespeare and actors (who maybe mumble half the words) and I'm bored.

This goes for Warner Bros.' A Midsummer Night's Dream.

Most of the photography is excruciatingly beautiful.   The whole picture is surprisingly fine.   When, in advance, you scan that line-up of Warner Bros.' low comedians, tough guys and blonde ingenues, you expect queer things when they take on Shakespeare. But, under Max Reinhardt's spell you get something miraculously fine and lovely.   You get a lot of pleasant shocks; you get, for instance, Dick Powell reading Shakespeare about as well as anybody you ever heard trying it.   You get excellent performances out of Ian Hunter, Grant Mitchell, Frank McHugh, Olivia de Havilland, Jean Muir, James Cagney, Victor Jory and, believe it or not, Joe E. Brown.   Eventually, however, you get sleepy.   And I blame Shakespeare for this, rather than Warner Bros.   Shakespeare is not right for a wide-awake evening in the modern cinema.   And the show is damnably long.

Perhaps it might be better if we went to this in a recital or concert mood, rather than in a movie mood.   But then I'm afraid we might find fault with what is known as the sound.   A sound track is not a symphony orchestra and does not intoxicate as such.   The Mendelssohn-Warner music has an inevitable kitchen-ware quality, especially noticeable during the overture, as you sit there looking at an illuminated blank curtain.

But anybody who can take about two-and-a-half hours of luscious photography, thoroughly intelligent direction, and gorgeous production of Shakespeare will have a good time at this M. N.'s D. Being Shakespeare, its plot does not gnaw at your vitals, and the humor is entirely of another age.   The surprise is, that the thing is so gratifyingly un-Hollywood.   In only a few spots does it go picture-postcardy.

--Don Herold in Life, Vol. 102, No. 2609 (December 1935), page 22.

☐ MR. DEEDS GOES TO TOWN (Columbia, 1936)

Just another of those cinematic masterpieces we have been
led to expect from Frank Capra when given a script he and Robert
Riskin have put on paper. I regret that Frank in each production
is showing a more marked trend toward dialogue as his medium of
expression. Mr. Deeds Goes to Town is definitely a talkie, but it
is a brilliant one and capital entertainment. It is notable, however, that its outstanding scenes get their strength from the camera.

When Gary Cooper, a small-town boy, is informed he has
inherited twenty million dollars, he keeps on playing his tuba; and
we see him again playing his beloved instrument in the village band
which has marched to the depot to bid him farewell as he leaves
for New York to take possession of his fortune. In perhaps a
dozen other places in the picture the camera steps to the front for
brief moments to take possession of the story, and in such scenes
Capra's direction is so effective it makes one regret that the burden
had not been shifted more often from dialogue to photography.

The story is a deeply human one with a sound psychological
basis. That is its strength. Superficially it is almost farcical,
highly hilarious scenes following one another in quick succession,
but underneath it all is a serious thought. A decent, clear-thinking,
unspoiled and experienced young American is taken from the quiet
of the village in which he was born, given great riches, and thrown
among the wolves and jackals who lurk in cities and hunt in packs.
In this instance the chase is not successful, as the young fellow has
a philosophy of his own, an elemental conception of right and wrong
which carries him through to final triumph.

Some inspired touches make Capra's direction a rare treat
to the beholder. There is a love scene on the steps of a house on
a foggy night, the setting being unattractive, totally lacking in romantic significance, yet for tenderness, beauty and emotional value
Cooper's avowal of love for Jean Arthur takes its place among the
great moments in motion pictures. I am sorry, however, that
Capra and Riskin saw fit so quickly to change the picture's mood
by showing Gary running out of the scene and falling over obstacles
in the street. It was not a place for laughs. It was all right to
have Gary beat a retreat, an action consistent with his character,
but as the atmosphere created by the scene had been one pleasant
for the audience to linger in, Mack Sennett technique should not
have been resorted to to take it rudely out of it.

But the production is too rich in virtues to be harmed greatly by a couple of minor faults. It is a credit to all those who had
a part in its making. Columbia spared no expense in giving it an
appropriate setting, Stephen Goossen's art direction being in every
way commendable. Joseph Walker's photography is excellent, some
night shots being particularly effective.

In no department is Capra's direction greater than it is revealed in the performances of all the members of the long cast.
One easily can understand why even our most prominent players are
eager to appear in a Capra picture.   Frank allows his people to be
natural.   There never is any acting in front of the camera when he
is standing behind it.   I have liked Gary Cooper every time I have
seen him on the screen.   His lack of stage training is the strength
of his picture performances.   Under Capra's sympathetic handling
he appears to better advantage than ever before.   His performance
is brilliant.

It was quite early in the life of the Spectator that from time
to time it had things in it about an ambitious girl who wanted to get
somewhere on the screen.   Every time I reviewed a picture in
which Jean Arthur appeared I wrote again that she had a future.
In Deeds she makes good all the pleasant things I said about her,
but it is Hollywood's fault, not hers, that it took so long for my
prophecies to come true.   She is an admirable little actress.

George Bancroft surprised me with the excellence of his performance.   When he was starring for Paramount he became quite
hammy, acting all over the place at the slightest opportunity.   In
Deeds he gives a really intelligent performance.   I see no reason
why he should not become a box-office asset again.   I am sorry
Lionel Stander has such an unpleasant voice.   I like him as an actor and can stand a little of his talking, but too much of it makes
his voice get on my nerves.

Douglass Dumbrille is an effective heavy.   One of the finest
scenes in the picture is a bit of acting done by John Wray, the
only scene which drew applause from all sections of the big preview audience.   H. B. Warner, Jameson Thomas, Gustav von Sey-
fertitz, Raymond Walburn--but if I keep on naming those who add
strength to the picture, I merely will reproduce the list you will
find at the head of this review.

By all means see Mr. Deeds Goes to Town.   It is entitled
to a place on your list of those you must not miss.
                                        --Welford Beaton in Hollywood
                                          Spectator, Vol. 11, No. 1
                                          (April 11, 1936), pages 19 and
                                          21.

                              *   *   *

When two artists like Frank Capra and Robert Riskin get together they don't need a great story.   This one of Clarence Bud-
dington Kelland is of the country lad suddenly inheriting
$20,000,000, going to the big city, being made a monkey of by a
gal reporter who learns to love him, and then tries to square off
her tabloid dastardies.   Kelland's one original gag is having the
boy tried on an insanity charge.   But what Capra and Riskin have
done with that material!   Grand comedy, wonderful characterization,

and a joyous spirit that builds and builds to the most original, dramatic and at the same time hilarious trial scene ever enacted.

Gary Cooper was not exactly the type for the hick role of Longfellow Deeds--more a Jack Oakie part--but he plays it with fine understanding and great skill. Jean Arthur--she of the deep rich voice--as the sobsister stands right up with Gary. They play a love scene in the rain that is the last word in tender beauty. George Bancroft does a city editor right. Lionel Stander knows dialogue timing as Charlie Chaplin knows pantomime. He never misses a syllable. Douglass Dumbrille is meaner than most meanies because he doesn't sneer and meanie all over the place.

And what a sense of comedy has Raymond Walburn, so gentle and dumb as Gary's valet. H. B. Warner makes a perfect judge, serious with a just perceptible sense of humor. Too many excellent performances to credit all.

Gags, direction and amazingly beautiful photography--and sets--that makes this a big picture. Night and fog effects suggest Whistler. If Grant's Tomb was a process shot, hats off to the processor.

At the finish of the preview at Carthay Circle, everybody in the audience was "pixilated," and you'll learn what pixilated means when you see the picture.

You'll also realize what Frank Capra learned in my art class--or perhaps it was my wrestling class.
                    --Rob Wagner in Rob Wagner's
                      Script, Vol. 15, No. 363 (April
                      25, 1936), page 12.

☐ MR. SMITH GOES TO WASHINGTON (Columbia, 1939)

Frank Capra is not a director from whom we expect the unexpected. In advance, just the title, Mr. Smith Goes to Washington, and the fact that Capra was to direct, were sufficient to make almost anyone predict success. Mr. Smith therefore, is neither a surprise nor a disappointment. It is Capra at his very best, which is incomparable.

While the political and patriotic theme may be more significant than the stories of other Capra films, I'm perhaps the only reviewer who wasn't flattened by Mr. Smith's oratory in the Senate chamber. He talked a lot of common sense, and it goes without saying that all of us should appreciate our liberties, but I doubt whether we needed Frank Capra and James Stewart to tell us just that. Rather, I admired a perfect example of resolute screen showmanship, the director's skill and resourceful use of his personal

idiom, his masterful handling of his actors, and the complete veracity of the Washington and Senate backgrounds.

Other directors might have given us a film equally dramatic,
quite as funny, possibly as stirring and poignant.   But they couldn't
have combined these elements as Capra does, with such apparent
effortlessness and spontaneity.   He has a genius for making the
short scene or the brief moment memorable.   He explores a situation thoroughly, permits a leading character to talk interminably,
yet none of his sequences ever sag, and he has never been guilty
of boring an audience.

Caring nothing about formal structure or integration, Capra's
films are loosely constructed and tangential, yet the material never
gets out of hand.   Mr. Smith has the inevitable flow of a river following its irregular course; sometimes turbulent, sometimes calm,
sometimes fast, sometimes slow, but always moving toward its pre-
destined, climactic meeting with the sea.

The climax of Mr. Smith, which must be one of the longest
sequences ever filmed--devoted to but one event and dominated by a
single actor--has a maligned and persecuted junior Senator filibust-
ering on behalf of his political life, honesty in government, and the
democratic ideal.   It is to Capra's credit, and to Mr. Stewart's,
that together they make this oratorical torrent--which has little
physical action--as exciting, as compelling as any of the screen's
notable pictorial achievements.   Its mounting intensity and almost
unbearable suspense stir the emotions as violently as the great natural disasters, the swarming of the locusts in The Good Earth,
the tempests and hurricanes, the battles and migrations which have
made motion-picture history.

Yet there is no spectacle.   While Senators yawn, an earnest
and awkward young man stalls for time, grows hoarse, becomes
disheveled, as he gives passionate utterance to his belief in human
decency, equality, and American ideals.   At this point one was not
conscious of the plot or the cameras or the actor: only the words
and their implications mattered.   In one respect, at least, Mr.
Smith Goes to Washington is unique in screen history: its long-to-
be-remembered thrill is a speech!

The circumstances which send Mr. Stewart to the capital are
not typical of all American political life, but neither is this instance
far-fetched.   Possibly the villains of the piece are a shade too ruthless in their methods and shocking lack of conscience, and Jean
Arthur a bit too wonderful as the Machiavellian secretary--although
smart women are notoriously powerful in Washington--but why not
charitably blame any distortions of truth on dramatic license?
Claude Rains is artificial in an artificial part, which goes for Edward Arnold, too.   Harry Carey is completely natural as the Senate's presiding officer, and so is Thomas Mitchell as a cynical reporter.   Jean Arthur's pliant personality has never been more attractive, which is saying much; and while I can't follow the crowd

in proclaiming the Stewart performance of Academy Award caliber,
hereafter I'll associate him with Mr. Smith although the familiar
mannerisms and excessive histrionic understatement were as much
in evidence as ever.   Mr. Stewart is so natural that he gets hysterical about it, but since this story makes provision for that and
the Academy vote has never been discerning, he probably has a
statuette in the bag.

       Mr. Capra has another sensational hit, democracy a popular
advocate, and my! how Washington has learned to act! I think the
Lincoln Memorial almost steals the picture, but so effective was
the photography that I'd have relished a camera-tour of the entire
city.

                              --Richard Sheridan Ames in Rob
                              Wagner's Script, Vol. 22, No.
                              527 (October 28, 1939), page
                              16.

                        *   *   *

       A picture of which politicians disapprove is not by that token
necessarily a good one, but the rumpus stirred up by Mr. Smith
Goes to Washington convinces me that the elements of importance I
see in it are really there.   Moving pictures, even those rare ones
which deal with the serious problems of democratic government,
generally are not considered worthy of senatorial attention.   Their
inaccuracies are dismissed with the graceful shrug reserved for
"entertainment."   Therefore when Mr. Smith succeeds in evoking
the capital's ire, we may safely assume that something more than
mere entertainment is involved, that the picture has touched a sore
spot, that, perhaps, it has even touched the truth.

       The truth partially delineated in Frank Capra's new film is
so obviously true that it is hard to understand why astute vote-
getters rush into print to deny it.   Political chicanery at some
time or another touches the life of every citizen; from his own experience he knows as much as this picture tells, and more, of the
operations of the machine bosses and their paid stooges.   So when
senators tell him that the film is a libel, my guess is that he will
stamp them fools or knaves or both, if indeed he has not already
done so.   It is in any case clear that official Washington's disap-
proval of Mr. Smith will have no effect on the picture's box-office
appeal except to enhance it.   The film grossed the phenomenal sum
of $110,000 in its first week at Radio City Music Hall, and will
probably repeat this record on a lesser scale throughout the nation's
cinemas.

       Though we laugh out of court the Senate's objections to its
photographic portrait, the new film has other detractors with a different base for their objections.   They are concerned for the artistic future of an admired director who seems to be repeating the
formula of his greatest success, Mr. Deeds Goes to Town.   No
question but that Mr. Deeds and Mr. Smith are one and the same

person. Both are young idealists who attack the citadels of corrup-
tion and triumph by force of sincerity alone. But the similarity is
so open that it seems intended, and I wonder if the plot structure
of the two pictures can be dismissed as a formula. It seems more
like an idea, a viewpoint, an avenue approach to those aspects of
the American scene with which Capra is deeply concerned. Here is
a man who has the faculty of interesting audiences in almost anything he chooses to show them but who persistently returns to one
set of circumstances which he peoples with essentially the same
characters every time. It looks as though Capra feels he has
something very important to say about these people. Whether or
not we eventually agree with him about their importance, it seems
imperative to examine closely an idea into which so much creative
energy has been poured.

The scene he sets in Mr. Smith is a familiar one--political
Washington, where silver-haired senators proclaim their independ-
ence of spirit and devotion to duty while tacitly following the orders
of the man back home who controls the votes. On the sidelines are
equally typical characters, a senatorial secretary and a political
reporter; they are not exactly corrupt, but they have had to acquire
a sort of protective cynicism in order to survive in a world governed by gangster morality. So far the picture is notably real, a
naturalistic portrait of the surface of modern life superbly acted by
Claude Rains, Edward Arnold, Jean Arthur, Guy Kibbee, Ruth Don-
nelly, Thomas Mitchell, the old standbys who lend Capra the veri-
similitude he needs. The first doubtful note is the appearance of
Mr. Smith himself. Would a naive leader of Boy Rangers ever get
a Senate seat? No, shout the scoffers, but Capra tells us it's all
an amusing accident, and certainly what happens to the boy is believable enough. He is duped by his political superiors and taken
for a ride by tooth-and-claw reporters out for a sensation at any
cost. This is his natural fate, and it enables Capra to point out
with cruel, ineluctable accuracy that Washington would make a
Zioncheck out of the sanest of us. Actually, the picture should
have ended with Mr. Smith discredited, made a fool of, relegated
to the lunatic fringe of politics. Had it done so it would have been
the truest and most devastating analysis of representative government yet on record.

But Mr. Smith triumphs, of course. He persists in the face
of criminal calumny, stages a filibuster to end filibusters, and
eventually so moves his opponents that they come over to his side.
We're left with the implication that all will be right with America
now. Now this conclusion, though wholly unbelievable, is important
just because it couldn't happen. In the middle of his picture, Capra,
as he always does, shifts from a portrayal of objective reality to
that of psychological reality. The obvious wish-fulfilment of the
ending is much more than a movie evasion of the truth. It is a
precise representation of the viewpoint of the average voter, a man
often forgotten by those of us who like thoughtful realism, but whom
Capra never forgets because they think alike. Both of these interesting people, the director and his sympathetic auditor, believe pas-

sionately in the American way of life and government.   Since the
depression, they have been forced to realize that something is
wrong somewhere.   But since, by hypothesis, the system itself is
right, then the trouble must be with the way it is managed.   Many
films of the past ten years (not to mention other channels of mass
opinion) have revealed the bitter conviction of everyday people that
they are being betrayed by the "men higher up" whom they have
entrusted with the reins of power.   And they are forced by their
own logic to conclude that the only way to set things right again is
to replace the corrupt leaders with idealists who, magically, will
retain their ideals in the face of the world, the flesh, and the devil.

      This thesis, expounded in Mr. Deeds Goes to Town, is ap-
plied to politics in the new Capra film.   Its significance, it seems
to me, lies not in its truth or falsity but in its persistence as an
idea and its popularity with audiences.   Individual idealism is no
solution for any practical problem, but it is the totem people worship when every other way out cuts across their thinking habits.
A film which embodies this phenomenon enjoys, to my mind, an
importance beyond itself.   It is to be evaluated less as a mirror
of life than as a document of human psychology, an index to the
temper of the popular mind.   Mr. Smith Goes to Washington is
such a film, and the classic example of its type.

--Richard Griffith in National
Board of Review Magazine, Vol.
14, No. 8 (November 1939),
pages 13-15.

☐ MODERN TIMES (Chaplin/United Artists, 1936)

      I once asked Charlie why he insisted on going ahead with
"silents" when all the world had gone talkie.   "For years I worked
in pantomime right alongside of the spoken drama, and many people
found it acceptable," he answered.   "It's a distinct art, and I like
it."   He might have added that it is also the one art understood by
every son of man.   And Charlie addresses a world audience.

      Talkies have been with us five years now and one wondered
if straight pantomime would still go over.   It does.   In fact I was
surprised how little one missed the spoken word in the face of perfect pantomimic action.   True, the action is fortified by sound, and
Charlie's sound effects and music are nothing less than superb.
The love motif, a wistful call to his mate, is exquisitely beautiful,
and the way he has gently interpolated "How Drunk I Am" in alcoholic sequences and "Hallelujah I'm a Bum!" into the mob scenes
is a triumph of musical accompaniment and recording.

      Charlie's pictures are always "proletarian" in their import,
so that one can read into them anything one wishes.   But the widely
advertised propaganda in this picture limits itself to the picture of

a frail little man's conflict with the Machine Age.   And his old
classical theme of Jack-the-Giant-Killer.   The boy-man up against
the monsters (cops) of authority.

For the rest, the laughs are from grand gags well done.

Yes, for the first time you'll hear the Chaplin voice.   As a
singing waiter.   He forgets the words he has learned so he substitutes a faked French song that he puts over by his inimitable pantomime.   He also proves that if he ever does speak, he will do so
in a voice that will hold his audience.

After reading the sneak-preview critiques I was not prepared
for the fine spirited performance of Paulette Goddard.   She has a
beautiful body, an intelligent face and she registers like a sharply-
cut diamond.   True, she seemed a bit high-strung, but this is her
first picture.   Besides this alert nervousness suited her character.
Best of all, she uses absolutely no make-up, which permitted her
to run the whole gamut of facial pantomime.   Altogether she makes
a fine start toward her goal.   Of course she had the greatest coach
in the world.   No wonder Marlene Dietrich expressed envy for her
opportunity.

I do think, however, that Charlie's greatest foil was Edna
Purviance (who, by the way, attended the preview and was just as
pretty as ever).   For Edna had a gentle, sweet calm and a mother-
liness that all womankind feels for "the little waif of the screen."

Charlie faces one big handicap these days.   He makes so few
pictures that each new one becomes an international event.   With
the result that everybody expects him to burst forth with something
tremendously significant, or at least mark a new and important
milestone in the art of the cinema.   But he prefers to go on in the
same Chaplin tradition of simply making an amusing picture of gentle satire and hilarious gags.   Personally I hope he never changes.
He has created a classical character that has swept the world.
That's enough for the first life time of any great artist.

This picture is in his best tradition, backed by the best musical accompaniment--his own!--that has come to the screen.   He
still holds the title of the world's greatest pantomimist.
                              --Rob Wagner in Rob Wagner's
                                Script, Vol. 15, No. 353 (Feb-
                                ruary 15, 1936), page 10.

*   *   *

Charlie Chaplin still walks funny.

His Modern Times is merely an elaboration of the old joke
about the man in the Ford production line who laid down his wrench
to scratch his ear and threw the whole factory out of gear, but
Chaplin still walks funny.   Modern Times is a funny picture, a

terribly funny picture, but its ingenuities are simply the ingenuities at which many in Hollywood are adept, many including Laurel and Hardy and Harold Lloyd and the Marxes and 100 gag men. It is not a great picture. It is not a profound, significant picture.

The one great thing about it is Charlie Chaplin.

And, at that, there is a great deal of bunk about Chaplin-- not in Chaplin, but around and about Chaplin. He is not (that is, not in his pictures) a deep, searching, penetrating philosopher or a subtle sociological observer and satirist. His calling his picture Modern Times and his inclusion of a lot of complicated Joe Cook machinery and Goldbergian gadgets, and alternate shots of people in a subway and sheep in a runway, do not make him one of our great sociological cynics. The observation that people are sheep is not new or deep.

But the fact remains that though Charlie Chaplin is often just a clown, he is oftener a great artist and a master pantomim- ist. The smartest comment ever made on Charlie Chaplin was ut- tered by M. M. Warburg, director of the American ballet: "After all, the greatest ballet dancer this country has produced--one of the world's greatest--is Charlie Chaplin."

Many critics have raved some pretty banal stuff about Chap- lin's profundity. Well, he may be as profound as the devil over a bottle of Scotch, but I maintain that Modern Times is simply a suc- cession of swell gags with overtones of ballet--not overtones of technocracy or undertones of any other ocracy. Chaplin is not only a genius, but he is practical showman and business man enough to keep his pictures on a pure clowning basis.

One time in Los Angeles, between chukkers of a tennis tour- nament, my attention was caught by a man on the fringe of the crowd under the stands, a man looking into time and space with the lonesomest, saddest, deepest eyes I've ever seen--an isolated think- er in a crowd of silly, buzzing picture people. I finally realized that this was Chaplin, and I knew that I'd love the guy, that I'd like to sit and cry gloriously far into the night with him about the ugh and phooey of man.

But that Chaplin and the Chaplin of Modern Times are two people, and I am a little impatient with many motion picture writers who try to make them the same.

The authorship and conception of Modern Times are super- ficial and commercial. The picture itself is little more than a suc- cession of robust belly laughs, and some of them pretty old. Chap- lin steps on a loose board with a brick on one end, and unconscious- ly socks a cop with the brick--that's a fair sample.

But Charlie Chaplin still walks funny--as funny as all get out--he dances--he capers--he frolics--he rises in elation and falls

in abject despair--and it all adds up into humorous beauty, into ballet art at its highest and best.

--Don Herold in Life, Vol. 103,
No. 2613 (April 1936), page 20.

☐ MONKEY BUSINESS (Paramount, 1931)

Had Ye Ed exhibited only his well-known half-wit, he would
have had this picture reviewed by Drs. Edward Huntington Williams
and Cecil Reynolds sitting en bloc, for only two great psychiatrists
could possibly sort out any rhyme, let alone reason, from this latest madness of the Four Shining Marx.

In Transatlantic, most of the passengers were unaware of the
drama going on right under their noses, but aboard the good ship
Hoosgow, everybody from director to cabin boys went violently insane. When the story--if any--opens, the four famous coca nuts
are disguised as kippered herrings, and from that moment on, when
they are not kipping the gals they are herring the crew. From
binnacle to bilge, up and down through the booby hatches, they pur-
sue their mad careers, acting the way they do because God loves
the Irish, and because, no matter how thin a pane of glass, you can
always break it with a hammer.

You don't get that. I thought so. It's because you don't
know how to measure the speed of a ship in knots. Nots that it
matters, for nothing matters when Thelma Todd is present in per-
sona au gratin. Yes, even Thelma is addicted to foolish powders,
and when Groucho begins his "attack," she wrestles him into a
rumba. Overcome by the proximity of her gorgeous beauty, Groucho
suddenly goes completely haywire and sits her down on her bumba.

Thus for seven reels the insanity keeps up, with the audience
howling its head off at the mental collapse of five proud dementia
precocks.

--Rob Wagner in Rob Wagner's
Script, Vol. 6, No. 144 (November 14, 1931), page 8.

*   *   *

Messrs. Marx, Marx, Marx & Marx in another outbreak of
assorted lunacy. It has no beginning and no end, as far as any
real plot is concerned--but if you're of that group who like gorgeous
nonsense, then by all means split your sides over the latest Marx-
ian antics as herein manifested. Groucho's absurdities rattle off
his tongue; Harpo is silent but mad; the other two are Marxes, too.

--Photoplay, Vol. 40, No. 5
(October 1931), page 51.

☐ MORNING GLORY (RKO, 1933)

So perfectly does the role of Eve Lovelace fit Katharine Hepburn that you'll believe it is her own life's story.   If it isn't, it might just as well have been, for this strange young lady has one of the most decisive personalities of the screen--more decisive in some ways than Garbo's--and she enacts a character that you'll never forget.

Eve is a stage-struck country girl from Vermont who is regarded as just another nut by the sophisticates of New York, but her superb belief in her own genius permits her to handle all kiddings and every test.

The story is too good to spoil by telling here, but I think you'll agree that, excepting for one or two holes, it is exceptionally creditable to Zoë Akins who wrote it and Howard Green who adapted it.

Adolphe Menjou must have liked his role because he plays it with rare understanding and sympathy.   Young Doug Fairbanks, who has been cruelly crucified in a series of tripe roles, proves that he is just about the best juvenile of the screen.   Mary Duncan as a big dramatic star overplays her sniffiness in the earlier sequences but rises to fine dramatic heights in the big scenes.   C. Aubrey Smith lends his gentle and polished artistry to a delightful role. Even the lesser characters interpreted by Fred Santley, Richard Carle, Don Alvarado, Tyler Brooke and Geneva Mitchell are all excellently done.

The art direction of Van Nest Polglase and Charles Kirk and the camera work of Bert Glennon are of the same high standard.

Finally, Lowell Sherman should be given some sort of Academy award for his direction, which is superb.

As fine as is the whole production, Miss Hepburn will leave the strongest impression in your heart and mind.
--Rob Wagner in Rob Wagner's
Script, Vol. 10, No. 234
(September 2, 1933), pages 9-10.

*   *   *

Followers of Katharine Hepburn should find this a complete evening of what they like.   It's Katharine at her superb best--and not much else--from beginning to end.

The story has to do with a naive but ambitious girl from Vermont who's determined to get ahead on the New York stage. Right at the start comes something that nobody but a Hepburn could handle--an immensely long monologue, in which she talks the arm

off everybody she meets.   But thanks to Hepburn art, she makes
you like it.

The rest of it is carried in pretty much the same way, with
Doug Fairbanks, Jr. giving one of his best performances, as the
young playwright willing to cast her, and Adolphe Menjou as a producer of mixed motives and morals.   Mary Duncan good, too--but
it's Katharine's show.
                                        --Photoplay, Vol. 44, No. 5
                                         (October 1933), page 56.

☐ MUTINY ON THE BOUNTY (M-G-M, 1935)

If you like your roast beef rare, cut thick, with lots of
gravy, this is your meat.   If you are fed up on Pollyanna and too
much jollity, you may relish two hours of sadistic brutality.   But
there is the danger that always accompanies tremendous exploitation; M. G. M. may have oversold the picture, and your expectations
will be too demanding.   According to the superlative ballyhoo, Leo
considers this "the biggest picture ever filmed." Undoubtedly it is
big; but to this critic, who is more susceptible to beauty than
blurbs, it is not a great picture.   The Informer, one quarter its
size, is four times as convincing.

Knowing the producer, director and most of the cast and
crew, and also knowing the heartaches that lurk in every picture,
I arrived at this conclusion reluctantly.   For these reasons.   While
the building of the ship is no doubt authentic, its handling is absurd,
and the storm itself ridiculously terrifying.   Sailing vessels running into heavy weather, leave up only enough canvas to give the
vessel steering way.   In the case of a typhoon, the hatches will be
battened down and the ship allowed to run before the storm under
bare sticks, which alone often gives it steering way.

Even on a steamer plunging ahead under 40,000 horse power,
not every wave breaks over the bow.   About one in four, when the
ship and wave happen to synchronize just right.   After a terrific
storm in the China Seas, the captain told me that he had "seen
green water" four times.   In other words, only four waves had
struck the ship hard enough to show green water as high as the
bridge.

But these movie storms!   Everybody on deck running hither
and thither; waves breaking continuously, with the decks awash from
stem to stern; and always the ship driving into the storm.   Where
do they get the power?   Even with auxilliary engines--which the old
sailing vessels didn't have--they'd have to comeabout and ride with
the storm.

And when a movie ship goes on the rocks--"Shoot the works,
boys!"   Yes, even I have seen a ship on the rocks, and it did not

come down like a box of matches. It took several days to do what the technical staff accomplishes in five minutes.

Perhaps this is carping criticism, but there are lots and lots of people who know the sea. So why be so utterly foolish about it?

I read the exploitation stuff about the hundred tons of equipment taken to the South Seas including safety-pins, fly swatters, Bibles, old coins, a hot-water bottle, a bottle of blood (!), a toy sewing machine and a harpoon gun. I was not impressed. The Tahiti shots of natives coming out in out-rigger canoes is old stuff. Any "library" could have furnished them with hundreds of feet. (Which would have saved the expense of shipping safety pins 4000 miles.)

The Tahiti stuff ashore was completely "Hollywood"--beautiful gals in immaculate smocks with wreaths of love-flowers on their heads, boys climbing after cocoanuts and the inevitable swimming gag, sirens and sailors diving out of bosky glens into the pool on Stage 4.

And speaking of cleanliness, you should note the snowy whiteness of Clark Gable's and Franchot Tone's shirts and pants after months and months at sea and ashore. Even after their bloody brawls. Must have had a steam laundry and mending machines aboard.

No, as big and ambitious as this picture is, it is a monotonous narrative utterly lacking in dramatic punch. And too, too Hollywood.

The acting and Frank Lloyd's direction are superb. But again the Hollywood mania for names. Franchot Tone is cast as a mealy young midshipman. But Franchot while giving a fine performance also gives every impression of being able to take bally good care of himself. He should have changed roles with young Eddie Quillan, who is the most convincing character in the whole piece.

Some day we may learn from the Russians that the play is really the thing. They cast for the part, and often you will find their greatest actors in inconspicuous roles. But of course that isn't good "exploitation. " We address our pictures to exhibitors rather than audiences.

> --Rob Wagner in Rob Wagner's
> Script, Vol. 16, No. 342 (No-
> vember 23, 1935), page 10.

*   *   *

Technically and going by precedent, this is no woman's picture; but Clark Gable and Franchot Tone are in the cast and the likelihood is that they'll atone for any weaknesses in that part of the business end.   And with that one possible vulnerable point covered up, there's nothing to stand in the way of Mutiny qualifying for box office dynamite rating.

At the Capitol on Broadway, and with no cutting since the Coast previews, Mutiny is running 131 minutes.   If that's a fault, it can be considered one only from the theatre operation point of view.   Audiences generally are not apt to resent it.   For theatres wanting it shorter and sweeter, clipping will not be difficult for there's plenty in the present footage that can stand it.   At two hours and 11 minutes Mutiny runs about equal to the average double bill.

The superfluous footage appears to be in the part, or parts, of the picture that give it most of its power.   These are the flogging scenes, the torture stuff and the relentless exhibition of sadistic and terrible cruelty practised on his men by Admiral Bligh (Charles Laughton).   These moments are all brutally interesting, but they are at times repetitious, and that means much of it can go out without ill effects on the general merit of the story.   Yet, even though repetitious, none seems out of place or extraneous in the 131-minute print.   Mutiny takes its time, and plenty of it, without being guilty of a single dull moment.

As a production of the type that used to be known as a "spectacle," as an example of superb screen authorship and as an exhibition of compelling histrionics, this one is Hollywood at its very best.   The story certainly could not be presented as powerfully through any other medium.

For plot the scenarists have used, with some variations, the first two books of the Nordhoff-Norman trilogy on the mutiny of Fletcher Christian.   Beginnings of the first book and the picture are pretty much the same, as are the details up to the arrival of the hunted mutineers on Pitcairn's Island.   Picture ends there, omitting the third book almost entirely.   Further credence to the facts on which the novel was based is lent by the picture, which credits, on the title sheet, the case as causing a new and more humane system of discipline in the British navy.

First hour or so of the film leads up, step by step, to the mutiny, with a flexible "story" backgrounding some thrilling views of seamanship on a British man-o'-war in the early 18th century, and the cruel Captain Bligh's inhuman treatment of his sailors.

It was a rule in the navy of those days, it appears, that any sailor who struck a superior officer was subject to 20 lashes on every ship in the fleet.   At the commencement of the picture, Bligh demands he be given his privilege of lashing the offender, despite that the man is already dead.   A pretty hard-boiled start for a picture, and not a pleasant appetizer for the weaker stomachs, but it serves to set the character of Capt. Bligh right off the bat and with no stalling.

From then on Bligh, through the cruelties he performs and due to the faithful portrait drawn by Laughton, is as despicable a character as has ever heavied across a screen. Hateful from scratch, Bligh gets worse as he goes along, and when the mutiny arrives audiences most everywhere will applaud, as did the more or less sophisticated clientele at the Capitol.

Delicate romancing amidst picturesque scenes in Tahiti by the English sailors is handled with finesse by the script, and the boys must have worn plenty of kid gloves in slipping this part of the story in with diplomacy. Polynesians are considered members of the white race by many experts, but whether they are so held by the majority of laymen is questionable. And Gable's and Tone's girl friends are very much Poly in appearance. But it's all done so neatly that kicks won't be numerous.

Laughton, Gable and Tone are all that Producer Al Lewin and Director Frank Lloyd could have wished for in the three key roles. Laughton is magnificent. Gable, as brave Fletcher Christian, fills the doc's prescription to the letter. Tone, likeable throughout, gets his big moment with a morality speech at the finish, and makes the most of it.

Support players are mostly characters, depending chiefly on appearance and makeup, but the caster picked wisely and there's ability behind everything, from bits to major assignments. Dudley Digges is splendid as the alcoholic ship's doctor, and Eddie Quillan often takes the play away from the lead trio with his interpretation of the shanghaied kid, Ellison. Herbert Mundin, as a nervous mess "boy," has everything to himself in the comedy department. Pair of girls called Maria and Mamo, opposite Gable and Tone in the Tahiti romancing, are dark-eyed beauts who look good at all times, and especially in profile when emerging from a swim, but the girls talk mostly Polynesian and there's no indication of acting ability either way.

Musical score by Herbert Stothart and camera work of Arthur Edeson are commensurate with all other phases of Mutiny, and that means aces.

--Bige in Variety, Vol. 120, No.
9 (November 13, 1935), page 16.

☐ MY LITTLE CHICKADEE (Universal, 1940)

Since Mae West and W. C. Fields, individually, are such big draws at the ticket windows that, together, they comprise a boxoffice natural, it doesn't matter much that this presentation of the two as a team does not amount to much as a picture. They went western in My Little Chickadee and such story as it has is a sort of Destry in reverse, obviously shot on the Destry sets, and

unevenly told. But it has a considerable quota of firecracker laugh
lines from the lips of its co-stars, it brings back the Mae West of
She Done Him Wrong, and offers Fields as a garrulously funny
fraud, so its robust boxoffice future can be predicted without reserve.

In the story, Miss West is a two-gun moll from Chicago,
given the gate by the first cowtown at which she stops. Aboard the
train, headed for the next town, she encounters Fields and acquires
the mantle of respectability by entering into a phoney marriage with
him. They are plunged into a typical, lawless community, where
she gets friendly with the town's boss, who promptly makes Fields
sheriff, a job he treats with considerable indifference, finally suc-
ceeding in having himself suspected of being a notorious bandit he
is supposed to capture, with Mae making a last minute rescue from
lynching. The story is rather a jerky affair and never goes anywhere in particular, being sacrificed for a gag at the drop of a hat
anywhere along the line.

Miss West never looked more alluring and is at her best in
her own particular style. Fields, too, is in excellent fettle all the
way, performing as a straight comedian without benefit of parlor
tricks. No one else in the cast matters a great deal, though Margaret Hamilton, Joseph Calleia and Dick Foran give good accounts
of themselves.

Faced with a difficult task and a script which proves that the
two stars of the picture--who receive the sole screenplay credit--
are better before the camera than behind typewriters, Edward F.
Cline turned in an excellent job of direction, and the production,
handled by Lester Cowan, is most praiseworthy. Jack Otterson's
art direction is also commendable, as are the musical direction by
Charles Previn and the score by Frank Skinner. Joseph Valentine's
photography is tops.

--The Hollywood Reporter, Vol.
56, No. 12 (February 7, 1940),
page 3.

*   *   *

My Little Chickadee should find plenty of admirers among
folk who cherish broad burlesque. It is unlikely to disappoint either
the followers of Mae West or W. C. Fields, its stars, who share
the screen quite amiably in spite of rumors of professional jealousy
and attempted scene-stealing. True, Miss West as Flower Belle
Lee, trollop in transit, and Mr. Fields, as the indigent Cuthbert J.
Twillie, gambler and sheriff pro-tem, match wits and wisecracks
when they arrive in a frontier town of the '80's. Having written
their own material, both seem satisfied (though they could have used
a good scenarist, as well as a deodorant for some of the dialogue!),
and if My Little Chickadee is a battle for laughs, it ends in a draw.

A major contributor to the hilarity is the goat who substitutes
for Miss West on her bridal night, greatly to the chagrin of Mr.

Fields. The film rejoices in gags of this sort, is less lively when
it depends on its meagre plot, and if you can't respond wholeheartedly to such traditional West lines as "I was in a tight spot,
but I managed to wiggle out of it," there are the curves, somewhat
streamlined since we saw them last. Occasionally Mr. Fields
seems to be trying just a bit too hard, but when he relaxes and
merely stands, facing the hostile world, with his carpet bag, his
expression registering resignation, hostility, and intense preoccupa-
tion with absolutely nothing, he is inimitable. Since his recent pictures are so spotty, I suggest that some enterprising producer acquire all the Fields movies, cut and arrange the best sequences
and merchandise the result as Gems from W. C. Fields.
                              --Richard Sheridan Ames in Rob
                              Wagner's Script, Vol. 23, No.
                              545 (March 9, 1940), page 17.

☐ THE MYSTERY OF THE WAX MUSEUM (Warner Bros. , 1933)

        Now I know the meaning of that queer gleam in Sid Grau-
man's eyes. He thinks I look like Napoleon or Jack the Ripper or
somebody and he's after me. You know that wax figger of Doug
Fairbanks in the lobby of the Chinese Theatre? Well, that ain't no
wax figger; it's Doug himself. Sid murdered Doug, stole his body
outa the morgue, and then, taking it to his million-kilowatt factory,
boiled it in wax--and there you are! At least that's the way wax
figgers are made if we are to believe Jack Warner and Mike Curtiz.

        And think of doing this to a nice girl like Fay Wray. But
alas, Fay looks like Marie Antoinette, and Lionel Atwill simply
couldn't wait to boil her in wax. Indeed, so horribly do Jack and
Mike attempt to out-horror all previous flickering horrors that instead of being horrified, you're likely to start laughing.

        But if the horrors pall, get a load of Glenda Farrell. She
is the newspaper gal who exposes the monsters. Glenda is a jolly
lass with thick lips, beautiful eyes, a charming lisp, and a smile
that would melt a bronze monster, let alone a wax one.

        The monstrous opus is shot in Technicolor. The long shots
are still too weak in color and inky in the shadows, but the close-
ups are ravishingly beautiful studies. Technicolor is particularly
flattering to blondes, and if Glenda Farrell's skin is as peaches and
creamy as it looks on the screen, I don't see how the cast and crew
could go on with their work. Dr. Kalmus' Techni Kulor Kosmetics
for the Komplection!--there's millions in it!
                              --Rob Wagner in Rob Wagner's
                              Script, Vol. 8, No. 208 (Febru-
                              ary 4, 1933), page 7.

☐ NAUGHTY MARIETTA (M-G-M, 1935)

Lilting music that trills its way throughout the picture and
thrills by its performance.   The lovely, familiar Victor Herbert
arias are at once the hero and heroine and raison d'etre of the production and, as sung by Jeanette MacDonald and Nelson Eddy, they
are something one can't afford to miss.   It's a picture that should
be labelled "Must See. "

There is in the picture another debt the public owes to itself
and that is the privilege of hearing Nelson Eddy.   He sings his way
through with the greatest of ease, with a voice that has a surprisingly great range, with a personality that is easy-going and charming, and he has all the physical attributes of a hero.   There's gold
in that thar voice for Mr. Eddy, the producers and the exhibitors.

Those are the outstandingly important features of Naughty
Marietta.   The plot doesn't matter, because it's delightfully hidden
by the music and direction, the acting and the spare dialogue.   The
whole thing is necessarily made up of individual credits.   Van Dyke
turns his talents on a musical and manages to give it the same
moving pace that he injects into all his pictures.   The big song
numbers have been staged very well and he has gotten that same
feeling of the actors having fun while working that impresses in
everything he does.

Herbert Stothart is the one to thank for the grand scoring of
the picture.   It must have been a terrific task and he has done a
gorgeous job.   And to continue with the music, Gus Kahn has contributed fresh lyrics that help tremendously in the pleasure of re-
newing acquaintance with old favorites.   The screenplay has been
cleverly and amusingly done by John Lee Mahin, Frances Goodrich
and Albert Hackett.

Jeanette MacDonald has the happiest role that's been handed
her in a long time.   She looks so beautiful in the costumes and her
voice is an inspiration.   Frank Morgan, good old Frank Morgan, is
a joy as the governor trying to forget what he married was Elsa
Lanchester in her first sizable part on the American screen and
there's an actress who should become a valuable factor in our fair
business.   She's grand, she's so realistically awful.   Harold Huber
and Edward Brophy as a couple of palsy walsys in Daniel Boone out-
fits are priceless.   Cecilia Parker is lovely and very charming as a
little maid.   Joseph Cawthorn, Douglass Dumbrille, Walter Kings-
ford, Akim Tamiroff and Greta Meyer are all excellent in supporting
roles.

William Daniels' photography does much to enhance the beauty
of the production, and for that production itself Hunt Stromberg may
take a bow.   Hunt seems to be clicking along rather merrily these
days.   All in all, this picture is something to shout about for the

whole family.

--The Hollywood Reporter, Vol.
25, No. 38 (February 18, 1935),
page 3.

☐ A NIGHT AT THE OPERA (M-G-M, 1935)

        Did you ever try to shoot swallows in a cyclone? It's easy
compared with reviewing a Marx Brothers film. True, there's an
"if any" story and some twenty-eight names on the credit sheet, but
all I could see were three utterly insane men running about doing
hilariously nutty things. Don't ask why they did 'em; even the authors (George Kaufman, Morrie Ryskind and James McGuinness)
couldn't have known. The result is the grandest maelstrom of madness that these boys have ever put over.

        The collapse of dignity is a basic formula for fun; so can't
you see what the Marx Brothers would do to grand opera? While
the opera was granding, it was glorious, with a huge symphony orchestra and the stars, Kitty Carlisle, Allan Jones and Walter King
singing their hearts out. But what do you think Harp did? He
slipped vulgar sheet music into the score of Il Trovatore, and just
as the chorus reached the heights, the orchestra suddenly burst into
"Take Me Out to the Ball Game"!

        On another occasion, when things were going big, Harpo did
a Tarzan up among the ropes and counterweights of the scene-loft,
with the result that opera principals were one minute singing in the
garden, the next minute aboard a battleship and the next--but why
go on? It is one of the best comedy sequences ever filmed.
There's another in a crowded stateroom--aw heck, I mustn't spoil
your fun.

        After all one must give credit to some of the behind-the-
scenes fellows--surely Sam Wood, whose direction is a fine balance
of light and shade, "the calm before the storm" stuff. And Cedric
Gibbons and his side-kicks, Ben Barre and Edwin B. Willis, who if
they didn't actually use the Philharmonic Auditorium, did some
magnificent cheating. Yes, and Herbert Stothart for both "grand"
and foolish music. Finally, Merritt Gerstad for wonderful photography.

        Let us hope that the Marx Brothers never get well!
                        --Rob Wagner in Rob Wagner's
                        Script, Vol. 16, No. 340 (No-
                        vember 9, 1935), page 10.

☐ NINOTCHKA (M-G-M, 1939)

     Our Ernst has gone back to the days of the Warner lot on
Sunset when his pictures were a series of "Lubitsch touches" and
each was an eagerly anticipated cinematic event. When the talkies
came along he tried to do big things with them and his pictures lost
the sparkle which distinguished his silent ones. "Lubitsch touches"
were not as much in evidence and Ernst became just one of the directors who make pictures. But now he is back; he has the micro-
phone licked and he gives us a new Garbo.

     There really is not a great deal one can say about Ninotchka.
It is too good. A reviewer sums it up completely when he says it
is superlative entertainment. We used to admire Garbo. Ernst
makes us love her. Her first scenes remind us of the old Garbo;
the rest of them reveal a new one, one tender in love scenes, provocative in others, a rare comedienne in scenes designed to make
us laugh. Garbo is alive in Ninotchka, alert, understanding, and
at all times delightful. But she is not by any means the whole
show.

     Melvyn Douglas plays his part in a manner which makes us
feel no one else could have played it. He is in turn a great lover,
an amusing comedian and a commanding actor. Ina Claire, too,
acquits herself brilliantly. And there are three priceless comedians
who play what practically amounts to one part. Sig Ruman, Felix
Bressart and Alexander Granach make every moment they are on
the screen a pure delight. They fairly bristle with "Lubitsch
touches" and give us some of the finest comedy to which we have
been treated in a long time. All the minor roles are handled as
brilliantly.

     Three writers are credited with having had a hand in fashion-
ing the screen play: Charles Brackett, Billy Wilder and Walter
Reisch who had, to start with, an original story by Melchior Leng-
yel. Which of the lot deserves the most credit I do not know, but
each could take a quarter of it and have plenty. To Cedric Gibbons
and his associates go great praise for one of the most visually attractive productions the screen has presented. Each Metro picture
adds to my admiration for the outstanding genius of Gibbons.
Photography by William Daniels is up to his usual high standard,
and one cannot say more than that in the way of commendation.
               --Welford Beaton in Hollywood
                 Spectator, Vol. 14, No. 13
                 (October 14, 1939), page 5.

               *   *   *

     With so many winds of controversy tangling maelstrom-like
wherever people are reacting to world events, this gay zephyr of a
picture is likely to be taken in some quarters for something more
significant than seems to have been intended, something perhaps

laden with a message--and a subtly malicious one at that.   It treats
lightly a subject that some can contemplate only with the utmost
seriousness, serious sympathy or serious repugnance: Soviet Russia.   To such seriousness, such light treatment is like making jokes
about religion.   To most people, however, Ninotchka will be what
on the surface it appears to be, a comedy in which--to put it at its
crudest--Garbo laughs.

What Garbo means as a box-office asset, as exploited to attract the mass audiences, is summed up pretty accurately by Lewis
Jacobs thus: "the ultra-sophisticated, neurotic woman of the world
who lives only for love."   Dramas have been devised or adapted to
present her in that aspect, which is probably the best solution possible to the enormously difficult problem of how to make her special
genius "glamorous" to the number of paying customers necessary to
keep her on the screen in such expensive productions.   But genuine
caviar remains caviar, whatever it is labelled for the general, and
whatever package it is sold in.   And those who have admired Garbo
for herself and not for what she was called or for the stories in
which she has been presented, will not be astonished that she can
laugh.   To go no further back than Camille and Conquest, it has
been obvious enough that there was something merry and simple in
her waiting to express itself.

Ninotchka is a girl who is the precise opposite of sophisticated and neurotic, or living only for love.   She is sincere, straightforward and honest, completely sensible about love whether it is
romantic love or love for her fellow-man, and never solemn or
pompous about anything, be it love or omelets or hats.   She is
capable enough to be chosen by Moscow for a mission to Paris,
wise enough, though in her own world she has never met them before, to see through the fripperies and sophistications of Paris,
human enough for her youth to blossom out in the enchanting air of
Paris in springtime, Paris does not change her--it merely expands
her; she has a good time and falls in love.

What happens is concerned with some jewels that had be-
longed to a Grand Duchess of the old regime, which had been sent
to Paris to be turned into cash.   The three men entrusted with the
business were too simple to cope with the lures and wiles of the
worldly capital, and the transaction hung fire.   Moreover, the Grand
Duchess was there, with a friend in the sly and charming person of
Melvyn Douglas to help her recover her jewels from the naive bar-
gainers from Moscow.   So the incorruptible Ninotchka was sent to
put an end to the nonsense and get things done.   Business gets complicated with romance and intrigue, but in the end the simple maid
from Moscow has her triumph over the slick duchess.

Probably nobody but Ernst Lubitsch could have directed this
sort of comedy so lightly and skillfully.   He has never in all his
years of directing done anything better.   His unique and clever way
of handling an incident in fresh visual terms, his cinematic tropes
which with loftier material would have to be called poetic (such as

the masterly indirection by which he suggests the whole by showing
only a part, as when we are made completely aware of what goes
on behind the doors of the royal suite merely by seeing the servants
in the hall outside)--this element of style which has become com-
monly known as the "Lubitsch touch" has never flourished so richly
before.   Its richness comes from a sort of kindliness that is new
in Lubitsch.   Certain coarsenesses hitherto characteristic are absent.   With many temptations to be sharply satirical he has used
barbs only on the Grand Duchess, and has told his story with the
smiling geniality of someone telling an amusing joke on himself,
not laughing at his subject but with it.   Perhaps the whole key to
his attitude is to be found in the little Moscow episode, where
Ninotchka gives an omelet dinner in her overpopulated room to her
three friends who have to bring their own eggs.   The Russians
themselves once made a comedy about the rooming situation in
Bed and Sofa: they were not so human and gently humorous about
it as Lubitsch has been.

    But Lubitsch has never had Garbo for his central figure be-
fore, which may well explain everything.   With her to irradiate his
technical skill with a personal glow and meaning the comedy becomes something more than deft showmanship.   Among a most
craftily chosen cast--Melvyn Douglas so smooth without ever over-
doing it, Ina Claire so brightly capable, the three Moscow emis-
saries who are apparently doomed to be labeled the Three Karl
Marx Brothers, and all the adroitly sketched-in minor people--
Garbo keeps things warm and human, steadfast, with a gay and
civilized spirit, to a simple ideal of human relationships, a lovable
personality expressed through the lovely and effortless skill of a
fine actress.   Is she true to the Party Line?   She is "wise and
sweet and witty--let's not say dull things about her."

--James Shelley Hamilton in National Board of Review Magazine,
Vol. 14, No. 8 (November 1939),
pages 11-13.

☐ OF HUMAN BONDAGE (RKO, 1934)

    This is a picture of English roast beef, cut thick and with
lots of gravy--a grim story of an over-sensitive, clubfooted fellow
love-bound to a "sow's ear," who under no circumstance could ever
rise to even the splendor of rayon silk.

    Leslie Howard is one of the screen's finest actors, but as
he is intrinsically a gentleman it was difficult to understand how he
could fall so grippingly in love with an ignorant, dumb-bell waitress
lacking physical, mental and spiritual charm.   That he makes one
almost believe the characterization is due to his superlative artistry.

    The production is more notable, however, for the extraor-
dinary performance given by Bette Davis, as the moronic waitress

who begins on a low level and then descends in a pilgrimage of de-
gradations that end in sordid misery, tuberculosis and death.   While
Bette is on the road to hell, first with Alan Hale and next with
Reginald Denny, two beautiful women, Kay Johnson and Frances
Dee, come into Leslie's life; but the moment Bette arises from
each debasement she returns to her love-bondsman, and he can't
resist.   A horrible character, but so authentic--wonderful how Miss
Davis mastered cockney speech!--and so magnificently acted that
one is jealous of every moment she is off the screen.   Truly one
of the greatest performances of the cinema.

Reginald Owen provided the one light touch in this cavalcade
of fascinating gloom as a lower middle-class Englishman with a
heavy British sense of humor and a passion for roast beef.

I hadn't read the book, but Lester Cohen's screen play can
stand by itself as a grand piece of construction, and John Cromwell's
direction is superb in every respect.   I know Maugham's England
well, and the sets by Van Nest Polglase and Carroll Clark, and the
costumes by Walter Plunkett, took me right back to Russell Square
(I lived next door to Leslie Howard's chambers!).   Max Steiner
delivers a perfect musical score.

I doubt if the five-and-ten gals will go big for the picture,
but it is a Scripter production if there ever was one.   Pandro Berman should be congratulated for his courage in shooting such a
story.   He helps raise the cinema far above the moronic level of
most pictures.
                              --Rob Wagner in Rob Wagner's
                                Script, Vol. 11, No. 278 (July
                                14, 1934), page 8.

                    *   *   *

In a way it is too bad that the picture John Cromwell has
made from Maugham's Of Human Bondage is so closely tied up with
the book.   It comes, like the famous son of the famous father, well
recommended to our attention; but at the same time it stands enough
in the shadow of a finer thing to blur the fact of its being a very
fine thing in its own right.   Its screen story is pretty much a story
of Philip and three women, with his periods of artistic and eco-
nomic bankruptcy no more than indicated, his childhood and successive intellectual adjustments cut away completely.   It becomes a
little happier and (more regrettably) cleaner, but gains in quicken-
ing of speed, in unity of impression.   And it moves beautifully, being one of the best examples of pure directing craft to be found.
Leslie Howard and Bette Davis have the main parts, and while the
one seemed at times to lack the flavor of earth you might expect
(a little too much soul, perhaps) and the other simply hadn't in her
what the highest scenes required, both leave you finally with the
sense of a happy and right choice.   Intelligence, spirit, all that.
As a matter of fact there was a whole troop of good people in it:
Kay Johnson, Reginalds Owen and Denny, Alan Hale, Frances Dee.

Whether or not the picture can properly be divested of the book's
overtones, it is easily one of the best screenplays of the year.

                              --Otis Ferguson in The New Re-
                                public, Vol. 79 (July 18, 1934),
                                page 268.

☐ THE OLD DARK HOUSE (Universal, 1932)

        There is something very refreshing about a good spooky pic-
ture like The Old Dark House, Universal's latest contribution to
witchcraft.

        When you see the stranded motorists in this picture come to
the old dark house at night seeking shelter from the storm and
Boris Karloff opens the door and frankensteiningly speaking does his
best to send funny little shivers up and down your back, then and
there you leave your cares (if you have any) out in the sleet with
the wind machines and overhead sprinklers.

        Aside from having a shuddering good time those who enjoy
fine characterization for its own sake will be amply repaid in this
story adapted from the novel of J. B. Priestley by Ben W. Levy and
directed by James Whale.

        Boris Karloff as the mute butler whom everybody fears is
going to find some hard liquor about the premises that will cause
him to run amuck, and who does find some eventually, injects sufficient menace to keep things tingling throughout.

        Melvyn Douglas plays the part of a whimsical beloved vaga-
bond so dear to the British heart (the story is laid in the wilds of
Wales).   One can see that Douglas, in common with most handsome
leading men, likes to play whimsical roles.   The hearts of the
feminine fans should go pitter-patter.

        Lillian Bond, who as Margaret, a chorus girl, has something
of the air of Katharine Cornell about her, is blown in by the storm
in the company of Sir Porterhouse, an English meat eater, played
by Charles Laughton.   Since the death of his wife Sir Porterhouse
likes to take a girl out once in a while just to be seen with a pretty
woman.   That is what the girl tells Douglas later on, and it must
be true because these two derelicts on the sea of life find a haven
in each other's arms without a qualm.

        Gloria Stuart as a young married girl and Raymond Massey
as her husband complete the roster of refugees.

        These two have the rather thankless roles of spookees or
recipients of spookery roles.

The four members of the family that inhabit the old dark
house, played by Eva Moore, Ernest Thesiger, Bremer Wills and
John Dudgeon, give an enthusiastic and finished performance in their
respective roles of sister, brother, mad brother and aged father.

The camera work by Arthur Edeson is finely attuned to the
requirements of the story.   The shadows are rich and black yet
never completely lacking in detail.   The faces are superbly chiseled
to reveal the play of emotions.   Here and there only does Edeson
descend to mere prettiness in a close-up and the result seems quite
flat by comparison.

Some evidence of the conflict between the traditions of the
screen and those of the stage can be seen.   Early in the picture
we are shown a storm in true cinema fashion including a landslide
for good measure.   Later, inside the house we have to imagine the
storm aided and abetted by such stage devices as the sound of thunder and panicky dialogue.   It would be interesting to hear a good
discussion on the relative merits, let us say, of one "Egad, we
are doomed!" pronounced with sufficient fervor by a capable thespian
as against one landslide put on by a well organized miniature department.

The picture ends quite abruptly.   In reality the story does
not really stop at all but the screening of it does.   The urge to
construct an epilogue in one's own mind is irresistible, for not until the characters are laid away one by one in their final resting
place does one feel content to say FINIS.

--Fred Westerberg in The International Photographer, Vol. 4, No.
7 (August 1932), page 32.

*   *   *

Here's another horror thing that will make you shiver.   A
group of travelers, including Melvyn Douglas and Lillian Bond, caught
in a terrific mountain rainstorm, are forced to seek shelter in a
house inhabited by mad people.   Not much story, but the characters
are excellent, particularly Boris Karloff and Eva Moore.   Grand
camera work.

--Photoplay, Vol. 42, No. 4
(September 1932), page 110.

☐ ONE HOUR WITH YOU (Paramount, 1932)

Beauty is the aim of every artist; if not beauty of subject,
then beauty of form, design and color.   Lubitsch's greatest achievement is in showing us beauty in manners.   With his impish sense
of humor he will develop situations so naughty that in less skillful
hands they would be blushful, if not vulgar.   But no matter what
his characters do or say, they do so with utterly disarming charm.

In this picture Charlie Ruggles becomes so stirred by Jeanette MacDonald's seductive beauty that he simply burns up with passion.   Seizing her by the shoulder he shouts in frenzy, "I tell you
if I didn't have such a splendid education I would yield to the animal in me!" And then loosening his grip, he adds, "I admit I
come of a very refined family, but should a refined gentleman not
have any luck?   Does one have to be a rough neck to have any
luck?"   Besides the humor of the lines taking the curse off such a
near-ravishment, that scene epitomizes Lubitsch's excellent taste--
his characters are too well-mannered to do anything offensively unpleasant.

Another delightful thing about Lubitsch is that he is bound
by no rules of the stage or screen, jumping from one form to
another as the whim strikes him, and making no excuses for the
incongruity.   One Hour with You begins like a musical comedy with
the Paris Police Commissioner (George Barbier) addressing in
rhyme a full company of gendarmes who respond chorally.   But
that ends the chorus.   From then on the story is played like an
intimate domestic comedy, except for a tuneful musical score (Oskar Straus) as background that is timed and themed to every gesture
and situation.

Chevalier, upon the urging of his wife (Miss MacDonald) sets
forth to call upon the alluring Mitzi (Genevieve Tobin).   Knowing
perfectly well the danger, he throws out his chest and holds tight
to the All-Good, the humor of the scene punched up to hilarity by
the accompaniment of a marche militaire.   The straight comedy is
also rule-broken by the characters suddenly breaking into song and
even turning to the audience to ask questions.

Lubitsch's high standing gives him an added advantage; he
can demand exactly the paints he wishes.   As Chevalier utters the
naughtiest lines and enacts the most intimate scenes without the
slightest sexiness, he has become Lubitsch's brightest color.

Jeanette MacDonald makes a perfect partner of the boyish
Frenchman, for she, too, can put over Lubitsch's exquisite continental humor with equal charm and sparkle.

Three others in this particular cast stand right up with the
principals, Genevieve Tobin who, though she has a very sloppy
stance, is exceptionally pretty, and surprised everybody at the
press-premier with her delicious comedy; Roland Young, whose repressed drolleries are one of the cinema's greatest treasures, and
who shines in this picture more brilliantly than ever; finally, Charlie Ruggles in his well-known role of the impassioned lover who always gets the raspberry.   He almost steals this picture from one
of the strongest casts in Movieland.

Unlike most of Lubitsch's pictures, One Hour with You has
no "big production" scenes.   It is a gentle little comedy full of
brilliant lines, delicious situations and ravishing music.   If it

doesn't click big, then American audiences are simply not well.
                    --Rob Wagner in Rob Wagner's
                        Script, Vol. 7, No. 164 (April
                        2, 1932), page 10.

                    *   *   *

    It has Chevalier. Oh, how it has Chevalier--this gay,
naughty, sizzling little farce. And, too, it has Jeanette MacDonald,
and behind it all, is Lubitsch. Ernst himself. Need more be said?

    It races and patters along its risqué, saucy way to snappy,
lingering music by Oskar Straus and Richard Whiting. And every
once in a while, Maurice steps right out of the picture, walks down
front, and takes us into his confidence.

    Maurice, a doctor (oh doctor, my operation), married to
Jeanette, is happy and peaceful until along comes his wife's friend
Mitzi. Played too Mitzyish for words by Genevieve Tobin. Mitzi
sets out to get Doctor Maurice. And poor Maurice hesitates, weak-
ens, and alas, succumbs.

    But Mitzi's husband, played by Roland Young, and how he
plays it, sets out to divorce Mitzi and names the philandering
Chevalier as co-respondent.

    Charlie Ruggles, as a would-be lover, is a howl.

    One Hour with You, as the musical version of The Marriage
Circle, is even better than the silent version. George Cukor, the
director, with Lubitsch as supervisor, turned out a picture a bit
naughty, but oh, so "nize."
                    --Photoplay, Vol. 41, No. 5
                        (April 1932), page 50.

☐   100 MEN AND A GIRL (Universal, 1937)

        Of course Deanna Durbin's name precedes the title in the
billing, so you know that a nymphomaniac isn't on the loose. Also
Leopold Stokowski is out of bounds, juicily performing all over the
podium to his own delight. But even though he can't be called a
self-effacing conductor, you can bear with him because he makes
music as exquisitely as Vladimir de Pachmann, despite his monkey-
shines. I suppose he himself performed the familiar Bach "Toccata
and Fugue" on the piano--which at first sounded like a harpsichord
--but I'm certain he supervised the dynamics of sound which made
the symphonic recordings in One Hundred Men and a Girl as exciting as Eugene O'Neill melodrama. If this Universal success, undoubtedly inspired and whipped into perfection by Joe Pasternak and
Henry Koster, had nothing else, it is to screen music what the

Rockefeller Foundation is to effective philanthropy. Within popular bounds, it does things in a big way musically, and I suspect it is destined for enormous popularity at the box office, which would mean well-deserved sables for the Mesdames Pasternak and Koster.

Few words are needed to say that a "hit" picture was deliberately devised and manufactured. The sophisticated elegance of Adolphe Menjou was more or less wasted in making him the indigent parent of La Durbin, who bustles about finding legitimate employment for out-of-work musicians. But a name's a name, and for good measure there's Mischa Auer and Alice Brady, very relaxing in monotone roles. Eugene Pallette gets to "puff and he puffed" more, but the stock comedy will pass muster. Somehow, it seems to matter that Deanna should wangle Stokowski for her jobless players.

One Hundred Men and a Girl is a wholesome, diverting cinematic exercise, burdened with no excessive brilliance or directorial intelligence, but pleasant to behold, and especially delectable to the ear. Miss Durbin is animated, enviably young, engaging at all moments and actually competent in her coloratura passages. The composer's works are snipped here and there, but never mutilated beyond recognition, and the best of One Hundred Men and a Girl may be likened to a Mexican fiesta. Festive, naive, possibly excessive, but nevertheless very nice if you're in the mood. I was, and I know that millions will be!

> --Richard Sheridan Ames in Rob
> Wagner's Script, Vol. 18, No.
> 428 (September 11, 1937), pages
> 10-11.

*   *   *

My idea of a musical film. Joe Pasternak, first guide of Deanna Durbin, has done a beautiful job in developing her. She's really the personification of pure, adolescent joy. Stokowski is a very real figure in the film. The theme is highly worthy; the story is original, and adroitly built up. Considering the setting--among unemployed musicians, the tone of the entire piece is extraordinarily gay. And it's not fluff. For one-line satire, it is difficult to think of a movie scene that tops the bit where one millionaire, reading his newspaper, blurps, "This is outrageous!" and the second millionaire automatically drawls, "What have they done in Washington now?" And for sheer pictorial climax, the rag-tag symphony orchestra grouped around the stairwell in the maestro's home is something to remember.... A German film about a symphony orchestra won a prize a year ago; Hollywood's entry is an infinitely better story, as well as a better frame for the symphony music.

> --Meyer Levin in Esquire, Vol.
> 8, No. 6 (December 1937),
> page 166.

☐ ONE NIGHT OF LOVE (Columbia, 1934)

Two girls in front of me were simply ga-ga waiting to learn the name of the "Major Studio Preview." They were probably hoping to see "Metro-Goldwyn-Mayer presents Clark Gable--" or "Paramount presents Gary Cooper--." When "Columbia Pictures presents--" appeared on the screen they both slumped in their seats, one even holding her nose in disgust and disappointment. Before the end of the first reel they were clapping their hands off!

Yes, this is the picture I had to yip about in advance.

The story opens with Grace Moore trying out for an opera job at a radio audition. Far away in Italy, Tullio Carminati, the great Italian teacher, is luxuriating on his yacht, listening in by short-wave radio. With him is his greatest pupil, Mona Barrie, who loves him.

Grace loses in the audition, but with her meager savings beats it to Italy to study. She rents an apartment in a musical mad-house. In every window a musician--fiddler, pianist, celloist, harpist, flutist, etc. An adroit "Lubitsch touch"--they are all playing the same music! Grace, fascinated by the orchestration, appears upon the balcony and begins to sing the aria. The orchestra assembles in the courtyard and so enthralled are the apartment dwellers that the affair ends in wild applause--joined by the audience, which is lifted right out of their seats.

Thus the picture begins with a bang! But can Victor Schertzinger maintain the high note of enthusiasm? You don't know Vic--nor Grace--nor Tullio--nor Paul Neal, the sound engineer, nor Everett Riskin, the producer.

Yes, Grace meets up with the great Tullio, who takes her as a pupil only upon the understanding that there shall be no sentimental nonsense between them. (He had learned that love and music lessons don't mix.)

Several years of training (darned interesting to the layman), during which Grace is treated like a slave. She believes in Tullio, but his discipline irks. And oh, how she'd like to eat what she craves! Lyle Talbot loves her and wants her to marry him. Several times she is tempted, and once, after she has successfully appeared in provincial grand opera, she revolts and decides to give up singing for marriage, freedom, and a square meal! "Let's go crazy," she shouts in her enthusiasm. They do--in one of the most hilarious sequences you ever saw.

But the call of the stage is too strong. She goes to New York and joins the Metropolitan. But without Tullio. It's to be Madama Butterfly. She is so nervous that collapse is imminent. Almost pushed on the stage, she suddenly looks down into the prompter's box, and there is Tullio!

And oh, boy, how that girl sings! For of course they both love each other, try as they did to deny it. And does the Metropolitan roof go off? Yes, all the same as the roof of your local movie theater when you hear this gorgeous number.

A swell story--Dorothy Speare, Charles Beahan, S. K. Lauren, James Gow, Edmund North (here's once when the whole syndicate gets named!)--full of fine feeling, and so constructed that the singing is not merely dragged in, but is an essential part of the pattern. And the story builds; each big singing number is finer than the one before it, reaching a climax in Carmen. I thought, of course, that that was the end, and when the story went on I dreaded an anti-climax. But top it they did--in Madama Butterfly.

Grace Moore is beautiful, and can act circles around a lot of our film favorites; and her voice is gorgeous beyond words.

I've raved before over Tullio Carminati, the handsomest devil who ever came from Italy, the home of handsome men. Also he has great charm, delightful repression and innate gentility--not at all the crazy and excited "wop."

Lyle Talbot does another of his frustrated-lover parts, and Luis Alberni, as Tullio's assistant, lends fine color to his master's profession. As does Jessie Ralph, Tullio's housekeeper.

As Grace Moore has been in several other pictures that created no sensation, the big success of this one is due to Victor Schertzinger, who is both a great musician and a great director. At the preview the audience burst into tremendous applause at least five times.

Yes, this is one of the most thrillingly beautiful pictures I've ever seen.

Even if "One Night of Love" is Vic Schertzinger's theme song, it is a rotten title for the picture, suggesting a night of love (!), whereas the lovers never got so far as a single kiss.

Columbia borrows the biggest stars of the major studios and gets more out of them than the lenders ever did. Can it be that little Columbia has better executive brains than the big fellers? It would seem so. Anyway, there is something queer about it.

                                    --Rob Wagner in Rob Wagner's
                                    Script, Vol. 12, No. 282 (September 1, 1934), page 10.

*   *   *

Without hesitation this film can be given top rating from an artistic and general cinematographic standpoint. It should do healthy business generally.

One Night of Love is basically an operatic film. It is
pointed, as much as such films can be, toward general appeal, but
it is nevertheless operatic.   There are no very important b. o.
names and the story is hardly novel, but this is a surprisingly effective and entertaining film.   It seems a question of selling Miss
Moore to get 'em in and word of mouth should do the rest.

It's the fact that the film is human, down to earth, that
helps most.   Even the operatic excerpts have all been carefully
picked for popular appeal.   And a lot of comedy has been shot into
the picture at every possible point.   Max Winslow is reported to
have had much to do with the making of this feature.

Miss Moore makes a splendid impression in the film, her
best yet.   In the dialog passages she is rather stilted, although
lovely to look at, has a clear singing voice and perfect enunciation.
She even manages to look well in closeups when she's singing and
that's plenty.

Story is one of those convenient little yarns spun around the
career of a singer.   She fails to win a radio contest so goes to
Europe on her own, has usual student struggles, sings in a cafe,
is discovered by Tullio Carminati, a great singing teacher.   He
drives her, mesmerizes her, makes her into a star.   She falls in
love with him, is jealous of another girl singer, and almost upsets
the applecart at the last minute of success at the Metropolitan debut in New York.   It works out well, of course, for a happy finish.

It's all handled carefully.   Carminati, as the teacher-lover,
is a perfect choice and manages to ease himself into a lot more
attention than might be expected.   He works in a semi-comedy manner with yet sufficient romantic appeal to hold the femmes.   Luis
Alberni, as his assistant, goes into his usual tantrums but is, too,
more effective than previously.   Lyle Talbot is the other man for
Miss Moore and Mona Barrie is the other girl.   Both do well
enough.   Jessie Ralph is excellent as the housekeeper.   Nydia
Westman is in for a bit, as are also Andreas De Segurola and
Rosemary Glosz.

One comedy high spot is early in the film when Miss Moore
can't pay her room rent so the landlady is pressed into singing the
Lucia sextette with her, Miss Westman, Talbot and De Segurola,
an idea lifted from La Bohème, but effective.

Besides singing the title song, which, incidentally, is used
only once, to open the film, Miss Moore sings "The Last Rose of
Summer," from Marta, "Ciribiri Bin," one of the most popular
Neapolitan songs, "Sempre Libera," from Traviata, "Habanera,"
from Carmen, and "Lovely Day" from Madama Butterfly.   Last is
probably the most effective and is used for the finale of the film,
on a stage similar to that of the Metropolitan, where it is supposed
to take place.   Full orchestral accompaniment in this number and
for Carmen.

Victor Schertzinger, who directed and helped with thematic musical composition, has handled the job splendidly.   He was chosen for the assignment because of his musical background, having at one time composed.   Choice is certainly justified.   He shows ingenuity especially in the Traviata number.   In that Miss Moore has just arrived in Milan, she is seen at the window of her room looking out at the square.   Camera moves from window to window picking up various music students at work--a pianist, a bass player, a piccolo player, a violinist, etc. --and then moves back to find Miss Moore.   She's excited by the growing clamor of tunes, throws open her window and bursts into song with "Sempre Libera," all the other musikos catching the cue and giving her accompaniment.   It's as musical a thrill as has been reached in sound pictures.

--Kauf in Variety, Vol. 115, No. 13 (September 11, 1934), page 11.

◻ ONLY ANGELS HAVE WINGS (Columbia, 1939)

Howard Hawks has, in Only Angels Have Wings, a tremendously engrossing picture.   When clipped judiciously to top of the bill playing time it will prove topnotch screen fiction of that particular brand which sets up a merry jingle at the cash register.

The picture is more than packed with "atmosphere," thrills and action, plus a goodly portion of romantic stuff.   It is distinguished by more than the usual number of colorful performances, and directed with a sure hand in every shift of mood.

Only Angels Have Wings drops its characters in a little South American seaport, transfer point for a rickety airmail service being pioneered by a handful of adventurous pilots who have found flying too dull or too exacting elsewhere.

Heading the clique is Cary Grant in a restrained but two-fisted characterization which makes much of his talent for sly humor.   In his position he is required to make quick decisions, judge his men with little sentiment and largely on their ability to deliver expressly what he demands of them.   Grant does this with just the correct amount of restraint to key the play on the light side without going overboard in this direction, while maintaining a steady pull on melodramatic nuances.

Obviously, director Hawks must be credited amply for his discretion in this direction, and for maintaining an unwavering impression that heroics of this calibre are everyday occurrences.

Into this select group drops Jean Arthur.   An entertainer of sorts and perfectly capable of taking care of herself, she takes flier Grant's measure, decides to miss her boat and thus becomes in-

volved intimately in the fortunes of the embryonic flying enterprise.
Miss Arthur proves again that she is an adept companion for Grant's
particular brand of screen fun.   Here, however, it is kept pointedly
out of the screwball order, but nevertheless qualifies as superlative
work.

Miss Arthur shares in an unusually colorful opening sequence
and succeeds in holding major interest, with Grant, despite stellar
trouping by supporting talent.   Outstanding in the latter are Richard
Barthelmess, Thomas Mitchell, Sig Rumann, while Rita Hayworth,
Allyn Joslyn, Victor Kilian, Noah Beery Jr. , John Carroll, Donald
Barry and Lucio Villegas register effectively.

Barthelmess gives an unusually impressive delineation of an
outcast flyer in a deadpan effort to re-establish himself among the
flying clan.   The part has mounting sympathy, with Barthelmess
making the most of it.   Mitchell's characterization of the veteran
pilot devoted to Grant and fighting the inevitable day when he will
be grounded is well in keeping with the superb work he has been
doing in the past.   Rumann is given a fat part as the bankroller of
the air enterprise and he rises colorfully to every situation.   Miss
Hayworth makes an unusually effective entrance as Barthelmess'
wife, and former sweetheart of Grant's.   Josslyn, Kilian, Beery,
Carroll and Barry are importantly presented as co-adventurers in
the flying venture.

The picture is packed with thriller stuff ranging from spectacular crashes to breathtaking moments in plunging ships, a flight
with a cargo of nitroglycerine, blind flying and ships sheathed in
flames.   All are spectacularly registered with every semblance of
authenticity.   Novel shots include that of a ship literally scaling a
mountain.   Unforgettable too is the fateful attempt by young Beery
to land in a fog under unusually suspenseful guidance from Grant
and his ground crew.

Jules Furthman's screenplay, based on Hawks' story, is a
superb work of playwriting and punchy dialoging.   It is invariably
pithy, always colorful.   Special mention is due both Joseph Walker
and Elmer Dyer for their outstanding camera work.

Excellent in production assets also are the contributions of
Roy Davidson to special effects, Lionel Banks to art direction and
others.
--The Hollywood Reporter, Vol.
51, No. 35 (May 11, 1939),
page 3.

*   *   *

If the public can stand the shock, this department is prepared to offer four entertaining films during the same week, two of
them of exceptional merit.   Their titles indicate their variety:
Juarez, Mexico, during the last century; Only Angels Have Wings,

a title connoting nothing, but belong to a spirited film laid in modern South America; Rose of Washington Square, 'way back when, in
New York; and Ballerina, an interesting import, starring a beauty
from the Ballet Russe.   In addition to being good pictures, these
films offer such sterling actors as Paul Muni, Bette Davis, and
Brian Aherne (and I suspect Cary Grant's name belongs with these!)
and such justly popular stars as Jean Arthur, Tyrone Power, Alice
Faye, and a rejuvenated Al Jolson.   Truly, there is occasion for
rejoicing among movie patrons, and the box office should feel as
jocular as the reviewers.

I'm prepared to risk the ire of perspicacious and cultivated
readers by confessing that of all these films I enjoyed Howard
Hawks' Only Angels Have Wings most.   One expects a great deal of
such a combine as Dieterle-Muni-Davis, devoting their talents to a
dramatic and significant theme such as the struggle between Maxi-
milian and Juarez for the mastery of Mexico, and the Warners'
Juarez is a conscientious and artful photo-biography, filmed on an
epic scale.   The Hawks melodrama, the most ambitious candidate
to be sponsored by Columbia since the last Capra film, attempts to
be no more than thrilling and affable, but it boasts some of the
most telling dialogue, most natural acting, choicest photography,
and incisive direction offered to film patrons in many months.

In no way important, Only Angels Have Wings is a dashing
and romantic movie, overlong and rambling but so ingratiating that
minor lapses are seldom annoying, and the marvel of it all is that
the film is fundamentally concerned with the dangers and bravura
excitements of commercial aviation--a subject that apparently had
Hollywood's scenarists licked.   But this time Jules Furthman and
Mr. Hawks did what I've long hoped for but feared impossible: they
subordinated the planes, the violent elements, and the imperturbable
Andes to some vivacious and agreeable people; to a convivial saloon
run by a Dutchman (Sig Rumann); to some birds (including condors,
seagulls, and parakeets), and they weren't ashamed of having made
a boisterous and naive movie, even though they threw in Richard
Barthelmess to cinch it.   They made a film that we are all glad to
participate in, where we want to step up to the characters and say
"Let me buy you a drink," and that's an accomplishment.

The human relationships remind one of early Hemingway,
some of the dialogue has Hemingway's bite, and Mr. Grant knows
how to deliver lines with enviable aplomb.   While he never poaches
on Gable's territory, he has the same drive and rough gaiety of
that star, while gradually surpassing him as an actor.   Miss Arthur
is the ideal woman among men, able to fend for herself, extraordinarily attractive without the aid of a wardrobe (most of the time
she appears in the same trim suit); and Thomas Mitchell and Allyn
Joslyn contribute effective performances.   Several players are excellent in small bits, and we all will welcome Mr. Barthelmess
impersonating a coward who redeems himself in the cockpit, first
by transporting nitroglycerine, and then by refusing to "bail out"
after giant birds have wrecked his plane, the motors are aflame,

and a landing in the jungle seems impossible. The role is actor-
proof and I fear Barthelmess' well-wishers did their friend an injustice by overpraising a performance which is merely competent--
but I'm glad he's back.

--Richard Sheridan Ames in Rob
Wagner's Script, Vol. 21, No.
509 (May 20, 1939), page 16.

☐ OUR TOWN (Principal Artists/United Artists, 1940)

One's reaction to Our Town is bound to be intensely personal
although the theme of Thornton Wilder's play is universal and its
characters should be familiar to and cherished by Americans fortunate enough to remember, with the clear eyes of youth, the serene
joys, the placid rhythms and comforting smallness of village life--
as once it was.

Some people may quarrel with the play's substance, contend-
ing that Wilder neglects to include the ugly animosities, the greed
and hypocrisy, the gossip and boredom which flourish in the small
town as elsewhere. Some may find his tenderly metaphysical approach to death too dulcified, unsupported by facts and accepted beliefs. Conceivably, there are folk unprepared by experience to appreciate Our Town; still others, whose power of imagination has
atrophied, will not be able to live it with its people.

But I cannot bring myself to think that the majority of discriminating filmgoers will fail to respond to Sol Lesser's beautiful
production of such a quietly persuasive, deeply perceptive and lumi-
nous bit of authentic Americana. Just as The Grapes of Wrath was
important because it exposed a festering social sore and aroused
indignation, so Our Town should mark a milestone in the cinematic
lives of those who live by the heart--those who seek reassurance,
those who want so desperately to believe in the innate goodness and
generosity of the individual man and woman. This department has
no desire to remind its readers of the distant cataclysm, the mass
suffering, or the acute national peril which make our current
thoughts hideous; but as Miss Millay has written: "Life must go on,
I forget just why...." Our Town supplies a partial explanation. It
comes like a miracle, when most needed, to comfort those no longer
able to think affirmatively, to offer respite from disillusion and
momentary pause before tackling the ominous problems of the future.
Its balm may be brief, and some may scoff "escapism" and "sentimental self-indulgence," but I honestly believe that Our Town should
prove a better remedy for jangled nerves and radio-racked ears than
capsuled sedatives or the attentions of a neurologist.

In its transfer to the screen, the Wilder play has lost none of
the qualities which made it an unusual stage offering. Obviously, a
motion picture requires some sort of scenery, but the settings pro-

vided by William Cameron Menzies and exquisitely photographed by Bert Glennon do not violate Wilder's original conception which invited the spectator to visualize for himself. While substantial, they possess some hypnotic quality, aided by Aaron Copland's music, which transports one back to yesterday and holds one spellbound throughout the story of two families, the romance and marriage of George and Emily, and the life of Grover's Corners as casually described and interpreted by Frank Craven, the narrator, who talks directly to the audience.

It would be hard to imagine any satisfactory substitute for Mr. Craven in the role he created. Attesting to the eloquence of Mr. Wilder's writing and Sam Wood's sympathetic direction, there are several scenes that are unforgettable: the ladies lingering in the moonlight to chat after choir practice; the realization of their love, when George and Emily are seated at a soda fountain; the straggling procession of umbrellas in the hill-top graveyard, and Emily's heartbreaking cry when she has returned to earth to re-live her twelfth birthday, "Do any human beings ever realize life while they live it?--every, every minute?"

Personally, I regret the omission of important dialogue in the wedding scene and the altering of the ending which deprives George of his most poignant moment. No doubt the "happy" ending is permissible, but I'm certain it did little to check the general flow of tears at the preview.

Since a perfect cast was assembled for Our Town, each member of which seemed intent only upon contributing his or her best to an artistic enterprise with no thought of personal glory, I shall let you meet them as the characters of the film, mentioning only Martha Scott and William Holden who, because of their youth and relative inexperience, deserve double praise for performances that will ever rank high in the annals of motion pictures. And it would be ungracious indeed not to dip my reviewer's colors to producer Lesser who, having given Our Town to a larger public, thereby cancels the black marks chalked up against him for his erstwhile unconscionable espousal of a boy soprano.

--Richard Sheridan Ames in Rob
Wagner's Script, Vol. 24, No.
559 (June 15, 1940), page 16.

*   *   *

Picture patrons everywhere are under obligation to Sol Lesser for giving them such an emotional treat as this film provides. Greatly human, artistically presented, brilliantly directed, superbly acted, Our Town comes to us as one of the finest bits of screen entertainment Hollywood ever sent out to the world. The simplicity of the story, the small-town atmosphere pervading it, the social unimportance of the characters, their humdrum existence are the ingredients so expertly mixed in this cinematic masterpiece that we are interested greatly even when we notice that the milkman is keeping up to date by delivering his milk in bottles instead of pouring it from a big can, as he does when we first see him.

And when the son of the doctor and the daughter of the town editor first hint at mutual love while talking about everything else but that, your emotions will be stirred as theirs are, a lump will come to your throat and a suspicion of tears to your eyes, for you will be viewing perhaps the most beautiful love scene the screen ever has given us. Certainly in my years of picture reviewing I can remember none to match it.

In paying tribute to the efforts of those who made Our Town, a reviewer, in estimating the relative values of the contributions or in endeavoring to list them in order of merit, is faced with the impossible task of comparing perfections. To achieve perfection, each part of a pattern has to be perfect; Our Town is a perfect picture, therefore everyone connected with it is to be commended for distinguished service to the art creation. But in a review of readable length there is room for mention of only a few.

Sol Lesser was wise when he selected the story material, but he was inspired when he selected Sam Wood to direct it. Sam was directing pictures in the long ago before the Spectator was born; and since then has made many notable ones, but neither he nor any other director ever gave us one directed with such tenderness, such understanding, such obvious evidence of an artist in love with his work. It is a gentle tune which Sam plays on our emotions, so softly played we are more aware of the effect than we are of its cause. He must have been satisfied with the results, for he could not have striven for more than he achieved. Perfection is the ultimate an artist can attain.

The director's tools were a feelingly written screen play by Thornton Wilder, Frank Craven and Harry Chandlee; a speck of New England designed by William Cameron Menzies and Harry Horner; a cast composed of most competent players; photography of warm quality by Bert Glennon; music by Aaron Copland; a group of talented technicians. The contributions of all of them were blended by the director into a softly played symphony of emotions.

In Martha Scott this picture gives the screen a girl who will become one of its greatest ornaments, who is a great actress because she is a great person who does not suggest the actress. Her eyes tell us she lives each scene; her beauty is made more beautiful by its spiritual quality. Admirable choice to play opposite her was William Holden, another young player who will rise to the heights if he always is fortunate enough to get such roles and such direction. To take the rest of the cast in the order in which they are listed on the credit sheet, we must pin distinguished service medals on Fay Bainter, Beulah Bondi, Thomas Mitchell, Guy Kibbee, Stuart Erwin, Frank Craven (a big medal for Frank), Ruth Toby and all the others who contribute bits to complete a perfect acting pattern. None of the performances is harmed by the loud talking which reduces the box-office value of nine-tenths of the pictures we are getting.   Sam Wood gives us a group of people, not a troupe of barnstormers.

--Welford Beaton in Hollywood
Spectator, Vol. 15, No. 2
(June 1, 1940), pages 5-6.

☐ THE PAINTED VEIL (M-G-M, 1934)

... and Scheherezade related the following: "Long, long ago there lived a maid married to a certain Doctor Purposeful, who neglected her because of his work.   They journeyed to far Cathay, and there, starved for love, Mrs. P. fell for the handsome and amorous proportions of Dr. Cadd, who took her places and did things.   But oh, dear Sultan, when Mrs. P. learned that Dr. Cadd was just that, she suddenly realized that her hard-working and plague-stricken husband was the real Peruvian Doughnut of Love, so she rushed to his side and threw herself into his weak but happy arms....   Yes, it's an old story; the Medes got it from the Babylonians and the Babs got it from old cuneiform records."

Yet W. Somerset Maugham claims that story as his own, and M. G. M. no doubt paid him big money for it.

In this version the maid is played by "GARBO," Dr. P. by Herbert Marshall and Dr. Cadd by George Brent.   The story is slow; the mise-en-scène ugly, and GARBO'S gowns pretty queer for the daughter of a scientist (Jean Hersholt).   In one sequence she looks very beautiful, but like a Crusader out after the Holy Grail instead of the unholy love of George Brent.   (Ye Real Ed says maybe that's the smart costume to wear when on such an errand.) In another sequence she swiped the hat of Chico Marx, who was working on the next set, and the preview audience gave it the heh, heh, heh.

Even the Big Production Stuff, a Chinese temple fete, while costly as heck, is more weird than beautiful.   As for plague stuff, nothing is uglier.

The actors all do well, especially Marshall, and GARBO in her sad, Garboish moments.   Richard Boleslawski does as well as could be expected with a story that has been filmed at least fifty times.

Only William Daniels, cinematographer, and Douglas Shearer, sound engineer, come off triumphantly.   A deafening silence, not of reverence, greeted the final fade-out.

The tall, Swedish actress who came to us a few years ago is the first talkie star to attain the supreme dignity of a single

moniker--Caesar, Napoleon, GARBO. Not to be outdone by a mere
movie gal, we sign this piece--WAGNER.

--Rob Wagner in Rob Wagner's
Script, Vol. 12, No. 301 (January 12, 1935), page 10.

*   *   *

I guess what they'll have to do with Garbo is to keep her
out of epics. The Painted Veil is just a plain, human story which
doesn't try to make history or play for posterity, and Garbo, as
its heroine, keeps her hair up, and I like her pretty thoroughly for
the first time, if ever.

She abandons the woman-of-the-ages pose that she usually
assumes, throws off her sinusitus, cuts out the old mystery hoke,
and walks among mortals as a sister and a housewife and a person,
and she's not half bad. Somebody--no doubt Director Richard
Boleslawski--cooled her down and lightened her up, and she's all
right. I think the girl may have a future in pictures. I still
wouldn't call her exactly beautiful, nor impressively intellectual,
nor colossally talented, but she is far above the average.

Categorically, The Painted Veil is merely another busy-hus-
band picture. (When will you women learn what sterling fellows we
busy husbands and daddies are, underneath?) Herbert Marshall is
so occupied with the fascinatin' cholera that he has no time to do
his home work as a lovin' husband. My, but he is a serious young
man--you can see that from the first--and he surely does take
cholera anything but laughingly. So Greta, his wife, is wide open
for George Brent who plays polo and around, and has a consular
job in China, where all this takes place and where there is plenty
of cholera for cholera connoisseurs. George is married, too, to
a society wife. Eventually Herbert finds out that he has lost his
wife's love, and there is where the story really starts.

There is a big Chinese festival scene in the picture which
doesn't help the narrative any and which must have cost Metro-
Goldwyn-Mayer a couple of hundred thousand dollars and which I
could have told them to leave out, for fifty percent of the net saving.

Garbo fans ought to rejoice in this new, modified and improved Garbo--if they can tell the difference.

--Don Herold in Life, Vol. 102,
No. 2599 (February 1935), page
32.

☐ THE PETRIFIED FOREST (Warner Bros., 1936)

When Warner Brothers invaded a realm which had held
Shakespeare as exclusively its own and put A Midsummer Night's

Dream on the screen with a hundred times the physical sweep and esthetic appeal the stage could give it, the champions of the theatre had to acknowledge that perhaps in the field of phantasy the screen did possess some advantages. But take drama, the dramatic play with its real people, plastic characters in a three-dimensional world--.

Well, Warner Brothers took The Petrified Forest fresh from a New York theatre and put it on the screen, spread it on a two-dimensional plane across which shadows move instead of living people, and the only large audience which has seen it thus far sat for eighty minutes in that tense silence which bespeaks complete absorption in what was occupying its attention. Here the screen met the stage on the latter's ground. It confined to one set all but a few feet of the action, converged its characters to a given spot, as the stage is compelled to, and there told its story.

Charles Kenyon and Delmer Daves added a washroom, a scene on the roof and two outdoor locations which were used briefly, but tell ninety percent of the story in the single setting the stage employs in its presentation of the Robert E. Sherwood play. The script retains all the scenes and situations included in the original, and in one hour and twenty minutes tells everything the stage requires an entire evening to tell.

So much for the mechanics. The screen version of Petrified Forest demonstrates the advantage the screen has over the stage in developing esthetic values to heighten emotional appeal. In the theatre the proscenium arch and footlights ban the audience from the world in which the drama is enacted. The mere presence of persons on the stage does not make the theatre more personal than the screen. The theatre audience sits in a world of its own, apart from that in which its players move, whereas the screen, through the medium of the closeup, can place each member of the audience at the elbow of each character in the photoplay, thereby giving the screen a greater degree of intimacy than is possible for the stage to attain.

Intimacy begets emotional response. Petrified Forest, more than any other picture I have seen, demonstrates that the screen is a more powerful medium for the presentation of a stage play than is the stage itself. I cannot believe the play in New York evoked the emotional reaction the audience accorded the screen version. Largely responsible for this was the greater cleanliness of the picture. Thanks to the League of Decency, it is free from the bawdiness that distracts the attention of the theatre audience from the theme of the drama. For the rowdiness in the play, Kenyon substitutes beauty in thought and expression to give the film version wider appeal than the play could attain.

Archie Mayo's direction reaches the peak of perfection in its demonstration of the possibilities of deriving the utmost in pictorial effectiveness through intelligent handling of a small group of people

for a full hour in a single confined setting without pictorial attractiveness on its own account.   It is a cheap little desert restaurant
with sand and parched desolation reaching from its windows to grey
mountains which provide a distant background.   Wholly within this
dot of space, tense drama is enacted so graphically and convincingly we do not question the logic of the confession of undying love for
one another which Leslie Howard and Bette Davis exchange within a
few hours of meeting one another for the first time.   It takes great
writing, great direction and great acting to achieve such a result.

Howard, Bette and Humphrey Bogart give magnificent performances.   No lines ever were spoken on stage or screen more
beautifully than Howard speaks those which expound his philosophy
of life.   And for Bette Davis it is another triumphant step in the
march which seems to be leading to her ultimate recognition as the
greatest actress on the screen.   She is superbly human and convincing.   Bogart plays with chilling conviction the desperate and
hunted killer.

Dick Foran is another who takes a long step forward by virtue of his performance in this picture.   Charley Grapewin, Genevieve Tobin, Joseph Sawyer, Porter Hall and Paul Harvey also
stand out.

Petrified Forest is another triumph for the Warner technical
staff.   We doubt our eyes when we reflect that the little restaurant
is not located in the center of the great expanse of desert we see
beyond its windows, that the miles of sand and sage brush, the
towering hills in the distance and the boundless sky are confined to
a stage on the Warner lot.   Sol Polito's camera is responsible for
the complete illusion, and also for striking portraiture results.

We must bow again to the production genius of Hal Wallis,
leader of the Warner forces.   He is piling success upon success in
a spectacular manner.   To Henry Blanke was entrusted the piloting
of Petrified Forest from stage to screen.   He was responsible also
for Pasteur and A Midsummer Night's Dream, two other tremendous
achievements.   A bow for him.

                              --Welford Beaton in Hollywood
                                Spectator, Vol. 10, No. 7
                                (January 18, 1936), page 9.

                    *   *   *

Stage and screen: to each according to its possibilities and
limitations.   The stage is bounded by three walls; the cinema claims
all the world its stage.   Dialogue on the stage has the advantage of
the electric physical presence of the actors; the screen gains advantage by the close-up.   We can see into the eyes of the characters.

This is a stage play screened in almost exclusively stage
technique.

Bob Sherwood has taken as his theme: You can't beat nature. We think we are conquering nature with our intellects. We have achieved speed, mechanical marvels and fourth-dimensional thinking. But nature is striking back with neuroses. We are headed for the jitters of extermination. Nature will win.

Leslie Howard, frustrated intellectual, wanders the world, arriving at an oil station in the Arizona desert. Close by is the Petrified Forest. Yes, that's where he belongs, in the Petrified Forest! But he meets Bette Davis, illiterate but soulful. Ah, perhaps she can carry forward the seed that is dying in him!

A tense situation arises when a bunch of bandits, fleeing from the law, hold up the oil station. During the long wait, with the threat of death hanging over all, the characters speak their minds. For one hour the play centers in that one room, and what a scene! Howard is at his excellent best, Bette Davis' wonderful characterization is another triumph. Humphrey Bogart, who played the bandit chief on the stage, repeats what is reported to be one of the best stage characters of last year.

Charley Grapewin delivers another of his classically humorous old man parts. Dick Foran, as the collegiate oil station assistant in love with Bette, gives a notable performance. Genevieve Tobin, married to the Eureka Bonding Co. (Paul Harvey), innocent autoists caught in the drama, cuts loose and confesses her marital frustration. Grand stuff. There are several other characters, each an integral part of the strange dramatic pattern.

The play is beautifully written, equally well adapted to the screen by Charles Kenyon and Delmer Daves and superbly directed by Archie Mayo. John Hughes' art direction is notable, and as might be expected, Sol Polito's camera work is perfect. Henry Blanke, supervisor, should be very happy over the preview reception to his challenging drama.

> --Rob Wagner in Rob Wagner's
> Script, Vol. 15, No. 353 (Feb-
> ruary 15, 1936), pages 10-11.

☐ THE PHILADELPHIA STORY (M-G-M, 1940)

If all movies were as good as The Philadelphia Story there would be no complaints about empty seats in ye olde theater corrals. Not only is it the finest entertainment that Hollywood has proffered this season but it is also one of the most enjoyable offerings I have ever witnessed on the screen. And this department has seen most of the cinematic material made since the days when The Birth of a Nation was just beginning to be a twinkle in the eyes of Daddy W. Griffith.

The Philadelphia Story will do more to enhance box-office prestige than any "Greater Movie Season" publicity campaign. It will not only do amazing business for itself but, through its diverting qualities, will cause patrons to try their luck in the shadow palaces for some time to come. Not an "epic" which employed millions and cost millions, but a smart, intelligent, and engrossingly human comedy that utilizes a small cast. But what a cast!

Philip Barry's play has been converted into a smooth, titillating film that moves easily and convincingly, due to the extraordinary inventive script prepared by Donald Ogden Stewart. It has more sex, per frame, than the Breen-Hays Office has permitted us in too long a period. Possibly that is one of the reasons for the unusual vitality and sparkle which are projected to the audience. George Cukor's direction possesses consummate balance. He has often erred in concentrating on one performer but this photoplay is scaled to a nicety of weight and contour. Each ingredient is fitted into its proper place and the result is a film-mosaic that may well be termed perfection ... until perfection comes along.

And perfection is precisely what Katharine Hepburn bestows upon the role of Tracy Lord. Here is another proof that an actress is only as good as the creative company she keeps. Given substantial theatrical wherewithal, Kit crashes through with an exhibition of histrionics that has been matched by few stage actresses and still fewer screen personalities. There is a dimensional quality that is very close to genuine genius, a warmth and spiritual emanation most rare. True, Kit indulges in no eye-poppings and rollings, no studied, psychopathic leerings and totterings, no hysterical twitchings and chorean tittups. Consequently the Academy may overlook her work when bestowing its annual Oscar for acting. But whether she receives the award or not will make little difference to those who are able to recognize a major actress when they have the rare opportunity of seeing one.

The photography is superb and in precisely the same category rests the Franz Waxman scoring. Both Cary Grant and Jimmy Stewart top all previous efforts. Ruth Hussey, traveling in fast company, never falters. She always keeps step with her high-powered companions. There is certainly starring talent in the lady. Virginia Weidler is nothing short of wonderful in a demanding assignment. Mary Nash, Roland Young (as a bottom-pinching uncle), Henry Daniell, and John Howard couldn't possibly be improved upon.

The Philadelphia Story has made my Christmas most merry. I think it will do the same for you. —Herb Sterne in Rob Wagner's Script, Vol. 24, No. 580 (December 21, 1940), pages 17-18.

☐   PINOCCHIO (Walt Disney, 1940)

As the third feature-length animated cartoon to reach the public, Walt Disney's Pinocchio, an adroit and fanciful elaboration of the tale that has delighted many generations of the young-in-years and young-in-heart, is bound to lack the impact of novelty. But since comparisons are inevitable, it is in almost every respect superior to the justly famous Snow White. The adventures of the puppet who becomes a real boy only after learning to be unselfish and brave are more engrossing and more likely to amuse the average adult than the make-believe of Snow White, who was less real than the seven dwarfs or the birds and beasts incidental to her story.

In this new Disney creation which proves beyond question that one of the world's most original artists has mastered his medium, technical advancement is of paramount interest.   Color is better.   The animation is less jerky.   Human figures have been realized as never before.   But the innocence has not been lost. Nor the vivid imagination, the quaint humor, the gentleness, the quick perception, the playfulness.   If the qualities which distinguish a Disney work could be accurately enumerated and analyzed, he might have successful imitators.   But no one can copy the imaginative processes, the captivating conceits, the unexpected quirks, inventions, and spirit of pure joyousness which characterize Disney's major efforts.   Unlike his short subjects which seem to have deteriorated, losing some of their pungency, freshness, and imaginative ardor--some, recently, have indeed depended on crudeness and sadism for doubtful comic effects--Pinocchio has that sweet and cuddlesome appeal of a puppy who makes logical restraint and sensible reproaches for foolish misconduct seem positively wicked.   Disney masterpieces have an irresistible tail-wagging quality that makes one want to pet them with all one's heart. Pinocchio is no exception.

--Richard Sheridan Ames in Rob Wagner's Script, Vol. 23, No. 541 (February 10, 1940), page 17.

*   *   *

"Cartoon," even "animated cartoon," doesn't convey any longer what Walt Disney does, it hasn't for a long time.   Otis Ferguson, looking for a word for Pinocchio, had to fall back on calling it a "Disney," which of course is condensing into a noun what everybody has in mind when he thinks of a Disney film, in fact what a lot of people have been doing.   Maybe it is the inevitable unique word for a unique thing.

Pinocchio goes far beyond anything Disney and his studio have done before.   The difference is a tremendous advance partly in the technique of animation, and even more remarkably--whether

significantly or not--in a change toward what might be called a romantic kind of naturalism.   The drawings are far removed from
the broad and simple and humorous lines of the early Mickeys and
Silly Symphonies, for which the word "cartoon" could be aptly used,
and have become more and more the careful, serious kind of picture you find in pretty paintings.   Look at the landscapes, the sea,
the fairy: could Edmund Dulac have done anything in which fancy
and fantasy were more governed by prettiness?

To some people the first sight of Pinocchio gives something
of the same kind of shock--the shock of difference--that one might
feel if confronted, without any period of adjustment, by an immediate change from silent films (the best ones) to talkies (also the
best ones).   It isn't merely that there is a great amount of dialogue, an almost inordinate amount, in Pinocchio.   The whole style
and approach seem to have changed, just as comic strips have
changed from being just comic slapstick to narratives of adventure
or romance.   And once more you are confronted with the question
of whether change is necessarily progress.   Or is it a matter of
taste?

Comparing Pinocchio with Snow White is inevitable: there is
nothing else to compare it with.   Snow White is so old it is ageless, and all her adventures are a part of racial memory, happenings we instinctively understand without needing to adjust ourselves
to them at all.   Pinocchio is foreign and strange, localized in Italian tradition and (though that makes little difference) pretty modern
as folk-lore goes.   Snow White makes an immense appeal to the
sympathies: who cares whether a puppet becomes a real boy or
not?   Snow White is a simple tale of goodness rewarded and wicked-
ness punished, with no explicit moral: Pinocchio is as full of morals, carefully emphasized, as a Sunday school story.

These comparisons are apt to crop up forcibly at the first
sight of Pinocchio.   But at the second sight they are forgotten, and
you can give yourself up to the extraordinary movement and skill of
it.   The animation has become something little short of magic.
The details--such details as the clock figures, the dancing puppets,
the under-sea adventures with all their marine creatures, are superb examples of the Disney tradition brought to perfection.   The
non-human characters are delightful: Jiminy Cricket, the amiable
satires implicit in Cleo the goldfish and J. Worthington Foulfellow,
the foxy ham adventurer, the cat, the terrifying whale.

In technique it is hard to imagine how Disney can go further,
though it is one of the qualities of genius that it can go beyond the
common imagination.   But there is many an admirer of his who
wishes he would leave human characters to human actors, and give
us more animals and bugs and flowers and fish.   What he could do
with The Wind in the Willows!

--James Shelley Hamilton in National Board of Review Magazine,
Vol. 15, No. 3 (March 1940),
pages 10-11.

☐ THE POWER AND THE GLORY (Fox, 1933)

Preston Sturges has put the bee on another old proverb: No man is a hero to his valet. In this story, while all the world thinks Spencer Tracy an industrial monster, only God and Ralph Morgan, Tracy's old-faithful secretary, know the truth. Mark Twain, in The Mysterious Stranger, dwells at length on our "make"; if we are made like a truck, we won't perform like a light buggy, and vice versa. Ralph Morgan knew Spencer's make. He knew him as a boy; as a young man who could neither read nor write at twenty-one. He knew about his marriage to Colleen Moore, a pretty young school teacher--their marriage and young son. He was aware of how Colleen urged her husband on to better things. He was also aware of how Colleen grew cross and irritable with the years and how the son disappointed Spencer by becoming a no-good waster. The world didn't know all these things and when Spencer fell for Helen Vinson people thought him a lecherous, heartless old devil. When finally Spencer ends his "brutal" life by suicide, only three people knew why he did it--his son, his wife and Ralph Morgan.

A Big Production usually is god-fathered by a syndicate of authors--the original playwright or novelist, the adapters, the con-tinuity writers, and often an additional-dialogue-by-er.

Perhaps the reason this is one of the best stories ever filmed is because it was written by a single author, Preston Sturges, and Jesse Lasky, with his usual fine sensitiveness, did not permit a bunch of other minds to come in and ruin a superb piece of work. Furthermore, Mr. Lasky had the nerve to permit a new and daring--to the screen--form of story telling.

The picture is notable in other respects. The cast is per-fect, right down to the two little boys, Billy O'Brien and Cullen Johnson, who portray the principals in their youth. Ralph Morgan is the narrator. You know the kind of performance he can give.

Spencer Tracy has done a lot of fine things on the screen, but never has he risen to such heights as he does in the role of the great railroad king. Whether as a young man or later on as a big shot, his inhibitions and repressions are portrayed with a profound understanding of the role.

Colleen Moore's come-back is nothing less than a triumph. Gosh, what a performance! First we see her as the Colleen we used to know, joyous and bright-eyed. Then in the next sequence, as an embittered old woman. And she looks as though she had grown old. Not merely old-lady make-up. (Hats off to Ernie Westmore for his work on both principals.)

The lesser roles are splendidly filled. Helen Vinson is ravishingly beautiful, and in the scene where she has to admit that Spencer's son is the father of her child she hits dramatic high.

Clifford Jones, as the no-good son, also delivers with fine sincerity.

In still smaller roles Sarah Padden and Farrell MacDonald lend distinction.

With such a story and cast it is no wonder that William K. Howard, one of the cinema's ace directors, was apparently inspired in his work.

Do I rave? Well, let me add bouquets to Max Parker for his sets, Louis de Francesco for his musical direction, and finally to Jimmie Howe for the most beautiful photography you've ever seen. The opening scene of the funeral in the huge, dimly lit church looks like the work of an old Dutch master.

> --Rob Wagner in Rob Wagner's
> Script, Vol. 10, No. 236
> (September 16, 1933), page 10.

*   *   *

The Power and the Glory will do business. It should do more than what will probably be its destined quota of box-office grossage, but grossage and "narratage" are a bit too radically apart to insure relative appeal.

This, Lasky's third production for Fox, is unique through this coined "narratage" style of cinematurgy. Its treatment has been consummately developed by director W. K. Howard and scenarist Preston Sturges.

Power and Glory, apart from its unquestioned niche in 1933's cinema annals as a prestige picture, will get money. It's no smash and its b. o. reactions may be spotty, but there is much in it that will command commercial attention. The reviewers in keys and hinterlands will gobble it up, and that's not going to hurt.

The two major elements against it are the cast deficiencies, lacking marquee strength and the fact that the theme starts and finishes on a tragic note. On cast, the four principal characters are performed by Spencer Tracy, who has never done better; Colleen Moore, whose comeback is distinguished; Ralph Morgan, ever-effective, and Helen Vinson, at her best.

As to theme, film starts with its ending--ecclesiastic services for the dead. Showing the finale of the life span of your central character is something that is by no means easy to offset. For average film fare it's like flashing the finale clinch at the beginning--an indisputable anti-climax.

And that's where the "narratage" comes in. Ralph Morgan is the narrator, detailing the highlights in the career of his friend (Spencer Tracy) who, even in death, is muchly maligned. Morgan

undertakes to show that Tracy, who fought his way up from an ignorant, unschooled trackwalker to the presidency of railroads, and
a tycoon of industry, was not the bad egg everybody painted.   He
argues that his strike-breaking methods, which cost many railroad
workers' lives, had another element to it; that his turning out his
first wife (Colleen Moore) in favor of Helen Vinson might have had
extenuating circumstances, etc.   The climax is Tracy's suicide
upon learning of his second wife's unfaithfulness, with the inference
that his own son (by the first marriage) figured in that marital
breach.

         As in true life, Morgan, in recapitulating the episodes of
his friend's career, skips haphazardly from highlight to highlight,
in loose and unrelated fashion, but never palling as he presents his
oral evidence of his powerful friend's other characteristics.   Morgan is the meek private secretary to the go-getting Tracy, a gentle
stooge who worries about the man who, since their childhood days
at the old swimming hole, evidenced prophetic marks as a natural
born leader of men.

         All these flashbacks are skillfully introduced.   It's never
mechanical or creakily artificial.   The montage is smooth and natural.   The camera illusions with the soft fade-outs visibly command the mind's eye to what Morgan is telling to his wife (Sarah
Padden).

         The "narratage" is made possible through this device--Mor-
gan and his loving wife, both now bent by years, reviewing the
dead man's career.   Morgan has just come from the services--
even the watchman at the railroad office's building expresses himself not sorry about the tycoon's suicide.   Morgan alone defends
him.   He also defends Tracy to his wife when he reaches the retreat of his home.   She, too, bears malice to the departed man.
Then the story unfolds in episodic, flashback fashion.

         It's well done in every respect.   Casting right down the line
is punchy for performance.   Howard's direction is truly unique and
distinguished.   His favorite cameraman, James Wong Howe, mani-
fests indubitable artistry with the cinematography.   Power and the
Glory rates somewhat like its title in the progression of soundfilm
technic.

                              --Abel (Abel Green) in Variety,
                              Vol. 111, No. 11 (August 22,
                              1933), page 22.

☐   PRIDE AND PREJUDICE (M-G-M, 1940)

         In this territory when one says a film is a Four Star film
one means it is worthy of being shown at the theater of that name
where patrons expect and get only superior motion pictures.   Last

year this house, never stigmatized by the double feature, showed only eight films, but their success was so great that the theater made the biggest profit of any house in the circuit.

Merely note the cast and credits, and you'll see why Pride and Prejudice belongs in the Four Star: Jane Austen's most popular novel, scripted by the literary Aldous Huxley and ace scenarist Jane Murfin; produced by Hunt Stromberg; starring Greer Garson and Laurence Olivier, who had previously scored personal successes in the two films that ran longest at the Four Star.

Pride and Prejudice is almost as good as the play of the same name, and I think it won't disappoint admirers of Dear Jane. The story, as most of you know, revolves around the impecunious and ambitious Mrs. Bennet who tries frantically to marry off her numerous daughters. The background is the elegant and mannered eighteenth century, but the story depends for its effectiveness not on plot or period but upon robust characterization. The mood is not that of farce, although there are farcical situations, and a certain balance and delicacy are required to make Pride and Prejudice the delicious antique that it is in book form. Robert Z. Leonard's production is not sufficiently stylized for my taste, and I'd like it better if he hadn't given farce free rein, but for general consumption and in all important particulars the picture is as attractive and "different" as any you are likely to see this season.

Mr. Olivier has a perfunctory role and plays it that way. Miss Garson is only pictorially effective as the high-minded heroine. The real acting plums go to Mary Boland as Mrs. Bennet, Edmund Gwenn as her mousy husband, and to Edna May Oliver as the imperious but altogether delightful Lady Catherine. Miss Oliver is the scene stealer in this show, but Marsha Hunt makes herself noticed, and it was a pleasure to see Karen Morley again. Some people admired Mary Boland's work extravagantly, but anyone who had seen Florence Bates in the same part would perhaps wish with me that Miss Bates could have imparted her special gusto to Mrs. Bennet.

--Richard Sheridan Ames in Rob
Wagner's Script, Vol. 24, No.
564 (August 17, 1940), page 16.

☐ THE PRISONER OF ZENDA (Selznick, 1937)

In spite of the gorgeous production, lively music, and splendid acting, I simply couldn't catch the spirit of this old swashbuckling drama. When Andy Hawkins wrote the story in 1896, kings and such were still "some punkins." Now they seem like the punks most of 'em were--silly wasters of an outworn social system. Nor could I adjust my mind to the time element--a curious mixture of the sixteenth and nineteenth centuries--revolvers and broadswords, cigarettes and moats!

Ronald Colman playing the old dual role--a Britisher masquerading as a Mid-European king--almost made the part live by
his excellent acting.   But the absurdity of a foreigner--even grant-
ing identical likeness, which doesn't happen except in twins--fooling
the real king's intimates, to say nothing of his own flesh and blood,
is simply too childish to be taken seriously.

Madeleine Carroll is exceptionally beautiful in the brittle,
porcelain manner of the make-up departments, but her acting is
uninspired.

Douglas Fairbanks, Jr. gives a sympathetic interpretation of
a royal rotter, but I felt he was always acting.   Next to Colman
are Aubrey Smith, Raymond Massey, and David Niven who heroical-
ly try--and almost succeed--in making their artificial characters
real.

Ronald swims a moat, climbs a castle wall, fights Doug with
broadswords all over the works, and emerges with his arm in a
sling, the screen's old-fashioned symbol of great physical injury.

But romantic housemaids may still like the dear old hoke.
                         --Rob Wagner in Rob Wagner's
                           Script, Vol. 18, No. 432
                           (October 9, 1937), page 8.

☐ QUEEN CHRISTINA (M-G-M, 1933)

Greta Garbo's performance in Queen Christina reminds me
of a story, the tag line of which was, "Well, I guess that's telling
'em, fat lady."   Those of my not so gentle readers who have heard
this ancient nifty will get the entire picture without further comment.   To the others an explanation is due:

In the days of the silent films, Garbo was considered the
last word.   When the talkies came along her first word promised
to be the last one.   In other words, as an exponent of the English
language, Miss Garbo was not so good.   Even her employers ad-
mitted that she was barely colossal, which in our language means
lousy.

But instead of folding up and scuttling back to her native
land, as so many foreign stars did, Garbo dug in.   She was not
going to disappoint her loyal American film fans.   She was not going to let down the Metro-Goldwyn-Mayer organization that had been
so good to her.   And, incidentally, she was not going to pass up
that Hollywood dough without a struggle.

So Garbo went to work, and Queen Christina is the result.
In my opinion it is the finest thing she has ever done, talkie or

silent. Not only has she made amazing strides in her conquest of
the English language, but with this improved diction her acting has
taken on added ease and grace.

She has more warmth, more human appeal than she has ever
displayed before, which means that she is a better actress. And
this includes her silent work. Even in those days her inability to
speak and understand English was a big handicap, because she did
not have this bond in common with her American film associates.

Having paid tribute to Miss Garbo's efforts, it is only fair
to add that she was fortunate in having Rouben Mamoulian as her
director in Queen Christina. With his great genius for scenery and
lighting, Mr. Mamoulian has provided a background of convincing
authenticity that amplifies every nuance of Garbo's artistry.
(Come, come Evans, be yourself.)

Well, anyhow it is a good movie, but I don't want Mr. Mamoulian or anybody else to think they were kidding me about the
historical facts of the story. Christina, according to reliable authorities, was not the sort of a gal who would abdicate a throne for
any one man. She took her fun in bunches, and the last thing she
would ever have done would have been to take a long boat ride with
a corpse. No indeedy. Chris liked her boy friends to be up and
about.

And another thing, Mr. Mamoulian. What is that bedroom
scene all about? You know, the one where Garbo goes all around
the room patting, petting and fondling the furniture.

Then there's that business of Garbo lying on the floor bunch-
ing a munch--I mean munching a bunch of grapes. In the first
place it can't be done. I tried it, and the juice skeeches out on
your chin and runs down into your ears. (And I would also be
pleased if Miss Garbo will give me her reactions when that one
grape missed her mouth and rolled down her back.)

One last squawk. I am not a sucker for happy endings, but
I do believe the finish of Queen Christina should be more pleasant.
Killing the hero in an unnecessary duel does little to add drama to
the tale, and leaves Christina with no reward for the sacrifice of
her kingdom other than a visit to her dead lover's home in Spain--
"built on a white cliff overlooking the sea." (And may I remind
the scenarist that just a few reels before this Christina had rebuked
her Chancellor with this question--"Must we always live for the
dead?")

--Harry Evans in Life, Vol. 101,
No. 2587 (February 1934), page
38.

☐   REBECCA (Selznick/United Artists, 1940)

         A notable picture: from the standpoint of writing, direction
and acting, one of the most beautiful examples of film craftsmanship Hollywood ever presented to the world.   In essence a sordid,
depressing story, with infidelity and crime included in its elements,
it comes to the screen as a gripping drama related with so much
skill and good taste we are conscious only of its perfection as art,
a perfect blending of human emotions presented against backgrounds
which in themselves are masterpieces of visual art.   A purely
psychological drama, it is not for the casual film patron in search
of light entertainment; it is too fine a creation to break box-office
records, a fact no doubt apparent from the outset to Producer Selznick and regarded by him complacently, as Gone with the Wind is
attending to the money end of his business.

         Rebecca is screened literature which retains its literary
flavor; viewing it gives you the feeling you have when you turn the
leaves of an engrossing book you are reading.   The preview audience was a cross section of the best minds in pictures, but there
was little of the usual preview applause.   Applause would have
broken the spell which gripped the audience during the entire running of the film.

         An admirable cast was selected for the picture, with one ex-
ception all seasoned players who long since had won their spurs.
The exception was Joan Fontaine.   I have been waiting for her to
get her chance.   In the Spectator of June 5, 1937, I reviewed an
unimportant picture in which she appeared.   I wrote of her: "Joan
will get there.   She is a lovely creature with a charming personality. ...   You may put her down as a young woman destined to reach
stardom rapidly. "   Apparently Dave Selznick is the only producer
who shared my opinion, and for both of us she more than makes
good in Rebecca.   Denied, by the dictates of her characterization,
the glamour of a feminine star's usual costuming, the part itself a
self-effacing, negative one, she rises to the heights, displaying
dramatic fervor and deep understanding of the role, astonishing in
one so young and with no previous experience in similar parts.

         To all others in the cast only the warmest praise can be
given.   To name them individually would be but to repeat the praise.
They responded to Alfred Hitchcock's direction by giving him one
of the smoothest groups of performances a picture ever was blessed
with.   Nor was there ever more brilliant direction, more evident
appreciation of the values of a story and ability to realize them.

         Only a perfectly written script could account for such per-
fection in its presentation on the screen.   The picture was strength-
ened as film entertainment by the liberties taken with the du Maurier book.   The mood of the story pervades the remarkably impressive photography of George Barnes as it also does the settings designed by Lyle Wheeler and Joseph Platt, and the interior decora-

tions by Howard Bristol. The film editing by Hal Kern and James
Newcom also figures as an asset of the production. Special effects
by Jack Cosgrove add materially to the picture as a whole.
                                        --Welford Beaton in Hollywood
                                           Spectator, Vol. 14, No. 24
                                           (April 1, 1940), page 6.

                              *   *   *

     David O. Selznick may have been pondering the truth of "un-
easy lies the head that wears a crown," but after the preview of
Rebecca he must have slumbered peacefully, serene in the knowledge that press and public had again acclaimed him a producer
without peer. His picturization of Daphne du Maurier's celebrated
novel, directed with unfaltering skill by Alfred Hitchcock, provides
absorbing psychological drama, expertly acted, rich in sombre atmosphere.

     Rebecca may depress or distress patrons who are uncom-
fortable in dark rooms, uneasy on stormy nights, perplexed or re-
pelled by frustrated or tortured human behavior. Faithful to the
novel, the film intensifies the plight of a young bride brought to
live at gloomy "Manderley," where the unseen but all-pervading
presence of the master's dead wife, Rebecca, almost destroys the
second marriage. Joan Fontaine portrays with marked feeling and
emotional honesty the inexperienced girl who tries to hold the love
of Laurence Olivier, beset by troubled memories. The Olivier
performance equals his magnetic impersonation in Wuthering Heights,
and of almost stellar importance is the contribution by Judith Anderson who plays the malevolent housekeeper who works with sinister
cunning to keep alive the influence of her late mistress. However,
all of the supporting players merit praise, including such veterans
as George Sanders, Nigel Bruce, Gladys Cooper, and the newcomer, Florence Bates, who plays her first screen role as rich Mrs.
Van Hopper.

     It is not too early to predict a brilliant film future for Miss
Bates who has already scored importantly in stage productions of
Pride and Prejudice and O Evening Star. As evidence of her vitality and dramatic gifts, the preview audience, which included just
about everybody who ought to know, responded to her scenes with
spontaneous applause.

     Needless to say, Rebecca rejoices in a beautiful physical
production, in perfection of detail, sterling photography, and sympathetic musical treatment. The screen play by Robert E. Sherwood
and Joan Harrison is both adroit and literate. Possibly, more vari-
able pace might have improved the film, and it could have been
shorter, but those of us who enjoy Mr. Hitchcock's lingering pre-
occupation with a mood or his facile shadings and camera explorations aren't likely to complain when he is overly generous. One
doesn't have to call Rebecca a "great" film or a "masterpiece" to
indicate its real excellence. By this time it should be enough to

report that here is a motion picture worthy of David O. Selznick.
                        --Richard Sheridan Ames in Rob
                          Wagner's Script, Vol. 23, No.
                          548 (March 30, 1940), page 16.

☐ RED DUST (M-G-M, 1932)

        The virile Gable is back again, in one of those he-man parts
that made him famous.   With him is Jean Harlow, in her most
likable role.   The result is a picture worth seeing.

        The story is laid on a rubber plantation in the jungle, with
Clark the owner, and Harlow a flip little "Sadie Thompson" type
with a heart of gold.   To this hole of red dust, coolies and storms,
comes Gene Raymond and his bride, Mary Astor.   Gable falls in
love with Mary and trouble begins.

        There's a lightness in the direction, a sparkle in the dia-
logue, and a grand punch ending.   Jean Harlow gets the most out
of every line and all but steals the show.

        Donald Crisp, Tully Marshall and Willie Fung contribute
strong bits.
                        --Photoplay, Vol. 43, No. 1
                          (December 1932), page 57.

                    *   *   *

        Think of all the novels you used to read behind the barn when
you were a kid--review the confession magazine for the past month
--attend a travelling salesmen's convention--and you'll be all set
for Red Dust.   The two principals are the screen's leading exponents of what the screen calls sex, Clark Gable and Jean Harlow.
And you've got to hand it to them.   The thing they are supposed to
do is done well.   I mean to say, the producers wanted to let everybody know, right away, what Red Dust was all about, and Clark and
Jean do the trick in their first scene.   It is one of those tropical
pictures in which "the rain and heat get you."   Two women--one
respectable, married--the other a tropical trollop ... both in love
with old red-antsy Clark.   The scene is a rubber plantation ... and
everybody's morals stretch a point.   Red Dust (the last word is
wrong by one letter) is an elemental treatment of the most frequently discussed human frailty.   I thought it was pretty awful, and I
believe it will make money.   (And the censors appear to have
learned this lesson about sex: you can legislate against it, but
you can't make it unpopular.)
                        --Harry Evans in Life, Vol. 100,
                          No. 2574 (January 1933), page
                          37.

☐ THE ROARING TWENTIES (Warner Bros. , 1939)

The Roaring Twenties isn't as good as the title, the background of the last, mad decade, or the participation of James Cagney and Mark Hellinger would lead one to expect. In fact, it isn't
a good picture at all. Flaccid, artificial, just another of the gang-
war things, with Cagney indifferent, the producer sat back in his
chair and believed a few old songs, some muddy montage, and
glimpses of bathtub gin in the making would take us all back to
yesterday. They take us back all right--but not to yesterday. Instead, I was unpleasantly reminded of too-numerous, almost mime-
ographed Cagney films.

Gladys George helps out, as the sympathetic dame Cagney
should have loved. She's good as herself, but far from convincing
if she's impersonating Texas Guinan whose vocal signature she
uses. Priscilla Lane sings, advantageously, "Melancholy Baby"
and "I'm Just Wild About Harry, " and neither improves upon or
detracts from a stock characterization. Jeffrey Lynn yawns politely at another nice-boy role--when he should growl, at Warner
Brothers, who have given him nothing worthy of his ability since
Four Daughters. Paul Kelly, another of the neglecteds, is briefly
effective; Humphrey Bogart does his grim facial calisthenics, and
Cagney simply doesn't care. Will anyone?

--Richard Sheridan Ames in Rob
Wagner's Script, Vol. 22, No.
528 (November 4, 1939), pages
16-17.

*   *   *

The Twenties have roared so often on the screen in the last
few years that you are inclined to listen for some new note in the
noise, some addition to the old formula to make clearer why those
years were so important and what they did to America. Or why
do it again?

The most immediate and cogent "why" is that it gives James
Cagney a chance to be his best, and that is always reason enough.
But there is perhaps more than that--other prohibition-gangster
films have been exciting reminiscences, assumptions that they were
dealing with something safely past and done with: this one, though
directly it seems to be pointing definitely backward, indirectly it
cannot, in these days of an approaching war danger, help opening
up a prospect of the future. Can't it, after all, happen again?
Liquor prohibition can be other things besides itself, it can stand
for other mistakes. And what war and its disillusionments do to
the individuals of one generation it is sure to do to the individuals of
another. And the desperations of unemployment don't need even a
war to make them profound and fatal.

The Roaring Twenties, being written by Mark Hellinger, has
a bit of the Broadway columnist's sentimentality about it, an almost

nostalgic regret, under its hard-boiled manner, for the exciting
glamour of a past day.   But a March-of-Time commentator sternly
keeps things in line, bridging the time gaps with cause-and-effect
explanations that the audience might otherwise have to figure out
for itself, or feel without figuring out.   There are three Americans
fighting in France, each reacting in his own way to the business of
killing, each rushing into or revolting from the expression of violence for which a gun in the hand can so easily be a release.   Then
the three are back home, and the jobs that were to be saved for
them while they fought for their country are not there; and prohibition has come: and instead of peace-time restraints upon the violence they have learned to give vent to, the quickest, easiest, least
hum-drum way to get ahead is to go on being violent, with shooting
as easy as spitting, and law-breaking smart and fashionable.

Then of course you have the regular gangster story, so
familiar that its meanings have become as deeply buried in formula
as in any cattle-rustling quickie.   It piles up climax after climax,
till it gets exhausting, and it has all been done so often before that
one forgets these things have happened in life, not just in movies.

But if you can forget the rest of the gangster cycle, and
look at this with a fresh eye, you can see that The Roaring Twenties is written with a lot of understanding, not only of people but
of what social forces do to people; that Raoul Walsh, whose talent
as a director has been frittered away on so many worthless things,
has here found something he can do his best with; and that what
was rampant in the Twenties did things not only to the Cagneys and
Bogarts but to the Jeffrey Lynns and Rosemary Lanes.   For here,
in what might to the casual glance seem only a bit of love interest,
are two decent people who might have been just innocent bystanders
but might as easily, and were, innocent participants, caught up in
the swirl of things and drifting on it, their own moral sense curiously blunted by the callousness about them.

Of course five-per-cent beer and repeal didn't bring salvation to America, nor did the wiping out of Nick and George and
Danny and Eddie accomplish any curative operation on society.
Other and deeper things were wrong, and still are, for all the triumphant optimism of the commentator.   But where are you going
to get a final solution of such problems--in the movies, the preach-
ers, the government, or anywhere else?

The picture, in addition to good writing and better than good
directing, has--best of all--a cast that is about perfect.   Actors so
easily and so often typed as Humphrey Bogart, Frank McHugh, Joe
Sawyer and Paul Kelly, shed their typiness and become individuals
again.   Rosemary Lane, whether it is impersonation or just being
herself, is inconspicuously exactly right, just as Gladys George is
more conspicuously just right as a sort of toned down, more sympathetic Texas Guinan.   And Cagney.   Once more, and never so
successfully, he takes every line, every movement, every bit of
business, and makes them so utterly an expression of Eddie Bart-

lett that they seem not something he learned or was told to do but
a spontaneous creation of his own.   An eloquent and perceptive
critic may sometime succeed in saying all that could be said about
James Cagney as one of the great actors of our time, the unique
embodiment of one of our time's most tragic figures--the toughened
(not tough) city boy who has to fight his way.   But a volume of analysis, though it might tell more, could not show as much as seeing him in The Roaring Twenties.

> --James Shelley Hamilton in Na-
> tional Board of Review Magazine,
> Vol. 14, No. 9 (December
> 1939), pages 11-12.

☐ ROBERTA (RKO, 1935)

A knockout, a honey AND a wow!   It's the musical you
meant to save all those adjectives for and one for which you try
to think up new ones.   Freddie Astaire's dancing feet and nimble
comedy have never been seen to better advantage and he scores
another triumph.   Irene Dunne comes into her own again as the
heroine.   Bill Seiter proves himself a master musical maker.
Kern crashes through with two new hits besides the well known
"Smoke Gets in Your Eyes."   And there's a fashion show for the
ladies that will make them swoon with the clothes worn by the
kinds of girls that make men stay.   It's the best guarantee of how
to get money in the bank that an exhibitor will get this year.

If you think that opening paragraph exhausts the rave possibilities, you stopped reading too soon.   Sam Mintz and Jane Murfin
have taken what was a pretty dull book originally and, using the
bare outline of the story, have hung a flock of laughs on it with
great lightness and gayety without neglecting the love story.   The
bare outline is about a football player who inherits a dressmaking
establishment in Paris.   A Russian princess becomes his business
partner and, after a few minor musical comedy complications, becomes his partner for life.

Freddie Astaire ... there's so much to say about him it's
hard to start and worse to stop.   His utter ease and casualness of
delivery.   His superb dancing and the superb dance routines ...
entirely the product of Astaire ingenuity.   Maybe it's better to say
just Fred Astaire and then we've said everything.   Ginger Rogers
doing an Indiana gal gone Polish Countess is grand and improving
with every new dance step.   Irene Dunne, beautifully photographed,
her voice beautifully recorded and speaking lines as though she
meant them, steps up another peg.   Helen Westley as Aunt Minnie,
thoroughly delightful.   Randy Scott, given his chance to get out of
westerns and turning that chance to such good account that you
wonder what's kept him away from feature pictures all this time.
Claire Dodd as the other girl is attractive enough and just about

adequate.   The rest of the cast is fine, with "Candy" doing his
singing act, just for a laugh.

    Pandro S. Berman has brought forth another winner in the
production line and given it everything, including a new fashion designer for pictures, Bernard Newman, who has done some very
lovely things.   Bill Seiter misses nothing in his direction and nothing slackens his pace.   It's a musical without a single time-taking
chorus number.   Cronjager's photography is beautiful and Max
Steiner's musical scoring a joy, particularly in "I Won't Dance"
and the arrangement of "Smoke Gets in Your Eyes" for a dance
routine.

--The Hollywood Reporter, Vol.
25, No. 31 (February 9, 1935),
page 3.

☐ ROMEO AND JULIET (M-G-M, 1936)

    It required great and laudable courage on the part of the
late Irving Thalberg to attempt the resuscitation of Shakespeare's
"star cross'd lovers" for the screen, and while the incantation has
not been unreservedly successful, the picture will undoubtedly remain one of Mr. Thalberg's more glittering memorials.

    The production has everything money can buy and, in one or
two instances, touches of inspiration ... a rare enough commodity
in the studio world.   The Industry stands in sore need of such adventurously artistic hearts and purses as Mr. Thalberg possessed.

    Like the measles, Juliet is something actresses know they
must experience before full adulthood is achieved.   Norma Shearer's
delineation of the gamut-role is surprisingly facile; it unquestionably
tops such earlier contributions to celluloid-Shakespeare as were
proffered by Theda Bara and Beverly Bayne.   There is a deft suggestion of youth about Miss Shearer's concept of the character, a
dewey quality to the early moments, a searching depth, a restless
probing of the emotions as the tragedy soars to its appointed culmination.   The oft-rendered lines are read with freshness, there
is vocal timing without the insult of exaggeration and the result is
as full-length a portrait of the Capulet problem-child as it is possible for a picture-trained actress to bestow.   Cukor's influence is
detectable in the hepburnesque hand movements (watch the balcony
scene closely), and in numerous inflections of the Shearer voice,
but these enhance rather than detract, at least for this admirer of
the great Katharine.

    The superb screen play is the work of Talbot Jennings.   At
one and the same time it achieves scope and fidelity to the original
and while the speeches have been shifted, cut and rearranged, the
changes make for added pace.   In this transposition Shakespeare is

happily without a new collaborator; there is no "additional dialogue by" line to infuriate, as was the case when The Taming of the Shrew was picturized by the then-twain Pickford-Fairbanks. Great visual beauty (rapturously entrapped by William Daniel's camera) grapevines its way through the cadenced verbal tapestry and the blending has been accomplished with effect and discrimination by George Cukor.

Despite ingeniously contrived background-shiftings, scenes of mob-movement, motion remains subservient to the dialogue and it is impossible for even superlative verboseness to impale attention on the screen. Even Shakespeare's verse is useless to genuine picture art.

Read quietly, Shakespeare loses a great deal of his virility, though the less tempestuous technique has come to be confused with what is termed "modernity" in acting. Power is vitiated when roystering melodrama is played in drawing room style and therefore only the stark climaxes--the death of Mercutio, Juliet's potion scene, Romeo's bearding of Tybalt--carry the logical impact.

Leslie Howard's son of the Montague household is a cerebral performance, an Oxford don yearning for crumpets-and-tea. Handicapped by an obvious maturity, Howard dismisses the dash of the character, concentrates on a careful, skilled reading that to some may atone for his lack of fire. Neither Shearer nor Howard ever suggest the hot-blooded Latins of the romance land; not for a moment do we see the impassioned, storm-tossed children of the script.

Expecting great things of Mercutio in the hand of John Barrymore, I was disappointed to find wit displaced by buffoonery, whimsicality become horseplay. Only in the death scene do we find the Barrymore of legend and then with sure thrusts does he draw blood from the character's heart with as fine a piece of acting as I've witnessed. Stripped of strutting, excessive stylization, Barrymore is still a beacon light among performers.

The supporting cast finds Basil Rathbone a glorious Tybalt, Reginald Denny excellent, Henry Kolker a subtle, well-knit Friar Laurence. Only praise can be found for C. Aubrey Smith, Andy Devine (delectably comic), Robert Warwick, Conway Tearle and Maurice Murphy ... a huge block of names but all demanding special mention. Edna May Oliver's nurse is a faulty casting choice; she skims only the surface of a role that should be fat but here is lean.

Settings by Messel and Gibbons wisely refrain from reality, have a lush beauty that rivals the rhythms of the speeches. Costumes are magnificent and Oliver Messel triumphs again, this time with the assistance of Adrian.

Romeo and Juliet is an extravagant and controversial picture
that should surge to hit proportions through those very qualities.
--Herb Sterne in Rob Wagner's
Script, Vol. 16, No. 382
(September 26, 1936), page 10.

*   *   *

Commenting in a recent Spectator on the box-office value of
Shakespeare, I wrote: "It looks to me as if producers are about
to overdo Shakespeare as a screen author.... Language alone,
even Shakespeare's, will not make pictures successful. And beauty
of production ceases to be box-office when audiences get too much
of it."

Since I wrote these lines I have seen what is probably the
finest presentation ever accorded Romeo and Juliet--the finest, perhaps, of the many fine things Irving Thalberg has to his credit as
a film producer. No lovelier Juliet than Norma Shearer could be
imagined, nor one with more talent to interpret the part. Nor
could one wish for more impressive reading of Romeo's lines than
Leslie Howard gives them. The Mercutio of John Barrymore is an
acting gem, the Nurse of Edna May Oliver, the Tybalt of Basil
Rathbone, the Lord Capulet of Aubrey Smith, the Paris of Ralph
Forbes--all the characterizations, in fact, are completely satisfactory.

The production reaches an artistic peak seldom seen on the
screen. There is as much poetry in its visual beauty as there is
in Shakespeare's lines. The whole undertaking is worthy of its literary inspiration, a triumph for its producer, a credit to the
screen.

And yet I see no reason for changing a word in the lines I
wrote before I saw Romeo and Juliet. It is not box-office. Shakespeare is not box-office. His appeal is intellectual. The screen's
appeal must be to the emotions. The sheer beauty of the "Pretty
Girl" number in The Great Ziegfeld stirred me emotionally; I sat
with a lump in my throat as "The lady with the lamp" moved along
the corridors of pain in White Angel, and I cried over the tragic
misfortunes of Nova Pilbeam in Nine Days a Queen. In White Angel
I did not see Kay Francis. I saw Florence Nightingale; it was
Florence Nightingale who stirred me. Nor in the English picture
did I see Nova Pilbeam. It was a simple girl I saw, a tragic play-
thing of cruel fate.

As I viewed Romeo and Juliet I thought of the beauty of Cedric Gibbon's sets and the superb quality of William Daniels' photography; I watched the fleeting, sensitive play of emotions on Norma
Shearer's beautiful face, estimated the value of Howard's Romeo by
comparing it with other Romeos I have seen; I enjoyed Barrymore's
interpretation of his role, so unlike that of any other actor I have
seen in the role. When Barrymore died I admired the manner of

his dying, but as he had joined us at dinner prior to the preview
and now was sitting behind us, I shed no tears over his demise.

Likewise, I admired the acting of Norma when she tried to
kiss death from the dead lips of her lover and then found a dagger
to bring an end to her suffering, but there she was across the aisle
from us, the same radiant creature I chatted with as we were going
in to our seats. It was she, the girl I admire as a girl and as an
artist, whom I saw on the screen. I was pleased that Norma did
everything so well, but I was indifferent to the misfortunes of Juliet. They reached my intellect, but did not pierce it to find my
emotions.

Shakespeare is not box-office, as I have said, but Norma
Shearer and Leslie Howard are. Whatever measure of financial
success the picture meets with will be due to draw names in the
cast. Perhaps it will make money, but it will be the last Shakespearean play to find its way to the screen. Box-office success
is incubated by the warmth of human appeal which can be developed
only by our complete absorption in the human drama being enacted;
and we can not become absorbed until we forget we are looking at
actors and see only the people they are playing.

Of course, there is the possibility of the discovery of a director who can make Shakespeare human, who can handle the Bard's
characters in a manner to make us weep over their misfortunes,
something that George Cukor's direction comes a long way from
accomplishing.

> --Welford Beaton in Hollywood
> Spectator, Vol. 11, No. 9
> (August 1, 1936), page 7.

☐ RUGGLES OF RED GAP (Paramount, 1935)

Will Rogers and dozens of others have worked the pants off
of the old story of the crude, country newlyrich husband and wife
who want to put on airs including a butler, so I don't see why any
producer wanted to go and produce Ruggles of Red Gap. And I,
personally, blushed watching Charles Laughton's attempts at comedy, as the imported manservant. Mr. Laughton is a great actor
in certain types of roles, but he gave me the creeps when he tried
to be funny in this picture. I would just as soon see Walter Hampden take Stan Laurel's place in a Laurel & Hardy comedy, or
sooner. In one spot, however, Mr. Laughton gets a chance to
show his mettle as an elocutionist: when he recites Lincoln's
Gettysburg address to a group of ashamed Americans who can't
remember a word of it.

> --Don Herold in Life, Vol. 102,
> No. 2602 (May 1935), page 34.

* * *

There are six names above the title of this swell picture.
All are effective enough to deserve that rating, but the ace credit
belongs to Leo McCarey, the director.   McCarey has turned out a
fast and furiously funny film which should have no trouble establishing itself as a box-office leader in almost every spot.   Besides
being amusing and well handled, it has the unusual elements of
combining adult and sophisticated class draw with that of family
audiences.

Film is a perfect example of what smart handling behind the
camera can do.   It could as easily have been a cheap, hoke comedy getting nowhere, and accomplishing little.   Original novel has
been a near classic for many years, and it has been made as a
film twice before, once by Essanay (1918) and by Paramount (1923).
Edward E. Horton played the name part the last time out and it
was a successful b. o. film.   But this time all the old copies have
been thrown away and yarn is handled from a completely fresh
standpoint--with gratifying results.

It's the fine casting that will probably stand out to most
viewers.   Charles Laughton is Ruggles, the British valet incomparable.   And he turns in a performance that will surprise some and
widen his appeal by far.   He's played comedy before (Henry VIII),
but here he is doing it differently.   It's not satire; it's not a
pathological character study.   Just plain comedy, and he's splendid,
especially when he uses that dead pan.

Charles Ruggles has, perhaps, the toughest assignment, and
Roland Young runs a small part into one of the high spot performances.   The women, too, are all happily spotted.

Story is a bit dated and would be dangerous if not so well
treated.   It plants Elmer (Ruggles) and his wife (Mary Boland) in
Paris.   Elmer has a fetish for checked suits, spurred boots and
ten-gallon hats.   Effie wants to play the lady.   They play poker
with the Earl of Burnstead (Young) and win his butler, Ruggles
(Laughton).   They take him back to Red Gap, state of Washington,
with them.   There Ruggles is mistaken for a British army captain
and becomes a celebrity.   That gives him the idea of freedom and
standing on his own.   He falls in love with Mrs. Judson (ZaSu
Pitts) and opens a restaurant.   And to round out the tale the Earl
comes visiting, meets Nell Kenner and marries her.

McCarey has kept this yarn flowing constantly and surely for
90 minutes.   None of it drags.   Adaptation and dialog are extra
good and a decided help, and just to top everything off McCarey has
a scene about three-quarters through the film which is so dangerous
and audacious that it almost startles.   He has Laughton, at that
point, reciting in full Lincoln's Gettysburg address.   It doesn't
seem to belong in merely reading of it, but it's so deftly handled
and beautifully done by Laughton that this serious moment turns
into the high spot of the picture.

On the other end of the pendulum, there is an early scene, in Paris, where Charles Ruggles and Laughton meet James Burke, latter being another rough-and-ready American westerner. They all go out on a binge together, and the sequence is just about the comedy high spot of the season.

If there is any criticism at all, it is that the timing is occasionally faulty, the laughs sometimes overlapping. But who can hate a picture on that account?

--Kauf in Variety, Vol. 117, No. 13 (March 13, 1935), page 15.

☐ SAN FRANCISCO (M-G-M, 1936)

When I first heard that familiar rumble and saw the chandeliers swinging, I looked for the nearest EXIT. Subsequent fans prepared by the earthquake publicity won't be so shocked. Or maybe they will. My first reaction was: What will Doctor Giannini and the California Chamber of Commerce say? For John Emerson and Bernie Hyman have put over an earthquake more terrifying and destructive than the combined wreckage of the four earthquakes I have experienced. Here I've been telling the Outlanders that our California earthquakes are a joke, that we use 'em to rock the babies to sleep, that in San Francisco it was the Fire. And now along comes MGM and not only rocks the publicity boat but capsizes it.

Yes, and in so doing it all but drowned a grand and colorful story (Robert Hopkins and Anita Loos). Indeed, I had become so interested in the efforts of Jeanette MacDonald and Spencer Tracy to bring Clark Gable to God that I was unprepared for the earthquake as they were. True, it took God Himself to bring the roughest barbarian of the Barbary Coast to his knees, but He was so long doing it that my interest in the principals was overwhelmed by the god-awful catastrophe. The net result may not be Art, but it's "entertainment"--that is, if Chaos and Old Night may be considered entertaining. Good showmen as they are, however, these MGMummers rose from the ashes and pulled a glory hallelujah, dissolving into a panorama of new San Francisco that had the previewers cheering.

Clark Gable looks like a ruffian, but the real Clark Gable, sweet and gentle, always shows through. That's why he's so good in raffish parts. He runs the roughest "spot" on the Barbary Coast. He gives Jeanette MacDonald, a little country gal, work. When "discovered," she is naturally torn between gratitude (love) and a career in the magnificent Tivoli. Both Jeanette and Clark are superb.

Spencer Tracy, one of the screen's greatest actors, played a surprise role. We first see him knocking the block off Clark in

a gymnasium. When dressed, behold!--he is a priest! A grand
friendship between Sin and Virtue. Later, a wonderful bit of writing and acting. Spencer disagrees with Clark. Bang! Clark
knocks him down. But now, as a priest, Spencer does not strike
back.

Jessie Ralph, former washerwoman, now an "aristocrat of
Nob Hill," gives a magnificent performance. Her son, Jack Holt,
well-groomed, sedately ample--and horseless!--you'll never know
him. But you'll like him a lot.

The tapestry destroyed by the earthquake is alive with colorful characters; Shirley Ross, Margaret Irving, Ted Healy, Harold
Huber, Ed Kennedy, Al Shean, William Ricciardi, and many others.

Herbert Stothart's musical direction is sparkling--two grand
songs, "San Francisco" (Bronislau Kaper and Walter Jurmann),
hilarious and stirring, and a beautiful one, "Would you?" by Nacio
Herb Brown and Arthur Freed. Cedric Gibbons' art direction is
wonderfully faithful to the terrible art of the period. Adrian triumphs over the same handicap.

William von Wymetal "montaged" the principal scenes from
Faust, a corking way of emphasizing the high lights! And how
Jeanette ate up those high lights!

Naturally, Oliver March's photography is gorgeous. But one
half the show must be credited to the montage sequences of the
earthquake by John Hoffman. These are absolutely sensational.

Last, but no means least, credit W. S. Van Dyke, top director of super-super-colossal specials.

To MGM: Yes, it is a lovely picture if you can get by with
it.

> --Rob Wagner in Rob Wagner's
> Script, Vol. 15, No. 373 (June
> 27, 1936), pages 9-10.

* * *

Truly a great achievement. The picture leads us into the
cataclysmic death scene of the old San Francisco, gives us a flash
of its rebirth, and ends with a view of what it is to-day. Still, it
is not a story of a city. It is a story of two people, as far apart
as the poles in birth, early environment, upbringing--the daughter
of a country parson and a young man born and raised on the notorious Barbary Coast. The mating instinct is the one thing they have
in common. The growth of their romance is the story, the earthquake but an incident in it, a terrific, stunning incident, but so
cleverly has the story been constructed and presented that our chief
interest in it is its effect on the relations of the two young people.

San Francisco is Jeanette MacDonald's picture. This talented and beautiful young woman amazes us with the wide range of her versatility. The most impressive dialogue in the production is that spoken by her eyes and interpreted by the camera, fleeting, sensitive impressions more illuminating than any words could be. And her glorious voice is a golden strand that weaves its way through the stirring narrative and makes beautiful even the most sordid scenes in which it is heard. Jeanette is easily our greatest singing actress, the only one whose voice and dramatic powers reach the same superlative heights. San Francisco is a triumph for her. It is impossible to conceive of anyone else in the part.

Clark Gable's role reveals extraordinary skill in the fashioning of a screen characterization. Psychologically it is sound, its compliance with the code and traditions of the Barbary Coast being consistent and logical. In essence it is the portrait of a man whom all decent people should scorn, a vulgar trafficker in liquor, gambling and women's legs, a man who scoffs at God and all the niceties of life, but so well drawn is it and so understandingly enacted by Gable, that we accept his point of view and give him our sympathy throughout.

San Francisco is a great picture because it has taken these two opposite characters and has brought them together in a great way. Metro has given it one of the screen's most imposing productions. The earthquake sequences are a fresh revelation of the apparently endless ingenuity of our technical men. They are terrific, stunning, but in the shaking to pieces of a modern city the personal significance of the upheaval is not overlooked. It is made poignant by the cries of individuals seeking individuals, husbands frantically searching for wives, mothers for children. To Gable but one thing matters--the finding of Jeanette. Thus is the great disaster reduced to its simplest human terms.

Spencer Tracy plays a priest, a boyhood companion of Gable and the only one who understands him when both become men so far apart in everything except the bond of friendship which still exists. It is a fine performance that Spencer gives. Jessie Ralph has one scene which will live long in the memories of those who see it. She has other scenes, but none which gives her such an opportunity to reveal what a grand actress she is. Jack Holt also adds strength to the cast.

San Francisco is more than just an outstanding piece of motion picture entertainment. It is an illuminating lesson in screen writing, in adherence to the principle that the public is interested first in people, and that no matter how overwhelming a production is, it must not overwhelm the people for whom our sympathies have been enlisted. Also it is a lesson in how a picture should be directed. W. S. Van Dyke made a marvelous job of it.

--Welford Beaton in Hollywood
Spectator, Vol. 11, No. 7
(July 4, 1936), page 12.

☐ SCARFACE (United Artists, 1932)

Leave it to Howard Hughes to wait for all the other boys to
release gangster pictures, and then jump in and shoot one that
makes their combined excesses look like so many taffy-pulls.
Never has there been such a delightfully casual killer as Paul
Muni; never have such expensive cars been riddled and wrecked;
and never has there been such a rat-tat-tat of machine gun fire
as punctuates every roaring reel of Scarface.

We once wrote the story of the cameraman for the S. E. P.,
and in order to punch it up, we put all the wildest episodes of every
cameraman into the life of our hero, with the result that the insurance companies were about to cancel their policies on the grounds
that cameramen were extra-hazardous risks.   We saved the situation by explaining our artistic privilege, and assuring the insurance
fellows that sometimes a cameraman sat for days on end watching a
gopher hole, or a rose unfolding.

Ben Hecht seems to have followed the same formula.   Indeed, an editorial title states that the episodes shown in this film
are all historical incidents.   I hate to think what sort of a risk the
insurance fellows would have regarded Scarface.

In order to square off the squawks of the censors, and the
statement of Will Hays that "the film glorifying gangsters is on the
wane," Howard Hawks, who directed this homicidal debauch, has a
police officer call the murdies "lice," "rats," and other unpretty
names.   But that doesn't in the least detract from the fascination
of the robust and handsome killer-lad.   For as unconscionable as
is Scarface in bumping off his enemies, he is good to his mother,
kind to his relatives, and worships his sister--all admirable virtues.   Besides, the gentlemen he bumps off are "rats" and "lice"
and should be killed.

It's a grand rough-house, and so long as there are gangsters
messing up one another with machine guns there is the same reason
to show us their bloody soirees as there is to film cowboys shooting
up a town, or to release a newsreel picture of the war in the East.
As for "heroizing" the ruffian, why not be truthful?   No doubt those
murderous fellows are good to their mothers, the same as other
tribesmen and nationals who shoot their enemies in what they consider legitimate warfare.

As you may have guessed, Paul Muni makes a swell gangster.   Osgood Perkins, while not so handsome, stands right up to
him in artistry.   Young George Raft also does a nice bit of work
as a sleek, silent, menacing "rat."

I'm rather strong for Karen Morley, but neither she nor Ann
Dvorak looked in the least attractive.   It may have been the photography, but Lee Garmes is usually so good I'm inclined to think it
is make-up.

Tully Marshall, Vince Barnett, and Edwin Maxwell have small parts, but they add great strength to a powerfully strong story.

> --Rob Wagner in Rob Wagner's
> Script, Vol. 7, No. 161 (March
> 12, 1932), page 10.

*   *   *

At the end of the gangster vogue in pictures comes Scarface, the best gangster film ever made. So tremendous, so perfect a masterpiece, it remains a picture that stands alone, and belongs to no era or vogue.

Brutal. Horrible. Fearless. Cold, hard killing for killing's sake. Such is Scarface. The story unfolds without fear or favor. An idea and its development in the mind of a hoodlum tells the yarn, with scenes as sharp as the report of the machine guns with which it abounds.

A glimpse at the luxury of his boss's home and the blonde-ness of his girl, played by Karen Morley, gives Tony the idea of acquiring plenty for himself. Knee deep through blood and horror he wades to the attainment of that idea.

Paul Muni, as Scarface, gives one of the finest characteri-zations the screen has ever seen. George Raft as his bodyguard comes a close second, his dying scene needing no words, no cap-tions.

On to his death, brought about by his love for his sister, we travel down the dirty path of gangdom.

Howard Hughes has issued an open challenge to every man and woman in America. And made a picture that will linger with us for many days to come.

> --Photoplay, Vol. 41, No. 6
> (May 1932), page 48.

☐ THE SCARLET EMPRESS (Paramount, 1934)

There is one fundamental law of drama--characters should never be forced to compete for attention with their environment.

The early Shakespeareans knew this, and sets were merely suggested, the action taking place before a plain wall, magnificent drapes or perhaps a single pillar of a great cathedral. Then came the realists, culminating in Belasco, who went so far in literal representation that he littered the stage with wagons, plows, corn-cribs--yes, even chickens and cows. Modern dramatists have for

the most part gone back to the Shakespearean symbolists. Von
Sternberg, on the other hand, has made Belasco look like an amateur.

Indeed, the strongest impression left upon me after preview-
ing this picture was of a score of historic characters simply overwhelmed by "production stuff," vainly trying to attract my attention
through noise, tumult and a perfect deluge of props.   Even looking
at it as a pictorial pageant I was disappointed.   Never once did I
feel the dignity of immense architectural effects, for the scenes
were mostly semi-close-ups jammed with a confusion of detail.
Even the wedding in the cathedral was staged in what looked like
an ecclesiastical junk room.

Furthermore, though the art department may have been true
to fact, the extraordinary assortment of huge plaster gargoyles,
griffins and other goofy grotesqueries canceled whatever beauty
might have been achieved amid all that horrible Byzantine art.   If
the Russian revolution did nothing else, it swept away that tawdry
trash.

Finally, if it was von Sternberg's purpose simply to unroll
a gorgeous tapestry, wherein the characters were mere incidents
in the pattern, he should have emphasized the major motif and shot
the thing in color.

I've never thought much of Dietrich.   She doesn't "glam" me
a bit, and as for acting--Heavens!   It's too bad that her Catherine
invites comparison with the Catherine of Bergner, for it shows up
Marlene's hopelessness as an actress.   Dietrich's idea of youthful
innocence is to go about with the surprised look of Little Miss
Muffett, her lips parted like an adenoidal mouth-breather.   That
might do as a moronic peasant girl, but not as a royal princess.
Bergner's Catherine won her troops by marching and drilling them
and showing an interest in the army; Dietrich's Catherine simply
leered at and slept with a few officers.

Another unfortunate casting is Louise Dresser as the bad-
tempered and tempestuous Empress.   Miss Dresser is so congeni-
tally sweet and lovable that she is about as vulgar and tempestuous
as a butterfly.

Best of all is John Lodge, who gives a magnificent performance of intelligent restraint in the character of Count Alexei, and
looks like one of Rembrandt's Dutch noblemen.   Next, Sam Jaffe
gives an unforgettable portrait of the half-witted Peter.   Third,
Ruthelma Stevens lurked in Peter's background, a fascinatingly
menacing figure.

Most of the minor characters are wonderfully well portrayed.
I was particularly struck with C. Aubrey Smith's likeness to--
George Washington!

As a final critique I would say that this picture belongs to Bert Glennon, the cameraman; the prop department (unnamed) and the musicians (unnamed).

--Rob Wagner in Rob Wagner's Script, Vol. 11, No. 280 (August 11, 1934), pages 7-8.

*   *   *

Just a lot of pretty poses by Marlene Dietrich, is what I would call The Scarlet Empress, and a goulash of photos of bells and banners and horses and pageants and mobs and ceremonies and all the other things showmen put in shows to hide the fact they have nothing to say. Director Joseph von Sternberg has nothing to say in this film. The author has nothing to say. Miss Dietrich has nothing to say ... not more than 120 words in the whole picture.

Of course pretty photos of Marlene Dietrich are nothing to be sneezed at. She is still about the most photographic thing in the world, but it is too bad that she can't have a director who would use her as something else than a piece of still life.

--Don Herold in Life, Vol. 101, No. 2596 (November 1934), pages 42-43.

☐ THE SCOUNDREL (Hecht and MacArthur/Paramount, 1935)

The Scoundrel is about one of those bad men who go through life tossing off women and epigrams. But the bad man gets his, this time. He drowns, or semi-drowns, or something, in an airplane crash, and comes back and finds that he is unmourned, which hurts him terribly. It starts out Oscar Wildey and ends up Eugene O'Neill screwy, with Noel Coward talking to himself over his shoulder. The firm of Hecht and MacArthur produced it.

Noel Coward is a busy and talented young man, but when it comes to acting I believe he belongs in the will-power class. His notion of acting is to hold his body rigid and bite out cutting remarks.

Sample dialogue:

Cora (on the floor, crying): "You don't love me any more?"

Anthony (Mr. Coward with his hat on): "That is an ungallant question that women always want answered gallantly."

This would have impressed me greatly about 1910.

The New York Times said: "The most dazzling writing this column has ever heard on the screen."

--Don Herold in Life, Vol. 102, No. 2604 (July 1935), page 23.

*   *   *

The Scoundrel is an elegant bit of snob appeal, aimed with conscious adroitness at the kind of people who yearn to eavesdrop on the intimate banter of the Dorothy Parkers and Alexander Woollcotts and have to satisfy their sense of familiarity with the great by always referring to Beatrice Lillie as Bee, though they have never been within even shouting distance of her.   Written and directed by Ben Hecht and Charles (Charley) MacArthur, who have shaken loose from Hollywood to give freedom to their talents, and starring Noel Coward, whom Princeton seniors rate very definitely above William Shakespeare, it ought to provide an example of what some of the professional clever people of our day can do when they really go to it.   Their effort has been hailed with such almost universal hallelujahs by the metropolitan reviewers that some exception seems to be called for, for the record.

There is no denying the cleverness and facileness of Messrs. Hecht, MacArthur and Coward: past performances have given them plenty of right to their reputations.   But The Scoundrel, aside from some entertainingly acid sketches of personages who make a business of being conversationally brilliant isn't at all a thing to which three clever people can point with pride, even with the excuse of having dashed it off at odd moments.   The first part of it, over half of the picture, isn't a motion picture at all in spite of Lee Garmes' dexterity in shifting his camera around: it is nothing but talk. The latter part, inexplicably turning into a miracle play, whether motion picture or not is simply incredible.   After several thousand feet of semi-satiric comedy, unexpectedly asking an audience to believe that Mr. Coward, suddenly plunged into a watery grave, cannot rest there unless someone sheds a tear for him, is asking too much.   After all, was it so fatally scoundrelly for Mr. Coward to have been unable to endure indefinitely the adoration of the clinging literary ladies who flung themselves at him?   He merely left them to their weeping--James Cagney would have slugged them, and got a cheer from the audience for it.   But through some perverse operation of the theatrical mind it seemed proper to regard his conduct as villainy, and to punish it by dragging his ghost through New York streets till the tears, and the miracle, occurred.   It takes more than cleverness to pull off such a miracle as that.

Mr. Coward, it must be said, looks reasonably like the publisher he is supposed to be in the first part, and remarkably like a ghost in the second.

--James Shelley Hamilton in National Board of Review Magazine, Vol. 10, No. 6 (June 1935), pages 10-11.

☐ SHANGHAI EXPRESS (Paramount, 1932)

With the eyes of the world at this moment focussed on China, this picture will be enormously interesting. Doubly so, as it not only gives one a slant at the international chaos of this war-torn country, but it is in my opinion a tremendously vital and beautiful picture.

Josef von Sternberg is at his best when directing in the Russian manner; that is, when his background is bigger and more important than either the story or the characters, and when he uses the Russian montage technique, as he did in a modest way in his first picture, The Salvation Hunters.

The opening shots give us a kaleidoscopic eyeful of the railroad station of Peiping (Pekin) the hurry and bustle of that international melting pot which never reaches the point of amalgam. Marvelous photography by Lee Garmes and wonderfully directed by von Sternberg.

Then aboard the train, the Shanghai Express, where we meet the strangest assortment of people, on various and mysterious missions, ever gathered in one place. We meet Marlene Dietrich under the name of Shanghai Lily, a notorious prostitute of the East; Clive Brook, a British medical officer; Anna May Wong, Shanghai Lily's Chinese maid; Warner Oland, Mr. Chang, a half Chinese revolutionist; Eugene Pallette, an American Rotarian out to see the world; Lawrence Grant, an American missionary; Louise Closser Hale, an American boarding-house keeper of Shanghai; Gustav von Seyffertitz, a German narcotic agent; and Emile Chautard, a broken French officer on a visit to his sister.

These are the principal figures that go to make up the rich mosaic of a vital and vibrating picture of life in the most exciting place in the world today.

But it is not only these personal affairs that grip one's interest. It is the entire mise-en-scene--the customs of the Orient, the human eccentricities of the various nationals, noises, strange and familiar, the feeling of movement on the train, the excitement of a hold-up by revolutionary bandits, the holding of the passengers for ransom. Indeed I never saw a picture that foot-for-foot packs as much vital color and exciting interest. Perhaps the greatest technical triumph of the picture is the way in which von Sternberg cuts the dialogue to the bone. Long stretches during which no lines are spoken are filled by the babble of foreign tongues in the crowd, the station and train noises, and Shanghai Lily's gramophone. And how the lines register when they are spoken!

Marlene Dietrich has a tough--in more ways than one--character to put over. Cast as a hard, disillusioned woman of sin, the temptation must have been great to go after sympathy by sweetening up the character. She didn't. She had loved Brook in the past, lost him, went on the town; and now that she was trying to win him back, her cynical smiles while unpleasant to the audience so exasperated the Britisher's sporting instincts that he was finally stirred to a declaration of love. While Dietrich can't compare with Garbo for "glamour" (favorite studio superlative) her characterization as Shanghai Lily is much more believable than Garbo's Mata Hari.

Clive Brook is also at his best. A splendid figure in his British uniform, he is particularly fine in delicate nuances of feeling, put over with the most subtle changes of facial expression.

The other characters are as clean-cut as cameos. Warner Oland and Anna May Wong are utterly convincing. These two must often laugh at the number of times Anna May has knifed Oland in the cause of ART! Eugene Pallette and Louise Closser Hale are indeed comedy relief in the midst of real drama, and their comedy is part and parcel of the whole pattern. While Lawrence Grant, von Seyffertitz and Emile Chautard, though smaller pigments on the palette, in the deft hands of von Sternberg shine forth brilliantly.

The programme gives "Gowns by Travis Banton" but who designed the sets? Those are the boys who should have credit--they and Lee Garmes. A dozen times I had to pinch myself to realize that this picture was not made in China.

A final bow to the sound engineers. Their work is marvelous.

With Shanghai Express and The Man I Killed to his credit, who says that Ben Schulberg isn't producing pictures?
                              --Rob Wagner in Rob Wagner's
                                Script, Vol. 7, No. 157 (February 13, 1932), page 8.

*   *   *

What a ride! Through the skill of Director von Sternberg and realistic camera work, you hop aboard the Shanghai Express and crawl through a revolution. Your fellow passengers are Shanghai Lily (Marlene Dietrich); an English officer (Clive Brook); a Chinese girl (Anna May Wong); a suave Eurasian (Warner Oland); a prim matron, a gambler, a querulous invalid, a clergyman.

The stage is set for drama, and the story mounts vividly as the camera moves from compartment to compartment and the train roars along. Miss Dietrich was never more beautiful, but her face seems immobile and the constant raising and lowering of her eyelids hardly compensates. Amusing is the perfect English of Anna May Wong in contrast to Dietrich's foreign accent. A fascinating picture.

                              --Photoplay, Vol. 41, No. 5
                              (April 1932), page 51.

☐ SHE DONE HIM WRONG (Paramount, 1933)

If you don't believe that "they said such things and did such things on the Bowery," you should see this picture in which Mae West struts her pulchritude and amusing stuff in Noah Beery's music hall back in the Gay 90's.

This was my first eyeful of Miss West, and I can easily understand how she stands 'em up in this hilarious picture. She's as gorgeous as Lillian Russell, has more IT than Clara at her Bowest, and exhibits a sense of humor that makes one purr all the time.

Furthermore she wrote this delightfully unmoral play of counterfeiting, white slaving, and Lady Lou's nonchalant prostitution that has the censors all over the U.S. puzzled. Puzzled because the immorality is so joyously submerged in colorful surroundings, amusing situations, and above all in Mae West's bright-eyed charm, that they don't know what to do about it. If I were King, I'd know what I would do; I'd show it in the schools as a picture of robust and healthy entertainment that would cheer up the children of these out-of-joint times.

Cary Grant is a personable secret service agent masquerading as a Salvation Army captain. He is the one who finally wins the very unladylike Lady Lou. Noah Beery, Sr. (why the senior? Let the boy be junior, but there is only one Noah Beery!) is a delightfully sinister character. David Landau delivers his usual good stuff. Owen Moore in a heavy role of a convict gives a wonderful performance, and Gilbert Roland makes a handsome Russian crook. Rafaela Ottiano, as Gilbert's bosom friend, due to those Gay 90 corsets, exhibits a cornice like a ten-story building. Dewey Robinson, a huge fellow with a back like a moving van, adds a bully bit. And Fred Santley who sings old songs in the music hall does so with spirit and high humor. Grace La Rue's exceptional talents were utterly submerged. Others of the cast, fine.

It is easy to note the naughty hand of Harvey Thew in the screen play, and the fine Italian hand of Lowell Sherman in the direction. Indeed Sherman did a swell job throughout and was smart enough not to burlesque that amusing old stuff. It's funnier played straight.

I rave because I purred for an hour and a half. And Mae West--gosh, she's a card!

                              --Rob Wagner in Rob Wagner's
                              Script, Vol. 8, No. 207 (January 28, 1933), page 8.

*   *   *

A brawly howl of a picture that for sheer first class spicy
rough stuff, takes the cake. So cleverly has Lowell Sherman directed the story, so real is Mae West's characterization, that a
great deal of the bad taste is overlooked in the perfection of the
telling.

Mae West as Sady Lou, a Bowery moll of the gay nineties,
grabs up the story in her be-diamonded hands and dominates every
scene from the moment she steps her buxom self into the film.

A singer in a beer hall, she does her man wrong while he
languishes in prison. He escapes and then the fun begins, with
Mae finally landing the man she wants. Cary Grant, Noah Beery,
David Landau and Owen Moore are nigh perfect. But remember:
not for auntie or the children.

--Photoplay, Vol. 43, No. 4
(March 1933), page 59.

☐ SHOW BOAT (Universal, 1936)

Serving as a valedictory for Carl Laemmle in its present,
and third, reincarnation, Edna Ferber's Show Boat comes tooting
around the bend again, inviting your sentimental attention even
though it is definitely outmoded. Like "Old Man River" the popularity of the Kern score just keeps rollin' along, and it accounts
for the major moments in the film directed by James Whale. As
a spectacular motion picture, Show Boat is deficient in many departments: background and atmosphere never dominate as they should;
there is little or no emotional pull to the story as a whole; the
dramatic climax is weak; many of the musical numbers are photographed without imagination; the film lacks continuous action,
rhythm and pace.

Some of the performances are excellent, within the limitations of the script. In my estimation, Helen Morgan walks, or
warbles, off with the show, but that doesn't mean that her face
isn't worth watching. It's the most expressive thing in Show Boat.
Paul Robeson sings "Old Man River" magnificently, and "I Suits
Myself" just as well, but he is obviously there to sing and lacks
acting opportunities. Allan Jones does his share of the musical
chores capably, but he is badly miscast as Ravenal, and the gambler's character is whitewashed until it has no vitality except in
the tenor register. Helen Westley misses Parthy by a mile, and
seems downright apologetic about it. Liking Hattie McDaniel, and
respecting her vigorous portrayal, I'm nevertheless certain that
she wasn't just the right colored gal for Robeson's wife--not if
realism was intended. Charles Winninger did Cap'n Andy in good
musical comedy style; Sammy White and Queenie Smith belong in

the same praiseworthy category; and the young woman who did the adult Kim was so bad that I can't blame myself for forgetting her name.

Irene Dunne is billed as the star of Show Boat and she endeavors to justify that rating. Like many others I am willing to concede that Miss Dunne has personal charm, rare beauty and an air of good breeding; she takes to costumes as a duck does to water, or maybe I should say swan, and I can easily imagine producers saying: "Here's a role that should be furnished with Irene Dunne." She's a genuine and lovely period piece--but as an actress she's still in a class with a rosewood spinet. Show Boat accentuates her beauty, and her stiffness, while her singing does little to alter this general impression.

Show Boat has no faults if a musical comedy should be presented on the screen as a duplicate of a stage success. That question has been gone over before: you know what you think, and how I feel. Certainly no one could fail to be thrilled by the musical portions of Show Boat. And as long as the movies are to be looked at, Miss Dunne is equally exciting. Between the two, most of the 10,178 feet of Show Boat are accounted for, so it should sail into popular favor.

> --Richard Sheridan Ames in Rob
> Wagner's Script, Vol. 15, No.
> 366 (May 16, 1936), page 10.

*   *   *

With quite a magnificent gesture Carl Laemmle, Jr. bows his way out of Universal. His Show Boat is an extraordinarily effective production, musically entertaining, dramatically sound and scenically beautiful. The story is a human one that will run its fingers, not too roughly, over the emotional strings of the audience. The telling requires two hours, one hour and ten minutes less than the Ziegfeld running time but still unusually lengthy. I termed the Metro picture a "marathon of motion." Show Boat is a shorter marathon of melody, of beautiful solos beautifully sung, of impressive ensemble singing in which the voices of negroes reveal their organ-like quality, of back-ground music of high quality.

The production is not just Show Boat done over again. It is a new Show Boat, one you never saw before, one only the screen could present with so much sweep, vigor and esthetic appeal. From a cinematic stand-point it is an interesting study. Its primary elements are a story and music, and so adroitly are they mixed we do not lose sight of one when our attention is engaged with the other. The direction of James Whale is brilliant; the editing of Maurice Pivar equally brilliant, the story sequences being woven into the musical interludes until the two blend into rhythmic unity giving the whole smooth and logical progression from first fade-in to final fade-out.

The treatment of the opening titles, always a problem for
an art department to display originality in something all pictures
have in common, never has been handled more artistically. The
credit titles are carried on banners held aloft in a pictorially attractive procession which moves past the camera with stately tread,
inaugurating the forward movement which never ceases until the end
of the picture is reached.

Early in the film comes "Old Man River," sung as only
Paul Robeson can sing it and as he never has sung it before. Its
scenic embellishment is arresting in its beauty, Robeson's magnificent voice and the camera's superb treatment of the artistic composition of the scenes combining to give the old song such new dignity that the large preview audience could not restrain its enthusiasm until the end was reached. In the middle of the number a
storm of applause broke, to be checked almost reluctantly to allow
the rest to be heard.

Generous applause marked the whole showing, genuine applause earned by the merits of the picture and not confined to the
studio contingent and its guests. Irene Dunne captured the immediate approval of the audience and held it by the wide range of the
versatility she displays. An innocent, unspoiled girl at the beginning, tender and appealing, she reveals herself in turn as an eccentric dancer, an accomplished vocalist, a backface comedienne,
and a distinguished and stately grande dame with warmly human
qualities.

When I saw Allan Jones for the first time, last October in
Night at the Opera, I wrote of him, "Young, handsome, stalwart,
a pleasing personality, a speaking voice with music in it and a
singing voice that gives music life and dignity, form a combination
the public will not be able to resist." His Show Boat performance
shows my enthusiasm was justified. He shares with Irene Dunne
the ability to be satisfactory as a player without the added attraction of a fine singing voice and knowledge of how to use it.

Paul Robeson deserves a place also among the actors who
contribute largely to the enjoyment of the picture. The cast is a
long one and each member of it ably sustains his part. Charles
Winninger, Helen Morgan, Helen Westley, Sammy White, Hattie
McDaniel, Queenie Smith and Donald Cook, in the more important
parts, give excellent performances.

In every phase of his direction James Whale is equally impressive. By the simple expedient of permitting his players to talk
naturally, he makes his story an intimate one and gains for the
people in it the friendly interest of the audience. He appreciates
the fact that motion picture audiences desire to see people living
their lives, not players acting parts, and realizes the way to do it
is to present dialogue as ordinary conversations, not forensic out-
bursts.

Screen play, lyrics, music, investiture, photography, costumes--everything in this really notable production deserves its own award of merit. The individuals entitled to it are enumerated at the head of this review. I would run out of adjectives if I attempted individual mention.

Show Boat is another chapter in the fascinating history the screen is writing for itself. I have no idea what we are headed for with these filmic marathons, but it is a gay course we are traveling.

--Welford Beaton in Hollywood
Spectator, Vol. 11, No. 3
(May 9, 1936), pages 7-8.

☐ THE SIGN OF THE CROSS (Paramount, 1933)

Ten years ago, when the world was calmer, we ate up those big Cecil DeMille Biblical pageants, but they seem hopelessly outmoded now during this terrifically disturbing period of the world's history.

Henry Ford was smart enough to capitalize on the kidding of his "tin Lizzie," and C. B. DeMille has been equally smart in welcoming kidding of his luxury complex. Indeed, he has deliberately pyramided the most popular ridicule aimed at him, his onyx bath tubs. The luxurious empress, Claudette Colbert, bathes in goat's milk, and if you don't believe it's really goat's milk, Props secured two cats to lick it up. Perhaps the idea was to stir our envy of the cats!

Yes, it's the same old story--Elissa Landi is the virginal Christian gal going about with her psalm-singing Christians who quite reasonably annoyed the Romans with their holier-than-thou smugness. Fredric Marchus, Superbus as heck in his hardware, saves Elissa from the mob and falls in love with her, as who wouldn't?--there's Aimee! But wicked Claudette's piercing black eyes look right through Fredricus' hardware to his superbus proportions, and she "desires" him--you know what that means! Nor can you blame her; Nero is a big, fat slob, soft and nance-like, while Fredricus is--well, the girls will understand.

Fredricus, however, sticks to Elissa, and finally he goes hallelujah and joins his sweetheart in lofty martyrdom. As they clasp hands and start up the stone steps leading into the arena where the twenty lions await a good Christian dinner, one feels that as the great door closes on them in the final fade-out they probably weren't et up at all, but on the contrary they hopped into their Buick and beat it for the Town House for a nice human dinner. The reason one feels this is because one is certain he will again see the beautiful mummers next week filming a scene on the sands of Santa Monica.

Another reaction I felt in viewing this picture: it is too slick--like a Bouguereau painting. The costumes, props, manners and customs are accurate beyond the highest-browed criticism; the crowds are directed with almost military precision, and even the dirt in the street has been deliberately arranged. All of which makes the production appear theatrical and unreal.

Nevertheless there's swell entertainment in it. Especially the fight stuff in the Colosseum.

--Rob Wagner in Rob Wagner's Script, Vol. 8, No. 206 (January 21, 1933), pages 8-9.

*   *   *

If there is such a thing as a $1.50 roadshow in celluloid in these times this is it. Sign of the Cross, through which Cecil B. DeMille returned to the business end of a megaphone, is the nearest approach to a twice-daily picture at twice-daily prices that Hollywood has delivered in a long, long while.

Later on general release and lower down in the price scale it should be a hit picture. That will soften the blow in the event of a road brodie.

Cross, firstly, has spectacle of a type they haven't seen in a long time, and, secondly, it has a double action scenario. The latter is going to stir up some two-sided sentiment wherever shown. It's going to make the church element dizzy trying to figure out which way to turn. The plot takes longshot chances with meddlers, much of it being some of the boldest censor-bait ever attempted in a picture.

But while the chances are being taken every now and then, they remain superficial, while basically the theme plays safe on and finally makes victorious the straight religious precept.

Religion triumphant over paganism. And the soul is stronger than the flesh. Religion gets the breaks, even though its followers all get killed in this picture. It's altogether a moral victory.

Neat, deft and probably beyond reproach is the manner in which the scarlet punches are inserted. Every sequence in which religion wins out is built upon lurid details. The censors may object to the method, but they can't oppose the motive, and in the way Cross was produced one can't be in without the other.

For example, the handsome Prefect of Rome (Fredric March) sees that he can't get to first base with the Christian maiden (Elissa Landi), so he calls in the village temptress, Ancaria (Joyzelle Joyner), for help. Ancaria is described as the hottest gal in town. "The most versatile" is the phrase used. She uses her arts on Miss Landi. In the street the other Christian martyrs are marching to their doom, singing hymns bravely as they go.   Their chants disrupt and finally drown out the temptress's routine, and she strikes the unmoved Miss Landi in the face.   Then, having lost, she walks.

This occurs during the last half of the picture and is the strongest plea for reverence up to then.   It represents religion's first victory over pagan oppression insofar as this narrative goes, and was staged in such a way that the moral cannot get over if the build-up is cut.

Besides Ancaria, who sounds like Aunt Carrie as the dialog is read but who looks and acts like an Empire wheel stripper, there is Charles Laughton's expert Nero, who doubles as the degenerate emperor and musical pyromaniac as Rome burns.   That he plays the lyre instead of the fiddle refutes a popular myth.   He blames the fire on the Christians, and that's the reason for all the killings.

It's likely more trouble will come from the women than the censors.   Some attempts herein to horrify for theatrical effects and dramatic results are unprecedented on the screen.   The slaughter by bow and arrow of the Christians as they meet for forbidden prayer on the outskirts of the city is done in minute detail and pretty ghastly, but it's just an appetizer.   Prior to that the off-screen torture of a boy by Roman soldiers and then a view of his wounded body are bad enough.

Most of the last half is taken up with a bloody festival staged by crazy Caesar in the arena.   When it seems the limit in horror has been reached, on comes another exhibition of artistic and novel murder until the closing of the show with the devouring of the Christians by lions.   Miss Landi meets the lions, accompanied by the now worshipful March, whose attempts to save the girl are thwarted by the jealous Mrs. Nero, who was on the make for March herself.

The slaughter opens with gladiators poking out each other's eyes and cutting each other to pieces with swords and pitchforks. Elephants crush the heads of chained men, crocodiles devour and gorillas mangle undraped women, boxers with spiked gloves dash out their opponents' brains and Amazon women pierce dwarfs through the middle and carry them aloft on their spears.   Nothing is left to incomplete suggestion.   Everything is shown in detail as far as it can be.

Most of it will be nearly nauseating to those with sensitive stomachs.   But all of it is holding.   It makes the heart pound faster for almost a solid hour, and although the first thought may be to turn away, there is something in the brutal slaughter that nails fascinated attention.   Because this takes place at the far end it will leave all audiences with a depressed feeling.   But it will cause them to talk, regardless, and that talk will attract others.   Cross will get more attention and trade as a curiosity than as an entertainment.

Cast is uniformly good, but only one exceptional performance was registered. That's Laughton's. With utmost subtlety and a minimum of effort he manages to get over his queer character before his first appearance is a minute old. The few laughs in a picture that's very weak in the comedy department are all Laughton's.

Misses Colbert and Landi and Messrs. March and Keith are called upon chiefly to look their parts, and they manage. Frequently some badly written and often silly dialog holds them down. This is true in the early moments, when there's more talk than action. Gradually the chatter becomes less of a factor in the story's progress, with everything toward the finish hinging on sight and sound effects.

Among the supers are some familiar faces that haven't been seen lately.

DeMille staged his spectacle in his customary way, turning in a job that for sight stuff hasn't been duplicated since the silent picture days. His eye for extravagant production effects and secret of getting the most out of mobs so as to make a regiment look like an army, have not left him. Mrs. Nero's (Claudette Colbert) bath in a pool of asses' milk just gives a slight hint.

If any picture around just now has a chance to go out and get big money it is Sign of the Cross.

--Bige in Variety, Vol. 108, No. 13 (December 6, 1932), page 14.

☐ THE SMILING LIEUTENANT (Paramount, 1931)

With Herr Lubitsch leading him by the hand, back comes Chevalier in one of the breeziest and most tuneful pieces of entertainment that we have seen in a long time. And what a relief this is, too, from some of the current types of pictures!

Here is Chevalier at his best, as an Austrian lieutenant in love with a girl orchestra leader (Claudette Colbert) but forced into marrying a princess of one of those George Barr McCutcheon kingdoms. It's really an educational film for girls who are inclined to be a little too old-fashioned!

If we must have man-and-woman and triangle stories in films, please let Mr. Lubitsch do them. He can put over a red-hot affair and dare the censors to say it is anything but a game of checkers. The audience just grins and chuckles and laughs throughout. It's a cure for these depression blues.

The music is so generally good that there is hardly any outstanding hit.   Miriam Hopkins is great as the princess, Claudette Colbert is lovely, and you will scream with laughter at George Barbier, as the king of the hokum kingdom.   And, girls, just between us, notice how those actresses sock each other!   Ja wohl, Herr Lubitsch.

                                        --Photoplay, Vol. 40, No. 2
                                          (July 1931), page 50.

                          *   *   *

To a voluntary intellectual exile from Hollywood and its works, Ernst Lubitsch's picture, The Smiling Lieutenant, is a conciliatory and delightful gesture beckoning to a forbidden land.

The formidable persuasiveness of Rob Wagner and Ted Cook lured me to see the picture, and the circumstance was aggravated by supping with Lubitsch before I saw it.   Under these conditions, the natural impulse is to retrench one's-self behind one's incorruptibility and be ready to yell "No!" and "Rotten!" with all one's strength, if only to affirm one's convictions.

But The Smiling Lieutenant was too sprightly and genial to permit such an attitude.   Its good-humored and delicate irony, its joyful roguishness and its cunning jibes at many hateful posturings, are quite irresistible.

The star is Maurice Chevalier, whose inexhaustible good humor, healthy vivacity and mischievous drollery entirely remove whatever objections there may be to his awkward acting and inadequate voice.   He has the swashbuckling quality of a Valentino, without the Italian's somberness and murky passion; he has the skittishness and tingle of a Fairbanks without Doug's Rotarian insipidity; he is gallant and light-hearted without being stupid.   And, believe me, mates, that's no simple thing to be.

The picture is a merciless bantering of that insane anachronism--royal etiquette.   It also expounds the interesting postulate that snappy clothes are sufficient to inspire a truly Cosmic Itch.   There are, of course, a few judicious tears for the sake of contrast, and laughter--never of the belly variety--peeps in and out constantly like champagne at a banquet of civilized people.

Along toward the end of the picture, when it appears inevitable that the lieutenant will have to seek eternal solace in the continental recipe of a ménage à trois in order to escape from the intolerable tedium of a royal wife who had the makings but not the manner, one wonders if Lubitsch will be able to maintain a high level of entertainment.   One expects the picture to double up and collapse.   But the director was too well equipped and far too deft with his naughtiness to allow this catastrophe.

The Smiling Lieutenant ends well under control, and crescendo.   And it ends where it started--in a bedroom.

The bedroom--but in discussing Lubitsch's bedroom the English word is tasteless; one should use the French salle à songer or salle à coucher rather than a mere prosaic chambre à dormir--the bedroom is Lubitsch's favorite and best stage.   He has a resource of innuendo and of gesture that can be fully exploited only in that whispering frontier between the boudoir and the pillow.   The characters of The Smiling Lieutenant are either on their way to bed, or on their way to make it possible to go to bed.   And they abhor solitude.   They are the most sociable, companionable and gregarious humans one can imagine.   Their center of consciousness is perilously but firmly fixed at a point equidistant from their dancing feet and their saucy heads.

Oskar Straus wrote the music for The Smiling Lieutenant, availing himself of copious quotations from Oskar Straus and of some new tunes.   The lyrics were not strikingly novel nor notably witty.   But they formed, with the rococo elegance of the music, grateful and amusing interludes between incidents dedicated to sparkling incidents concerning the functions of nutrition and propagation.

Lubitsch, incidentally, does not scruple to drag in music by the hair; entirely without rhyme or reason, as it should be done. For, whenever pictures begin to tamper with rhyme or reason, they become ridiculous, just as actors become ridiculous when they attempt to appear intelligent.   But when they are their unreasonable and fantastic selves, without a by-your-leave, they are always enchanting.   Compared with the comedians of the screen, the "serious dramatists" are infantile.

No review of The Smiling Lieutenant would be complete without an appreciative word about the acting of Claudette Colbert as the pert and sentimental fiddle player who accepts the lieutenant's invitation to dinner and stays to breakfast; about the more subtle and difficult work of Miriam Hopkins as the dowdy princess who discovers fluffy panties and keeps her husband; about the bluff and hearty king who shows too well the alleged horrors of inbreeding, or about the bit which shows a soldier springing up from behind the hydrangeas to salute an officer who strolls through the park at night.

Well, it is a healthy thing that pictures are beginning to take up seriously the worship of the Venus Who Laughs.   If The Smiling Lieutenant would only start a run of this sort of thing!   Elegant, knowing, witty and swift.   The only trouble is, these things are so damned hard to do--and it's so easy to be serious and dull in the carnal style!

--Jose Rodriguez in Rob Wagner's
Script, Vol. 5, No. 127 (July 8,
1931), page 8.

☐ SNOW WHITE AND THE SEVEN DWARFS (Walt Disney/RKO,
1937)

It is so easy to take Snow White as a natural culmination of
all that Walt Disney has done before, and bring out all the superlatives to express delight in it, that one might overlook the most
important fact about it aside from its being the first feature-length
cartoon: that it is a landmark, of a significance hardly to be cal-
culated, in the development of the motion picture.   That is not to
say that animated cartoons (a term hitherto used for the mechanics
Disney uses, but totally inadequate as description) are likely ever
to supersede the use of human actors on the screen; but Snow White
definitely proves that there is a field in which hand-drawn and hand-
colored pictures, employed in the Disney way, are as much more
effective than the usual fashion of catching human beings against
solid sets and backgrounds with a movie camera, as a painting is
more effective than a photograph.   The screen has not yet seen a
better medium for translating certain creations of fantasy and
imagination into visual images than the Disney drawings, and no
photographing of actuality could come within leagues of being so
vivid, both in what it shows and what it suggests, as (for one out
of innumerable instances in this film) the flight of the wicked queen
from the pursuing dwarfs, with the flesh-hungry vultures perched
on the ominous tree-branch overhead.

What Walt Disney himself, or others following in the way he
has opened, may do hereafter in this medium is for the future to
disclose.   For the present it is joy enough to have Snow White and
the Seven Dwarfs, such a fairy-tale as the child in man has never
had to delight in before.   From the first glimpse of the castle
where the jealous queen keeps the lovely Snow White in rags and
drudgery to the last glimpse of the Prince carrying the Princess
away on his white steed, it creates a world of charming unreality,
peopled with lovable wild creatures of the forest, with the even
more lovable and amusing dwarfs, and such human beings as never
lived outside the pages of a picture book.

The outline of the Grimm tale has been followed quite faithfully, except for a more romantic ending in which the Princess is
awakened from her Sleeping Death by the Prince's kiss.   But upon
it has been hung a vast richness of detail of the kind only Walt
Disney has ever put into pictures.   The little wood animals and the
birds that befriended Snow White, created with an affectionate,
gently amusing touch that must surely make everyone who sees
them feel kindlier to wild creatures--the seven dwarfs, each one
so much an individual with engaging traits of his own that it is hard
not to pick a favorite and hard to pick one: Dopey, Bashful,
Grumpy--which?   All the life in the little house--the house-cleaning,
the washing of the dwarfs for supper, most of all the dancing party
--is enchanting.   And to keep the drama alive, with a note of suspense always in the air, there is the queen, so wicked that the rats
in the dungeon flee from her and her grimly evil raven shrinks in

horror from her, plotting to kill the maiden her magic mirror tells
her is more fair than she.

The thing that might have been most feared is that human
beings and human voices would not come through the animation
process happily.   The nearer to living persons they had to be the
less convincing they might have turned out.   Animals and dwarfs
could be unnaturalistic and still be quaint and attractive.   In fact,
it is only when the dwarfs talk together in comedian fashion (re-
semblances in speech to some screen comics will be caught) that
they are least interesting.   Snow White herself, mostly through the
grace of her movements, manages to escape almost completely the
effect of being just a flat line-drawing trying to be a photograph,
and the Queen turns out to be a personality that no actress could
by any of her arts embody.

It is astonishing how these pictures create a life in a world
of their own, totally unreal in fact but absorbingly real to the en-
tranced imagination.   It is a pity that the film on which so much
beauty and fine feeling exist should ever perish, for it is hard not
to believe that it would delight generation after generation, as long
as fairy-tale glamour and kindly humor and the myths of dwarfs
and animals have the power to charm.
                              --James Shelley Hamilton in Na-
                              tional Board of Review Magazine,
                              Vol. 13, No. 1 (January 1938),
                              pages 10-11.

                    *   *   *

To say of Snow White and the Seven Dwarfs that it is among
the genuine artistic achievements of this country takes no great daring.   In fact, outside of Chaplin, Disney's is the one Hollywood
name that any corn doctor of art and culture dare mention without
fear of losing face, or on the other hand of having to know too much
about the subject.   There is this to be said of Disney, however:
he is appreciated by all ages, but he is granted the license and
simplification of those who tell tales for children, because that is
his elected medium to start with.   It is not easy to do amusing
things for children, but the more complex field of adult relations
is far severer in its demands.

Snow White is a fairy-tale, surely the most vivid and gay
and sweet in the world; it is done in color, photographed on different planes to give depth, and it runs almost an hour and a half.
Some of the short cartoons have been more of a riot, some have
been more tender even.   But this is sustained fantasy, the animated
cartoon grown up.   The fairy-tale princess is just what you would
have her; the witch is a perfect ringer for Lionel Barrymore (not
by accident, I take it); and the seven dwarfs have been perfectly
humanized by somewhat the same technique, though each is more a
composite of types, not quite identifiable.   The animals of course
are as uncannily studied and set in motion as they have always been.

The Disney artists and animators are practically zoological, nearer to the actual life of animals than any who have endowed it with human traits for purposes of fable. Take the young deer in the little scene where the forest life first gathers around Snow White: shy but sniffing forward, then as she starts to pat it, the head going down, ears back, the body shrinking and tense, ready to bound clear; then reassurance, body and head coming up and forward to push against the hand--half a dozen motions shrewdly carried over from the common cat. Or take the way (later) the same deer moves awkward and unsteady on its long pins in the crush of animals milling about, as it should, but presently is graceful in flight, out in front like a flash. Disney has animals that are played up for comedy, like the turtle here, the lecherous vultures, the baby bird whose musical attempts are a source of alternate pride and embarrassment to his parents (on a finale he will get as high as eight inches straight up from the limb); but even in these cases, the exaggeration is based on typical form and trait.

The story is familiar in its simple fantasy. The castle, the stepmother with her black arts, Snow White escaping in the forest and keeping house for the little men; the witch seeking her out with the apple of living death; finally the young prince coming to break the charm. But all of Disney's fantasy starts out with a simple frame of story: the main body of the thing is incident. And the incidents start from a firm base in the realism of the everyday, serving to steady the fantastic (dwarfs, witches, alchemy) either by complementing it with the matter-of-fact, or by becoming fantastic through a seemingly logical progression from their common shape and function. Thus the fairy-tale dwarfs, in their diamond mine and home, go about their business in a highly natural manner, digging, appraising, grading, leaving the dirty dishes and going to bed. And thus the birds and animals, invading the empty house with the shy fits and starts appropriate to them as real birds and animals, fall to helping the girl clean up with highly unnatural abilities (the squirrel's tail for a bottle brush, other tails for brooms and dusters; the birds winding up cobwebs, flying with sheets).

I was disappointed to see the comedy faltering at times here. Such things as running into doors and trees on the dignified exit, the jumbled consonant (bood goy, I mean good doy, I mean...), headers into various liquids, etc., are short of good Disney. For the most part, the thing is as ingenious as ever, the idiosyncrasies of each dwarf quickly established and made capital of--Grumpy, Dopey, and Sneezy in particular--the flow of comedy through animism still on that level at which Disney's men have never been equaled. Witness the organ pipes in that wonderful music-hour sequence, made of penguins, the vent holes being choked off with little clappers, Grumpy frequently losing patience with his stops and whacking them shut by hand.

It is not all comic and quaint. The imaginative transformation of the stepmother, her mission, flight, and death (the vultures banking slowly down in the dark air), make a suspense and chase

interval that will put your heart back a few seconds; and there is
something not mawkish but gentle and nice about the little girl,
her face and singing and adventures in friendliness with every living thing. Something beautiful about all of it, I think, because it
does not try to be wise about fairy-tales, or fairy-talish about its
birds, rabbits, people. And all of it, the whole feature-length
true motion picture, is nothing but a hundred-odd thousand colored
drawings, photographed, and set to music.

The art work is fine, particularly the castle at night, the
scenes in the woods, the march home of the little men. The color
is the best ever, though it is true that its pastels would be up
against more difficulty in a film less deliberately imaginative. And
the music is as much a part of the picture as it always is in the
Disney scorings, with nice songs and a rollicking chant and swell
background stuff for the moods of the story.

Disney gives credit to his directors, animators, musicians
in a way that is heartening to see and a list as long as your arm;
but while it is true that his pictures are built on the conference
method, good ideas being kicked around until they suggest others,
there is the fact that he apparently has known how to pick his men,
train them, and give them free rein to contribute their individual
best. A film is a collective enterprise anyway and should be made
that way; but in general there are too few men of talent at the top
who have the leadership and patience, the exaltation of job over
ego, to do it. Walt Disney is a pioneer in more things than his
conception of and tireless experiment with the animated cartoon as
a reflection of life. Now that the best picture of 1937 has been
adjudicated, awarded, etc., the best and most important picture
for 1938 is called Snow White and the Seven Dwarfs.
                                    --Otis Ferguson in The New Re-
                                    public, Vol. 93 (January 26,
                                    1938), page 339.

☐ STAGECOACH (Walter Wanger/United Artists, 1939)

One of the greatest of all Westerns. And one of the most
interesting Hollywood possibly could have for study. It is superb
entertainment, but take it apart and we discover all the story it
has could be told comfortably between the two ends of one reel of
film. That interests me because one of the beliefs the Spectator
has expressed at intervals during the past decade is that the story
is not the thing of most importance to screen entertainment, that
what really matters is the manner of telling what story there is--
that it is the medium that entertains. Film producers as a whole
know too little about their medium to give them confidence to test
a theory. Walter Wanger apparently is an exception. Stagecoach
is evidence of his willingness to put to a test the theory that the
medium, not the story, is the thing. He takes us with a stagecoach

on a trip across a stretch of Western territory at a time when
prowling Indians made it perilous.   After one brush with the Red-
skins, the coach gets through; at the destination one of the passengers kills the three desperadoes who had killed his father and
brother.   There you have all the story there is.   And for one
hour and thirty-three minutes it is gripping entertainment.   It is
a Grand Hotel on wheels.

Only great screen craftsmanship could elongate so slim a
story without stretching it too thin in spots.   In Dudley Nichols,
writer, and John Ford, director, Wanger had a team with many
notable screen achievements to its credit, but no other I can recall matches Stagecoach as an example of cinematic skill.   Quite
extraordinary is the manner in which Dudley has strung together a
series of little incidents, snatches of dialogue, gems of humor, to
enlist our interest in a strangely assorted group of people--a young
woman of commercial virtue, the refined young wife of an army
officer, a drunken doctor, a timid whiskey peddler, an escaped
prisoner on his way back to jail, a pompous banker who is absconding, a stagecoach reinsman who is not brave but bravely carries
on, a United States marshall, resolute, fearless, sentimental.
They are the people whom the stagecoach carries into and out of
danger.   Another, a professional gambler with a gallant side, falls
victim to an Indian bullet.   Each of these people has his or her
individual problem, and all of them are worked into the script with
a literary version of the skill a juggler displays when he keeps an
equal number of balls in the air simultaneously, each ball being a
separate unit, but it is as a group they hold our interest.

When John Ford was given the Nichols script he must have
seen it as a series of pictures, could not have read it as a story
in words.   Its literal translation in screen terms would have
achieved poor results.   It essentially was a script we had to see,
one containing only one chase and a triple killing.   And Ford makes
us see it, and makes the seeing continuously thrilling.   It is a production of tremendous physical sweep, of pictorial grandeur, of
superb beauty which the preview audience greeted with rounds of
applause.   Photography has the velvety warmth of masterly graded
light and shade, not the gaudiness of technicolor which cheapens
so many screen productions.   To the cameras of Bert Glennon and
Ray Binger we are indebted for some of the most imposing pictures
that ever adorned a screen.   Through all the feast for our eyes to
feed on, Director Ford weaves strongly the thread of human values.
He gives us no hero, no heroine--just the people I have mentioned,
each to himself being the most important, but to you and me being
only one of the group.   The forward progression of the story is
one of the most brilliant exhibitions of sustained filmic motion the
screen has given us in recent years of the talkie era.   We have
the feeling all the time that we are pressing onward with the characters, going with them on their perilous journey, hoping with them
that they will reach their destination in safety.   And for that, we
have John Ford to thank.

As for the individual mention of cast members, no more evenly balanced set of characterizations ever has been presented, the prominence of the individual player being dependent entirely on the length of his or her role. Hundreds appear in the picture and all of them are merely human beings whom we are permitted to see as they live their lives. Claire Trevor, as the prostitute, earns our instant sympathy and retains it throughout, her performance being the most penetrating she has to her credit. John Wayne seemed born for the part he plays, but the same might be said of the others in the most prominent roles, Andy Devine, John Carradine, Thomas Mitchell, George Bancroft, Louise Platt, Donald Meek, Berton Churchill. In all its technical aspects the production maintains the high level of the writing, direction and acting. Cutting the film presented some nice problems, particularly in a sequence in which a few score mounted Indians attack the stagecoach, and which, incidentally, is an intensely thrilling sequence. Otho Lovering, editorial supervisor, and Dorothy Spencer and Walter Reynolds, editors, deserve praise for their skilful assembling of the film. The excellent results achieved with the sound recorded by Frank Mayer have much to do with the success of the production.

--Welford Beaton in Hollywood
Spectator, Vol. 13, No. 28
(February 18, 1939), pages 5-6.

*   *   *

One swellelegant Western that even the carriage trade will go for. A whale of a good story that has brilliant direction, writing and acting. No stars or come-ons, but an all-star cast of players that does itself proud. Play it and play it heavily, and give a good western a chance to pay through the box-office.

It has long been suspected that it was possible to have a western in which the hero didn't have to pose as a cattle rustler, or horse thief, or bandit in order to clean up the frontier or picture. This is the story and picture to prove it, and one that takes a group of people for a stagecoach ride to Lordsburg and packs in all the drama, action, humor, pathos and love story that could be wanted in a month of Sundays.

On this memorable ride go the Ringo Kid, escaped from jail in order to wipe out the Plummer gang that framed him; a sheriff who wants to save his life by keeping him prisoner; a dance-hall girl; a real lady out to join her husband and who has a baby on the way; an absconding bank president; a whiskey drummer; a drunken doctor who has been run out of town; a gambler and, of course, the stagecoach driver. And this group meets up with a band of Apache Indians on the warpath and outrides them to safety, and to the finish of the Plummer boys when they get to town.

The writing and directing by the pair who gave the world The Informer is plenty on a par with that picture, and, besides

all the ingredients included for the tried and true western fan, is
the intelligent handling of swell characters and a new way of making old situations suspenseful.

The cast is a strikingly good one.   Claire Trevor and John
Wayne, as the girl and jailbird, do one grand job of the love interest and make it better than legitimate--they make it something
for which an audience can root.   Thomas Mitchell as the drunken
doctor is superb, and Donald Meek as a liquor salesman is something that cannot be missed without great loss.   John Carradine is
most impressive as the gambler.   Louise Platt does beautiful work
as the officer's wife.   Berton Churchill is blusteringly pompous as
the thieving banker.   Andy Devine and George Bancroft trade laughs
and scenes, and add a great deal to the general entertainment value.
Duke Lee, Tom Tyler and Joe Rickson as the Plummer boys are a
dainty dish to set before a hero on a dark night, and Tim Holt,
Chris Martin and Elvira Rios are standouts in supporting roles.

Bert Glennon's photography, too, is a standout in a world
of breathtakingly beautiful and scenic westerns.   The music score
is well put together and aptly sticks to American folk tunes, well
orchestrated and neatly placed.   And, all that, plus the Indians,
is something worth going to see and something that's worth playing.
                          --The Hollywood Reporter, Vol.
                            50, No. 2 (February 3, 1939),
                          page 3.

☐ A STAR IS BORN (Selznick-International/United Artists, 1937)

That fabulous place, Hollywood--which someone, even years
ago, called as much a state of mind as a place--is far too vast
and complicated a thing for one movie to present completely; but
A Star Is Born covers a surprising lot of it.   Directly or by implication it manages to enclose within its frame a good deal of
Hollywood the town, Hollywood the institution, and the business of
making pictures in Hollywood.   Along with this, by an indirection
that is sometimes subtle and sometimes more than a little barbed,
it provides a comment on the perpetual and insidious interaction
between Hollywood and the public, each with its tremendous effect,
so hard to analyze and so impossible to deny, upon the other.

In pattern a Cinderella story, this film happens to tell the
one Cinderella story that today's life has many a time proved a
true one.   A girl going to Hollywood, completely unknown and without experience, and leaping with almost no trouble at all into stardom! Oddly enough the train of circumstances that accomplishes
this near-miracle is entirely credible, because the characters involved in it seem lifelike, with understandable dispositions and motives.   Whether they are typical, in such a combination, doesn't
particularly matter so long as they are convincing.   The whole

Hollywood tale is convincing, as a matter of fact. It is only its
framework--its prologue and epilogue--that is hard to swallow without gagging: some grandmother business, excessively sentimental
and fabricated, in which May Robson repeats yet once again her
conception of a barking old vixen with a lot of spurious philosophy
and a heart of caramel-fudge under her boorish domineering.

The main part of the picture is as good as a visit to the
cinema capital under the auspices of someone who knows all and
tells a good deal--with due regard to the discretion.   You enter at
once upon the holy of holies, Sid Grauman's Chinese Theatre, with
its footprints of stars immortally embedded in cement--and the essence of Hollywood is with you.   In an entirely natural way you
progress from outer to inner, from lower to higher.   The cheap
little hotel, later on the Trocadero, finally the magnificent estate
of the established luminary; Hollywood Bowl, the Central Casting
Office (with a kindly Peggy Wood to explain just why you should be
discouraged and go back home), the studio with its workings: at
length in the swim, in the money, in the fan's heaven.   Your
dreams of those glamorous careers keep happy pace with Esther
Blodgett as she mounts the golden ladder and becomes Vicki Lester
--through the make-up man's magic hands, through the camera
tests, through the press-agent build-up (but not through the weary,
nerve-racking, heart-breaking hard work of getting the picture
made) to the triumphant preview.   And fame and an Academy
Award.   Which is all held together with remarkable humanness by
Janet Gaynor, who (under direction of a high order) easily makes
the whole thing seem as if it really happened.

But against this rising of one star is set the falling of
another.   The man who gives her her first chance is already,
though he doesn't realize it, slipping from his pinnacle, and his
is no fairy tale but a grim picture of disintegration.   A charming
and generous, even an intelligent man he is, but a screen idol
whose day is done, contemptuous of the public adoration that raised
him so high, but with that adoration gone unable to find a foothold
to stop his downward plunge, finding in drink the only thing that
keeps reality from being unendurable.   And finally even drink cannot keep life endurable.   It is a tragic part (though oddly enough
the trade is beginning to talk of it as a "light" part for Fredric
March, which probably means that it is recognized as a human
part, with lights and shades and no whiskers or strutting bun-
combe), splendidly written and magnificently acted.   Fredric March
has never had a better chance to show what a fine and honest actor
he can be.

This collapsed idol is not the villain of the piece, however.
The real villain, as a little thought discloses, is the gargantuan
monster which has grown up with the movie industry, that octopus
of public curiosity that seems to be an inevitable part of public
adulation, reaching into the most sacred intimacies of its gods and
goddesses and leaving them no possible hope for a normal private
life.   Just a nice friendly interest, maybe?   Just take a look at

the funeral near the end of A Star Is Born and figure out what a prominent movie personality can do, continually hounded by such interest.   Lionel Stander is given the unhappy job of personifying this universal characteristic as the press-agent in this film, who must keep the public clamorous and satisfied at the same time, and as he does the thing with characteristic gusto and terrific honesty he is going to be vigorously hated by many an audience.   The part is likely to work as libel on publicity men, who don't really deserve being mixed up in another Frankenstein-and-his-monster confusion.

Altogether, if you want to look at it that way, this film is a pretty keen comment on things as they are, leaving out a lot of aspects of Hollywood life but treating those which it does use with remarkable honesty.   William Wellman deserves some hearty appreciation for the idea, for the way he has used the help of his collaborators, and for the final manipulation of actors and technicians in bringing it all into its final shape on the screen.   (Incidentally, he has made the best use of Technicolor to date, for dramatic purposes.   Technicolor is the ideal medium for telling the truth about some of the things in this film--which may be a compliment with a double edge.)   And finally, if you don't care to bother about looking under the surface, you can go to this picture with the assurance that you will see the best movie about Hollywood that has yet been made, and be excellently entertained.

--James Shelley Hamilton in National Board of Review Magazine, Vol. 12, No. 5 (May 1937), pages 8-10.

☐ STATE FAIR (Fox, 1933)

After the ugliness of prisons, gangsters and hi-octanic sex, this picture comes like a breath of fresh air blowing away the miasma of our recent celluloid debauch.   It is a gentle story of farmer folk preparing for, attending and returning from the State Fair.

The opening sequences show Will Rogers chambermaiding Blue Boy, a huge hog; and his wife, Louise Dresser--what a delightful married couple they make!--preparing her pickles and mincemeat for the fair.   The two charming children, Norman Foster and Janet Gaynor, simply can't wait.

Then aboard the truck, Blue Boy and all, for the long ride. The camp in the woods; the kaleidoscopic excitements of the fair itself; the awards; and the return home.   Simple, but loaded with charm and amusing incident.

Baptist picnics and state fairs are notoriously dangerous to the libidos of the young, and this one is no exception.   Janet meets a city feller, Lew Ayres, who, refreshingly enough, is not a slicker out to do her wrong.   On the contrary, this meeting develops into one of the sweetest love stories on the screen.   This time it is the boy who is "wronged"!   Norman falls for Sally Eilers, a beautiful trapeze gal, and Sally--oh, oh, oh!   "Say, Melissa," snorts Will Rogers, "that boy of ours has spent the last three nights with that friend of his.   Don't you thin--?"   Maybe the scene, delicately handled, in which we hear, but do not see, the young couple in bed is good, but somehow this note of "sin" seemed to me to take the bloom off the rose.

The fun is in the fair itself: Norman getting the better of the booth fellow by winning everything he throws rings at; the roller coaster, the cooch dancers; and best of all, the pickle and mincemeat judging--that, and the hog judging.   High humor, folks.

State Fair, from the novel by Philip Stong, is made into a screen play by Paul Green and Sonya Levien.   Henry King has directed with delicacy, good taste and a fine sense of fun; and the camera work of Hal Mohr is beautiful beyond words, the night stuff particularly so.

Recently Will Rogers told me he would much rather work in stock than to be starred.   He is right.   In this picture there are five or six stars, and each shines more brightly because of the constellation.   Will is at his best; Louise Dresser is as charming as she is beautiful; Janet Gaynor fits her innocent role perfectly, even her lisp being appropriate to the part; Sally Eilers could easily have "wronged" stronger men than the country boy; Norman Foster and Lew Ayres are entirely convincing.   Frank Craven and Victor Jory in small parts are terribly amusing; one of the best laughs is the pompous speech given by Congressman Goodhart, the actor unnamed on the program.

A swell boost for Duncan Cramer, responsible for the beautiful sets, and for Rita Kaufman for the costumes.

Of course we all know that, at present, life on the farm is no such idyll of peace and contentment, but it used to be, ought to be, and when I am King, it will be!

City folks will love this story.   I'll be interested to know how it goes in the farm-mortgage belt.
> --Rob Wagner in Rob Wagner's
> Script, Vol. 8, No. 208 (Feb-
> ruary 4, 1933), page 6.

*   *   *

Based on Phil Stong's best seller written around a country fair, Henry King has nicely caught the spirit of the simple story and has turned in a production that has the charm of naturalness and the virtue of sincerity.   No villain, little suspense, but a straightforward story of a rural family who find their great moments at the state fair, where paterfamilias captures the title for his prize hog, the mother makes a clean sweep in the pickle entries, the boy gets his first vicarious but satisfying taste of romance, and the girl finds a more lasting love. Well cast, sumptuously produced, intelligently directed, and done in very fine photography, State Fair promises to be a winner all the way down the line.

Those who have never sat in the grandstand for the horse trots or thrilled to the high dive will appreciate the novelty. Those who know their rural America will find it ringing true. Just enough of the general atmosphere has been used to give the local color, but most of the happenings are backgrounded against other than the fair locales.

Of chief interest is the debut of a new romance team in Janet Gaynor and Lew Ayres. His rather flippant style gives a needed tang to situations which sometimes in the past have been too saccharine. The combination should give Miss Gaynor a fresh hold on her fans, and it will not hurt Ayres. It is a charming romance between these two. There is interest, too, in the less wholesome romance of the boy with the girl of the acrobatic act. Norman Foster and Sally Eilers handle this capably, while there is just enough of Will Rogers' quaint humor and Louise Dresser's country dame to temper the more hectic moments. For a moment Victor Jory steals the screen as the concession owner who gypped young Frake the year before and smilingly prepares to repeat, only to find that his erstwhile victim has spent the twelvemonth interval in practising to ring the prizes and is practically a dead shot. There is even a humorous twist to the porcine romance of Blue Boy, the prize hog, who comes to life only when he meets Esmeralda, the red-headed sow.

Over all Henry King has wielded a sympathetic megaphone, getting his effects through naturalness rather than stress, and knitting the whole into a consistent and acceptable sequence of events.

The picture shows some very beautiful scenes, particularly in the grove where the farmers camp, and a travel shot on a moonlight ride down the road between the rows of the tall corn for which the state is famous.

State Fair is a picture that will do much to restore faith in the ability of the cinema to appeal without recourse to sensation or sex.

--Chic in Variety, Vol. 109, No. 8 (January 31, 1933), page 12.

☐ STELLA DALLAS (Goldwyn, 1937)

Barbara Stanwyck's performance in Stella Dallas is one of
the most brilliant to the credit of any screen actress since the dawn
of talkies.   There is little trace of the real Barbara, which, by
virtue of their lack and much else, she must display in the standard
film roles she is called upon to play.   Here we have her as a sow's
ear out of which her husband vainly tries to make a silk purse.   It
is a sensitive, beautifully shaded characterization, one which definitely places Barbara among the truly great actresses of the screen.
In my review of every picture in which I have seen her I have accorded her warm praise, for even in parts which offered her little
scope to display her ability, there was in evidence the divine spark
which becomes a blaze in Stella Dallas.   I was confident that all
Barbara needed was an opportunity, and the canny Sam Goldwyn
gave it to her.

Sam really is the hero of the picture, with Merritt Hulburd
distinguishing himself in the chief supporting production role.   A
Goldwyn picture always is cast with regard only for the adaptability
of the players to the parts assigned them.   By the cleverest publicity campaign in the entire history of screen entertainment, Sam
Goldwyn has made his own name mean box-office, which permits
him to cast his pictures without regard for the box-office strength
of the players he selects.   He does not start at the head of the
box-office list and work down it until he comes to a player he can
secure.   Stella Dallas, without any of the big ten, male and female,
will be one of the greatest draws in years because Sam looked for
talent instead of names.

Mother love always is box-office, but never before has it
been presented more poignantly than we have it here.   The strength
of any screen offering lies in its emotional appeal, and Stella Dallas
is so strong in that respect that it keeps tears never far from audiences eyes and the lump always hovering in the vicinity of the
throat.   It is a symphony of heart beats, a human document which
no art except that of the screen can write so graphically.   It brings
us a new King Vidor.   The touch of genius always has characterized
his direction, but never previously has he attained such emotional
heights.   His handling of his players is inspired.   He gives us only
human beings who are the people they play, plumbing the depths of
their emotional resources until their hearts, not their minds, carry
the picture's messages to us.

Under Vidor's sympathetic direction, young Anne Shirley fulfills the prediction I made in December, 1935.   Under the heading,
"New Star Is Rising," I wrote then of her performance in Chatter-
box, "One can see Anne's future in her fine eyes.   They reflect
everything that is clean and sweet, with a hint of latent emotional
fire ready to burst into flame when her opportunity comes."   Her
opportunity came in Stella Dallas, thanks to her selection by the
astute Sam Goldwyn, who could see in Anne what her own studio
apparently never saw.   And I repeat that in her a new star is rising.

And while on the topic of new stars, I would like to point to another.   It is Tim Holt, son of Jack.   He is not on the screen many minutes in Stella Dallas, but quite long enough to register that he has a future which ultimately may lead to Jack's chief distinction being the fact that he is Tim's father.   In case you think I am too impulsive, I would remind you that after seeing Tyrone Power in an even briefer appearance in his first picture, I predicted for him in these pages everything that has happened to him since.

John Boles was a happy selection for the leading male role in Stella Dallas, a role with no particular high spots, but to which a gentlemanly personality is essential.   Barbara O'Neil makes a fine impression, and Alan Hale is brilliant in the role of Ed Munn, the cheap sport who was played by Jean Hersholt in the silent version of the story.

It was important to the story that the background of Stella Dallas be planted to justify later her rather vulgar point of view when she married above her social station.   A bit played by Marjorie Main in itself tells that part of the story.   Drab, slovenly, long-suffering, the impression we get of her in the home in which Stella was raised, makes reasonable everything which later is developed in Stella's character.   Miss Main is an artist and her contribution to the picture is out of all proportion to the length of her part.   The wisdom of Sam's casting is in evidence down to the bottom of the list.

Those who had to do with the story as it appears on the screen were Harry Wagstaff Gribble, Gertrude Purcell, Victor Heerman and Sarah Y. Mason.   The praise I have given the production as a whole could have been earned only by a picture made from a perfect script.   Richard Day's art direction, Rudolph Mate's photography, Omar Kiam's costumes, Alfred Newman's music, Julia Heron's set decorations, and Sherman Todd's film editing all played their parts in making Stella Dallas one of the greatest pictures the sound screen has to its credit.

--Welford Beaton in Hollywood
Spectator, Vol. 9, No. 12 (July
31, 1937), pages 7-8.

*   *   *

The silent films coddled sentiment as the legitimate offspring of the medium.   Pantomime, softly augmented by a good musical score, bowed the emotions through a series of tear marathons that were eminently successful and satisfying.   With the advent of dialogue came remakes of story material that had once before hit the bull's eye of popularity.   Way Down East, Over the Hill, and Seventh Heaven were less than acceptable to those who remembered the originals.   The old plots and the new technique never quite merged.   Now comes Stella Dallas, following a hit predecessor of 1925.   Veteran fans will be pleased to learn that it is better than

the first version. What is more, it will probably be one of the
most widely liked pictures of this or any other year.

Mother love is an ageless dramatic standby. Utterly natural
development and simplicity of treatment come from King Vidor, who
has his best effort since the memorable The Crowd. The dialogue
must be fabulously adroit, for one is never conscious of it ... a
roll of the drums for Victor Heerman and Sarah Mason.

One believes in Stella, child of millhands magnificently etched
by Marjorie Main and Edmund Elton. The girl marries out of her
class. (There is a swell romance-bit in a nickelodeon of 1919 with
some brief footage of a movie of that period. Unless these eyes
betray me, the idols were Herbert Rawlinson and Sylvia Breamer.)
The girl is brash, raucous, finds it impossible to dispense with
vulgarisms. Husband and wife separate, and the child becomes
sensitive and, in the after-years, discerns that mother is rayon instead of silk. Heartbreak for both.

The heroine's wardrobe should have been less exaggerated.
True, the woman was coarse and common, but she had the perspi-
cacity to realize her faulty taste when her husband revisits her at
Christmas. One of the scenes I found most touching was Stella
snipping the excess lace and trimmings from her dress in order to
win the approval of the man she had lost and still respects. Later,
when she tries to "set" her daughter in society, she out-sadies
Sadie Thompson. It just doesn't convince.

Barbara Stanwyck, blondined, gives a major show that will
be remembered; it is certain to shoot her stock sky high on the
movie exchange. Anne Shirley is deft and engagingly young, realizing all the dramatic nuances of a difficult role. Noteworthy contributions by Barbara O'Neil, Alan Hale, George Walcott, Tim Holt
and Dickie Jones. John Boles does nothing to animate a priggish
assignment. Fine musical setting by Alfred Newman, with ex-popu-
lar songs used to plant period feeling. A "must."

                              --Herb Sterne in Rob Wagner's
                                Script, Vol. 18, No. 426 (Au-
                                gust 28, 1937), page 10.

☐ STREET SCENE (Goldwyn/United Artists, 1931)

An almost perfectly produced and acted picture. Not a flaw
has slipped by the eye of director King Vidor. It's the pinnacle of
his directorial career.

Just one question worries us. Will it be box-office? Does
the public really want a true cross-section of life presented as it
actually happens? We hope it goes big; big money on this would
encourage more really excellent pictures.

Here are the humor, the pathos, the gripping drama which comes to just one street of one city. You've seen it again and again; you've read it as reported in your daily paper.

The picture moves rapidly, adroitly and dramatically. If you saw the stage play, which was a Broadway hit, you will be amazed to see the advantages of sustained interest given by the picture presentation.

There are thirty-four main characters--mostly from the original New York cast. Sylvia Sidney, Estelle Taylor, William Collier, Jr. , and Lawrence Wagner are the main screen contributions. Each of the thirty-four does his share so aptly that all must share honors.

However, Beulah Bondi, as Mrs. Jones, has the advantage of more lines than the average player. She makes the most of it. She almost steals the picture! Estelle Taylor is good as Sylvia's mother.

--Photoplay, Vol. 40, No. 5
(October 1931), page 49.

*   *   *

Elmer Rice's play of Street Scene, which Samuel Goldwyn has converted into a striking motion picture, well might have been called Just Folks. As contrasted with the high and mighty usually employed as the backbone of a screen story simplicity and simple persons here come into their own.

For camera material the tale reverts to the Biograph days when with almost unvarying regularity the hero of a picture was one who worked with his hands and the heroine was one unacquainted with the feel of silk stockings.

Biograph with its simple stories simply told became the world's leading motion picture maker. Even for the comparatively short period that its chief director, Griffith, was unknown and unidentified to the multitude nevertheless the impression grew among exhibitors that somewhere in the Biograph organization was a man who stood out above his confreres in competing companies.

So here a man writes a story around the doings of human beings in a single city block. Actually the locale is restricted to an area nearer to three or four twenty-foot city lots. These human beings do much the same things done by their brothers and sisters in thousands of other spots all over the world--scarcely more or less. Yet with it Elmer Rice wins the Pulitzer prize. And why should not the award go to the person who can keep his people near to the soil--even though some of them inevitably must be soiled?

The tale is of absorbing interest throughout its entire length. At one time or another all of the thirty-four members of the stated

cast are heard from, briefly or otherwise. Disregarding the implication contained in that statement the interest centers on a few,
and from them never departs.

Principals among these are Sylvia Sidney as Rose in whose
home a skeleton has taken shape; William Collier, Jr., as Sam, a
Jewish lad not overpugnacious by nature, abused by the bully of the
block and in love with Rose; Estelle Taylor as Mrs. Maurrant,
mother of Rose, tied to an uncongenial husband and secretly meeting Sankey, the milk collector, played by Russell Hopton.

One of the best performances of the production is that given
by Beulah Bondi, as Ma Jones, the chief gossip of the block--which
is a statement of major dimensions. She follows not the prescribed
routine of overemphasis; rather she rests her work on restraint and
deliberation, with a high degree of success. Matthew McHugh as
Vincent, the grinning apelike pride of the Jones family, is practically perfect in his most repellent part.

David Landau as the father of Rose, the man who when he
shoots down his wife and the milk collector contributes the tragedy
to the story, is convincing in his bitterness toward life in general.

Sylvia Sidney is near her best as Rose, as near as we have
had an opportunity to see her on the screen. Her really great part
has not yet come to her--one where we may see her not always in
drab or unkindly surroundings but one wherein she may have a
chance to radiate gayety and be a part of a less unlovely atmosphere.

Willie Collier, Jr. does well in a difficult part. King Vidor
directs.

--George Blaisdell in The International Photographer, Vol. 3,
No. 9 (October 1931), page 29.

☐ THE STRUGGLE (Griffith/United Artists, 1931)

Many will decline to believe that this subject is a D. W.
Griffith document, but rather a crude bit of propaganda to which
Griffith has lent his name.

As a commercial production, or even as a propaganda picture, it is practically valueless; because as a film it is void and
without form, and as propaganda it isn't plausible either for the
wet or the dry partisan side. Quite as astonishing as the Griffith
connection is that of John Emerson and Anita Loos.

For key city uses the film is pretty completely out, although
it is conceivable that it might have its uses in minor spots and then

only on the ground that <u>Ten Nights in a Barroom</u> may still be profitable in minor territories.

On the theory that the subject is promoted propaganda it's a
wasted effort because it deals with prohibition in a serious controversial way when anybody could have told its promoters that the
Eighteenth Amendment can't be handled in any other than a comedy
vein on the screen. Prohibition is like the institution of the nagging mother-in-law, a subject so bristling with annoyance and head-
ache in actual experience that in mere defense humanity has to believe it's funny.

Advance notices set up the pretense that the picture is meant
for an anti-prohibition social moral, but no such aim is discernible
in the film itself. The story of a mill worker who brings on his
own destruction and that of his wife and child by drinking, certainly
is no plea for personal liberty in the matter of bending the elbow,
legally or illegally. The subject of the Eighteenth Amendment
doesn't enter into the matter one way or the other.

Worst of all the picture is just dull when it isn't in the highest degree maudlin, untouched by logic or humor and an utter bore.

Picture was made in New York, Audio-Cinema studios being
employed for the purpose and using the new and improved Western
Electric equipment, the first subject turned out on that apparatus.
Probably the one cheerful angle of the unhappy incident is the suggestion that comes with watching Hal Skelly's performance as the
wretched hero that, given a spot and an opportunity, he would
achieve something as a dramatic actor. His performance here has
a good deal of vigor, be it ever so wasted in a vain role. As
much cannot be said for Zita Johann, from legit and in her first
film, who was perforce restricted to a flat and colorless reading
of the hopeless character of the drunkard's sorrowful wife.

Audience at the premiere gave its own verdict by giggling at
passages apparently meant to be the most moving, and also by de-
parting in squads before the footage was half over.
                                        --Rush in <u>Variety</u>, Vol. 105, No.
                                        1 (December 15, 1931), page
                                        21.

                    *   *   *

Old Demon Prohibition Rum makes bum out of honest working man. Papa, full of red-eye, gets D. T.'s and chases tiny tot
around ruined garret, à la Lillian Gish while audience snickers at
phony thunderstorm. "Father, Dear Father, Come Home with Me
Now" and <u>The Face on the Barroom Floor</u> done in the manner and
with the technique of the early Biograph pictures. New invention
of talking pictures makes characters actually talk. Sodden wreck
rolls in gutter while radio squawks "Abide with Me." It's all too
sad. Hal Skelly tried hard to save it, but even his good work was

of no avail.   Directed by D. W. Griffith, who sixteen years ago
made The Birth of a Nation.

--Photoplay, Vol. 41, No. 3
(February 1932), page 98.

☐ A TALE OF TWO CITIES (M-G-M, 1935)

One morning, seven or eight years ago, Ronald Colman
called for me at my house and we went for a walk into the Hollywood foothills.   He told me then he hoped he someday would play
Sydney Carton in The Tale of Two Cities.   Ronnie's enthusiasm for
the part never wavered; many times since that morning talk he has
mentioned it to me.

And now Metro's lion roars out an introduction to Ronald
Colman's appearance as Sydney Carton.   The Dickens masterpiece
is presented on a massive scale, a great, honest, painstaking production dignifying the screen and of vast credit to its makers.   No
one who keeps abreast of film progress or takes an intelligent interest in the recurring demonstrations of the immense sweep of the
screen as a purveyor of entertainment, can afford to miss The Tale
of Two Cities.

With tremendous power the motion picture camera paints on
a gigantic canvas justification of the French Revolution, puts reason
behind the uprising of a crushed and outraged people, and then goes
on to show the little reason behind the people's handling of the power they bought so dearly with blood--pure cinema, all of it, ampli-
fied pictorially by printed titles superimposed on some of the scenes.
In its massive record of the tragedy the camera asks no aid from
the spoken word.

No other art could paint so impressively, so tragically, the
deadly drama of the guillotine, the heroic unyielding of its victims,
the stupid blood-lust of those who used it with such unreasoning
cruelty.   It is terrible history written terrifically.

With marked fidelity the screen recreates the Paris of the
deadly day when the Bastille fell, to this day the nation's national
holiday.   Cedric Gibbons and his associates have wrought wonders
in providing a production to do justice to the greatness of the drama, and Oliver Marsh has photographed it in a manner which develops all its pictorial values.

The story does not fare so well under the competition of the
weight of its scenic investiture.   The revolution is both hero and
villain and by contrast the individuals are unimportant.   Sympathy
for them is not developed, making the intimate scenes slow the
progress of the more impressive mass drama.   When I viewed
The Story of Louis Pasteur my eyes filled with tears and a lump

came to my throat when Pasteur merely stood in surprise as he caught his first glimpse of the scientists gathered to do him honor. When Colman mounted the steps of the guillotine I, dry-eyed, appraised the excellence of his acting.

And it was not Ronald's fault that I surveyed unemotionally his great sacrifice to the love he bore a woman, that my reaction to the grief of Elizabeth Allan was intellectual, not emotional. Their performances are in every way meritorious, but I was viewing history being made, watching a nation being convulsed with horror, and individuals were to me mere dots on a mighty canvas covered with things of more importance.

To be wholly successful a motion picture must focus the attention of its audience on the fates of individuals, and all its elements must be aimed in that direction and serve as a background against which is written in intimate terms the drama of a group of people for whom our sympathy is aroused.   Impersonal drama can not stir our emotions, and it is the emotional response to what it offers that makes the screen universally appealing.

The Pasteur picture focuses our attention on an individual, first as an unknown scientist struggling alone against the odds of unbelief, then as a recognized benefactor of mankind, gathering as he goes and with accumulating force, our sympathy for him and all who concern him, until his final triumph profoundly stirs our emotions.   All the elements in the picture are blended to accomplish that single end.   No scene is inserted to check the steady trend of our emotions toward it, no setting so imposing as to attract our attention to it as an individual element.

The Metro picture overreaches itself in its effort to entertain us.   It gives us so much that it employs our visual sense too fully to permit us to develop sympathy for individuals who are merely frail strands shot through a great pattern woven with sturdy ropes.

And still there is not a performance in the picture that is not outstanding on its own account.   Nor is the direction at fault. Jack Conway has done a notable job, one of which he justly can be proud.   His handling of the masses of people in long shots is extraordinarily effective, and many of his individual scenes are set with little acting gems for which Conway's intelligent direction was responsible.   An instance of this sort is the judge, played by E. E. Clive.   We see this veteran actor not a half dozen times and only in shots of seconds' duration; what he says in these brief intervals is what any judge might say, but when you note the manner in which Clive says them you will have a demonstration of a skilled actor responding intelligently to intelligent direction.

It was fine to see again so many stalwarts of the silent days whose acting ability and popularity with audiences the industry of late has ignored to its own loss.   Mitchell Lewis, Tully Marshall,

Harry B. Warner, Claude Gillingwater, Lawrence Grant, Robert
Warwick, Ralf Harolde, John Davidson and Tom Ricketts, members
of the cast, are players of reputation whose steady employment
would benefit the box-office.

In a picture in which the bits are done as well as the bigger
parts, it is only the length of their roles which make the principals
stand out prominently.   Colman's performance is a sensitive, understanding delineation of a not too admirable character.   Blanche
Yurka registers strongly in a dramatic role, and others who do
splendid work are Edna May Oliver, Reginald Owen, Basil Rathbone, Henry B. Walthall, Donald Woods, Lucille La Verne and
Walter Catlett.

Herbert Stothart has provided an impressive musical score,
and Dolly Tree's costumes are an important element of the production.

--Welford Beaton in Hollywood
Spectator, Vol. 10, No. 4
(December 7, 1935), pages 7-8.

☐ THREE SMART GIRLS (Universal, 1936)

Usually it is about as safe to take exploitation blurbs seriously as it is to walk into the den of a famished tiger. "The Surprise Picture of the Year" is the way Three Smart Girls is being
advertised.   It's that all right, and also the best film Charles
Rogers' New Universal set-up has turned out.   Liberal credit is
undoubtedly due coproducer Joseph Pasternak.

Not only does this provide an introduction to a talented singing star, but it also marks the local début of Austrian director
Henry Koster.   Koster displays an acute knowledge of the screen's
demands, handles his actors with a naturalness which is as rare as
it is welcome.   Symmetry and motion are among his strongest assets.   He seems slated to land among Hollywood's top-flight mega-
phoners.

Screen play by Adele Comandini is noteworthy for its humor
and spontaneous spirit.   A simple tale of three young girls brought
up in Switzerland by their divorced mother.   The woman still loves
the man she's lost and when she reads of his approaching second
marriage she grieves.   Daughters take things into their own hands,
escape to New York and finally manage to extricate papa from the
coils of a brazen enchantress.   Incidents and dialogue sparkle and
flow, the romantic angles are handled with grace.   Joseph Valentine's lensing is great and the same must be said for the John
Harkrider sets.

Deanna Durbin, a fourteen-year-old songstress with a high
clear voice which she uses effortlessly, makes a most auspicious

bow. Totally without the humbuggeries flaunted by most sub-debs, she has a crisp, fresh and delightfully wholesome appeal that will take her a long way on the success road.

As her sisters, Nan Grey and Barbara Read do well, and there is a most persuasive portrait by Charles Winninger who has burst his Captain Andy shackles at last. Ray Milland is at his best in light comedy while Mischa Auer takes care of the eccentric steps of the entertainment. It's absurd to cast Alice Brady as Binnie Barnes' mother; she looks more like her sister. Alice, more restrained and therefore better than she's been of late, is one of the major hits of this hit picture. Nella Walker hasn't much to do but her graciousness is most attractive.

> --Rob Wagner in Rob Wagner's
> Script, Vol. 16, No. 393 (De-
> cember 12, 1936), pages 13-14.

☐ TOP HAT (RKO, 1935)

If I had to have somebody bothering me with noise in the apartment above, I don't know anybody I'd rather have doing it than Fred Astaire. Miss Ginger Rogers has this kind of Astaire trouble in Top Hat, and goes upstairs to tell him to cut out that tap dancing so she can sleep. This is the start of another Fred Astaire dancing film, which is of more significance to the world right now than the Ethiopian war or the dissolution of the utility folding companies. A film perfectly blank except for a few Fred Astaire dances would be well worth sitting through, and I dare some producer to give us just such a film some time; I'll wager it would succeed--and save him a lot of money.

Top Hat comes as near to being a carbon copy of The Gay Divorcee as the law would allow RKO to make without paying royal-ties to Cole Porter, and RKO rates a kickinthepance for not trying harder to think up something new. I'd like, for example, to see them give Ginger Rogers a part which would not require her to pout through most of the picture. For the first three-fourths of this film, she has no twink; seems to be just a good-looking girl speaking lines for money. She is utterly unimpressive as a lofty lady. But when she went into her single song, there towards the end, I wondered if, after all, the girl hasn't a touch of talent.

> --Don Herold in Life, Vol. 102,
> No. 2608 (November 1935),
> page 50.

*   *   *

The theatres will hold their own world series with this one. It can't miss and the reasons are three--Fred Astaire, Irving Ber-lin's songs and sufficient comedy between numbers to hold the film together.

But on story Top Hat is a masquerade, and behind the very
thin mask is Gay Divorcee. That won't make any difference because Roberta has spaced Divorcee and Hat while Astaire's routines,
his singing and Berlin's melodies and lyrics are of such strength
as to smother any other consideration. It's Irving Berlin's initial
film chore and the first time he and Astaire have ever worked together, stage or screen, the result being a piece of work worth
everything it will get and it'll get plenty.

Productionally the film is all it should be. This includes
photography and recording, the latter particularly acute and deserving more than mere mention because of the balance necessary
between the instrumentation and Astaire's dancing. It is also true
that the picture is too long. Cut 15 or 20 minutes, and to the
first three numbers, it could have been sensational. But in that
case what would become of "Cheek to Cheek" (expected to be the
main commercial melody) and "Piccolino" which it is hoped will
evolve into another "Cariocca" or "Continental"? "Piccolino" is
tuneful, interesting, fits and makes a satisfactory finale but the
expectation that it will repeat on the same scale as the two preceding C&C's seems optimistic.

Astaire's sock routines are up forward starting with "No
Strings." He does this alone. It is the hot ditty of the batch,
then "Isn't It a Lovely Day?" with Ginger Rogers for probably the
best dance they've ever done together, trailed in turn by the title
item, "Top Hat, White Tie and Tails," the boy number. This
latter inclusion is dynamite because pictures have never seen anything like it. It is the same number Astaire did in his Ziegfeld
show (Smiles), practically the only change being the melody. Nevertheless the number is a classic of its kind and had the picture been
shortened and the dances rerouted so as to finish with this smash
it might have sent them out of the theatres yelling. Reminding that
Astaire still has another pip boy number in the files from Funny
Face.

Rather a shame that the numbers, as they stand, couldn't
have been arranged so that "Lovely Day" would hit next to closing
instead of "Cheek." The story needs a builder-upper through the
last half hour and "Day," as presented, would be it. A lot of people are going to have a tough time deciding which tune they like
best between "Lovely Day" and "Cheek." However, there can be
no question as to either of the dances concerned. The Astaire-
Rogers routine to "Day" is outstanding, that for "Cheek" is nice
but not important.

Berlin wrote 11 songs for this picture of which the five used
consume approximately 30 minutes, or about one-third of the running time. This cuts them down to an average of around six minutes each, a happier solution than when the musical display splashes
run near the 20-minute mark. It might also be noted that Hermes
Pan, who staged the production numbers, has kept away from the
animated pinwheels and revolving swastikas which often make audi-

ences crosseyed. In addition he has made a marked effort to sub-
jugate the chorus to the principals. Smart.

For the title number Astaire works in front of around 30
boys all in tails; in "Piccolino" Miss Rogers and Astaire have
about 28 mixed couples behind them. "No Strings" is the longest
number in the film due to the premise on which it is based. Astaire keeps Miss Rogers, in the apartment below, awake by his
dancing and upon finding this out he scatters sand on the floor,
does soft shoe and lulls her to sleep. Eight minutes for that, only
four or five for "Lovely Day" and each a gem. There are no music cues, the numbers leaping direct from the dialog and Astaire
is into them before the house realizes it.

But the danger sign is in the story and cast. Substitute
Alice Brady for Helen Broderick and it's the same lineup of players as was in Gay Divorcee. The threat is that it can become
Astaire's stock company so the sooner they break it up the better.
Besides which the situations in the two scripts parallel each other
closely. In fact, it's like the Walla-Walla gag--they liked it so well
they used it twice. Astaire is again the American dancer in London, carefree and unattached (leading up to "No Strings"), thence
the meeting minus benefit of introduction with Miss Rogers, his
pursuit of her around London (and into "Lovely Day") with the mistaken identity thing again via Miss Rogers believing Astaire is
Miss Broderick's husband although her spouse is E. E. Horton.
There will also be some difficulty ascertaining just what and who
Miss Rogers is in the story. After which comes the change in
locale to Venice, carnival night and into "Piccolino" for the finish.

The story similarity carries over to include the group behind
the camera. Pandro S. Berman also produced Divorcee, Mark
Sandrich directed that one as well as this, and Dwight Taylor did
both books. Indeed, Taylor did the book for the show, Gay Divorce, upon which both pictures have been based. It's okay this
time because the jobs Astaire and Berlin have turned in are so
superlative, but if Roberta hadn't been in between the result might
have been much less satisfactory.

Meanwhile, the studio is taking a chance of jeopardizing the
best piece of property it's got, Astaire, through burning him up
extremely fast in asking him to do five numbers a picture. It
shouldn't be overlooked that Astaire is also now on the air as well
as phonograph disks. Regarding these records (Brunswick) theatres
should buy a couple of sets of the platters for lobby or marquee
amplification.

Outside of "Piccolino" the orchestrations on the records (Leo
Reisman and Johnny Green bands) are actually better than in the
picture. These are the first records for which Astaire has ever
danced and his voice more than stands up. Vocally he's a surprise
with this score all three ways--sound track, air, and disk. Which
also means that Astaire is getting further and further away from
the stage all the time.

His dancing, of course, remains a modern rhapsody in
cleats.   It will again awe professionals and fascinate the public for
he is head man as an interpreter of rhythm.   A brass ring for a
couple of rides around the Equator would not uncover similar for-
mations, or sequences, of steps because there is no one like him,
and that goes back long before his picture debut.   Aside from that
his edge on the screen is that both men and women like him, not
always the case as regards masculine stars.   This seems to be due
to a modesty of manner and a personality which boils down to the
word "class. "   And now his singing.   He always had that same
sense of rhythm in his reading of a lyric but his voice has gained
in melody and range.   Astaire has come a long way vocally.

For the rest of the cast Edward Everett Horton bears the
brunt and is the secondary pillar around which the story revolves.
His is the comedy burden which he splits with Eric Blore, his
valet, and Erik Rhodes as a dress designer.   The writers will
probably be surprised, themselves, at the laughs in the picture.
That the material is far from unusual, is particularly evidenced in
the case of such an expert comedienne as Helen Broderick, but
they giggle at it, are amused and that's all that's necessary with
numbers like these in between.   This marks Miss Broderick's
feature film debut.   That her material isn't what it should be is
unfortunate, but she shows enough here to stick on the Coast because she is one of the stage's top comediennes and screens well.

Miss Rogers has little to do in this picture and never opens
her mouth vocally until the concluding "Piccolino. "   She is again
badly dressed while her facial makeup and various coiffeurs give
her a hard appearance.   At the end they manage to soften this impression.   With one of the best figures in Hollywood, it's a mystery
why this girl consistently appears to such disadvantage.   It should
also be said that she's a better trouper than this film allows her to
be.

Top Hat could practically be transplanted to a New York
theatre as a book musical for the simple reason that it so closely
traces a book that was a previous show.   For $4. 40, however, the
comedy would need considerable brightening.   At 40¢ it will meet
the obligation.

This is Sandrich's second directorial effort with Astaire.
He seems to work well with the star and despite a disinclination
to cut has made the cast play superior to the script.   Under any
analysis, however, the picture's enthusiasm springs from Astaire
and Berlin.   It would be something of a task to hoot one with this
duo.

                              --Sid in Variety, Vol. 119, No.
                              12 (September 4, 1935), page
                              14.

□   TRADER HORN (M-G-M, 1931)

        I have been to Africa. I have been up and down the Ubji-
Ubji; I have seen the jag-u-ar in mortal combat with the dic-dic
and the iglutz ravening off ingagii; I have tom-tommed with the
Lallapaloosas and fought with the Kokomoes. As far as I'm concerned, they can now junk all previous African films, dramatic or
travelogic. Trader Horn tells the whole story and tells it better
than the combined footage of every explorer who ever emerged with
a can of film.

        During intermission sophisticated Hollywood was figuring out
trick shots, but the tricks were all those of artistic privilege and
are not in the least pertinent. Mr. Van Dyke told the essential
truth; he assembled an amazing array of local truths to put over
the larger truth--the tragic violence of the African jungle and the
lure of the veldt.

        So convincingly did the ingenious director present his sub-
ject that I felt I was looking upon actual, unpremeditated action until I would suddenly say to myself, "But where is the camera?"
The thing must have been more or less staged.

        For instance, there were long shots across the veldt that
showed practically every animal in Africa, the taking of which must
have spread over the two years the company was there. Yet so
expertly were they cut into shots of the three adventurers trekking
across country with Horn, pointing out and describing the wild
creatures, that the illusion is perfect.

        The jungle fights are absolutely terrifying in their vicious
horror and violence and the killing of the charging lions by the
colossal black, Omoolu, with a spear as big as a tent-pole, is
without doubt the greatest dramatic moment ever filmed--or likely
to be. One Intermissioner feared censorship on the ground that
such killings "just to make a picture" were outrageous. But those
animals were sentenced to violent death at birth, for according to
the law of the jungle, every animal is sooner or later killed by his
natural enemy. There is no dying of old age in the jungle. As
soon as even the most powerful animal grows weak he is gone.
No, Van Dyke set out to show us the tragedy of primitive animal
and human life and his record is complete.

        If old Trader Horn is a good sport, he should share his book
royalties with Harry Carey, for Harry has personalized the venerable author in a way to immortalize the dear old fakir. His performance is convincingly superb.

        No doubt it was good "production" to hang all this gorgeous
material on Trader Horn, and Dick Schayer did a marvelous job of
marrying realism to the fancies of that fascinating book. After all,
the story was a mere thread upon which to string a bunch of epi-

sodes that will stir the sluggish hearts of even our tired, oh, so
tired business men.

In fact, Richard even included a pair of pretty legs. Miss
Edwina Booth furnished them and they were perhaps the only Hollywood note in the picture. Bessie White once told me that "the
vertical rays of the tropical sun" ("or the tropical rays of the
vertical sun"--she couldn't remember which) were almost fatal to
the bodies of the white race, and that she and Stewart had to wear
strips of flannel felt under their clothes the whole length of their
spines for fear of the paralytic effect of those same rays.

Bessie was wrong. The African sun isn't as strong as the
sun at our Santa Monica beaches. After eighteen years of practical
nudity in the jungle, Nina's skin was as white as snow. Furthermore, she cared naught for the barbs and thorns of the underbrush
and wore her blonde hair in a long flowing mantle. Nor had she
lost her inherent modesty, for though she draped her herbivorous
skirt to reveal all of her legs, she was brassiered as chastely as
a Fanchon and Marco chorine. In fact, whenever Nina was shown
with her jungle captors, one fully expected the horrid savages to
cut loose into a musical-comedy extravaganza with squirt lights
and an acrobatic band. This "white fetish" stuff was necessary for
the "romance" of the story and Mr. Metro G. Mayer was quite
right in dragging it in. It's terrible art, but no doubt grand box-
office.

Duncan Renaldo is a pleasing chap, but he was a mere feeder for Harry Carey and an essential boyfriend for the white virgin
of Ubji-Ubji.

But after all the story rests on the capable and courageous
shoulders of Harry Carey and Omoolu.

Without waiting for the other eleven months, I rank Trader
Horn as the greatest picture of 1931.

> --Rob Wagner in Rob Wagner's
> Script, Vol. 4, No. 103 (Janu-
> ary 31, 1931), page 6.

*   *   *

Without a single murmur of ballyhoo about "authenticity"
Metro-Goldwyn presents herewith a film that has all of the African
animal pictures tied to the mast for action and convincing realism.

The movie rights to the novel by the venerable Mr. Horn
were obviously purchased for nothing except the privilege of using
a good boxoffice title--the big idea from start to finish being the
animals, with some honest-to-goodness talking pictures of native
tribesmen thrown in as an added attraction. This combination, together with adequate performances by Harry Carey, Duncan Renaldo,
Edwina Booth and a big black fellow named Mutia Omoolu, provide

two hours of excitement that will be enjoyed by everybody except
people whose nerves are upset by the capers of wild beasts.

In addition to the usual shots of game that are seen in all
African travel films, Trader Horn offers some closeups of scraps
between jungle animals that will make you sit on the edge of your
seat and hold your breath. No doubt these scenes were framed,
nor would we be surprised if some of the beasts are native born
Americans, but the effects obtained are none the less convincing.

This is equally as true of the scenes in which the natives
go through the motions of roasting Trader and his friends alive,
while the drums beat wildly and the savage-looking warriors sing
their tribal ditties.

The chiefs and medicine men argue the matter out in their
native Swahili, or whatever it is they speak--the white girl (who
has been living with them since childhood and is, of course, regarded as some sort of high priestess) intercedes in a mess of
jargon that might very well be the same language--and the whole
business is carried out with amazing naturalness--particularly on
the part of the black men.

Toward the end of the film the story degenerates into one
of those things in which two men love the same woman. Harry
wants her--Duncan wants her--and then our evening was almost
ruined when the girl we were with (a blonde) said, "Do you suppose she will commit Harry Carey?"

Director W. S. Van Dyke deserves a big hand for this fine
piece of showmanship ... and an added burst of applause for Clyde
De Vinna's excellent photography.

> --Harry Evans in Life, Vol. 97,
> No. 2520 (February 20, 1931),
> page 20.

☐ TROUBLE IN PARADISE (Paramount, 1932)

You haven't seen the real Herbert Marshall until this picture
hits your theater. And hits is what we mean, for you'll hear the
impact echoed in audience applause. Besides the finished performance of Mr. Marshall, this film has all the other qualities that
make real entertainment.

Marshall plays a super-crook and super-lover. How women
will envy Miriam Hopkins and Kay Francis! And the clothes those
girls wear prove that Paris hasn't cornered all the dashing and
novel style ideas. But that's incidental. What we want to say is
that they turn in two charming and capable performances, Miss
Hopkins' animated, Miss Francis' more subtle, each in keeping

with her role.   Aided by Charles Ruggles, Edward Horton and C.
Aubrey Smith.

The theme and dialogue are sophisticated, in tune with the
times, but Ernst Lubitsch directs with such finesse that it doesn't
offend.   Neither will the story be over the heads of an average
audience.

It's about two crooks and a rich Parisian widow, and is one
of Lubitsch's best productions, so we don't have to tell you not to
miss it.

And don't forget--here is your first opportunity to see the
Herbert Marshall who captured the New York stage in a screen
play that gives him a chance to be his fascinating self.
                                            --Photoplay, Vol. 43, No. 1
                                              (December 1932), page 57.

☐ TWENTIETH CENTURY (Columbia, 1934)

What a comedian is this Jack Barrymore! I've yipped my
head off to get him out of romance and let him do his stuff; and
how he does it when he has stuff to do! Not only that, his joyous
spirit becomes contagious and he carries everybody else with him.
Walter Connolly and Roscoe Karns are two of our very best troupers; they reach heights in this wild farce that must have surprised
even themselves.

But most remarkable of all, you should see what Jack Barrymore does to Carole Lombard. For a long time I've been twitting
her masque-like face and lifelessness. She fairly explodes in this!
Amusingly enough she is cast as a beautiful but lifeless doll who
has come under the stage direction of the great John Barrymore.
Floppo, tears. "Try again; this time scream so that you can be
heard in the last seat in the balcony." At the proper moment John
jabs her in the fanny with a pin! Eureka! At that instant both the
play's imitation and a real screen actress are born. Too bad
someone didn't stick a pin in Carole several years ago. She had
it all the time, but it took a pin in the impish hand of Jack Barrymore to effect the miracle.

Yes, Jack, as a producer, is a supreme egotist, exhibition-
ist and congenital damn-fool. But he's the genius of Broadway, so
that his courtiers stand for anything. And oh, the comedy that
fellow gets into his part! Perhaps he is having diabolic fun kidding
David Belasco. In any event no red-nosed comic ever threw his
heart into such hilarious business as does Jack.

While Carole is being built up into a big star she becomes
inoculated with Jack's tempestuous temperament, quits him and goes

to Hollywood.   The main action takes place on the Twentieth Century Limited, with Jack trying to get her back.   "My God, Lily,
when I saw you in that picture you were like a sapphire dropped
into lard!"

On the train are two of the twelve apostles of the Oberam-
mergau Passion Play--Herman Bing and Lee Kohlmar.   Wonderful!
Jack will engage them, do the Passion Play and cast Carole as
Magda!   A financial sugar-daddy appears and finances the play to
the tune of $200, 000.   He turns out to be an escaped lunatic who
has been going about pasting "Come to Jesus" stickers on everybody and everything.   Etienne Girardot plays this part superbly.

Charles Levison, perfectly cast as a rival producer, also
hits high in every scene.   And Ralph Forbes, as Carole's Hollywood cutie, gets into the spirit of the thing and farces like nobody's
business.   Even Dale Fuller and Ed Kennedy, in bits, ring the bell.

In the end--but why tell more?   You've simply got to see
the most outrageously funny picture of the year.   Charles Mac-
Arthur and Ben Hecht wrote the darned thing and their dialogue
alone is priceless.   Howard Hawks has directed himself straight
up to an Academy award.

--Rob Wagner in Rob Wagner's
Script, Vol. 11, No. 271 (May
19, 1934), page 8.

*   *   *

John Barrymore, who stars, is quoted in the Music Hall's
house ads as saying, "I've never done anything I like as well ...
a role that comes along once in an actor's lifetime."   Which is
wholly believable; the role as it shows up on the screen, and after
the cutting that must have been done, still looks like a field day
for the profile guy.

It's Barrymore's picture, no doubt of that, with something
left over for Carole Lombard, who manages to shine despite practically stooging.   But whether it will prove a customer's picture
on general release seems doubtful.   For all its good points, and
it has several, there are numerous bad ones, and the latter tend
to make it a long shot for grosses outside the large cities that
boast a cosmopolitan clientele.   For the rest of the country it will
need extra campaigning.   The laughs are certainly there, but they
must have selling.

Bad point No. 1 is the very nature of its plot, a departure
in detail but not in theory from the legit original of last season,
which had a fair run on Broadway.   Twentieth Century appears
limited to two minor groups of auditors--the theatrical bunch that
has known counterparts of Oscar Jaffee, eccentric impresario
(played by Barrymore), and that portion of the lay public that appreciates and understands trade satire.   The first group never sup-

ported any show venture, stage or screen, and the latter is too
much in the minority to count at the box office.

Good points are the breathless pace of the picture, probably
due equally to the adaptation by MacArthur-Hecht and the direction
of Howard Hawks--and Barrymore.   Give Barrymore a chance to
go off his nut, not too much, but just enough, and it's a pleasure.
Producer Jaffee, who not only goes off his nut, but stays off for 91
solid minutes, is a character that's right up his foyer.

In the show the action commenced on the train and remained
there, but for the finale in Grand Central terminal.   In the picture
it doesn't board the train until about the third reel.   For the first
section the Hecht-MacArthur team performed some expert plot-
grafting and the result is that the addition to the original classes
with the original itself.   But while successful in the manner that it
blends with the original, the additional literature is unsuccessful in
that it fails to bring the original down to the level of average com-
prehension.

In the first half the authors paint their puppets and plant
their dynamite, meanwhile keeping it interesting (for those who will
get it) with racy dialog, fast action and biting satire.   On the train
the theme is carried out, only the action is still speedier.

For those not knowing in advance what it's all about, the
action, despite its quality of pace, is likely to prove confusing to
anyone walking in after the beginning of the picture.   Because a
large percentage of picture house patrons walk in at any point in
the running, this picture's drawbacks in that respect are bound to
cause trouble.

Those who see the picture from the beginning probably will
find a reasonable amount of sense in the subsequent happenings.
At the opening the characters are drawn logically and clearly enough.
They're a pack of legits led by a wild-eyed gent, who in any line
of endeavor other than theatrical producing and directing would surely be classed as a loon.   There's no midway explanation for the
wild man's antics.   If they don't get the characterizing at the start,
they won't get it at all.

Lily Garland (Lombard) walks out on producer Jaffee to go
to Hollywood shortly after he makes her, double, and that happens
early in the picture.   From then on it's a chase.   Jaffee goes
broke trying to land another Lily Garland and Lily goes big in Hollywood.   The way Jaffee and his boys try to frame Lily into coming
back into the legit fold paves the road for some of the craziest
trouping since "Dr. Dippy's Sanitarium" was mothballed with other
noted full stage dramatic sketches of the past.   Barrymore is given
the opportunity to do such things as imitate a camel while describing
a scene in the Passion Play he's going to put on.

Miss Lombard, looking very well, must take Barrymore's
abuse as his mistress and hand-made star for the first few hundred

feet, but when she goes temperamental herself she's permitted to
do some head-to-head temperament punching with him.   But the
beautifully dialoged scrapping scenes may prove too inside-stuffy.

There's fine support for Barrymore from Walter Connolly,
Roscoe Karns and Etienne Girardot.   Karns has the press agent
part which had the cream tag lines in the stage version, but which
has shrunk away.   Ralph Forbes as an American society boy and
ex-footballer talks too much English for his assignment and strikes
the only sour note on the casting sheet.

--Bige in Variety, Vol. 114, No.
8 (May 8, 1934), page 14.

☐ VIVA VILLA (M-G-M, 1934)

Trot out that frequently misused word "epic."   Dust off all
the adjectives you haven't even thought of since All Quiet on the
Western Front and The Big Parade.   Dig up a whole flock of syno-
nyms for "stupendous" and "colossal."   Then shout Viva Villa at
the top of your lungs.   David Selznick has given it everything that
makes it a showman's picture--including, of course, an advance
legitimate news campaign that money could not buy.

Mexico should have no quarrel with this presentation of its
Revolutionary bandit hero.   Pancho Villa, as written by Ben Hecht
and magnificently realized by Wallace Beery, is a simple soul.
As a boy, he watched his father flogged to death for the sin of
protesting when his lands were confiscated by tyrannical overlords,
already wealthy.   The lad flees to the hills and emerges a Mexican
Robin Hood.

To this uncouth, untutored bandit chief, there is only one
wrong, the oppression of peons--only one law, death to the oppres-
sors.   His cruelties are inflicted as a child is cruel, without
thought that there might be another way to gain his objective.
Primitive, barbaric death is to him a triviality.   What matter if
men die today or tomorrow!   They are destined to die someday
anyhow.   Yet, despite his grossness, he is essentially a gay fellow, worshipped by all peons, followed adoringly by his band of
cutthroats.   It is a vivid, unforgettable portrait of the man Villa
that Beery and M-G-M give us.

Certain liberties have been taken with history, more by
omission and suggestion than by deviation from basic fact.   Many
characters are entirely fictional, others patterned after real people.   For example, General Pascal is more than a little suggestive
of Huerta.

The simplicity of the characterization of Villa actually vies
with the massive spectacle of the production.   In this respect, the

picture is more than masterful.   Not often is there maintained such
a close affinity between human interest in a character and the grim,
uncompromising horror of guerilla warfare.   Battles, fought by
ragged men on horseback, have a graphic intensity that will leave
you limp in your seat.   Yet it is no slight upon the impressiveness
of imposing spectacle to say that the real power of the picture lies
in the humanness of Villa--a glorified portrait, if you will, but
nonetheless an always engrossing one.   Without doubt, Beery has
never given a finer performance than his Pancho Villa.

Second only to Beery is Henry B. Walthall as Madero, a
portrayal that ranks with his Little Colonel of Birth of a Nation.
Madero is the quiet, saint-like revolutionary leader for whom Villa
campaigns and from whom he learns his first refinements--such as
adding a "please" to the command "Shut up!"   To avenge the as-
sassination of Madero, "the little feller," Villa returns from exile
to stage a second revolt against the villainous General Pascal,
played extremely well by Joseph Schildkraut.

Stuart Erwin wanders through the story as an American
newspaperman who makes friends with Villa.   To make good the
reporter's false dispatch to his paper, Villa captures a town, "just
the way Johnny said it was done."   Chalk up another excellent job
for Erwin.

Leo Carrillo scores heavily as Sierra, Villa's lieutenant.   It
falls to Sierra's lot to commit most of the cruelties of the revolution, but in Carrillo's hands the assignment retains sympathy, in
itself an achievement.

The other parts are smaller, but Katherine DeMille as Ros-
ita, one of Villa's many wives (he always marries his girls if only
for the evening); Frank Puglia as Villa's father, Phillip Cooper as
the boy Pancho, David Durand as a young bugler, and George E.
Stone as the poetic letter-writer, all make outstanding their opportunities.   Fay Wray has one of the best scenes of her career, a
powerful one, when she is horsewhipped by Villa.   Donald Cook is
convincing.

Direction is credited to Jack Conway, to whom was given
the tremendous task of filming the version made in Hollywood
around the scenes obtained in Mexico.   No greater tribute to his
work can be made than that it is impossible to tell which is which,
though fifty percent of the credit for the picture's sweep and power
must go to whoever shot the Mexican sequences.   And to Vorkapich
must go credit for a crashing crescendo of tempo reminiscent of
the Birth of a Nation climax, when the word spreads from hill to
dale, "Villa Wants You!"

Photographic credits are divided between James Wong Howe
and Charles G. Clarke.   Together they have filmed scenes of remarkable beauty and breath-taking action.

A word, too, about the musical score of Herbert Stothart, which is in perfect accord with the theme.

It is to be expected that Viva Villa, which ran a few min-utes over two hours at the preview, will be cut again before re-lease.

--The Hollywood Reporter, Vol. 20, No. 13 (March 26, 1934), page 3.

*   *   *

The marriage of History and Art is likely to be a little tough on History--at least in motion pictures. For no matter how low-down and mean the principal character, he must be washed-up enough so that the fans will like him.

Well, the "historic character" cycle is in full swing, with Catherine, Henry VIII, Christina and Rothschild all enjoying certain kalsominings. Now comes Pancho Villa, an ignorant, illiterate, physically dirty peon whose so-called patriotism was rooted in sav-age vengeance and expressed in unconscionable cruelty.

The only person M. G. M. could have selected for such an unlovely part was Wally Beery, generally loved because of his good nature. Yes, Wally, one of the best actors on the screen (remem-ber him in Grand Hotel?) is again cast as a big, happy-go-lucky, moronic slob, a role he seems destined to play to his flickering end.

Comparison between Thunder over Mexico and Viva Villa, both dealing with the identical subject, is inevitable. In the former, Eisenstein pictured the Mexican Revolution as a sullen revolt of in-articulate peons. M. G. M. presents it as spectacular comic opera. Eisenstein's characters, both peon and haciendado, looked authentic; everybody in this production looks like a Hollywood actor. Even Leo Carrillo! Eisenstein's treatment was as grim as the historic facts; M. G. M. treats the subject as entertainment punched up by thrills and punctuated by laughs.

Because of Mexican sensitiveness, M. G. M. also had to di-gress from many local truths. The peons of the revolution were for the most part bare-footed and ragged. Even the Federal Army was sartorially a joke. The present Mexican authorities insisted upon dressing 'em up. Curiously enough they seem not to have been disturbed by the ruthless cruelty of both sides.

Well, if Viva Villa couldn't be truthful, it could at least be entertaining, and accordingly this picture will no doubt be swell box-office.

Wally Beery gives a notable performance, although a bit over-sentimental, even maudlin at times. (He stops in battle to pick up a dying kid bugler who blows his own taps!).   But he's always amusing.

> --Rob Wagner in Rob Wagner's
> Script, Vol. 11, No. 271 (May
> 19, 1934), page 9.

☐ WAY OUT WEST (Hal Roach/M-G-M, 1937)

Laurel and Hardy in bordertown, or How Slapstick Came to Brushwood Gulch.   Acceptable, if you like.

> --Frank S. Nugent in Cinema
> Arts, Vol. 1, No. 2 (July
> 1937), page 97.

☐ WHAT PRICE HOLLYWOOD (RKO-Pathe, 1932)

Here you are, movie customers!   All the lights, laughs and heartbreaks of Movie-Town!   One of the fastest, most interesting pieces of entertainment ever to come out of Hollywood!   Mustn't miss it!   Gorgeous Constance Bennett gives her finest performance as the little blonde Brown Derby waitress who wants to get into the movies.   Catching the eye of a famous but liquorish director, magnificently played by Lowell Sherman, she goes to a big première with him.   Into the films she goes, and the joys and glooms of a star's life follow.

Neil Hamilton does a great millionaire play-boy, and Gregory Ratoff's cartoon of a producer is amazing.

Almost everything in this picture has actually happened in Hollywood.   A great director really went down and out as Sherman does here.   It's a pretty true picture of what goes on--and reveals startlingly just how hard it is to stay married in Filmland.   The movies have always chided Photoplay for tipping off technical secrets of pictures.   Here they give it all away themselves!

All in all, one of the finest, most fascinating movies ever made.   It grabs the interest in a death-grip, and holds on.   Its authors, our own Adela Rogers St. Johns and Jane Murfin, know every inch of the Hollywood scene.   And they've concocted a swell talkie and a box-office knockout!

> --Photoplay, Vol. 42, No. 3
> (August 1932), page 51.

*   *   *

Not bad, this new Constance Bennett picture, not bad at all. Perhaps one wouldn't go so far as to say that the star earns her

reputed fabulous salary in this one, but if she was worth thirty
thou a week in earlier efforts--and the producers should know--she
is worth at least sixty grand in this.   I could never see her either
as an actress or a beaut before.   She has a new stance, a more
natural make-up, she has humor, shading, and infinite appeal.
She's her father's daughter, worthy of the Richard Bennett of, say,
The Dark Purple.

     Support is excellent.   Lowell Sherman, consistently suave,
gives one of his best performances.   Neil Hamilton does justice to
a suitable assignment.   Gregory Ratoff is not surpassed in his particular métier.   It is always a treat to see Louise Beavers and one
is grateful for even a hazy glimpse of Phil Tead.   Many clever
directorial touches by George Cukor.   Margaret Pemberton designed
dazzling duds for Miss Bennett (lingerie by Juel Park).   The story
by Adela Rogers St. Johns Hyland has poignant reality.   Jane Murfin had a hand in the adaptation.

--Rob Wagner in Rob Wagner's
Script, Vol. 7, No. 182 (August
6, 1932), page 8.

☐   WHITE ZOMBIE (United Artists, 1932)

     If you're just a fiend for horror pictures you'll take this
and like it, but if weird screams and tom-toms don't make your
blood curdle any more, you'll find this just a little funny.   It concerns the half-dead who rise from their graves.   They are known
as zombies to the natives.   Madge Bellamy returns--not so good
in talkies as silents.   Bela Lugosi is his old Dracula self.

--Photoplay, Vol. 42, No. 4
(September 1932), page 110.

☐   THE WIZARD OF OZ (M-G-M, 1939)

     The advertisements stress the fact that a new world was
created for The Wizard of Oz but to me it seems more important
that M-G-M and Mervyn LeRoy aided by Victor Fleming, who directed; Herbert Stothart, who did the music; and a trio of accomplished writers which included Script's own Florence Ryerson, have
elevated the artistic standards of musical extravaganza to a point
unequaled in screen history.   My capitulation to The Wizard of Oz
was so complete that I neglected to bring out the critical yardstick
and admired the Frank Baum fantasy as extravagantly as any child.
For that matter, my theater-going commenced with The Tick Tock
Man of Oz and I suppose it was comforting to discover that because
of the resourcefulness of the screen's craftsmen the wonderful Land
of Oz endures as a magical and captivating province of the imagination.

The film has been so felicitously contrived, the actors are
so uniformly appealing, atmosphere and illusion so persuasive that
the story and its characters ought to amaze and delight all of those
Young In Heart to whom the production has been dedicated.   With
charming simplicity Judy Garland plays the little Kansas girl
whirled off into an enchanted world by a cyclone.   There she be-
friends a Cowardly Lion (Bert Lahr), a Tin Woodman (Jack Haley)
and a daffy Scarecrow (Ray Bolger) who accompany her to the Emerald City where they encounter the awesome Wizard (Frank Morgan) who turns out to be a genial old humbug.   Margaret Hamilton
is the terrifying Bad Witch, Billie Burke the benevolent fairy, and
Singer's midgets play the grateful Munchkins.

Ballyhoo is the business of the publicity department, but I
don't envy it the task of equaling in words the visual splendors of
The Wizard of Oz.   Go to it boys, but I doubt whether you can extol this remarkable attraction too extravagantly.   Not when it's a
cinemasterpiece.

> --Richard Sheridan Ames in Rob
> Wagner's Script, Vol. 22, No.
> 519 (August 26, 1939), page 16.

*   *   *

One of the greatest technical feats the screen has to its
credit: A picture which would make Mervyn LeRoy famous if it
had been his sole contribution to the screen.   Visually a cinematic
masterpiece, its creation of Munchkinland being one of the most
remarkable achievements ever offered as entertainment by any medium.   To Cedric Gibbons and his associates in the Metro art department goes unbounded praise for the strikingly original and highly picturesque settings to which the cameras of Harold Rosson and
Allen Davy do such justice.   The special effects which are to the
credit of Arnold Gilespie are enough in themselves to make the
picture remarkable, the Kansas tornado being one of the most wonderful things the screen has done.   Another visual treat is provided
by Bobby Connolly who staged some artistic and picturesque scenes.

But The Wizard of Oz is much more than a visual treat.   It
is a really human document, one with a lesson in it, one of the
few to which grandfather can take his grandchild and both of them
find entertaining.   The scenic embellishment is beyond description
so no words of mine could give you even an impression of what
you will see when you view the picture.

Noel Langley's adaption of the screen play by himself, Florence Ryerson, and Edgar A. Woolf, makes a fascinating story when
brought to the screen under the intelligent and feeling direction of
Victor Fleming.   The story revolves around the adventures, actual
and in a dream, of Judy Garland, and to me the outstanding feature
of the production is the astonishingly clever performance of that
youngster.   Ray Bolger as the Strawman, Bert Lahr as the Lion,
and Jack Haley as the Tinman are such unique characterizations

that they are liable to attract the most attention. Billie Burke as
the lovely fairy queen and Margaret Hamilton as the witch also
stand out in a manner which will attract much attention to them.

But all through the picture moves the little Judy, holding it
together, being always its motivating feature, and so natural is
she, so perfectly cast, one scarcely becomes conscious of her
contribution to the whole. I have read all the other local reviews
of the picture and have not found in one of them the praise which
in my opinion is due this accomplished child for whom I predicted
great things when she made her first appearance on the screen.
Her performance in the Wizard of Oz strengthens my conviction
that in a few years she will be recognized as one of the screens
foremost emotional actresses.

I saw the picture in a Metro projection room where the
sound was more terrific than I hope it will be in the theatres showing it. Margaret Hamilton's impersonation of the cruel witch is
enough in itself from a visual standpoint to give children cold
chills, but the screams which accompany it will drive them nuts
unless more care is exercised in the theatres than was exercised
in the projection room on the Metro lot. Those who objected to
the ferocity of the witch in Snow White will have grounds for complaint about the one in The Wizard of Oz, but I do not think there
will be enough complaining to keep the picture from being a terrific box-office success. Like Snow White it is a piece of screen
entertainment which can be shown every year from now on.
--Welford Beaton in Hollywood
Spectator, Vol. 14, No. 10
(September 2, 1939), page 10.

☐ THE WOMEN (M-G-M, 1939)

For Joan Crawford, The Women does more than it does for
that deplorable, futile, immensely funny feminine minority photographed so accurately and flagellated so unmercifully by Clare
Boothe (an assassin in the best Booth tradition, plus an "e") in
the notorious play now adapted to the screen with great gusto by
Anita Loos and Jane Murfin, and shrewdly directed by George
Cukor at the risk of life and limb.

Miss Crawford with great relish and visible effect plays a
heartless, boorish home-wrecker whom you hate yourself for liking,
but hers is the most surprising and vivid performance in a saucy,
slanderous comedy replete with engaging impersonations. Rosalind
Russell furnishes plenty of competition as another home-wrecker
whose weapon is lethal gossip. Mary Boland has the best role
she's had in years as the nincompoop and nymphomaniac countess
fatuously addicted to "L'Amour," and somehow she has a streak of
decency possessed by none of the others except Marjorie Main, the

maid at a Reno dude ranch, whose knowledge of men is surcharged
with worship and disgust.   And Norma Shearer, the film's heroine,
damned by the author in an introduction to the printed play as "too
damned nice," whose charm and beauty mark her for attention in a
story which gives her nothing to do except look for sympathy.

Paulette Goddard is more than ever a treat for the eye, although her behavior is appalling--the fight scene is excessive even
if those girls would undoubtedly claw and kick to the finish--and we
may thank wise casting for the appearance of Mary Nash, Lucille
Watson, and Phyllis Povah, actresses all, in finished performances.
As you must know, there are no males in the cast, although the
girls talk of little else, and I doubt whether any male could survive
the competition or maintain his equilibrium in such a picture.   It's
fun to watch, but as a he-man star confessed to me at the preview,
it would be hell to be in.

Naturally the film, which will bore the unsophisticated as
much as it will horrify or nauseate the right-minded to whom
Whistler's "Mother" is both good art and spiritual nourishment,
hushes in places where the play was vehement.   Not much of a
loss, although Miss Povah is deprived of some audacious cracks
as an expectant, but not happy, mother.   Surprisingly, a play
which shocked many and annoyed quite a few has reached the screen
without losing its thrust, and while there are concessions to popular taste such as Adrian's elaborate fashion show, and the dialogue
has been tempered as well as tampered with, the film should not
displease the playwright who exulted in the indecent exposure of
her own sex.   Whatever women may think of The Women, it was
written by one of them, and she's still at large.   The handsomely
produced, gayly improper, wickedly accurate estimate of a frac-
tional part of the feminine whole should vex and amuse feminine
patrons, and I'm afraid it will give their paying escorts the time
of their lives.   Until they pay for copies of those Adrian gowns!
                              --Richard Sheridan Ames in Rob
                                Wagner's Script, Vol. 22, No.
                                520 (September 9, 1939), page
                                21.

*   *   *

Certainly one for women; also for men who can enjoy a good
natured poke at the feminine predilection for gossip, vicious and
otherwise.   The characters are drawn with broad strokes, and at
no time is the meaning of a speech or a scene at all obscure.   The
only fault that can be found with the production is that it is too long.
One hundred and twenty minutes of constant feminine chatter is a
bit too much.   But for those who can appreciate brilliant screen
craftsmanship, The Women will prove to be a constant delight.

First honors, of course, must go to Hunt Stromberg who
visualized the whole thing and placed it in the hands of those who
so brilliantly could realize his conception of what the completed

production should be.   George Cukor's direction is extraordinarily
clever.   I cannot recall any other picture which gave us so many
practically perfect performances.   The most important members
of his cast derive their importance solely from the importance of
the parts they play, and not by virtue of the manner in which they
play them.   Girls who appear in but one or two scenes, acquit
themselves as competently as those who are seen most often.   Only
brilliant direction could achieve such results.

Continuing to regard the production as a whole, I would give
next honors to Cedric Gibbons and Adrian, whose contributions
made it possible for Oliver Marsh's and Joe Ruttenberg's cameras
to make the production one of the season's outstanding visual treats.
Here again, of course, Cukor's direction figures as one of the picture's assets, his composition of scenes giving them great pictorial
value.   Against the background of the Gibbons sets, the women
wearing the Adrian creations are grouped by Cukor in a manner
which must have delighted the artistic souls of Marsh and Ruttenberg.   Certainly The Women as a whole is a lovely thing to look
at, a striking example of the screen's ability to achieve the ultimate
in visual beauty.   The pictorial effectiveness of the production will
be one of the leading factors in making it the box-office success it
will prove to be.

The story is amusing, one which will make no great demands on the intelligence of the audience.   Its humor is elemental,
but it is dressed so beautifully and enacted so brilliantly, it will
appeal as much to the intellect as it will to the sense of humor.
This makes it a somewhat remarkable comedy, one which will appeal to all grades of intelligence.   None of the dirt which characterized the play is to be found in the picture.   This will cause
Broadway to sigh but the box-office to rejoice.

To distribute acting honors would be to drain my stock of
laudatory adjectives.   In any event we have to give Director Cukor
credit for the excellence of the performances of those we have seen
in many roles and who merely give an extra glow to the kind of
characterizations they have made familiar to us.   Not so, however,
with Joan Crawford.   Here she plays something she long has wanted
to play--a hard-boiled, designing, hateful woman, and plays it with
the rare skill only to be expected by those who have followed her
career.   I hope her success in the role will do something towards
lessening the conviction of producers that leading women always
must be cast in angelic roles.

Another performance which attracted my attention is that of
Joan Fontaine.   Her first appearance on the screen prompted me to
predict in print that she had a brilliant future ahead of her, but
George Cukor is the only director she has had since who realized
some of the possibilities I thought I saw in her first performance.
Paulette Goddard is another comparative newcomer who is to be

credited with a valuable contribution to The Women.
                        --Welford Beaton in Hollywood
                          Spectator, Vol. 14, No. 11
                          (September 16, 1939), page 6.

☐ WUTHERING HEIGHTS (Goldwyn, 1939)

        Having the nerve to attack a brooding, tormented classic
like Emily Brontë's Wuthering Heights for commercial movie purposes, whether he merely subjugated or actually conquered a mass
of unyielding material entitles Samuel Goldwyn, his scenarists,
Hecht and MacArthur, and his diligent director, William Wyler, to
critical praise, and the daring of their collaborative enterprise
merits comment because such ventures are exceedingly rare in
Hollywood.   No doubt the sagacious Goldwyn believed that he had
a bludgeoning melodrama, moody and mystical, with just a hint of
modern psychological interpretation to offset the weary explorations
of the gifted authoress into the tortured characters of her time and
place, that would appeal to the matinee audiences of today.

        I hope he was right, feeling that Wuthering Heights is a
women's picture; that they who like to suffer vicariously over a
doomed love affair will ultimately repay Mr. Goldwyn for his well
intentioned effort.   As for men, I think they may be bored by the
film, or at the least squirmy; but viewed objectively, it has much
that is meritorious, and my only personal complaint would be that
with all the necessary cutting and understandable syncopation, the
makers of Wuthering Heights were overly conscientious in their approach to a revered classic and might have fared better if they had
thought more of motion pictures and less of their literary obligations to Emily Brontë.

        However, the story has tension in its cinematic adaptation,
and lacking a more descriptive word, the "atmosphere" has been
created anew, while the actors knew what they were about.   Always
a bit vague and what-am-I-here-for, as if waiting for direction,
Merle Oberon really surpassed herself as the hapless heroine,
Cathy, who loved the stable-boy (Laurence Olivier) and married
another man.   The strange story of a love that found fulfillment
only in death, is kept from being merely just another melodrama
by its location, period atmosphere, the vitality of acting such as
that contributed, in addition to the principals, by Flora Robson,
Geraldine Fitzgerald, and David Niven.   But there are times when
everyone's artistry is insufficient to do the trick, and the film is
regulation Hollywood in spite of commendable efforts to probe frustrated emotions.

        As an earnest film, and one that is outstanding in lighting,
photography, costuming, and general good taste, Wuthering Heights
merits praise.   Just whether it will affect you as something you

ought to like, which permits your attention to wander, or whether you can believe every reel of it, is the question. This much I'm willing to grant: the film merits a second look, which I'm having, but until then it seems to me a case of love's labor lost, strayed, or possibly stolen.

--Richard Sheridan Ames in Rob Wagner's Script, Vol. 21, No. 504 (April 15, 1939), pages 17-18.

* * *

People to whom Emily Brontë's only novel seems uniquely great might naturally have shuddered when the news came that Wuthering Heights was to be made into a movie. Many of them did. Then came the further news that Samuel Goldwyn was to do it, and the wise ones knew they might as well control their shudders till they actually saw it. You never can tell about Mr. Goldwyn--he has done some pretty fine things. The waiting is over now, the shudders unjustified. The picture is the best that Mr. Goldwyn has ever made. Moreover, it isn't a picture that only the serious art-lovers will rave about and the rest of the public stay away from--it has dramatic grip and emotional power to catch and hold any intelligence that looks to the screen for something besides laughter.

There's no point in comparing the film too closely with the novel: it's an extremely difficult novel to dramatize, covering two generations in time, with practically two sets of characters and a piling up of violent passions and incidents that no play or movie could hope to include. The one important and supremely desirable thing is that the character of one man be made understandable in its atmospheric and emotional setting. That is the heart of the book, and it has been made to live again in the movie with surprising power. Nobody can deny the cleverness and movie knowingness of Charles MacArthur and Ben Hecht, but they usually content themselves with doing a quick and easy job, with tongue in cheek and plenty of solicitude for the lowest in public taste. Here, with intelligent respect for their material, they have done their very good best, and wrought a script that has integrity and superb dramatic effectiveness.

Wuthering Heights was a house on the Yorkshire moors, where two children, a brother and sister, lived with their father. A pleasant house in spite of its austere natural surroundings, to which the father brought a dark and gypsyish orphan boy named Heathcliff, to make one of the family. But even as children the three were strangely bound together by love and hate: between Heathcliff and the girl Cathy grew an almost mystical sympathy and oneness of feeling, as if they were two strings of an instrument which vibrated equally to any tenderness or wild violence that touched them, while the brother Hindley from the beginning hated the strange boy intruded into the household with a bitterness that

became an obsession. Then the father died and Hindley became
master, with full power to work his hatred upon Heathcliff, brutalizing him into the lowest of stable servants. But instead of running away, for love of Cathy Heathcliff stayed, and so the three
grew up.

The torturing ties of love and hate grew with them, to become dark and terrifying passions when Heathcliff and Hindley were
men and Cathy a woman. Only death could still them, only in
death could peace come to those stormy souls. There the film
ends, after Heathcliff has finally fled from his torture and Cathy
turned to the mind calm of an affectionate marriage with a neighbor's son, and Heathcliff returns, rich and vengeful, to take a
bitter and ultimately unsatisfying payment from those who made his
boyhood and youth so miserable. It is a tragedy of the degrading
and brutalizing of a strong man's personality, and of the fatal workings of hate usurping the place of love. An enormously difficult
tragedy to portray, whether in words or in pictures, but this film
does it, with beauty and power and amazing clarity. Why Heathcliff was what he was, tortured, torturing himself and others--why
Cathy held fast to him though a part of her wanted to escape from
him and never could--probably only an Emily Brontë could ever
make that plain. But Emily Brontë is allowed to speak for herself
on the screen, through writing and directing and acting and all the
instruments of movie making that make no condescensions to un-
intelligence but by reaching up to the level of their material achieve
a height that few pictures of this kind attain.

It is necessary to say of William Wyler's direction only that
it is superbly equal to its opportunities. And so is the acting.
Naturally Laurence Olivier dominates everything. He has a chance
to, and is able to. His Heathcliff is one of the screen performances that has to be called great. Rex Downing, who acts Heathcliff as a child, sets the key for Heathcliff as a man (as Sarita
Wooden does for Cathy), and Olivier takes up the role as youth and
plays it on into embittered manhood with increasing power to a
magnificent climax. Merle Oberon manages Cathy almost beyond
her natural capacity--she just isn't genius enough to put Cathy on
a level with Heathcliff. But what actress is? Geraldine Fitzgerald
strikes the topmost note among the women, with a heart-breaking
moment of which even the memory is poignant. The others fit in
beautifully, in their necessary but subordinate places.

The picture isn't without minor, if negligible, faults. The
musical score is particularly unfortunate, syrupy and banal and
completely missing the feeling it should heighten. The very ending, of ghosts moving hand-in-hand through the snow up to the crag
that represented the only moments of happiness in their mortal
lives, is trite and unimaginative. Some such ending is necessary--
Emily Brontë herself had it--but it should have been much better.
Inspiration faltered at the final moment.

Probably Samuel Goldwyn is ultimately responsible for the
quality of this picture. He takes too lively an interest in his pro-

ductions simply to have allowed this to be good of itself, without
having a positive hand in it, and the praise that will come to him
from it ought to make him not only proud but eager to stay on the
high level he has here reached.

--James Shelley Hamilton in National Board of Review Magazine,
Vol. 14, No. 4 (April 1939),
pages 16-17.

☐ YOU CAN'T TAKE IT WITH YOU (Columbia, 1938)

The distance between Tibetan Shangri-La and the uproarious-
ly peaceful parlor of the Vanderhofs is geographically impressive.
But cinematically Frank Capra has traveled almost as far since his
first success, That Certain Thing; and You Can't Take It with You,
newest of his films in pursuit of happiness, again proclaims him
the master of the human touch.

This Columbia film, which vastly improves upon the Kauf-
man-Hart Pulitzer prize play of the same name, may be described,
without reservation, as unsurpassed entertainment.   But once its
universal appeal has thus been certified, a reviewer finds himself
at loss for words with which to recapture the mood of a comedy
that is also both tender and wise; a capricious study of a family
of eccentrics which restates the case for individual liberty so
challengingly that it might be called "The Battle Cry of Freedom--
of the ego"; a creative collaboration in which the whole is greater
than any of its parts, so that the spectator walks home jingling a
pocket philosophy--"Be Thyself"--instead of remembering scraps of
dialogue or actor-autographed performances.

Technically (especially in early sequences) You Can't Take It
with You violates several canons of orthodox screen craftsmanship
by loafing where others would hurry, by exploring already known
character territory, by playing cat-and-mouse with climax, by the
prodigality of directorial "touches."   But the end more than justifies
the means, and after Grandpa Vanderhof has thanked "Him" for the
last time, when eager hands are passing around steaming food, with
the whole family reunited as the film ends in a babble of happy
conversation, then you realize that you have more than a superficial
knowledge of all these people--thanks to the Capra method which
has never been more apposite to the material.

Loath to extol individual performances, because all are excellent and properly subservient to a well integrated story, I must
single out Edward Arnold for praise because for some years I round-
ly abused him as incapable of a real characterization.   I now with-
draw that charge, congratulating Mr. Arnold on a flawless portrayal
of the robber baron who found himself human after all.   And since
much was naturally expected of Lionel Barrymore, who did not dis-

appoint, the most surprising virtuoso performance was Donald
Meek's, as the emancipated gadget-maker whose funny little face
became beautiful when transformed by joy.   The actor who made
the biggest impression in the shortest time was Harry Davenport,
as the judge who was not only just, but archly benevolent.

Perhaps the most hilarious line in the play is Mischa Auer's
explosive answer to a question regarding his nationality: "I'm a
Russian from Om-s-s-s-k-k-k-a!"   And M. Auer looked the part.

James Stewart and Jean Arthur (radiant in her return to the
screen--so there must be no grudges) have the romantic assignments.   There is the same adroit use of won't-you-all-join-in music that Capra perfected in It Happened One Night, and the screen
obviously gives more elbow room to the subterranean fireworks than
the stage ever could.

As the latest achievement of Frank Capra, You Can't Take
It with You hardly requires recommendation.   It's only a question
of when and how many times you are going to see it.
                                        --Richard Sheridan Ames in Rob
                                        Wagner's Script, Vol. 20, No.
                                        477 (October 1, 1938), page 8.

☐   YOUNG MR.   LINCOLN (20th Century-Fox, 1939)

As meticulously fashioned as The Informer and Stagecoach
although unlike either, John Ford's Young Mr. Lincoln provides a
personal triumph for Henry Fonda, who portrays four of the prairie
years in the life of our best-loved president.   The film is slowly
paced and not enriched with much narrative incident, but the insight
and quality of the direction.   Mr. Fonda's characterization, and
the stirring theme combine to make Young Mr. Lincoln one of the
year's most enjoyable films.   It is not great or novel cinema.   It
is not noisily entertaining, but it has veracity and sincerity and
rough, simple beauty, and it is not unworthy of the man who inspired it.

The picture might just as well have been titled Lincoln, the
Lawyer, because unlike the Sherwood or Conkle dramas, Lamar
Trotti's screen play is chiefly concerned with young Abe's practice.
Its amusing and pungent climax re-creates with mounting excitement
a famous trial in which Lincoln saved two brothers (Richard Cromwell and Eddie Quillan) from the gallows and earned the undying
gratitude of their mother (Alice Brady).   Ann Rutledge, Mary Todd,
and Stephen Douglas affect the heart or ambition or the progress of
the gaunt prairie figure, but with the exception of Miss Brady's
warm and glowing performance the whole picture is, and rightly,
Mr. Fonda's.

As a recent Script cover indicated, Fonda's physical resemblance to Lincoln is uncanny, obtained, with little make-up
artifice, by adding the mole, altering the nose, wearing the hair
long--and Bert Glennon's photography must be credited for the
perfect illusion.   But more importantly Fonda projects his characterization beautifully, making us feel, after the first few moments, that he is Lincoln, the gangling, quiet but forceful, humorous yet earnest youth whose fists are as quick as his wit.   Fonda's
portrayal is a miracle of naturalness but I suspect he and his director carefully thought out every nuance of character, the facial
expressions, the walk, the slow gestures and inflections.   Few
screen characterizations have been so honest or compelling and
my admiration was aroused by Fonda's skill in uniting strength
with tenderness and suggesting the spiritual depths of a great leader not yet aware of his destiny.

--Richard Sheridan Ames in Rob
Wagner's Script, Vol. 21, No.
512 (June 10, 1939), page 16.

* * *

Notable for the manner in which it creates for us a young
Abraham Lincoln we can believe, but not notable as a piece of
screen entertainment which makes the most of the possibilities inherent in its story material. Its early footage sketches briefly a
few incidents which played a part in determining the path Lincoln
was to follow through life, and introduces some of the people whose
names have become known because of their association with the
greater name: then we sit through several reels of a trial which
would have made The Springfield Murder Case a more appropriate
name for the picture than Young Mr. Lincoln.

And even as a murder mystery the picture has its weaknesses.   It does not even hint at the manner in which the young
lawyer unravelled the mystery and pointed the finger of conviction
at the man who committed the crime.   The trial serves merely to
give members of the capable cast opportunities for clever characterizations, but the weakness of that lies in the fact that the people
they play are unimportant and contribute little to our understanding
of the forces which shaped the career of the backwoods boy who
became the greatest American.   And I thought that was to be the
purpose of the picture.

Stephen A. Douglas, Ann Rutledge, Mary Todd and a few
others whose names are linked with that of the Great Emancipator,
are virtually extras who have no part in motivating the story, but
much footage is devoted to the buffoonery of country yokels whose
sole mission is to make the audience laugh.   This robs the production of the impressive dignity its theme demands and keeps it from
becoming the great Lincoln picture it could have been.

But Young Mr. Lincoln at least can boast the fact that it
gives us a great deal of Lincoln.   Henry Fonda's characterization

of the central character is masterly, its chief virtue being its
startling faithfulness to our conception of what Lincoln must have
been when young.   His walk, his gestures, his unruly hair, his
humanness--all but his voice--live again on the screen with such
fidelity that as long as Henry Fonda continues to appear in pictures
his name will be associated with that of Abraham Lincoln.   In giving
us his Lincoln, Fonda gives us something which will be an imperishable screen memory.   His performance crowds into the background those who appear with him, but even so, Alice Brady, Donald Meek, Richard Cromwell, Eddie Quillan, Ward Bond give us
something to remember.

No one can quarrel with the manner in which everything in
the picture is presented.   Technically it is a superb achievement.
It is the irrelevance of the comedy scenes, their lack of harmony
with the spirit of the production, not a lack of skill in the manner
of their doing, which makes so much of the footage drag.   John
Ford's direction could not have been improved upon.   He gives us
a series of striking living portraits, tender scenes which play on
our heartstrings, groupings of pictorial and dramatic effect, and
to him goes none of the blame for such moments of dissatisfaction
as the picture will cause.

Of outstanding virtue is the photography of Bert Glennon
which brings us some shots of great beauty as well as a series of
striking portraits.   Physical re-creation of the period of the story
by Richard Day and Mark-Lee Kirk, art directors, also is a notable contribution to the picture.   Lamar Trotti is established too
well as a screen writer to be charged with such weaknesses as the
story has.   He has made a clever job of the kind of job his studio
wanted, and no writer can be expected to do more than that.   Alfred Newman's score is one of the picture's big assets....   Film
editing by Walter Thompson and sound recording by Eugene Gross-
man and Roger Heman reach technical perfection.
                                    --Welford Beaton in Hollywood
                              Spectator, Vol. 14, No. 5 (June
                              10, 1939), page 5.